Close !

no new jails!

Solidarity!

CITY TIME

City Time

On Being Sentenced to Rikers Island

David Campbell *and* Jarrod Shanahan

NEW YORK UNIVERSITY PRESS
New York

NEW YORK UNIVERSITY PRESS
New York
www.nyupress.org

Please contact the Library of Congress for Cataloging-in-Publication data.

ISBN: 9781479828999 (hardback)

ISBN: 9781479829040 (library ebook)

ISBN: 9781479829033 (consumer ebook)

This book is printed on acid-free paper, and its binding materials are chosen for strength and durability. We strive to use environmentally responsible suppliers and materials to the greatest extent possible in publishing our books.

Manufactured in the United States of America

10 9 8 7 6 5 4 3 2 1

Also available as an ebook

Dedicated to anybody serving city time right now.

Hold your head.

CONTENTS

Introduction 1

1. Intake 27
2. The People of City Time 47
3. A Day in the Life 67
4. Doing Time 84
5. Work 110
6. Special Occasions 124
7. Food 148
8. Hygiene 171
9. Clothing 191
10. Substance Abuse and Mental Health 204
11. Interpersonal Relationships 227
12. Institutional Relationships 259
13. Release 280

Acknowledgments 289

Glossary 291

Notes 295

Index 313

About the Authors 319

Introduction

On a small island in the northern reaches of New York City's East River sits a vast complex of human cages overlooking the glimmering Manhattan skyline and the bustle of nearby LaGuardia Airport. A single bridge controlled by the New York City Department of Correction (DOC) connects the penal colony to East Elmhurst, Queens. Rikers Island is at once unlike any other place on earth and also quite banal, a sprawling network of local jails concentrated on a single island. While the people locked up there are surely prisoners, they are not technically held in prisons, which are administered by state and federal authorities. The captives of Rikers Island are in the custody of the City of New York. Most are detainees awaiting trial, and a much smaller number are already convicted and awaiting transfer to state prison facilities.[1] Another subset of the island's incarcerated population consists of inmates doing "city time"—sentences of typically one year or less, served on Rikers Island rather than in the state prison system.[2] The present study deals with a distinct group within this unique segment of New York City's incarcerated population: adult men serving city time on Rikers Island.

Doing city time is very different from serving time in prison. It is commonly defined by its comparative idleness, limited mobility within the facility, high turnover, and high degrees of unpredictability in daily life.[3] City time is also highly distinct from pretrial detention, because city-time inmates have a fixed, fast-approaching release date, unlike pretrial detainees, who generally do not. In the early 1970s, New York City prisoners with determinant sentences were even called "Time Men" by pretrial detainees with indefinite stays.[4] Today this distinction is typically made by the color of one's uniform: "Greens" are serving set sentences, while "Tans" are detained.

Writing in 1976, journalist Ronald Goldfarb advanced the hypothesis that jails are "the poorhouse of the twentieth century." According to

Goldfarb and related views, jails warehouse poor people who are out of work, substance dependent, or simply unruly and lower class, a status defined by their position on the bottom of the racial division of labor.[5] As jail and prison populations climbed in the early 1980s with the onset of what we today call mass incarceration, former California state prisoner John Irwin formulated "the rabble management hypothesis," by which jails are understood to respond not simply to lawbreaking but to the public existence of socially "offensive" populations of racialized poor people. Jails, Irwin postulated, are warehouses for people who refuse to follow the informal rules of gentrifying cities, such as the imperative to remove petty street illegality or public displays of poverty from neighborhoods designated for intensive capital investment, as would happen over the following decade in Times Square.[6] In recent decades, scholar Ruth Wilson Gilmore has examined the role incarceration plays in managing capitalist crises by unevenly targeting racialized populations for whom there is no steady employment available.[7] Recent studies by scholars Kelly Lytle Hernández, Judah Schept, Lydia Pelot-Hobbs, Melanie D. Newport and Jack Norton, Jacob Kang-Brown, Jasmine Heiss, and Oliver Hinds of the In Our Backyards Initiative have examined the fraught histories of local jails at the intersection of capital accumulation and white supremacy.[8] Jarrod Shanahan, coauthor of the present study, has built upon this tradition to craft a political and economic history of Rikers Island, historicizing many of the trends explored herein.[9]

These accounts instruct us that the jail is merely a stopgap measure, and a particularly violent one at that, for larger social problems attendant to capitalism and its inherent racialized inequality. This does not, however, mean that the jail is not an important lens for understanding society. As repositories of problems that a society is unwilling or unable to fix, jails tell us a great deal about the broader social context in which they operate. Looking closely at incarceration on Rikers Island, then, is an instructive way to learn about New York City, its social organization, and the global capitalist society of which it is a key nodal point. Examining the day-to-day life that plays out amid these brutal conditions also allows us to glimpse the most basic potential for mass struggle against them, and the possibility for alternative forms of social organization, in all their potentially explosive contradictions. And just as the jail represents distinct experiences of incarceration deserving of sustained study, so too must city time be explored in all its specificity.

City Time

As mass incarceration receives long-overdue scrutiny in popular culture, far too little has been written about the experience of short-stay incarceration like city time. Jails account for the highest number of people caged each year—some ten million, or roughly one in thirty Americans. "Given the reach of America's jails," writes ethnographer Michael Walker, who has experienced incarceration, "I'm struck by how little we know about them."[10]

Most existent writing falls into the categories of grand historical and theoretical narratives of state-level incarceration, sensationalist accounts of violence and predation against or among incarcerated people, or heartfelt tales of tragic individuals struggling for survival and redemption. In the sizable body of literature surrounding mass incarceration, we have found scant recent accounts chronicling in more sober terms what exactly incarcerated people do all day, how their social world is structured, and how they relate to the fact of being a human being locked in a cage. Still fewer of these accounts are set in jails. Despite its considerable media attention, this is also true of Rikers Island; as former Rikers writing teacher Jennifer Wynn argues, Rikers "not only hides prisoners from public view, but in a double sleight of hand it keeps *in* those who want to get out and keeps *out* those who want to get in."[11]

A potential remedy for this deficiency of insight comes from prison ethnography, which rigorously studies the social life unfolding within human cages. But as sociologist Loïc Wacquant argued in the 2001 essay "The Curious Eclipse of Prison Ethnography in the Age of Mass Incarceration," prison ethnography actually declined with the rise of mass incarceration. Wacquant cites real barriers between scholars and the social life of carceral facilities, enforced by both carceral administrators and academic disciplinary bodies like institutional review boards, which stymie many would-be researchers.[12] But even for scholars who gain institutional access to carceral facilities and are escorted to the other side of the prison wall under guard, doubts persist over how real anything they are witnessing actually is; anthropologist Manuela Cunha remarks that such studies can best be described as "quasi-ethnographies," as they are conducted on a version of reality highly curated through the "institutional filters" of the authorities.[13] All the while, US society is saturated with pop-culture images of prisons and jails, giving people the mistaken idea that they understand life behind bars. Formerly incarcerated scholar Jason Warr bemoans this "cultural ignorance" and the unearned certitude that proliferates it.[14] Even citizens who attempt to bridge this divide through activities like tourism of defunct prisons balance, in the words of scholar Michelle Brown, "voyeurism and civic mindedness."[15]

This trend is so dramatic that we encounter many otherwise well-informed people, including activists against mass incarceration, who believe that every incarcerated person in the United States is forced to perform productive labor for private corporations, and that this generates profits large enough to justify the immense costs of the US prison system. This is not the case; when incarcerated people work at all, most of their labor simply reproduces the facility where they are held through basic services and upkeep, while the small number of incarcerated people who labor for private corporations generate a profit for these parasitic private institutions, not the system itself. Considering its immense expenditures and scant returns, if mass incarceration were a for-profit enterprise undertaken by the United States government, it would be the most disastrous business venture in world history.[16]

At the same time, hard-working journalists and activists in many places record the violence and depravity of life behind bars. This work, though necessary, comes with its own risks of skewing public perception. A constant emphasis on extreme acts of violence committed at a place like Rikers Island, while surely important to emphasize, can give the general public the idea that these facilities are teeming with sadistic individuals who unceasingly harm one another all day long. There are certainly horrendous cases of violence among incarcerated people that deserve public scrutiny. But simply focusing on violence and predation, while ignoring the countless unremarkable days of ordinary boredom and wasted human potential that characterize life behind bars for many remarkably average people, can have an undesired effect. After all, if Rikers Island's jail facilities are packed wall to wall with people constantly committing horrible violence against each other, who on earth would want to let any of them out?[17]

The book you hold in your hands is a small step toward redressing these trends. It reflects its authors' personal experiences and observations of city time, organized as systematically as possible, to present an account of daily life in a social world kept locked far away from public view.[18] The material not appended with footnotes comes from notes taken within these facilities during our respective stints of incarceration, when we used golf pencils, unwieldy soft, plastic prisoner pens, and the all-too-scarce contraband civilian pen, to write on odd scraps of institutional paper, legal pads, and the back pages of books. Names were anonymized at the time of note taking, both for our safety and to protect the anonymity of people often depicted as breaking the institution's rules, and sometimes the law. We have also drawn from a larger body of Rikers-specific research, and other jail and prison writing, that helped us make sense of our city time, including documents obtained by Freedom of Information Law requests and visits to the New York City Municipal Archives. While we do not claim to have crafted a transhistorical or transspatial narrative of incarceration, we cannot help but notice some basic recurring themes attendant to locking large groups of disaffected people in squalid cages with little to do all day and nothing to look forward to except release.

Today there is no shortage of interesting theoretical accounts of mass incarceration, but an alarming dearth of day-to-day empirical facts about how it is lived. Therefore, while we episodically strive in this book to make sense of what we experienced with the use of theoretical abstractions, we are primarily interested in reconstructing the institution's rules, rituals, traditions, interpersonal relationships, object ensemble, and other everyday practices of city time at Rikers Island, as these phenomena presented themselves to us. In depicting the variegated social worlds unfolding beneath the monolith known as Rikers, we aim to add a bit of nuance and insider perspective to the discourse around this notorious facility and the behemoth carceral system of which it is a part. Accordingly, we aim to underscore not just the brutality of city time but the banality, stupidity, and waste that characterize every second of it, and the complex social relations that nonetheless thrive in the thrall of captivity.

In academic parlance, *City Time* is a "participant-observer ethnography." This means that we experienced city time both as scholars studying it and as inmates, part of the phenomena under study. David spent a full year at C-76 and C-74 between October 2019 and October 2020, at the height of the COVID-19 pandemic at Rikers. He was caged in C-76, in housing units 1-Upper and 12-Lower, and in C-74, in housing units Mod 4–Lower North and Mod 4–Lower South. Jarrod spent the month of June at C-76 in 2016. He was caged in housing units 1-Upper, 11-Lower, and 10-Upper. Our study benefits from the balance of these two perspectives, rooted in two very different, yet also both common, lengths of city time.

City Time did not begin as a research project. We were both arrested for protest activity and were locked up begrudgingly, not as part of a deliberate study. Walker dubs this an "organic ethnography."[19] It is by virtue of bad luck, then, and not scholarly foresight, that we nonetheless took up the challenge made to pioneering prison ethnographer James B. Jacobs by an incarcerated man at Stateville Penitentiary: "Instead of doing your bull shit research from an armchair, why didn't you come in as an inmate so you could find out what it's all about, you phony cock sucker."[20]

During his brief sentence in 2016, Jarrod took extensive notes about his experiences and daily life in the facility as part of a planned ethnography. Upon release, however, he decided that he had spent insufficient time there to write about it with confidence, and pivoted instead to a historical study that became the book *Captives: How Rikers Island Took New York City Hostage*. We became acquainted in 2018, at a time when David was navigating the city's Kafkaesque court bureaucracy and had yet to be sent away. We remained in close touch. Despite never having conducted fieldwork, David was advised by a member of his defense committee who had trained as an anthropologist to approach the experience as a participant-observer, and to take detailed notes of his observations to that effect. During David's incarceration, we corresponded frequently via letter, telephone, and video visits, and planned in detail a program of study that, over time, turned into this book.

"*The Price Is Right* was on in the day room," wrote rapper Lil Wayne, during his own city time at Rikers. "I tried to play along, but just kept thinking about how this place is wrong."[21] The narrative effort of *City*

Time unfolds within this contradiction. Research has shown that city time on Rikers actually increases recidivism and provides no benefit to public safety.[22] It merely takes people already facing numerous challenges—crises of mental health, substance abuse, and housing chief among them—and adds further chaos to their lives by forced immersion in a setting that offers no solutions to these problems but only multiplies the abandonment, indignity, distress, danger, and trauma that have led them to this point in the first place.

The violence and utter meaninglessness of short-stay incarceration is reflected in every facet of city time. It is a world defined by the pointless squandering of the most precious thing a person has: the time remaining in their life. The crushing boredom that suffuses daily life is symptomatic of a social order that simply has no use for the people locked up there, or else, can think of no better way to handle their behavior than forcing them to sit idly for a set stint of time in a dangerous, disgusting place that will leave them worse off than when they entered. In this context, the profound apathy of Rikers Island's correction officers, called COs, toward the men in their custody is an honest, if callous and inhumane, reflection of the inmates' social role. Even their good-hearted attempts to imbue the endeavor with a little bit of dignity, such as referring to male inmates as "gentlemen," seem to only make matters worse.

Amid these conditions, however, inmates forge an elaborate social world and carve out ornate networks of survival, care, and even enjoyment, in defiance of their supposed disposability. In the process, they demonstrate a level of creativity and ingenuity that is at times stunning, creating ad-hoc, self-organized micro-societies against all odds, and providing for a variety of wants and needs with a pitifully sparse assemblage of available objects. And while city time is premised on the need to remove its captives from society, the brevity of their sentences testifies to the absurdity of this thesis: they are, from the beginning, scheduled to return in a matter of mere months or even days. All the while, most city-time inmates promptly demonstrate their ardent desire to live in an organized social world, to abide by commonly agreed-upon customs and rules, and to color their existence with as much meaning as possible.

Like Lil Wayne, these men are forced to "play along" with the dictates of incarcerated life, enacting a kind of perverse normalcy in a deplorable institution that ought not to exist at all. The resulting social world is no order we would be happy to inhabit in the outside world, but one that nonetheless demonstrates the remarkable, if contradictory, capabilities of some of society's most powerless people to create community and purpose in one of the most hostile settings in New York City.

Inside/Out

We are hardly typical city-time inmates. We are socially designated as white and were locked up in a system where the white population hovers around 10 percent.[23] Even among the small subset of white men incarcerated at Rikers, our path to city time was nontraditional. We were both sentenced in cases related to political activism, irreducible to any illness, desire for financial gain, or immediate dictates of survival. Moreover, while both of us indulged in reckless and foolish behavior as adolescents and young adults, white-skin privilege shielded us from the worst of the punishment system, and our Rikers experiences represented our first times spending more than a night or two in a cell. We are both college educated, and though we had each lived in New York City for nearly a decade when arrested, neither of us grew up there. Neither of us was economically indigent at the time of our incarceration, and we had political support networks that enabled us to post bail and navigate our cases unincarcerated, until we accepted noncooperative plea deals and began our sentences. We also received a high volume of mail and visits that was remarked upon by COs and inmates alike.

Similarly, neither of us had preexisting social ties like gang or neighborhood affiliation, or socialization in other disciplinary institutions like adolescent detention, that would have facilitated a simpler, if more fraught, integration into the jail's social networks and institutional life. This made our acculturation to Rikers life more difficult, and erected barriers to our subsequent analysis. Our perspective surely suffers from our not being more integrated into these social worlds, especially the internal cultures of the gangs. Moreover, as atheists, neither of us ventured into worship services, and cannot speak from experience about the spiritual life of the island. As cisgendered men, we were largely excluded from the social world of trans people. One of us has queer sex on the outside, but we both elected to stay out of the jailhouse sexual subculture, drastically limiting our perception of this largely clandestine world. We did not require serious medical or mental health treatment, engaging with that infrastructure only on a cursory level. Finally, we remained in "general population" and did not experience protective custody or punitive segregation, also known as solitary confinement.

In response to these limitations, we have largely erred on the side of not speaking with authority on things we simply do not know enough about. We regret these omissions and the further exclusion from the discourse of underrepresented dimensions of jail life, such as the plight of transgender and disabled prisoners, or those battling chronic illness.[24]

In a recent memoir reflecting on a time when he left academia to become a factory worker, the revolutionary scholar David Ranney wrestled with the question of what exactly he could definitively say about the social world he encountered. Even after years spent laboring in multiple factories, Ranney nonetheless felt a certain social distance from his coworkers, exacerbated by his presence as a white man in heavily Black and Latino shops. "I was both an outsider looking into the world of factory workers," Ranney reflects, "and an insider looking out at the outside world."[25] As inmates, and especially as new arrivals, we too were outsiders looking into a social world foreign to the ones we grew up in and inhabited as adults. Nonetheless, we were quite literally *inside*, stuck in the jails twenty-four hours per day, just like everyone else.

Michael Walker, whose arrest and incarceration at LA County Jail interrupted his professional career as an academic, reflects, "I was an inmate, not a scholar impersonating an inmate. The distinction is important," he argues. "When you know you cannot go home . . . you are sure to gain a deeper understanding of the groups and the setting that you are examining." Yet, Walker clarifies, "There is a difference between living in a particular community and being from a particular community."[26] English novelist and anthropologist Alison Spedding similarly remarks, of her time locked in a Bolivian jail, that the experience was defined by both a commonality of position—being locked up—and the large cultural gulfs that often yawn between the "customs" of those who undertake advanced degrees or pursue creative work, and the more traditional values and life paths of the average incarcerated person.[27]

Ultimately, David Ranney, writing from the "outside in and the inside out," resolved to simply represent factory life as it revealed itself to him. Similarly, when Jarrod expressed uncertainty about how to relate to his short time, former political prisoner Daniel McGowan reminded him that he was being granted access to a world that requires far more documentation than it presently receives, and his objective could be to simply remedy that. In *City Time*, we follow this guidance. By necessity, our observations and analysis must inhabit the tension between being markedly atypical among Rikers inmates but also having a level of access to Rikers that is impossible for writers and scholars to attain unless they actually go to jail—which we encourage only as an unavoidable consequence of political activity or other prosocial illegality.

There are a number of thoughtful reflections on the role of the outside researcher conducting ethnographies in carceral facilities they are free to leave.[28] Fewer studies exist of the unique position of the ethnographer who is simultaneously incarcerated. The small but important field of "convict criminology," established in part by John Irwin, has produced notable ethnographic works, alongside a methodology that puts a high premium on jail and prison research done by incarcerated people themselves.[29] In a technical sense, we fall in this tradition, but we feel little affinity with academic criminology and its pretense of objectivity. We both went to jail as a result of our political commitments—against capitalism, white supremacy, and the forces of reaction—and have no interest in checking these commitments in order to perform objective scholarship. We have not been concerned with the supposed imperative of "achieving an insider's understanding while maintaining an outsider's objectivity," as convict criminologist Richard S. Jones puts it, and are still less concerned about the possibility of, in his words, "going native."[30] *City Time* is instead driven by our preexisting allegiances and our experiences as inmates, which only strengthened our opposition to the entire social order represented by the jail and its keepers. When we talk about life on Rikers, then, any illegal or disallowed behavior we discuss is already common knowledge. Otherwise, we leave it to the investigators to earn their paychecks.

For narrative ease, we make a number of declarative statements that describe the social world of city time as it presented itself to us. We do not feel the need to hedge each observation with the qualification that it might not be a universal truth. "I can tolerate all men till they come to 'however,'" Goethe's young Werther complains of his rival, Albert, "for it is self-evident that every universal rule must have its exceptions. But he is so exceedingly accurate, that, if he only fancies he has said a word too precipitate, or too general, or only half true, he never ceases to qualify, to modify, and extenuate, till at last he appears to have said nothing at all."[31] We nonetheless wish to be clear from the onset that we consider the observations that follow to represent our own experiences, and the scholarly work we have done to make sense of them, rather than final statements on the nature of Rikers Island, or life behind bars. Similarly, when we speak of "city time" in the abstract, we mean city time for sentenced men serving their time in general population. When discussing things specific to our experience that are no longer true, or that may never have been universally applicable, we use the past tense. Descriptions of practices that are certainly (or almost certainly) still ongoing, or that are broadly applicable for life behind bars, are given in the present tense.

We are aware of the recent movement toward "humanizing language," which trades loaded terms like "convict" for softer designations like "incarcerated person," " resident," or even "person with justice system involvement."[32] While this language poses the risk of inadvertently obscuring violent or uneven power relationships—as when police murders are euphemistically rechristened "officer-involved shootings," or when Jarrod's minimum-wage grocery-bagging job earned him the lofty title of "associate"—we nonetheless understand and applaud the imperative to humanize incarcerated and formerly incarcerated people, and have used this language wherever possible.

We realize, then, that readers who prefer human-centered language may be disappointed to see that we generally refer to the incarcerated men we encountered during city time as "inmates." Our reason is simple: this is how the men serving city time refer to themselves and each other, with near universality. This is also why we occasionally use the institutional term "Greens" to discuss sentenced adult men in contrast to "Tans," pretrial detainees. Though we sometimes opt for "prisoner" or "incarcerated person" (and generally eschew "inmate" in favor of these terms in our other writings on incarcerated life), it felt both disingenuous and inaccurate to avoid the term "inmate" here, as it is, for better or worse, the language preferred by the vast majority of city-time prisoners we encountered.[33]

We are also attentive to the changes within even the short window separating our city time. When Jarrod was locked up in 2016, most of the jail's visible record keeping revolved around pens and paper. COs relied on telephones, heavy log books, and frequent hand-tabulated counts to make sure everyone was in the right place. Jarrod was issued a plastic ID badge to clip to his uniform, which he simply showed to COs upon request. He often observed that no visible object in his dormitory was unique to the twenty-first century. By David's time, however, computers were becoming more common in the COs' "Bubbles," and ID bracelets were scanned throughout the facilities where he was held. Similarly, during Jarrod's time, cameras were only beginning to appear in housing areas at C-76, and a grating sound, rumored to be workers installing them in nearby dormitories, echoed throughout the day. When David arrived in 2019, cameras were ubiquitous.

Above all, our respective bids are distinguished by two watershed events. The first was the temporary closure of the C-76 facility in 2019, after David had spent two months there. C-76 had housed sentenced men since 1964, including Jarrod. During David's time it was shuttered as part of a ten-year plan to close Rikers (though it was later reopened, befitting the seriousness of that plan).[34] David was then transferred to the C-74 building, where he experienced many differences, including a phenomenon that was rare for city time at C-76: a degree of integration with Tans, pretrial detainees. This also meant that writing a comprehensive account of city time became still more impossible, given the dispersal of sentenced men across numerous buildings, in countless novel situations. The second event was the COVID-19 pandemic, which uprooted whatever remained of the ordinary daily routines at C-74. This also gave David a very particular experience of Rikers as a global epicenter of

COVID-19.[35] Despite these and other differences, however, our basic daily experiences largely corroborated each other, which has led us to provide sketches of institutional life, however tenuously, with some confidence.

C-76: The Eric M. Taylor Center

Since 1964, the predominant site of city time for men in New York City has been the C-76 building, short for its original city budgetary designation as "Capital Project Number 76." Alongside its numeric designation, C-76 was first dubbed the New York City Reception and Classification Center, then the Correctional Institution for Men, and is known today as the Eric M. Taylor Center (EMTC). Among COs and inmates, it is usually called "the Six building" or simply "the Six." The grounds of this low-slung facility sprawl horizontally across thirty acres on the southwest side of the island, near the primary staff parking lot and the mouth of the bridge connecting Rikers to East Elmhurst, Queens.[36] Its facade is brick dappled with shades of beige and brown and punctuated by steel-framed windows, slatted with seven panes of grubby glass that open obliquely, like vents, with the laborious rotations of an inmate-operated hand crank. C-76 is comprised of three sections, the North Side and the South Side, which opened in 1964, and the Annex, which opened in 1970. The North Side contains two floors of traditional cell blocks, four in total, boasting 136 cells. This is the kind of special accommodation afforded to "protective custody" inmates like Lil Wayne, who spent eight months there in 2010.

The vast majority of the building's approximately 1,850 beds, however, are spread across twenty-eight rectangular dormitories, massive open rooms with stationary single beds, connected to the main building only on one side. This so-called chevron design gives the building the distinct aerial shape of three Ks, with two joined back to back by the number eight.[37] These dormitories are identified by a number from one through twelve, denoting distinct three-story structures emanating from the building, along with the level (lower, main, or upper). 12-Main, for instance, is stacked between 12-Lower and 12-Upper, and overlooks 11-Lower, 11-Main, and 11-Upper across a disused courtyard. From many dormitories and passageways of C-76, prisoners may gaze at the Manhattan skyline, the comings and goings of nearby LaGuardia Airport, and the vanishing point where the Buono Bridge connects Rikers to the freedom of the outside world.

C-76 is a building of long corridors of polished tile, concrete, and glazed block, connecting dormitories with a high-school-style cafeteria, cage-lined infirmary, institutional chapel, visiting area, mailroom, disused recreation gymnasium, basement barber shop, and other spaces for sustaining and reproducing the jail. The hallways are streaked with a red line on either side, creating a narrow passage close to the wall, to which inmates are supposed to confine themselves. When moving in supervised groups, they are instructed to cling to the right-hand side of the hall, a behavior that quickly becomes second nature. Multiple checkpoints, complete with metal detectors and sometimes locked doors, stretch the passage from one end of the jail to the other, though these are often abandoned and most inmates are free to roam the halls without restraints or accompaniment, provided they can account for their destination if asked.

"If you grow up in the projects and the public school system and then go to Rikers Island, it almost feels like no big deal. It feels like, oh, we know this setting. I'm willing to bet that the same architect designed all three things," explains hip-hop artist Fat Joe in *Rikers: An Oral History*.[38] Fat Joe would absolutely win that bet, at least when it comes to C-76: its architecture firm, Brown & Guenther, also designed a number of public schools and housing projects in the Bronx and throughout the city.[39] This is a common sentiment expressed by those familiar with the island. "It wasn't until I worked in a jail setting that I realized the . . . colors on the walls were the same colors used in the hallways and stairwells in the projects," writes former Rikers CO C. René West. "A color I would call institutional gray, drab yellow, or drab yellow and orange colors. The floor areas in jails are very similar to the lobby areas in many of the project apartment buildings; and the inmate's housing areas have the same tiles on the floor." Working as CO, West came to suspect that the message this architecture sent to inmates from New York City's housing projects was, "Welcome home."[40]

Figure I.1: C-76 as depicted in the 1968 proposal for the construction of the annex, shown here in the foreground amid a fanciful profusion of trees. The reality is much less inviting.
Source: Brown Guenther Battaglia Galvin Architects, *Preliminary Plans: New Housing Addition to New York City Correctional Reception and Classification Center for Men*, May 29, 1968. Courtesy of New York City Municipal Archives.

The lion's share of city time at C-76 plays out in its dormitories. The dormitories of its Annex, typical of the facility, measure 72.5 by 50 feet, and feature space for sixty-four beds. At the entrance to the dormitory sits a narrow hallway gated on both sides by heavy doors meshed with weathered iron. The "A gate" leads outside, while the "B gate" leads into the house. This hallway contains a storage closet and the COs' private bathroom, both of which are usually locked. Situated on one side of the entrance hallway is the day room, a small metal-and-plexiglass-enclosed common area open in the daytime, where inmates can watch television, play games, eat meals, or, in some dorms, simply sit at a proper table and chair. On the other side is the bathroom. In some houses, semi-opaque plexiglass and metal grating provide only partial privacy for the inmates' bathroom, showers and all. At the mouth of this hallway is the COs' station, commonly called "the Bubble," an enclosure best compared to a toll booth. There the so-called A officer engages with inmates from behind plexiglass, fielding requests for razors,

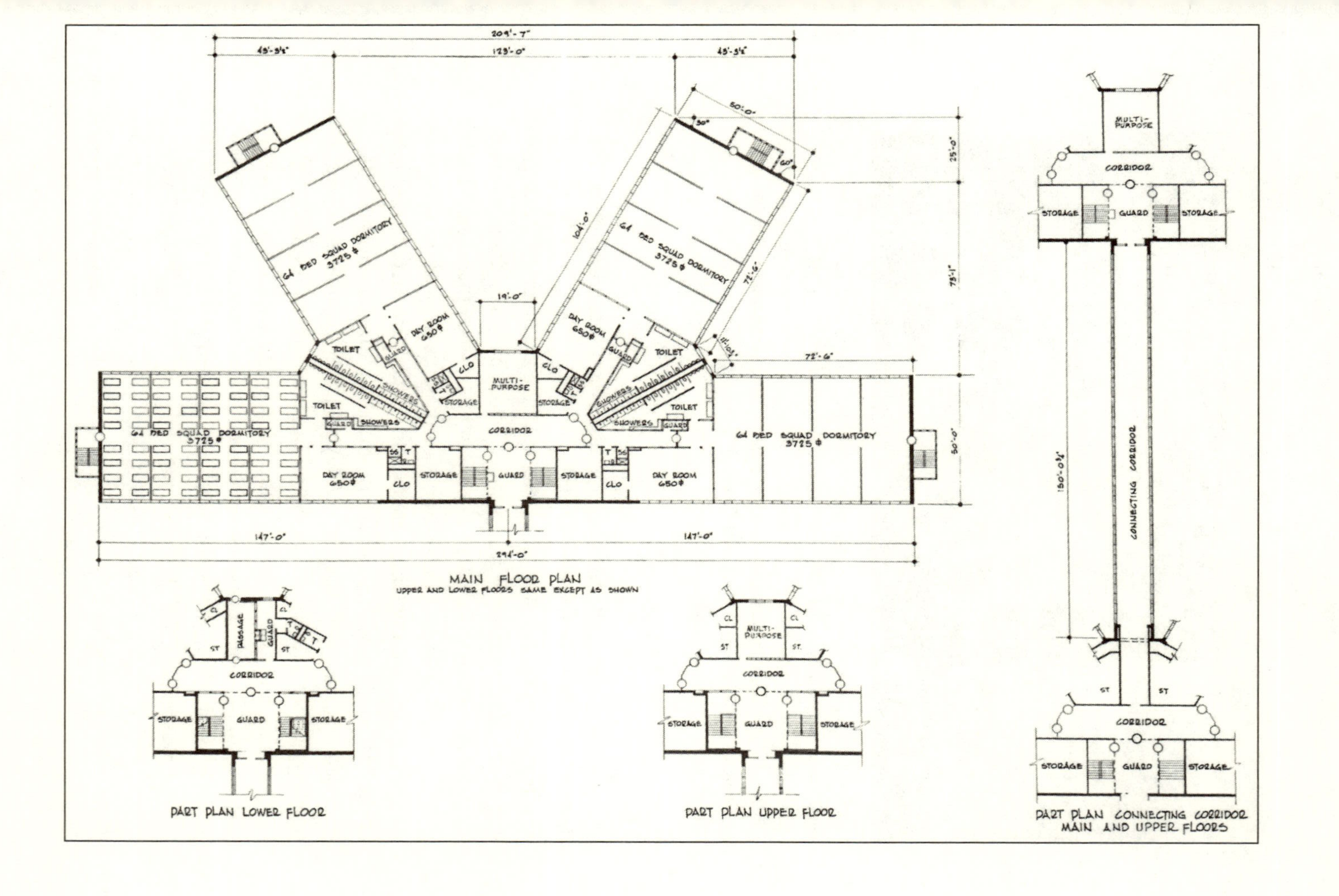
209'-7"
45'-3½"
123'-0"
45'-3½"
50'-0"
30°
60°
64 BED SQUAD DORMITORY
3725 ϕ
64 BED SQUAD DORMITORY
3725 ϕ
104'-0"
72'-6"
25'-0"
73'-1"
19'-0"
DAY ROOM
650 ϕ
DAY ROOM
650 ϕ
TOILET
GUARD
SHOWERS
CLO
MULTI-PURPOSE
STORAGE
CORRIDOR
GUARD
72'-6"
64 BED SQUAD DORMITORY
3725 ϕ
64 BED SQUAD DORMITORY
3725 ϕ
50'-0"
DAY ROOM
650 ϕ
STORAGE
GUARD
147'-0"
147'-0"
294'-0"
MAIN FLOOR PLAN
UPPER AND LOWER FLOORS SAME EXCEPT AS SHOWN
CL
PASSAGE
GUARD
ST
CORRIDOR
STORAGE
GUARD
STORAGE
PART PLAN LOWER FLOOR
CL
MULTI-PURPOSE
ST
CORRIDOR
STORAGE
GUARD
STORAGE
PART PLAN UPPER FLOOR
MULTI-PURPOSE
CORRIDOR
STORAGE
GUARD
STORAGE
150'-0¾"
CONNECTING CORRIDOR
ST
CORRIDOR
STORAGE
GUARD
STORAGE
PART PLAN CONNECTING CORRIDOR
MAIN AND UPPER FLOORS

ibuprofen, toilet paper, and permission to leave the dormitory, along with episodic romantic attention, while the "B officer" holds court at a small table set up just in front, on the floor of the dorm.

Beyond the Bubble and into the depths of the dormitory stretches Broadway, a six-foot-wide corridor bisecting C-76's rectangular barracks. On either side of Broadway sit rows of rusted iron bed frames, four to each side, situated roughly three feet apart and bolted to the floor. Their harsh surface is evenly dotted with drainage holes; a low lip around its perimeter keeps the mattress in place. Narrow aisles branching off Broadway create sections of eight beds apiece, with roughly five feet in the middle, which often becomes social space with an explicit sense of community, including hostility to outsiders. In some houses, a low divider provides a modicum of privacy between the heads and feet of respective beds, but there is in any case little privacy to be had in the dormitories where city time is served. "Here is the somber monotony of a world created to lock up everything with security, suspicion and certitude," wrote former Rikers chaplain Pierre Raphaël, "to put everything in boxes and pigeonholes, far removed from every kind of fantasy or initiative."[41]

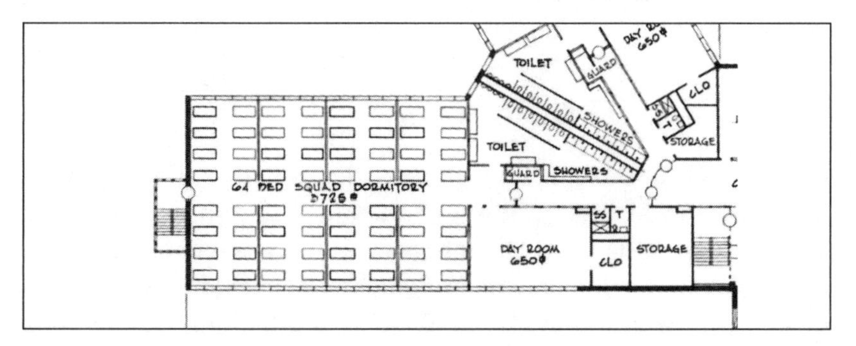

Figures 1.2 (*facing page*) and 1.3: Layout of the C-76 addition, including the 12-Lower dormitory with amenities typical of the facility. Note the layout of beds, the positioning of bathrooms and day rooms off the entrance hallway, the small COs' "Bubble" simply labeled "guard," and the strip of hallway running down the center of the dormitory known as "Broadway."

Source: Brown Guenther Battaglia Galvin Architects, *Preliminary Plans: New Housing Addition to New York City Correctional Reception and Classification Center for Men*, May 29, 1968. Courtesy of New York City Municipal Archives.

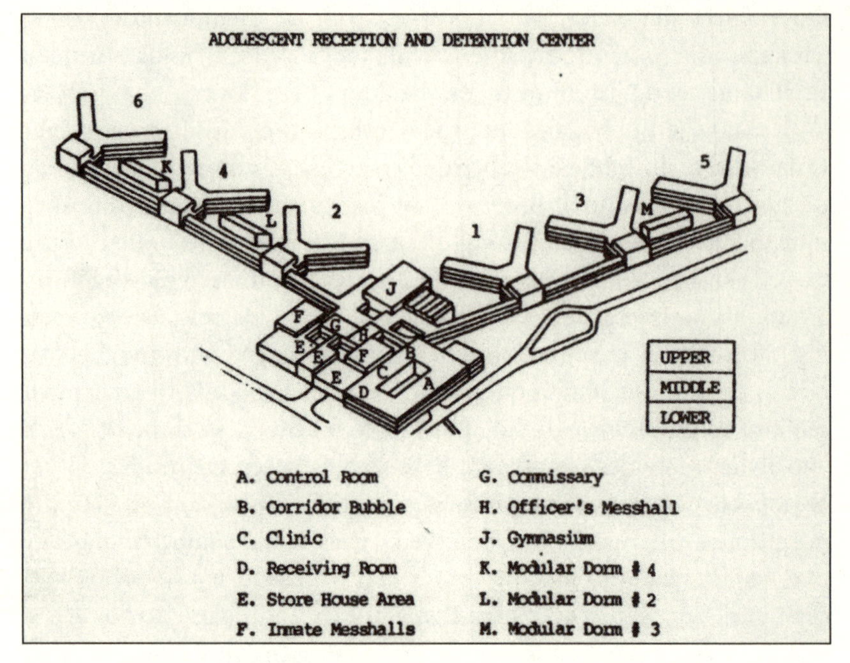

Figure I.4: A diagram of C-74 from 1985. Figures K, L, and M are the modules, designed as temporary measures but still in use today.
Source: New York City Board of Correction (BOC), *A Study of Violence and Its Cause at the New York City Adolescent Remand and Detention Center* (New York: BOC, 1985), 11.

C-74: The Robert N. Davoren Center

David spent most of his time at C-74, the Robert N. Davoren Center (RNDC), which has primarily functioned since its 1972 opening as an adolescent facility. Though just across the street, C-74, which dwarfs C-76, stretching across fifty acres to its immediate east, might as well be a world away.[42] Like C-76, it is a building of chevrons and long corridors, and from the outside, largely resembles C-76: three stories of nondescript brick in "warm buff color" and endless rows of steel-frame louvered windows.[43] This facility has two central wings, emanating in an obtuse V shape from a cluster of support facilities, thirteen hundred feet in each direction. When it opened in 1972, RNDC counted 1,080 cells and a single dormitory. In the early

1980s, DOC added 300 beds in three "module" (or "mod") dormitories that stretched across the chevrons, along with 108 cells.[44]

RNDC is generally known as "the Four building" or simply "the Four." But, confusingly, the chevron-shaped wings projecting from the main hallway are known in C-74 jargon as "buildings." Thus, an inmate in C-74 may speak of "the Six building," meaning the chevron-shaped wing of C-74 bearing this number, only to have the person he is speaking to interpret this as C-76, which is another facility entirely. The same problem arises with "the Five building," as this is both a wing in C-74 and a nickname for AMKC, or C-95, another facility on Rikers. To avoid this confusion, inmates in C-74 who are acquainted with the problem will sometimes refer to the other two facilities using the "C," as in "C-76," rather than simply "the Six" or "the Six building."

Each "building" in C-74 has a north side and a south side, designated by those names. They each have three floors, meaning that people in C-74 speak of housing units such as "6–Upper North," or "6–Upper South," "4–Main South," "4–Lower North," and so on. The two arms of the V-shaped main RNDC structure itself are likewise referred to as "North Side" and "South Side," despite their intersecting at an almost-right angle. The North Side contains buildings 2, 4, and 6, and Mods 4 and 6. The South Side contains buildings 1, 3, and 5, as well as Mod 5. The 1 building was closed during David's time in C-74, and housed no inmates. The mods are essentially giant two-story trailers joined to the main hallway by a short corridor with a gate. The mods contain four dorms of approximately fifty beds—Mod 4–Lower North has forty-eight beds, and Mod 4–Lower South, fifty.

Most of the spaces designed for functions other than warehousing humans can be found at the crux of the North Side and the South Side. Here, a three-way intersection is closed off by a series of gates operated by a CO in a plexiglass control booth, from which a red light can be seen flashing during C-74's daily occurrence of "alarms." This booth affords a view down both main hallways as well as toward the shorter hallway from which emanate the DOC staff area, social-services office, clinic, visiting floor (including a blind-turn staircase that has allegedly been the site of many stabbings and slashings over the years), Intake, and kitchen. The North Side, where David was held, affords access to the kitchen, or "KK," mail room, chapel, and upstairs gym, the staircase descending to the "Peace Center," downstairs gym and yard, video-visiting/ remote-court center, office of the captain on duty, commissary, and mess hall. The South Side hallway affords entrances to the chaplains' offices and the law library.

Surfaces are largely the same in C-74 as they are in C-76: the walls in the main halls are made of the same glazed block, coated in eggshell enamel.[45] The floor is also polished concrete, and also bears a bright red line running parallel to the wall with a few feet's worth of distance between the two, across which inmates are instructed not to walk when moving to and from the housing units. The walls have a handful of uncaulked seams large enough for rats to crawl through. They bear the occasional feeble attempt at inspiration via thoroughly uninspiring murals: a child behind barbed wire reaching for an enormous butterfly, a formerly incarcerated man going to college and becoming a suit-toting professional, and even an abstract splatter-paint work. Every seventy-five feet or so on the walls of the main hallway, a warning appears, stenciled in black block letters:

ATTENTION ALL INMATES
DONT SUBJECT YOUR FAMILY AND FRIENDS
TO ARREST BY ASKING THEM TO SMUGGLE
DRUGS OR CONTRABAND INTO THE FACILITY

C-74's buildings contain cell blocks, not dorms, but otherwise strongly resemble the wings of C-76. The mods are completely different from the buildings. Entering Mod 4 from the main hall, one passes through a double door that can be locked, but rarely is, and then immediately encounters a barred black metal gate. Beyond this sits "the bridge," the empty landing-like space in front of the Bubble and between the two dorms on either side. An inmate must get the attention of the Bubble officer, usually by yelling "On the gate!" or simply "Yo, CO!" to get the gate open, as it is controlled from inside the Bubble.

The outer surface of the Bubble is equipped with a small black scanning device so inmates can scan their ID wristbands upon entering or exiting the dorms. The door to each dorm has a plexiglass window, perhaps two and a half feet square. Entering the dorm, one finds the

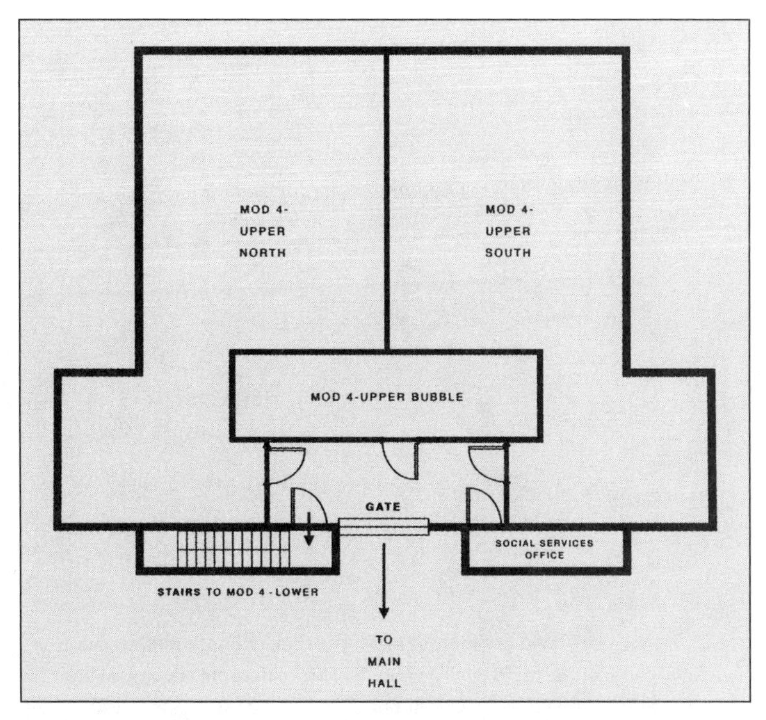

Figure 1.5: An approximate floor plan of Mod 4–Upper, recreated from a sketch by David. The layout of Mod 4–Lower is identical. Illustration by Chloé Maës, 2023.

day room straight across, along with the "day room corner" section, a stretch of perhaps ten bunks in the front of the dorm, running from the entrance to the day room along the concrete block wall separating it from the main space of the dorm. There are also two small columns here, which provide some relative degree of privacy for certain bunks and from certain angles—about as good as privacy gets in this environment.

The columns, like the walls of Mod 4, are clad in rough white plastic paneling, likely PVC, held together at regular intervals by flat white plastic seams and round button-like fasteners, a sort of tamper-resistant plastic rivet. This is a far cry from any surface in C-76, or the original C-74 structures. The windows, too, are remarkably different—unlike the louvered windows present elsewhere, these are actual sliding windows

Figure I.6: A sketch by David of the front of Mod 4–Lower South looking out from inside the day room at the main entrance on the left, "day room corner" section (bunks are not in the frame) and columns, the Bubble, phones, cleaning closet, and entrance to the bathroom on the right. Courtesy of the authors.

with heavy-duty metal screens and diamond-pattern metal grates, commonly referred to as "bars."

Turning away from the day room to look down the length of the dorm, one finds the bulk of the sleeping space: one line of bunks along the inner wall, which separates the sleeping space from the bathroom, and another along the outer wall, prized for its windows. One bed in particular, "the corner bed," sits in the far corner of the outer wall and the short end wall capping the length of the dorm. This bed is unanimously accepted as the dorm's best real estate, as it has no neighbor on one side, as well as two windows.

On the opposite end of the real-estate social scale are the "Broadway beds": a double row of bunks running head-to-toe down the middle of the dorm, between the two lines of wall beds. "Sleeping on Broadway" is largely reviled because one has practically no space to call one's own. The mod bathrooms offer slightly more privacy than those in

EMTC, but only thanks to the inmates' creative reappropriation of the environment. Yet as a rule, personal space is all but nonexistent. This is the case because city time is a world of forced sociality, whether the inmate likes it or not.

Remembering Our Numbers

It was a bout of short-stay incarceration that inspired Jamaican musician Toots Hibbert to pen the song "54–46 That's My Number." In it, Hibbert reflects both on his own experience with incarceration and on the profound realization that, at the exact moment he is singing, someone else stands in his state-issued shoes. "54–46 was my number," Hibbert croons, "right now, someone else has that number." As our own experiences with city time recede into the past, and increasingly take

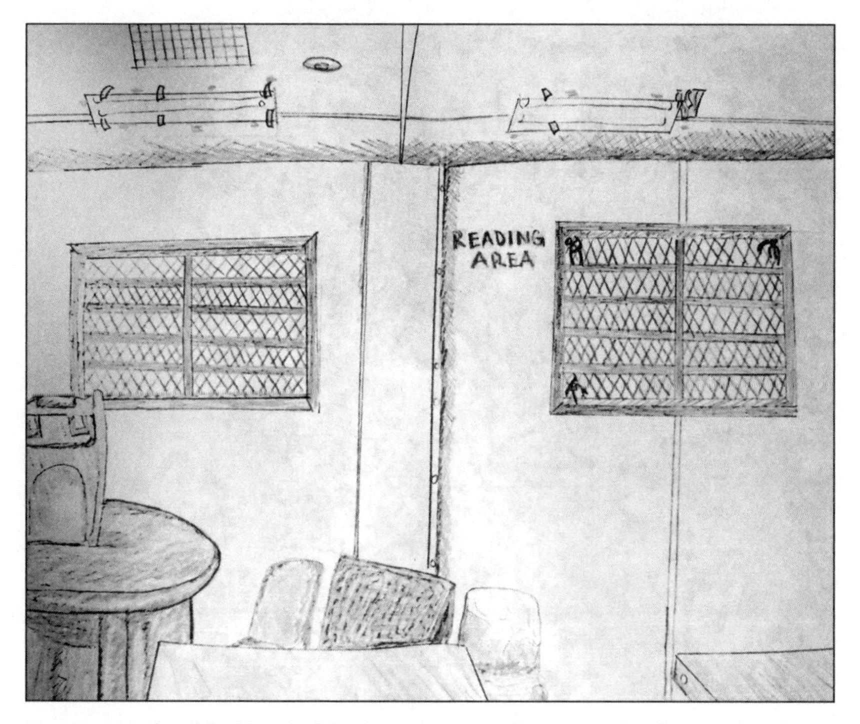

Figure 1.7: A sketch by David of the day room in Mod 4–Lower South. Note that the square corners on the tables are not accurate. Courtesy of the authors.

on the contours of a strange and awful dream, we must emphasize that the subject matter of this book is being lived by real people as we write, and, barring the creation of a liberated society free from human cages, as you read it. Every morning the lights come on, and every night they go off. All the while, the boundless complexities of human sociality play

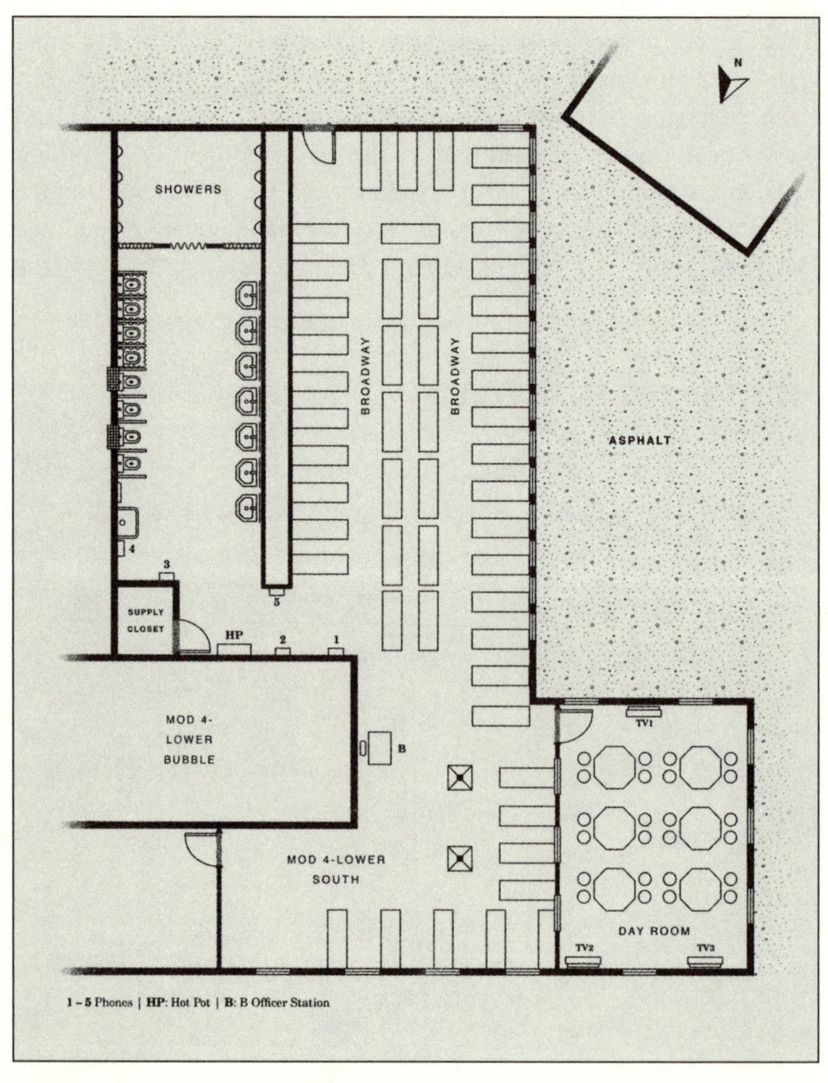

Figure 1.8: An approximate floor plan of Mod 4–Lower South, recreated from a sketch by David. Illustration by Chloé Maës, 2023.

Figure 1.9: A sketch by David of the bathroom in Mod 4–Lower South, looking toward the showers from the entrance. Note the unofficial inmate sheet-curtains tied up around their lines, to prevent removal by staff.

out within the harsh confines of grubby concrete walls. Rikers Island is, after all, a 24/7 operation. Short-stay incarceration most often sends people back to the streets within a few months, but city time never stops.

1

Intake

City time begins with intake, when the new inmate is processed into the jail. Intake is found in many institutions, including workplace training for new hires in almost every occupation and orientation for new students at universities. The particular type of orientation that takes place in jail, however, is characterized by the surrender of legally recognized freedom, the inculcation of a new set of statutes and customs to replace those in the outside world, and, above all, the violent compulsion—usually just below the surface, but sometimes overt—to accept one's place in this new order.

Sociologist Erving Goffman evoked the medieval concept of *civiliter mortuus* to describe the intake process as the moment of "civil death," when a person forfeits the formal rights of an ordinary citizen and becomes a prisoner.[1] New arrivals undergo a process of "loss and mortification"; they are stripped of their outside possessions, including their street clothing and personal grooming equipment, are assigned a number that will be more significant than their name, and are issued Spartan institutional clothing and grooming supplies to replace those they use on the outside. Also lost is the emotional comfort that comes from items representing free life on the outside. "The admission procedure can be characterized as a leaving off and a taking on," Goffman writes, "with the midpoint marked by physical nakedness."[2] The free person is thus stripped down, literally and figuratively, and established as an inmate.

Central to intake is what Goffman calls "the welcome," a process in which "staff or inmates, or both, go out of their way to give the recruit a clear notion of his plight."[3] Beside the supposedly practical matters associated with intake—searching for contraband, ascertaining medical history, providing a uniform, outlining the rules, and so forth—there is an equally if not more important process of communicating to newcomers that they are now living in a place where they are insignificant and powerless. Inmates are made to understand that most of the liberties even a working-class person can enjoy on the outside are suspended, and that they should therefore follow the rules and avoid causing trouble in order to simply survive. This message has many carriers: the harsh architecture and filthy neglect of the intake pens, the humiliating process of the strip search, the endless waiting and unapologetic inefficiency of the whole process, and, of course, the verbal instructions and advice offered by COs and inmates alike.

In our experience, while COs may inform new arrivals of what is expected of them, mostly through threats, insults, or scarcely comprehensible commands, the inmates themselves take a more active role in orienting newcomers to the social setting where they will cohabitate. The first process is the *institutional intake*, the official mechanisms through which newcomers are taken into the facility, in Goffman's words, "to be shaped and coded into an object that can be fed into the administrative machinery of the establishment, to be worked on smoothly by routine operations."[4] But equally important, and largely neglected by Goffman, is what we call the *social intake*, in which other inmates acculturate and acclimatize the newcomer to the de facto social order structuring inmate life.

Given that we both had the privilege of posting bail, and thus began our city time directly from the outside, this is how our narrative is framed. From what we gather, however, the intake process is similar for those already housed on the island prior to conviction, including the forfeiture of street clothing and other small benefits of innocence in the eyes of the law, and the new inmate's subsequent processing into the distinct world of city time.

"Because I Said So": Institutional Intake

The judge is clad in a black robe and ensconced in polished wood paneling, just like on television. But in real life, the scene is much shabbier. It is hard not to notice the run-down furniture, dirty windows, and wrinkled vestments of the judge sneering down from a bench propped up higher than everything else in the courtroom save for the bold, gilded words embossed above the judge's head: "In God We Trust." Beside the judge's venerable bench sits an ominous door leading from the contrived civility of the courtroom to the world of human cages. Burly COs clad in unnecessary bulletproof vests patrol this portal, ferrying captive people from the jail, a world of unvarnished violence and neglect, to the courtroom, where brute force appears cloaked in the highest Enlightenment ideals.

By the time we crossed this threshold, we had eyed it with morbid fascination in dozens of grueling and often pointless court appearances. Passing through this door, we began our city time. We started out in a set of "pens," the colloquial term for cages of different sizes, often filthy and lacking basic facilities like sinks and toilets, where prisoners languish for hours on end at nearly every step of their movement through DOC custody. Jarrod was shuttled into a small, dilapidated cell with a disused bathroom overlooking Manhattan rooftops. The CO processing him was training a trio of cadets, and used Jarrod to demonstrate the proper methods of searching a detained person for weapons. He explained that they should always be polite and respectful. "Some court officers make fun of me for being polite to prisoners," he added, "but my philosophy is you say please—once." The cadets nodded eagerly.

We were questioned at length about our professions, medical histories, and gang affiliations. The COs processing Jarrod, a Latino man, and two Black women, joked that it was not too late for him to join a gang before he got to Rikers. "Now is a good time to get covered," one of the women told him. Jarrod asked if they had a form for that. The man threw up gang signs with his hands while the two women laughed. Meanwhile, the man chewed on cherries, throwing the pits on the floor. One of the women yelled at him, saying he was feeding the mice. Picking them up would be the responsibility of inmates bused in from Rikers Island.

This process was a rush from one filthy pen to another, with broken toilets, clogged sinks, and nowhere to sit or lie down without great discomfort, just to wait for hours on end before being transported to begin again. As we lost track of time, it dawned on us that it no longer mattered. We were patted down and asked the same questions over and over again as we changed custody from one cluster of COs to another, slowly making our way to the ground floor of 100 Center Street, through a series of elevator rides in which we were commanded to face the back wall. Amid the squalor and stale air of the sunless pens, and the still more dismal gloom of detained men headed to Rikers and the state prison system, a small, home-printed sign hung over one guard station bearing the words, "The worst prison of all is fear of what other people think."

Jarrod was escorted toward the bus by an East Asian male CO. A white male CO playfully shouted, "Why are you messing with the white guy?" Jarrod's escort replied, "I have to, for our numbers. It can't just be Black and Latino guys in here!" Such banter between COs sometimes uses the inmate as the butt of a joke, but usually ignores the inmate altogether. In transit, COs often stopped and talked among themselves as if we were inanimate objects—a sentiment further betrayed by their frequent reference to us as "packages."

Reaching the ground floor at last, we entered a short corridor leading into a foul-smelling outdoor loading dock stacked high with clear plastic trash bags containing unfinished detainee meals, allowing a narrow path alongside an idling DOC transport bus for us to board. These vehicles resemble heavily armored school buses, with metal grating over the windows, one row of double-seater pens along the left-hand side, and another row of single cages along the right. Jarrod traveled with a group of women from the Rose M. Singer Center, the women's jail on Rikers, who had been transported to 100 Center Street to work. "Hurry up and get us on the bus before a rat jump out!" one commanded the CO overseeing their transfer. The overpowering smell of garbage boarded the bus along with the passengers, and never left.

Worn and rusted metal doors and locks jangled incessantly as the bus bounced around the sinuous Lower Manhattan streets. Outside, New York City street life went on as usual, with nobody paying particular attention to what is, after all, a very common sight. Jarrod was transported in June, and the heat was stifling. The bus crawled across gridlocked Chinatown streets for upwards of fifteen minutes, making its way east to Bowery in stop-and-go traffic, only to loop around and return to the loading dock in a similar crawl. One of the COs had forgotten something. "CO, turn on the air conditioning!" one inmate yelled. Laughing, the CO replied that there was no air conditioner, and while the women had "grounds for a civil rights lawsuit," they would have to wait until its success in court to get their justice. The atmosphere was convivial. These were people who clearly spent a lot of time with each other.

Jarrod's bus crawled through the Lower East Side in search of the elusive "better way" across Manhattan in midday traffic. There was much grumbling by inmates and COs alike, including one woman exclaiming, "Where are all these people going at two o' clock in the afternoon?"—a phrase Jarrod had heard hundreds of times in his years of work as a New York City truck driver. At last the bus reached the United Nations building and entered the Midtown Tunnel to Queens. The bus then traversed a maze of industrial streets heading toward East Elmhurst. David's driver, in contrast, opted for the Manhattan Bridge and made much better time.

A noxious smell hit Jarrod's nostrils, and one of the women on his bus exclaimed excitedly, "Oh, we home!" an instant before the bus turned the corner and revealed the entrance to the Rikers Island Bridge. The bridge itself is a mile-long span with a slight elevation in the center that jolts passengers momentarily off their seats at the midpoint. Meanwhile, on the right sits LaGuardia Airport, so close to Rikers that its runways practically touch the island, with Citi Field, home of the Mets, looming behind it in the distance. "We're home!" other women on Jarrod's bus reiterated, cheering, upon reaching the other side of the bridge.

The intake area at C-76 ("Intake") features much of the same dirty and decrepit pens one finds throughout the chain of custody in the city's punishment system. Jarrod was uncuffed and herded into one pen with a putrid, unflushable toilet and a sleeping man whose tray of food, stripped only of its meat, was being devoured by a swarm of flies. A gentle sea breeze wafted in through windows covered in rusted iron grating and overgrown with greenery on the outside, emitting the smell of salt water, vegetation, and morning dew that permeates the island's windows to battle in vain with the odors of sweat, feet, piss, shit, burps, farts, and bleach that otherwise dominate the atmosphere.

Next, we turned our money over by feeding it into an electronic machine that resembled a MetroCard dispenser, got photographed, and turned over our civilian clothing, including our shoes. We were then ordered to strip to our underwear and hover above a BOSS chair, which looks a bit like a drugstore blood pressure machine but can supposedly identify metal contraband stored in the anus and mouth. We were then led into a small booth, open on one side, and told to remove our underwear and squat down, exposing our anuses. The male COs who oversee strip searches at Rikers fiercely guard their masculinity by performing shock and revulsion at the sight of male penises and anuses, which must in reality be quite routine sights to them after only a few days on the job. The muscular, heavily tattooed white male CO inspecting Jarrod barked an inaudible command, which Jarrod incorrectly interpreted to mean "spread your ass wider." When Jarrod did this, he learned that the CO had meant the opposite. "OK! OK!" he shouted, as if in great physical pain, "You're done!"

The visual inspection of the anus does not actually reveal any contraband unless the new arrival has been very careless in stashing it, and is thus far more about the performance of guard vigilance and inmate subservience than anything practical. Sociologist Harold Garfinkle called these rituals "status degradation ceremonies," performances in which the subordinate position of a class of people, in this case newly arrived inmates, is inscribed and repeatedly emphasized.[5] Incidentally, these searches are notoriously futile at Rikers; we were both reproached by several men in the intake dormitory for knowingly turning ourselves in to custody without contraband stashed on (or in) our bodies. (Jarrod did not disclose that he had in fact smuggled a flashlight into the facility in a pair of reading glasses, for the purposes of reading after lights out.)

After the strip search, we received "greens," ill-fitting forest green jumpsuits stamped "DOC" in six-inch white letters across the back, and so-called Air Patakis, flimsy, flat-bottomed Velcro shoes with no arch support. Generally speaking, Patakis run large, and all the clothes run small. Nothing really fits.

We got dressed and were ordered to escort ourselves to the clinic down the hall. It was an introduction to the fairly lax transport practices at C-76, where inmates are sometimes allowed to simply roam the halls unescorted. A befuddled Jarrod was dispatched to the clinic with no escort. He knocked on the door repeatedly, until someone on the other side shouted, "Come back later!" Confused about how to proceed, he just sat down on a nearby bench. When the door finally opened, Jarrod was greeted by a Black female CO loudly berating a crying man in a cage: "He's crying like a little boy," she taunted, "and he a grown-ass man!"

The C-76 clinic is a cramped office reminiscent of a food stamp processing center or drop-in center, worked by the same kind of civilian bureaucrat one would encounter in one of those spaces, and overseen by

COs posted up near the door. We had our vitals taken, underwent a perfunctory discussion of mental health, and were asked about dietary restrictions. Almost as a joke, Jarrod remarked that he was a vegan, and to his surprise, was sent a few cubicles down to a thirty-something Jamaican dietician with a big beard and large golden necklaces, one of which was the scales of justice. In the background, a professional shoplifter debated with the nurses whether his trade was morally wrong. Hearing this, the dietician remarked to Jarrod, "Who makes those rules? Who says 'Thou shalt not steal?'" He paused, before answering: "The rich! They say 'Thou shalt not steal' so we don't steal their things, and 'Thou shalt not kill' so we don't kill them! They don't follow those rules, only us!" He shook his head, and Jarrod followed in kind, before they both went on with the business of inmate intake at a facility where the poor are held captive at the behest of the rich. At least Jarrod was promised some vegan food.

David got his first glimpse of DOC's disorganization during his initial clinic visit. He was paired with one nurse who asked him a battery of questions about medical conditions, addictions, and so on, and then asked him to step into a bathroom and provide a urine sample. When he came out, he was paired with another nurse who asked him the exact same questions. A few days later, he was sent to the clinic again, only to repeat the entire process because his blood and urine samples had apparently been misplaced.

After processing in the clinic, we were returned to an intake pen. More waiting. Jarrod was, at last, issued his ID card and taken to the intake dormitory, where he received a flimsy and uneven rubber-coated mattress, two sheets, a green plastic cup, toothpaste, a toothbrush, a towel, and a small bar of soap. When David served his sentence a few years later, the DOC had switched from ID cards to ID bracelets, which he was cautioned to wear at all times. When he was finally moved from the holding pen to the intake dormitory, a CO unlocked a hallway closet as David and two other transferees waited beside him, fumbled inside for a moment, and then began throwing flaccid vinyl pillows, mattresses, sheets, and horse blankets onto the floor in front of them. One of the three had been to Rikers before; he immediately scooped up the least deflated-looking mattress and pillow. Though the other two were issued cups at this time, the CO could not find one for David. "Sorry, man," he said as he locked the closet, "just ask the floor officer in the morning." It ultimately took three days for David to get a cup.

Musician and New York City counterculture leader Ed Sanders, who served city time at Hart Island in 1962 following a sit-in at the Atomic Energy Commission, recalls his own intake: "We were processed into the citadel. . . . We were given some stiff black shoes, loose jeans, [a] blue shirt, towels, and [a] thick green overcoat. Never in my life had such a negative rush of immediate boredom stormed my soul."[6]

The Incomprehensible Order

One's first time entering a massive caged dormitory filled with captive men can be quite overwhelming, and is a crucial moment for the new arrival. "When you walk into a house on Rikers Island, it's all eyes on you. . . . Everybody lookin' to see if they know you from somewhere . . . to see if you a rat, gang member," explains one formerly incarcerated YouTuber.[7] "I noticed the garbage in various corners of the huge room," recalls Marcos Perez, who served city time in the early 2010s. "The steam from the bathroom carried the odor of numerous people relieving themselves. Further in, people sitting, standing, talking, and arguing. . . . Then the silence and attention turned toward me as I slowly walked in, looking for a bed of my own."[8] So too did we take in this intimidating setting as much as possible, without appearing doe eyed, before making our way to the harsh bedframe that would serve as home base for navigating an unfamiliar and threatening terrain.

In the days after our arrival, we received the second half of the institutional intake, in which we were instructed by demonstration how the facility was to be run. We learned that rules and policies were selectively enforced, and often just made up, depending on the day and the CO in charge. Jarrod had a very difficult time getting a copy of the *Inmate Handbook*, which is supposed to be made available to every new arrival. While David was later able to grab one from a stack in Intake, during Jarrod's time, they were scarce in C-76, and men who showed up to the 11-Lower dormitory with the handbook saw it confiscated as "contraband" by COs who were sick of hearing that they violated inmates' rights. A common motto within the DOC describes the job as "care, custody, and control."[9] One CO during Jarrod's time, a Black woman who spent much of the day bellowing obscenities at any inmate looking in her general direction, spelled out exactly what this means on Rikers: "It's called 'care, custody, and control': I don't care, you're in my custody, and I'm in control."

The COs' rule by belligerent force begins immediately and constitutes the most visceral aspect of institutional intake. Those arriving at a new house are often berated by COs for their personal hygiene, humiliated in front of other inmates with a variety of schoolyard taunts, and warned in harsh tones to do what they are told, not cause any trouble, and basically "shut the fuck up," as some COs were quick to command. Questions of any kind about how the house functions are generally treated by COs as a major inconvenience, or else eyed suspiciously. COs are commonly instructed that nearly every request from an incarcerated person, including asking for basic amenities like toilet paper, is likely the beginning of a complex process of seduction that will lead the CO to ruin.[10] When David, newly arrived, asked a CO how to sign up for a clinic visit, she responded with disgust that he was "a real smart-ass" and simply walked away. On a more basic level, the freedom to not care about inmates' basic needs, except when the spirit moves them, is a coveted part of Rikers COs' daily work. Accordingly, they made it clear from the onset that regardless of what was said on paper, they did not have to lift a finger to do *anything* for an incarcerated person, unless they damn well wanted to.

This applied to daily schedules, which were hopelessly opaque. The times for elective daily activities like sick call or law library were not announced in advance, and often conflicted, with no warning or recourse. Inmates, for example, had to decide if going to sick call, their daily chance to (maybe) see a doctor, was worth possibly missing their daily trip to the yard, if it was called while they were out. And if they missed sick call because they could not hear the announcement over the impossibly loud dormitory noise, it was their fault for not paying attention, and they might have another chance to get it right tomorrow. Everything was called abruptly, as inmates who had been waiting around for hours were suddenly summoned with excited shouts, belittled for taking too long, and threatened with being left behind. This false urgency, coupled with vast stretches of dead time, whether at the behest of a CO's whim, or the jail's lumbering bureaucracy, called to mind the old military adage: "Hurry up and wait."

With no efficient system in place for addressing the dormitories, COs simply bellow commands on the spot, and become incensed when they are not immediately followed by inmates who often cannot even hear them. Meanwhile, the COs very publicly prioritize small talk among themselves, often loud and without concern for being overheard, over the needs of inmates, however pressing. "At first their carefree banter seemed to have nothing to do with me," recalls Michael Walker, "but then I got it in my head that they were ignoring me on purpose—like they wanted me to feel unimportant."[11]

Though DOC policy calls for daily orientation sessions to be conducted by COs for all newly arrived inmates, neither of us ever saw or even heard of such a thing at Rikers, nor had anyone we met while incarcerated there.[12] On the contrary, most of what we learned about the institution from COs we gleaned not from their explicit instruction but by watching them operate. As Gresham Sykes argues, "The incomprehensible order or rule is a basic feature of life in prison."[13] This was also observed over a century ago by New York City political prisoner Carlo de Fornaro, who served eight months of city time on Blackwell's Island in 1910. "As there are no written rules, and nobody informs us of all the unwritten rules on our entrance here . . . this apparent forgetfulness is really meant to give the warden and the keepers an unchallenged power of persecution over suspected and unruly convicts."[14] More recently, longtime federal prisoner Michael G. Santos recalls remarking to an uncooperative guard, "Living in the unknown is just part of being a prisoner. Isn't it?"[15]

When pressed for explanations, COs most often default to a parental "because I said so." They do this partly because it is simply easier for COs to bark commands than explain themselves, which enables them to tailor their work to whatever is easiest and most convenient for them, inmate needs be damned. It also derives from the COs' quasi-military structure, in which those who interact with inmates mostly fall at the bottom of a harsh chain of command, and receive similarly unqualified orders on a last-minute, need-to-know basis. In this sense, COs simply extend this hierarchy to their relations with inmates, rudeness and all. But their refusal to provide information is also more fundamental. As Sykes argues, "Providing explanations carries an implication that those who are ruled have a right to know—and this in turn suggests that if the explanations are not satisfactory, the rule or order will be changed."[16] Refusing to explain themselves is both a symptom and a source of COs' unchecked power.

This command over daily life becomes so powerful that many COs become accustomed to dictating the very nature of reality. When Jarrod took a urine test in the clinic, the CO told him to place the cup on top of the blue trash can, and pointed to a red trash can. Jarrod hesitated for a split second, looking at the can, and then at the CO. "Put it on the red trash can!" the CO emphasized, as if he had said that the first time. Flummoxed, Jarrod complied, and received a look as if to say, "Was that so difficult to understand?" Similarly, Jarrod was dispatched to the mail room, and having not received mail for several days, hastened to make it there within a matter of minutes, only to find nobody inside. Upon his return, he was told, "You must have taken too long to get there."

This attitude in particular is the cornerstone of the longstanding practice among Rikers COs of covering up their own transgressions, including violence against incarcerated people, by getting their stories straight with their coworkers, and converting their lies into institutional truths through the alchemy of paperwork. A 2014 Department of Justice investigation into adolescent facilities at C-74 and C-76 found systematic embellishment of paperwork, sanctioned up and down the chain of command, to routinely cover up incarcerated people's injuries and make COs' wrongdoings, and even the formal processes in which COs must explain their uses of force, vanish through the invocation of bureaucratic word magic.[17]

"Officers were always told not to start shit outside their jail," recalls former Rikers CO Gary Heyward, "because when it comes down to writing reports and coming up with lies to cover your ass, you'd rather they come from officers from your jail that you have a bond with, that you trust."[18] Former CO C. René West recounts being instructed by a senior officer on how to fabricate disciplinary write-ups, or, in the institutional language, make them "more juicy." "When he was finished making my report 'more juicy,' it was a completely different scenario. A small curse like 'fuck you bitch' turned into a threat to kill my mother, rape me, or to visit me once he was released."[19]

In his first week, David was told by an officer in the Bubble that he could not leave for his visit because there was "an alarm." When he asked what that meant, she frowned and impatiently told him, "Ask your fellow inmates, sir." About a month into his sentence, David tried to give a small load of laundry to the institutional laundry services. The CO scowled and turned away, saying, "Can't you just wash it yourself?" Incidents like this are emblematic of a CO mindset based around abdicating the responsibility they are hired to take on, especially the "care" portion of the department's motto, and becoming indignant when asked to fulfill it. Most new arrivals, therefore, are left to rely on other inmates.

"This Is Jail": Social Intake

Jarrod was struck by how often inmates stated the obvious fact that they were presently located in jail. "This is jail!" was a popular refrain in a number of situations. It could refer to the lingering surprise that one had transitioned from free life to being incarcerated: "This is jail!" uttered incredulously. Lil Wayne notes in an early entry to his Rikers diary, "I traded a coffee pack for a pack of noodles. Damn . . . I'm really in jail!"[20] It could be an imperative, a reminder that the setting called for steely resolve: "This is jail," meaning "toughen up." It could be a simple, dismissive statement of fact, almost like a shrug: "This is jail," so what do you expect? Above all, it was the affirmation that this was a social setting with particular rules different from those of the outside world. "This is jail," and you had better behave accordingly. This sentiment figures prominently in social intake, the process by which inmates instruct the new arrival in the written—and largely unwritten—rules structuring daily life in the facility.

Former Rikers detainee Russell "Half" Allen dramatizes his own experiences with social intake at C-74 in the novel *Gladiator School*. "Listen kid," an old-timer named Mr. Thomas tells the young Half as they exit the DOC bus on Rikers, "I want you to stay focused and stay to yourself. You didn't come here to make friends. You do your time, and you get your ass home. That's the plan, you understand?"[21]

For those who come from neighborhoods and other social settings with considerable overlap with Rikers, or have previous experience with incarceration, learning the ropes in a new facility is a matter of parsing out minor local differences, such as the governing rules of a particular building or dormitory. For this, there is a vibrant network of communication, publicizing local knowledge throughout the facility. As one incarcerated man tells rookie CO Rakin Mohammad in the novel *Across the Bridge*, written by former Rikers CO Steven Dominquez, "Word travels quick here, big dawg. Rikers isn't as big as you think it is, especially for a person like me who comes in and out of this bitch."[22]

For inmates like David and Jarrod, whose prior knowledge of jail life was largely restricted to popular culture and anecdotes from other nontraditional inmates, much of the social world is mysterious. Yet it is urgent to learn it as quickly as possible, at the risk of making a disastrous faux pas. A codefendant of Jarrod's who was locked up at C-76 before him described it as "an endless hermeneutic" in which almost every social interaction and daily activity comes with a set of structuring norms that are invisible, and initially bewildering, yet necessary to decipher and observe.

Jarrod's social-intake process began before he even boarded the bus. Waiting in line at the city courthouse on the day he was to begin his sentence, Jarrod sparked up a conversation with a young man who claimed to frequent the island, and who broke down his time strategy: "Don't look at the calendar, don't look at the clock." Such pithy proverbs are plentiful throughout the system. Shortly thereafter Jarrod received another from an inmate with experience in both city and state facilities. He explained that the key to navigating the push and pull of macho posturing in the jail is presenting a stern front while actually practicing benevolence and kindness to those around you or, in his words, "being nice, without looking like a bitch doing it."

Jarrod also benefited immensely from the insights of a codefendant who wrote a step-by-step guide explaining what Jarrod could expect. It began, "I think it's safe to say that it won't be nearly as bad as you're expecting it to be. If you just stay within yourself, stay thoughtful and humble, you'll be perfectly fine." This kind of firsthand knowledge, which really only comes from word of mouth, proved invaluable in mitigating the fear that accompanies uncertainty in such a hostile setting. David was put in touch with a number of formerly incarcerated activists, including Jarrod, before his sentence began. Though all offered useful advice for serving time, David found that nothing can truly prepare a person for the first time behind bars.

The most important part of social intake begins in the dormitory. Among the first instructions new arrivals get from their fellow inmates is a rundown of the hygiene standards, often emphasizing the prohibition of naked showering and the necessity of covering oneself while using the toilet. These commands echo throughout the intake dormitory. Another early lesson revolves around use of the dormitory's telephones. While these are technically free for anyone to use any time they are turned on, lines of gang affiliation and other soft-power dynamics structuring dormitory life often dictate otherwise. Socks placed on phone receivers communicate the presence of these rules, and it is incumbent on the individual to figure out what they mean. The results of ignoring or disobeying them could be violence, or at least public humiliation signaling vulnerability.

Other house rules may govern the maximum state of undress permitted in the dorm, who can touch the TV and when, who can open the windows and when, who can sleep in which bed or "section," where to walk in order to avoid disrupting what little privacy is available, and even how to use the Cambro drink dispenser for ice cubes or beverages. Inmates also share information about the personalities of individual COs, which rules are enforced and by whom, what kind of tacit agreements exist between them, such as the proper protocol for smoking without getting in trouble, and scheduling information like when the house goes to commissary. Often enough, all of this is readily communicated by one or more inmates who pull the new arrival aside to tell him the ropes. If the arrivant is lucky, this will be somebody known to him from another house or the street. If not, as the reader is likely aware from popular culture, overenthusiastic interest shown by a stranger could be the sign of a predator.

Accordingly, we were both warned to refuse any act of generosity shown by strangers upon our arrival. Leaving nothing to chance, we both insisted on offering objects for trade in exchange for the first items we wanted—writing utensils, relatively worthless commodities in the jail economy—lest we be ensnared in a web of extortion. David flat-out refused another inmate's offer to give him a couple of packs of ramen noodles until he could go to commissary. In all likelihood, with the benefit of hindsight, the people who offered these items were probably just being nice. It is much more common for sentenced men on Rikers to share food and hygiene products with each other, even with new arrivals, than might be assumed. This is not to say that extortion and other forms of predation do not exist but that most people David and Jarrod met were simply trying to make the best of a bad situation, and were willing to help others when they could.

Since city time is often served in multiple locations, beginning with the intake dormitory and then spread across any number of houses with different de facto rules, social intake never really ends. Even a seasoned inmate arrives at a new house in need of basic information. Upon transfer, Jarrod was pulled aside by a few inmates and politely yet firmly told, "This is a work house. We keep things quiet here, and don't want any trouble."[23] This sentiment was repeated, almost verbatim, by the dormitory's COs. This was no coincidence; Jarrod soon observed how a compact had been reached, under which COs overlooked minor infractions (smoking, for instance, was constant and almost always ignored) in exchange for a quiet and orderly facility. In this house, open belligerence toward staff and other inmates, which might be a path to shotcaller status in a more chaotic dormitory, was frowned upon. People looking to make good names for themselves by causing a conflict were more likely to turn the whole dormitory against them than win its respect.

The first bed David picked was empty, but as soon as he put his belongings down on it, one of the men next to it let him know that he might want to move: it was a "hot" bed, and had contraband stashed in it. David settled on a bed across the dorm next to a thirty-something Black man he did not know, and two Black men he had been with in the intake dorm the day before. Jarrod arrived in the intake dorm and soon realized he had an entire section to himself, even as the rest of the dorm was getting crowded. He later learned that shortly before his arrival, two inmates serving short "skid bid" sentences had quarreled in this section. One shoved the other, who fell, hit his head on the bed next to Jarrod's, and died. Before the week was out, however, the bed in question was the scene of a lively game involving bouncing a marble-like Fireball hard candy off the metal, trying to sink it into one of the frame's ventilation holes. Soon it was taken by a new arrival, and the stigma forgotten.

The designated intake dorm, 1-Upper, was a chaotic place because its population was always transient, meaning that no enduring power structure could ever be built. Both inmates and COs told David that incarcerated men generally spent as little as two days but no longer than two weeks in 1-Upper. David arrived there near midnight, and just picked a random bed in the near-empty dorm. There was nobody running the dorm, and nobody had much of anything, having just arrived from the street or another facility. There were no books, nothing to write with or on, and no commissary food or hygiene products, since no one had been able to go to commissary yet. The other inmates there quickly learned that David was a first-timer, and helped him learn the ropes. One guy demonstrated how to tie his sheet around his mattress properly so it would stay put. Another showed him how the phones worked and offered him a phone call.

Once David arrived in his first long-term dorm, and settled in next to his acquaintances from the intake dorm, some inmates immediately offered him commissary food while others explained how the phones and the bathroom worked. One man in his section, a Puerto Rican in his fifties, offered to hook him up with "the best jail job there is" (in his opinion, the bakery). "Write your number down here, and I'll talk to my boss," he said. David, not yet in a jail mindset, confusedly asked the man if he meant his phone number. The man sucked his teeth and shot him an incredulous look. "No, man—your book and case number!"

The same man also enthused over how David had chosen a good bed, because it had a view of the moon at night. After nightfall, he squinted and pointed a finger up at a white disk above the neighboring wing of the building. "See?" he told David. "The full moon!"

It was a searchlight.

Naming Conventions

Social intake also establishes how inmates will be identified. If one does not know another's name, he is nevertheless likely to have heard his last name called out by a CO at some point, and to therefore use that name until he learns the most commonly accepted or preferred nickname. David witnessed this play out countless times with new arrivals: they began by addressing others by their last names, but were within no time calling them by their street or jail names as if they were old friends. The exception, of course, occurs when inmates see familiar faces upon entering the dorm, as often happens on Rikers, where the population is spontaneously rotated between housing units by the administration and where very few are first-time offenders. This means that many men recognize one another either from the outside world, from other housing units on the same bid, or from previous bids.

In an environment where old friends are always leaving and new faces always arriving, inmates give each other nicknames primarily as a matter of convenience. Some people's nicknames were bland descriptions, such as "White Stan" or "Black Stan," nicknames used in one dorm to avoid the confusion of living with two Stanleys. David was often called "Red" by those who did not know his name for the color of his beard, a common jail and prison practice. If a guy was from somewhere other than New York, he was likely to be referred to by the name of that place, especially if he had an accent. Thus, "India," "Jamaica," "Colombia," and "DR" (Dominican Republic), but also "Baltimore" and "Chicago." Strangely, this practice was sometimes even applied to those from less exotic locales, such as "Jersey" or even "Brooklyn." Latinos who at least vaguely fit the preconceived notion of what Mexicans look like were uniformly referred to as "Mexico," and a man from the nation of Georgia that David met was, to his constant consternation, referred to as "Russia." Irish or Irish American people, in accordance with general jail and prison convention, were referred to as "Irish" rather than "Ireland," possibly because the former is easier to pronounce quickly and repeatedly.

Another basis for giving someone a nickname was resemblance to a famous person. This practice gave rise to "Richard Gere," "MLK," "Scottie Pippen," "Abraham Lincoln," and many, many more. This naming convention served the double function, as do many street names or nicknames, of being good for a laugh—after all, imagine serving time with Scottie Pippen and Richard Gere.

Nicknames might likewise be good for a laugh if they stem from a description of a person's behavior or demeanor: "Scratchy" (a man with pruritis), "Bugout Sam" (a mentally ill man with violent, unpredictable mood swings), "El Presidente" (a somber Latino man with a dignified bearing), and "The Don" (a raspy-voiced Italian American with a scar on his face and a calm disposition).

Elderly folks are generally referred to as "OG" ("original gangsta") and Muslims as "Ack" ("brother" in Arabic, a term of endearment also common on the outside).

Others had typical macho street names like Rambo, Crusha, and Jungle. Gang members often had gang-specific nicknames, and would not tolerate any other designation. For all inmates, whether or not they accepted the names others gave them said a great deal about their personality and place in the social hierarchy. Some found their names disparaging or insulting—and indeed, nicknames could often be a tool of humiliation. For example, David witnessed inmates dubbed "Fartboy" and "Dirty Bird" against their will.

Jailhouse Argot

A new arrival quickly learns, if he does not already know, how to speak in a way that does not attract the attention of COs or other prying ears, and to keep it unclear to those who are not privy to the conversation what exactly he is talking about. This skill is practically second nature to many incarcerated people, cultivated over either previous stints or years of growing up in working-class urban neighborhoods. But others, like us, had to learn to say things like "I got that for you" instead of "You can have that newspaper you asked for when I'm done reading it," or "thanks for that" instead of "thanks for that jar of peanut butter you lent me." In general, asking people where they got things is highly taboo. Instead, you ask them if they have more, if you can have them when they go home, if they can they get you some, and so on. The reason is simple: in an environment where everything is overheard and scarcity and desperation are the rule, any stray word might invite a horde of others asking for the same. Talking this way also avoids inadvertently incriminating oneself or the person one is speaking to, as it is often impossible to know if the authorities or a snitch might be listening.

In time, this became second nature for us, too. Around the middle of his sentence, after he had fully transitioned to using jailhouse argot but when it was still fairly new, David was sometimes surprised to hear himself speak. Whereas he had never addressed people as "bro" in the outside world, David soon found himself tagging this word onto his sentences as a marker of in-group camaraderie. The only other word used this way, generally speaking, was the n-word, which was not really an option for him; when he used "dude," people sometimes laughed or asked him if he was from California. David also found himself formulating questions in a way more typical of working-class New Yorkers, such as "Let me get that?" instead of "Can I have that?" After a few months, this manner of speaking came naturally, allowing David to blend in as much as possible.

There are other particularities of incarcerated speech, though it is often difficult for us to parse out whether they are specific to Rikers, the world behind bars in general, New York City, African American Vernacular English, or the street vernacular spoken by people of all backgrounds that is so heavily influenced by it. Men looking for a way to respectfully attract the attention of another inmate they do not know will often address him as "big dog" or "big man," regardless of his physical stature. The use of "good lookin'," a common slang expression meaning "thank you," is ubiquitous. "Thanks" is rarely heard, and almost never does anyone say "thank you." This may be the case because thanking someone is an expression of indebtedness, which puts the thanker in a submissive position vis-à-vis the person being thanked, carrying implications of weakness.

Just Another Inmate Lying

One of the first and most essential skills any city-time inmate must acquire is the ability to get a read on the people around him. Besides the obvious factors like race, ethnicity, age, and size, there are a number of more subtle cues inmates pick up on. When a new arrival enters a dorm, for example, he is immediately scrutinized by the residents: how he walks, how he looks around the room, how he speaks to other people, how clean or dirty his clothes are, how old or new his shoes are. If he has braids, dreadlocks, or cornrows, the length of hair grown out underneath his coiffure can give an approximation of how long he has been locked up. The same holds true for fingernails and beards: though they are not always a sure sign that an inmate has been in for a long time, if they are grown out, that is likely to be the case. How much the person is carrying in the way of personal belongings, too, can serve as an indicator of social status, financial resources, gang affiliation, or length of time behind bars.

This sort of interrogation via gaze is not lost on the new arrivals, who are well aware that they are both subject and object at the same time.

This dynamic holds true even beyond an inmate's initial arrival in a dorm, as the forced proximity of their living conditions means inmates are constantly evaluating each other's actions and refining their opinions of each other. Thus, many inmates take great pains to impress others with their manliness or feats of criminality. To hear them tell it, most inmates had never lost a fight and were always moving serious weight, living the good gangsta life before their arrest. The fact that many inflate their personal histories is well known, as evidenced by the common jailhouse saying, "You know what 'jail' stands for? 'Just another inmate lying.'" For comparison, this sort of fish tale was generally much less tolerated upstate, according to those who had been there.

There are also questions that every inmate is expected to answer if asked by another incarcerated man, such as "What're you in for?"—a question so ubiquitous everyone seemed to accept it as normal. Neither of us ever heard anyone speak ill of the practice, and in fact it was almost taboo to criticize it. The same went for asking another inmate's release date or sentence length. These questions often went together: "What you in for? How long you got?" or "How long they gave you?" and "When you go home?" This seemed to be primarily a feature of life among sentenced men, who generally avoided asking these sorts of questions of pretrial detainees, who were often facing much more serious charges. For this reason, many pretrial detainees seemed generally less forthcoming with this sort of information, even if they could not avoid it altogether: refusing to discuss one's charges, or giving indirect answers, aroused as much suspicion among them as it did among sentenced men, and could easily put someone in danger.

Above all, the combination of institutional and social intake forces the inmate to become callous to experiences that would ordinarily inspire disgust, terror, and heartbreak, and to accept the setting of the jail enough to eke out a bearable day-to-day life within its walls. It is a simple matter of survival. In his C-76 diary, Lil Wayne recounts witnessing an attempted suicide. "And because I was in jail," he recalls, "I was like, damn, that nigga is crazy . . . oh well, what are we eating tonight?"

"Jail desensitizes a lot of things," Weezy concludes.[24]

2

The People of City Time

During our time, the majority of city-time inmates were locked up for nonviolent misdemeanors. In 2019, when David began his city time, six thousand people received city sentences, constituting 11 percent of the daily Rikers Island population. The most common charge was misdemeanor minor theft (1,150), meaning that the items stolen totaled less than a thousand dollars. The next largest numbers were for misdemeanor assault (400), misdemeanor drug possession (400), misdemeanor criminal contempt, which most often means violating a restraining order (230), and felony assault (220). The figure for drug possession was particularly significant, as diversions into "alternatives to incarceration" and a decrease in prosecution of misdemeanor drug cases had, in recent years, significantly diminished the prevalence of inmates with that charge.

Roughly half of these six thousand people served thirty days or less of city time, largely for theft and drug possession. Fifty-five percent of these received their sentences while detained, meaning that they were not out on bail, and the rest navigated their cases while unincarcerated. Inmates who served longer sentences (up to and in some cases exceeding a year) tended to be charged with assault, felony theft, and domestic violence. Of these, 79 percent received their sentences while already detained.[1] The high rate of misdemeanor theft charges, coupled with such high percentages of people unable to make bail (few, if any, of these men were denied bail altogether) underscores a truism of city time that is nonetheless worth repeating: these are men from the lowest rungs of the city's working class.

This data also supports our experience that city-time facilities, especially the intake dormitory, house a combination of people who are simply passing through, and others hunkering down for upwards of a year in captivity. Straddling this dividing line are the so-called weekend warriors, who have secured a sentence of consecutive weekends, ostensibly to serve their time while retaining employment and respecting familial obligations. These aristocrats of sorts among city-time inmates were few in number, and remained in the intake dormitory, where they tended to sleep as much as possible between their Friday evening intake and their Sunday evening release. One weekend warrior told Jarrod that the trick was to take as many downers as possible immediately before coming in, to minimize the amount of time spent awake on Rikers Island.

We found misdemeanor theft convictions to be largely the domain of men who cycle in and out of the shelter system and other precarious housing, and support themselves financially through shoplifting, either as one hustle among many, or as dedicated professional shoplifters, self-identified "boosters." Likewise, in a city where the elite have a famous appetite for illegal drugs, the men convicted on drug charges tend to be from heavily policed neighborhoods with high populations of working-class people of color. A 2013 study found that one-third of overall Rikers captives hailed from the South Bronx, Brownsville, East New York, Harlem, and Bed-Stuy neighborhoods.[2] When David began his time, the population of sentenced men was roughly 51 percent Black, 30 percent Latino, and only 12 percent white.[3]

Assault convictions seemed a bit more democratic in their distribution than drug and property crimes. It was this charge, for instance, that led Jarrod and David to Rikers, albeit in the context of protest activity. We also met men with assault convictions who were not as far down the class ladder as the average booster or habitual drug user, including some with lucrative jobs on the outside. The average domestic violence case was a bit more elusive for us to pin down, as we knew statistically that many inmates were locked up on "DV" charges, but they rarely admitted it. For example, Jarrod met only one man who spoke freely of his charge, albeit with the caveat, "The bitch set me up!" David met a number of men who were somewhat open about their DV convictions, but who always tried to downplay it, saying things like, "I slapped my girl around a little, you know how it is." Anyone telling a convoluted story about his charges that did not quite add up was assumed to be in for DV or something similarly inglorious, like sexual assault or indecent exposure. These inmates also seemed to be higher up the class ladder than the typical fodder for street arrests, though in most cases were still firmly working-class.

It is always a fraught undertaking to speak of large agglomerations of human beings using simple, abstract categories. Even within reasonably objective categories like geographic origin, income bracket, and family units, human beings evince almost boundless variance and defiance of classification.[4] For the purposes of acquainting the reader with the rough contours of city time, however, we have formulated four basic categories that account for the lion's share of the inmates we encountered inside.

The Inmates

Hustling and Boosting

The fast-talking street hustler is a ubiquitous presence in city time; we both encountered many inmates disparaging C-76 as a "shelter" due to its high rate of homeless men convicted of low-level property crimes. These men demonstrated high rates of drug addiction, particularly to heroin, coupled with severe and apparently untreated mental illnesses like schizophrenia. We met very few street hustlers whose lives were not defined in large part by one of these factors, and many who seemed wracked by their disastrous combination. While most of the street hustlers we met relied heavily on the city's shelter system, they did not receive city time for simply being homeless. And while petty drug possession and sale lands some street hustlers in city time, far and away the most common charge is misdemeanor theft, stemming from shoplifting, or as its practitioners call it, "boosting." In our experience, these self-identified "boosters" account for the vast majority of street hustlers serving city time.

For a short time Jarrod bunked next to one full-time booster, a middle-aged Black man who identified himself as homeless. He had been at Rikers two weeks prior, and was already back. He told Jarrod he liked one particular "white boy judge" who always gave him fifteen days instead of the sixty that the district attorney requested. Shortly before his arrest, he had been boosting air freshener liquid at Duane Reade. As he loaded boxes into a duffel bag, a yuppie confronted him. "Is that what you all do," the man said, "steal from the store like that?" Continuing to load boxes into his duffel bag, the booster replied, "Yeah, man. You look like you got a good job. I don't. And I been looking." The yuppie replied,

"Don't you see these cameras?" The booster said, "Man, I got out of jail last week. Difference between me and you is you're scared to go there and I'm not."

Dormitory life sometimes felt like a citywide boosters convention; large groups of them, prominent in the daily call for methadone, recounted their exploits with pride and enthusiasm: outsmarting sales clerks, securing lucrative fencing deals, and outmaneuvering the police. They often sounded like middle-aged men recounting their high-school-football glory days at the local bar—and true to form, the average booster was approaching this age. These rap sessions involved elaborate exchanges of information around the security protocols at various businesses; whether employees are permitted to interfere, whether they have facial-recognition software, whether they call the cops, and so forth. The most vocal boosters were self-identified professionals, akin to convict-criminologist John Irwin's professional thief, who treated their occupation with seriousness and derived pride and identity from their work.[5] With keen precision they spoke of calculating the smallest items with the highest value, balanced with their ability to easily find a fence to pawn it off. For example, Jarrod met one man who stole nail polish from CVS in large quantities. He had a deal with a Chinatown nail salon, which bought his inventory and even requested particular colors and brands for the future. David met one booster who proudly claimed that his trade had gotten him banned from every Duane Reade above Fifty-Ninth Street.

Boosters work hard for their money. Jarrod bunked next to another middle-aged man who recounted his lucrative racket filling a sack with Häagen-Dazs in Midtown Manhattan and quickly hopping on an uptown bus by asking departing passengers for their tickets. Once in Harlem, he and his partner would sell containers that retailed for five dollars for only two dollars to bodega owners, selling out before they even melted. Stealing an average of one hundred containers per run, he and his partner would split two hundred dollars.[6] He estimated that he had stolen seven thousand dollars' worth of ice cream from Duane Reade. Unfortunately, their corporate office also made estimates: they compiled surveillance footage of him stealing over one thousand dollars' worth of ice cream, sufficient for the state to charge him with grand theft. He was sentenced to a "bullet" (a "city year," or eight months after time reduced for good behavior) but was perfectly comfortable at Rikers; he ordinarily lived in a homeless shelter, and did not find Rikers much different. Like Irwin's professional thief, many boosters treat short-term incarceration as an occupational hazard. They are distinguished from other professional thieves, however, by the pettiness of their trade; instead of occasional big jobs that carry potentially long prison sentences, boosters are always at work, in low-yield, low-risk undertakings. If thieving is a profession, they are what we might call its precariat.

In addition to the professional boosters, who were more likely to be gregarious and boastful, we also encountered many street hustlers whose lawbreaking was rash, uncalculating, often pathetically inept, and doomed to failure. David met one man who robbed a bank with a note demanding eight hundred dollars, which he received, only to be captured waiting for the bus outside. Some of these men were withdrawn almost altogether from the life of the dormitory, wandering in a state of confusion that earned some of them the derisive distinction of "zombie." A subset of "zombies" only seemed to get out of bed for their daily dose of methadone. These particularly abject inmates seemed to be on the outside what the charming and gregarious street hustlers are on the inside: tragic men caught in an unending cycle of poverty, substance abuse, mental illness, and bad decisions, whose only agenda seemed to be escaping reality by getting high, and supporting this habit by any means necessary.

'Bout That Life

The main gangs on Rikers are Crips, Bloods, Trinitarios, and Latin Kings, though, during David's time at least, the "Folks" (Folk Nation) and "Salvatruchas" (MS-13) were also present in significant enough numbers to warrant occasional mention. Jarrod, who sports short hair, tattoos, and an athletic build, was approached by a gang intelligence officer and clumsily accused of being a member of the Aryan Brotherhood. "I am aware of twelve of you on the island," the CO told Jarrod, who did not envy—or pity—the men up against those odds.

The 2023 NYC Mayor's Management Report for the Department of Correction estimates that "at least 14 percent [of inmates] are affiliated with a security risk group [SRG], or gang."[7] The accuracy of this figure is somewhat debatable: as evinced by Jarrod's Aryan Brotherhood anecdote, the DOC sometimes tries to label neutral inmates SRG (David witnessed at least two other cases of this), and many gang members are of course unknown to the authorities, despite the creation of an "interdepartmental gang task force" to combat the rise of gangs in Rikers in the mid-1990s.[8] The Bloods are widely accepted by both inmates and COs to "run the island," as by far the most numerous and well-connected gang there. In fact, the Bloods as they exist in New York City can be traced to Rikers Island itself. An incarcerated New Yorker known as Omar "OG Mack" Portee created the gang in C-73 in 1993 as a way to defend against the Latin Kings and the Ñetas, two then-dominant Latino gangs.[9] The Bloods, according to Rikers folk knowledge, displaced the Latin Kings in the late 1990s and have been on top ever since.

Those who are "'bout that life" generally espouse what is thought of as the typical "gangbanger" worldview: the pursuit at all costs of material success, represented by flashy luxury commodities, conspicuous romantic connections with traditionally beautiful women, willingness to break laws to make money and to use violence against one's adversaries, a code of not "snitching" or cooperating with authorities, and an overall culture of toughness in the face of danger or adversity. Importantly, not all gang members fall into this category—those who, despite enjoying formal membership in a gang outside, do not glorify these themes and instead go about their time quietly are not included here. Likewise, this category includes many inmates who are not gang members at all. Regardless of whether they are dedicated to a gang subculture, or are simple neophytes who play with the identity while at Rikers, what they have in common is great interest in the same themes and lifestyle as the mainstream current of gang members, such as the drama of high-risk criminal feats and the flashy material and social benefits of a life of crime, and they act accordingly. These are prisoners who identify with being "'bout that life."

There is nothing terribly novel about this persona in the annals of working-class criminal identities in the United States. The brazen, affluent, and smart-mouthed gangster has been a central figure of US pop culture since at least the earliest days of cinema.[10] Since the commercial success of so-called gangsta rap in the 1980s, a ready-to-hand gangbanger ethos has been marketed to young people of color through mainstream entertainment like music, television, and film. This means that apart from any involvement with street life, then, gangbanger is a stock identity that is readily available in the confusing transition from youth to adulthood. Thus, while this sort of identity at a place like Rikers usually derives from membership or adjacency to a gang on the outside, in its more abstract form it extends far beyond this framework, and can be adopted by just about anyone.

Gangs are organizations of localized affinity that have, since the nineteenth century, thrived in New York City's working-class communities hemmed in by ethnic and racial segregation coupled with exclusion from lawful, well-paying labor markets.[11] In neighborhoods where enduring segregation and poverty compound a generally stagnant job market to make lawful social advancement all but impossible, gangs offer the promise of social status, money, and power through participation in black-market economies, albeit at the cost of great risk to one's freedom and very life. Far from constituting a life apart from the rest of their communities, however, membership-based gangs like the Bloods and the Latin Kings also blend into ordinary social groups, as was demonstrated in the 2016 "Bronx 120" raid, when NYPD's so-called gang intelligence resulted in a sweeping indictment of scores of young people for "gang activity," which in many cases amounted to social ties with people accused of being in gangs.[12] Many gang formations, consisting of groups of friends organized on the basis of minuscule geographic areas like blocks, fall somewhere in between.

The term "gangbanger" is rarely heard on Rikers. Gang-affiliated city-time inmates eschew this noun in favor of its verbal counterpart, "to bang." New arrivals, for instance, are asked, "You bang?" meaning "Are you in a gang?" The term "banger," meanwhile, is really only used in reference to a weapon, a rudimentary homemade knife. Yet the gangbanger label is not a pejorative one to the men serving city time. While it may be imposed on them to their detriment by schools, cops, courts, and now the jails, the designation simultaneously provides them with the tools for making sense of their captivity and their position in the social worlds on both sides of the bars. It also provides a structure of social belonging; men group together around being 'bout that life, sometimes drawing on social bonds that exist outside of the jail, like preexisting gang or neighborhood ties, and sometimes fabricating new ones in the dormitory house.

Those who are 'bout that life accept its consequences and appear ready to see it through, no matter the cost. Among their leaders are men who have done prison time upstate, and adopted the identity of a seasoned convict. They hold social rank over men who have not served state time or otherwise distinguished themselves heroically in gang, street, or carceral culture, but only aspire to this status. Of course, city time is not doled out for offenses like murder and big-time drug dealing, which are synonymous with truly making a name for oneself in this regard. Most of the men who claim this identity during their city time are in for minor crimes that few rappers would celebrate in song. Many have not done time upstate or committed themselves to a life of crime in any substantial way. We witnessed a number of such inmates testing the waters by adopting clumsy tough-guy personas, attempting to cozy up to the more dedicated gang members, and generally acting like lost young men still grasping to find their way in the world—or at the very least, get through the ordeal of city time in one piece. Many of these neophytes or wannabes seemed to be searching for a sense of themselves in a world defined by their exclusion from many avenues of subsistence, self-expression, and social mobility. Those who try this identity on for size are nonetheless playing a dangerous game in the process, at an important crossroads in their lives.

Some Bullshit

Given the disproportionate infusion of police and courts into working-class communities of color in New York City, many ordinary men with no aspirations to a life of crime wind up in the meshes of the city's punishment system. Some of these men may experiment with the "'bout that life" identity. But many just wish to get through their time, return to their lives, and forget all about their city time. These men do not celebrate crime or their forays into criminalization. When they are asked what they are in for, a common refrain is, "Some bullshit."[13]

The inmates in for "some bullshit" are testaments to the racial and class biases of the punishment system. They are men of color locked up for things that we could not imagine a white person, especially of means, doing jail time for. Some of these are drug charges, involving possession or sale, that do not underlie a glorified life-of-crime identity; after all, plenty of people outside of that lifestyle use and distribute drugs, but young, working-class Black and brown men are far more likely to be stopped and searched, whether on foot or while driving. Others are even more tragic. Jarrod bunked next to a young Latino man who had assisted his cousin in transporting a television that turned out to be stolen. David worked alongside an undocumented Guatemalan immigrant who had been arrested twice for driving without a license, then fled the state. This is not to say that these men were faultless in the eyes of the law, but it is to say that many of these crimes would have resulted in instant probation, especially for first-time arrestees, in the white worlds that David and Jarrod hail from.

These men were largely familiar with the social world of the gangbanger, having grown up in communities where these subjectivities and forms of organization are common. They would make sure to distinguish themselves as streetwise and not to be messed with. But they were not chasing after gang status or glory in the social world of the jail. To whatever extent they represented street culture, it was to get themselves enough respect to not be preyed upon, and maybe enjoy some of the perks that come with familiarity with powerful cliques, like access to contraband. These men spoke of eagerly returning to their law-abiding lives, as blue-collar workers or entrepreneurs, and were decidedly not "'bout that life." The "some bullshit" inmates' careful negotiation of proximity to gang culture, and their studied removal from active participation, was in all likelihood a dance they had long cultivated on the outside.

You Don't Belong Here

A fourth category includes both of us: cases of bad decisions, bad luck, or initial forays into criminal activity by people who are noticeably atypical in the jail population. Similar to the "some bullshit" inmates, they defy others' typical image of someone who gets locked up at Rikers. These inmates, whom John Irwin called "square johns," are often told, "You don't belong here."[14] (David often heard this from sympathetic COs.) They can stick out like a sore thumb—often to their great displeasure, as conventional wisdom holds that inmates who look out of place are likely to have been locked up for sexual assault.

At Rikers, we found that "you don't belong here" inmates are locked up for multiple-offense drunk driving, domestic violence, drug possession, and strange petty crimes, like that of Jarrod's section mate, a young Latino man who spoke in full paragraphs and carried himself with the refined bearing and mannerisms associated with upper-class gay men, eliciting sideways glances from the other inmates. He landed in Rikers after he drunkenly set out for ice from a hotel room party, accidentally wandered into a restricted area of the hotel, and wound up in a confused tussle with a worker who attempted to physically remove him. He was charged with assault, on top of what was recast as trespassing. David met a man similar in demeanor, perhaps of South Asian or Middle Eastern ancestry, who claimed to have signed some paperwork that ended up featuring in one of Mayor de Blasio's multiple financial scandals of that period, and been sentenced to four months.

David and Jarrod presented their fellow inmates with this same puzzle: What could these men have done to receive city time? David became aware of unsettling rumors that he was inside for a sex crime, which were thankfully quashed. Jarrod was regularly asked *which* drug he was in for, and one group of inquiring prisoners did not believe he was not an addict, until one of them pointed out his muscles and the decent quality of his teeth as evidence Jarrod was telling the truth. Ironically, of course, the inmates who "don't belong here" are in fact locked up along with everyone else, and in considerable enough numbers to always have a few kicking around the dormitory. Often, the "you don't belong here" distinction was simply applied to inmates who were not Black or brown—by Black and brown inmates (and COs) who understood how much less likely these people were to get locked up, even for offenses, like drug use, that cut fairly evenly across all demographics.

"Let's face it," one city-time inmate told former Rikers writing teacher Jennifer Wynn, "for a white man to go to jail he gotta be a real fuckin' idiot."[15]

The COs

The New York City Department of Correction, constituting 3 percent of the city's total workforce, is extraordinarily large for a captive population of New York City's size. At the beginning of David's time in 2019, there were around 9,789 uniformed COs overseeing roughly 6,808 incarcerated people, even before COVID-19 occasioned a dramatic decrease in the latter, with no commensurate cuts to the COs.[16] As the federally appointed monitors overseeing Rikers as part of the *Nunez* litigation noted in late 2020, "The size of the Department's complement of Staff, particularly the number assigned to the jails, is highly unusual and is one of the richest staffing ratios among the systems with which the Monitoring Team has had experience."

Nevertheless, Rikers COs and their powerful union, the Correction Officers Benevolent Association (COBA) consistently argue that the island's failures to provide safe and constitutionally sound conditions for incarcerated people stem from understaffing, and demand more COs as a response to nearly any negative publicity, including abuse by COs. As the *Nunez* monitors argue, however, the bountiful overstaffing on Rikers might actually exacerbate violence, as "problems are precipitated, exacerbated, and catalyzed by the number of Staff who are present at the scene . . . [a practice] resulting in an excessive show of force that becomes counterproductive and likely catalyzes the need to use force in the first place."[17] Who are these staff?

Relations with inmates are mostly handled by rank-and-file guards, who insist on being called correction officers, or COs. Their supervision is attended to by captains, or "caps." Jail wardens and their various deputies and assistant deputies, also known as "deps," handle administrative tasks that require practically no interaction with the incarcerated. "Among the City's uniformed agencies," writes the Mayor's Office of Criminal Justice, "DOC stands out in terms of both gender and race."[18] While many readers may imagine Rikers to resemble the state prison system, where a workforce of overwhelmingly white COs oversees a captive population of overwhelmingly dark-skinned men, the vast majority of New York City's COs are Black and Latino. During David's time, white people made up 11 percent of rank-and-file COs and only 8 percent of uniformed higher-ups, a rate almost identical to the white percentage of DOC's incarcerated population. Meanwhile, Black people made up 59 percent of COs, and 74 percent of uniformed supervisors, and Latinos made up 24 percent of COs and 14 percent of uniformed supervisors.

The gender divide among rank-and-file COs was almost even, with 45 percent of COs being women. Among captains and supervisors, women were the majority—Black women in particular.[19] Until the mid-twentieth century, the small number of women who worked as guards were only employed in facilities for women. In the early 1970s, a series of lawsuits—backed by 1972 amendments to Title VII of the 1964 Civil Rights Act, and supported by the Equal Employment Opportunity Commission—opened up employment for women in men's jails and prisons. By the 1980s, women had established a small but secure foothold in US male facilities, despite the sexist attitudes of male guards and prisoners alike, and legal challenges by the latter to exclude women on the grounds that their presence violated incarcerated men's privacy.[20] At Rikers, where a relatively small group of women COs were first assigned to men's prisons under the 1984 tenure of Commissioner Jacqueline McMickens, herself a former CO, women today can represent upwards of half the workforce in a given male facility.[21]

Prospective Rikers COs must have a high school diploma and sixty college credits, or else two years' full-time work as a cop or either two years' full-time or six years' part-time military service with an honorable discharge.[22] As of 2021, new hires receive a base pay of $47,857, which does not include the considerable overtime COs are forced to work, which can more than double a CO's pay. It also includes twenty-four paid holidays and vacation days per year. After five and a half years on the job, this base pay jumps to $92,073 per year before overtime, and thirty-eighty paid days off.[23]

Becoming a CO requires taking the civil service exam and undergoing 640 hours of training at the DOC Academy, stretched across sixteen weeks. This intensive program emphasizes the basics of doing the job by the book, including daily custodial duties, best practices in interacting with incarcerated people, handling emergencies, understanding the chain of command, and, perhaps most importantly, filling out paperwork.[24] Academy training protocol, however, might not get much further than the paper it is written on. Former Rikers CO Gary Heyward paraphrases one trainer who told the class, "We are telling you how to do this shit. You ain't necessarily going to do it this way when you get inside the jails, but if you fuck up, don't say that we ain't teach you the right way to do it. These lessons are to cover our asses, not yours, when you fuck up." Sure enough, Heyward was instructed on his very first day at Rikers, "Everything that you learned in the Academy, forget about it. It's a whole new ballgame in here."[25]

A 2015 report by the New York City Department of Investigation (DOI) expressed shock and dismay at widespread social and familial ties binding COs with incarcerated people, which it attributed to DOC's failure to properly screen prospective hires. DOI based its findings on "over 200 hours of interviews with DOC staff and site visits and review of more than 75,000 documents related to the hiring process."[26] But if the department wanted a rich illustration of the deep social interconnectedness across DOC's bars, its investigators could have looked no further than the steamy pulp novels of former Rikers CO Yolanda "Yoshe" Dickinson, who worked as a CO from 1997 until 2004, when she was fired for "undue familiarity" with an incarcerated man. Writing under the pseudonym Yoshe, Dickinson subsequently released *Taboo*, the first of a series of "street lit" books set on Rikers Island, chronicling the sexual misadventures of Rikers COs with prisoners and each other.[27]

Yoshe's likely exaggeration of certain salacious details to sell books seems to have paid off: during his time, David found *Taboo*, with its central motif of pervasive back-room sex between incarcerated men and female COs, to be popular reading among sexually frustrated inmates—and at least one CO. Beyond the tales of forbidden romance, however, Yoshe's books depict the rich social fabric connecting Rikers COs and prisoners that one finds in neighborhoods like Brooklyn's Bedford-Stuyvesant. *Taboo*'s protagonist, Correction Officer Sierra Howell, navigates fraught networks of kinship bridging Rikers with Black New York, where she lives and searches for love alongside many of the island's incarcerated people and correction officers, and their families and friends.[28]

"Working in an all-male prison was a walk in the park; literally," recalls Robin K. Miller, who began her career as a Rikers CO in C-76 in 1983. "I grew up in the Brownsville housing projects, so for me, it was like walking down Stone Avenue. I recognized many faces and was never afraid to walk within the realm of incarcerated men."[29] This sentiment is echoed by Heyward: "For me, this job is mad easy. Shoot, coming from where I come from, it's just like hanging on the block."[30] More recently, a female CO of color told researchers, "I can relate to them because I am where you are from. Now, if you take me and put me in Maine, I would probably be fucked up. But because you have me with people from the Bronx, Brooklyn, Manhattan, like where I'm from, it's easier."[31]

Enduring segregation and structural racism in these neighborhoods makes employment in the DOC one of the most realistic and lucrative jobs available for young people seeking to avoid unemployment and criminalization. "With excellent health benefits and a pension after twenty years of service," writes former Rikers CO C. René West, "working as an officer is like hitting the blue collar jackpot."[32] West recalls the slogan of her and her fellow recruits: "Hired in my 20s, retired in my 40s, can't touch this."[33] Many New Yorkers who become COs, West argues, are thereby able to escape dependency on sex work and public assistance—or even becoming prisoners themselves.[34] Several COs affirmed to David that their friends and family members had passed through DOC custody over the years, serving as reminders that their own lives could easily have been much different.

When the revolutionary scholar Angela Davis was held at the Women's House of Detention in 1970, the COs, largely Black women, apologetically told her "they had been driven by necessity to apply for this kind of job. Apparently it was one of the highest-paying jobs in New York City that did not require a college education."[35] The main factors that seem to attract young COs are the salary, job security, and what former Rikers CO Gary Heyward emphatically calls the "BEN-O-FITS."[36] But the perks are not just monetary; former CO West also describes the newfound social status that came with being a uniformed peace officer, no longer a civilian, and encouraged to think of oneself as superior to those around one, in communities where continuing segregation and limited upward mobility make social advancement difficult.[37] Heyward similarly describes the "made-man status" of a secure city employee, coupled with the additional cachet of being a uniformed officer: "Everyone in the hood will know that nigga got a gun and a muthafucking badge."[38]

The same status dynamic is at work on the island itself. Former CO Umar Abdullah, during an interview with the podcast *Road to Legacy*, describes how he was initially afraid to start working at Rikers, despite being six-foot-five and in good shape, and how that changed once he got a taste of power: "When you're walking in and you've never done that before, into the facility and around the inmates, you're still in a civilian mindset. But when the inmates start walking away from you, that's when the mindset starts changing. Oh, wait—they're moving away from me like they're scared of me. Wait a minute, I'm a officer!"[39]

The relationship many COs display toward their job is rooted more in pragmatism than ideological support for "law and order" politics. "The correction officer exam was one of the many civil service exams I took in my early twenties," recounts West, who argues that her path to Rikers was less of a calling and more of a game of chance.[40] Summarizing his study of jail COs in California, ethnographer Michael Walker cautioned his reader, "If there is an expectation that more forethought than 'I passed the test' goes into becoming a [CO] you might be disappointed."[41] One of David's steady officers, who was later sentenced to federal prison time for smuggling contraband into Rikers, wrote to him in a letter from prison that he had started working as a Rikers CO "fresh out of college" at the age of twenty-one, and described it as "one of the worst decisions of my life," citing brutal working conditions, systemic corruption, dehumanization of incarcerated people, mandatory overtime, poor morale, and high rates of depression and even suicide among staff. Given that most COs see little higher calling than the paycheck and pension, and have to suffer greatly to obtain these, it is extremely common for Rikers COs to be in a foul mood, especially at the beginning of their shift. As one exasperated inmate in Jarrod's dormitory told a particularly belligerent CO, "I don't know how you can come from the town," meaning the free world of New York City, "in a worse mood than I woke up in."

Between COs and prisoners, there are both spectacular cases of corruption and ordinary favoritism. But it seems to be more common that COs refuse solidarity based on common racial, social, or geographic backgrounds, at least when it conflicts with the powerful solidarity binding them to their fellow COs. "Yeah, we're both brown," one female CO told a belligerent inmate in Jarrod's dormitory, "but I gotta stick with the blue." During her 1970 stay in New York City custody, Angela Davis spoke with a number of Black women COs, and later reflected how "some of them were keenly aware that they were treading in ambiguous waters. Like their predecessors, the Black overseers, they were guarding their sisters in exchange for a few bits of bread. And like the overseers, they too would discover that part of the payment for their work was their own oppression."[42]

Jarrod witnessed another instance of a Black inmate scolding a Black female CO for betraying Black people. "You don't let nobody mess with your paper on the streets," she responded, without missing a beat. "I don't let nobody mess with mine in here." This retort, framed in Black working-class argot, defended the CO's employment decision through its moral equivalency to the dog-eat-dog world of street culture. David and Jarrod both witnessed how COs are regularly berated by inmates for being traitors to Black and Latino people because they took jobs as COs; most often they just shrug, or even laugh it off, commonly invoking their pay when they do.

"I never felt that taking this job was a 'sell out,'" reflects West, "which is a term often used to describe a minority officer. I knew many inmates would prefer to see a kind, understanding face that tried to ensure they received the minimum standards instead of someone who would kick them in the face or throw them off the top dorm tier in the housing area if given the opportunity."[43] By contrast, many COs have also adapted to their position by adopting a warrior identity opposed to prisoners, christening themselves "New York's Boldest," as a rejoinder to NYPD's affectation of "New York's Finest." ("New York's Bravest" was already taken by the firefighters.) Initiated by guards, the slogan was later officially adopted by DOC leadership to flatter its guards.[44] This identity represents the working-class machismo that underlies the COs' approach to their job, in which they conceive of themselves as a cross between police "patrolling the toughest precincts in New York," as the current motto of the COBA insists, and an occupying military force.[45]

A CO's job is dirty work. COs labor in the same squalid and morose facilities where inmates live. They are regularly forced to serve mandatory overtime, keeping them on Rikers for upwards of eighteen hours straight. West recounts how female COs in particular are consistently degraded, verbally abused, and sexually harassed, not only by incarcerated men but also by their male coworkers. The violence of the incarceration that COs oversee bleeds into their relations to each other. COs who rock the boat are penalized by physical threats or transfer (which "means you lose your steady work hours, workdays, and working area"), arbitrary suspension, and even termination.[46] Getting in the good graces of supervisors, by contrast, translates to plum work assignments, with the least prisoner contact, and the ability to cut out early or get food delivered.[47] The COs inhabit a malicious, predatory, and dysfunctional social world. But long hours spent in the repressive environment of Rikers jails, working schedules that make traditional life routines difficult, and shared conditions that can be dangerous and would seem abhorrent to the vast majority of people all combine to make COs develop intense bonds of solidarity. "Like the police," write sociologist James B. Jacobs and former guard Harold G. Retsky, "guards may sometimes view themselves as a society apart."[48]

The social being of Rikers COs, forced as they are to work long days in a repressive environment overseeing the dehumanizing captivity of other human beings, often determines their consciousness, coloring the way they relate ethical and political questions, and supporting a conservative worldview. "Most of the guards are Black, usually from working class, upward bound, civil service oriented backgrounds," observed the Black revolutionary Assata Shakur, who was held as a pretrial detainee at Rikers Island's Correctional Institution for Women on multiple occasions between 1974 and 1977, and penned analysis that could largely have been written during our city time. "They identify with the middle class, have middle class values and are extremely materialistic." In one sense, these COs had few illusions. "Most are aware that there is no justice in the amerikan judicial system and that blacks and Puerto Ricans are discriminated against in every facet of amerikan life," Shakur continues. "But at the same time, they are convinced that the system is 'somehow lenient.' To them, the women in prison are 'losers' who don't have enough sense to stay out of jail. Most believe in the bootstrap theory anybody can 'make it' if they try hard enough."

This "middle-class" ideology, which Shakur argues helps the COs to forget that the main differences between them and the incarcerated people are "chance and the civil service list," is a powerful tool in helping COs rationalize the work they do.[49] We certainly found this to be true. One CO David knew, whose own brother had passed through Rikers in the past, insisted that most prisoners had made a choice to "stay in the street and do dirt."

Meanwhile, COs of color are subject to the same kind of structural racism and sexism that privilege white male workers throughout much of the US workforce. This leads to considerable grievances behind the scenes, including acrimony against white COs and captains, whom they perceive as discriminatory or undeserving of their professional advancement. It also leads to competition among COs of color, who are pitted against each other by the DOC bureaucracy, as are men against women. The united front that guards present to prisoners, then, is tenuous at best.[50]

As an important factor countervailing disunity, the collective identity of Rikers COs and the insular solidarity of this society apart is bolstered by their unions. Rank-and-file COs are enrolled in COBA, while their superiors are in the Correction Captains' Association, and the Assistant Deputy Wardens'/Deputy Wardens' Association. With the largest membership by far, and situated farthest from management, COBA leads the pack in guard militancy and public advocacy. Its history dates back to 1903, long before municipal unions were legally recognized as bargaining agents, and culminates in the present, when the union is among the city's most powerful.

While COBA has won lucrative pay increases and benefits for its members in this time, the foremost issue animating the union's activism has been the freedom of COs to use violence against incarcerated people however they see fit, free from bureaucratic oversight or civilian investigations. Echoing police unions, COBA's message is as simple as it is consistent: COs do the most dangerous and most important job in the city, and ought to be given as much power as possible, and otherwise left alone, by civilians who do not have the nerve or competence to do the necessary work of keeping the bad guys behind bars. Much like the CO workforce itself, COBA is a majority-Black organization. COBA members defy the cliché of jails filled with Black prisoners, guarded by whites, but are no less strident than majority-white guard workforces in their opposition to reform, civilian oversight, rights for incarcerated people, or anything that limits the power they wield in the workplace of Rikers Island.[51]

The Civilians

During David's city time there were roughly 2,027 civilian workers employed by DOC, compared with 8,949 uniformed COs.[52] Most manual occupations, like cleaning, cooking, laundry, and basic maintenance, are done by inmates. Civilian workers are concentrated in inmate programming, facilities maintenance, security, and central administration.[53] Additional civilian workers are employed by the New York City Department of Health + Hospitals, following Mayor Bill de Blasio's decision to recover DOC health services from the private contractor Corizon in 2015, amid scandal over inadequate services. During David's city time, there were roughly 426 full-time employees in DOC's healthcare services, stretched across medicine (138), nursing (232), and mental health (56).[54] Smaller pockets of civilian workers populate civil-society programming for a tiny fraction of DOC inmates, like education and prerelease counseling, provided by nonprofits like the Osborne Association, the employer of *Inside Rikers* author Jennifer Wynn.[55] David also worked alongside a small number of civilian cooks, perhaps twenty all told, in the kitchen at C-74. These employees handled food-preparation activities that required the use of knives and the enormous metal implements that come with operating an institutional kitchen.

C-76 and C-74 were designed to be facilities run by civilian correctional experts.[56] But beyond intake, the typical city-time inmate does not see many of them. The experience of civilian workers seems to be one of great discomfort, characterized by the same rule by threats and violence that COs use to police the inmates and each other. This is especially true in covering up violence against incarcerated people. Former Rikers clinician Mary Buser was cautioned by a civilian colleague, "You make a little too much noise and find your tires slashed."[57] This is corroborated by Homer Venters, former chief medical officer of Correction Health Services, who describes a repressive environment for civilians on Rikers, where anyone who opposes the brutal rule of the COs, including someone as high-ranking as he was, is berated and threatened by COs extending all the way to the top of the COBA hierarchy.[58] Kimberly L. Sue, who worked on Rikers from October 2018 to October 2020, recounts how these threats need not be explicit: "When a security officer strolled into my cubicle, I was immediately on guard. . . . It was not technically in my job description to work for them; however, it seemed impossible to deny them their requests."[59]

Though our evidence is much more anecdotal, civilian kitchen workers generally seem constrained by the same economic and social factors as the COs, and, as one might imagine, come from the same neighborhoods. Other civilian workers, like medical staff, seemed to include a higher proportion of immigrants. Doctors on staff varied between the rare progressive physician who actually wanted to help (one doctor David saw said his previous career in "third-world medicine" prepared him well for Rikers) and those who, either due to years on the job or simply because they arrived that way, generally showed themselves to be jaded and disinterested in their patients' health. Among inmates, medical staff were rumored to be "quacks" who had been sued for medical malpractice or otherwise fallen from professional grace before turning to Rikers.

Among the civilian program workers, those engaged in the most effective forms of social work were often ex-prisoners themselves. Sometimes these civilian workers had done considerable time, such as the Fortune Society representative, a regular appearance in one of David's dorms, who had done eighteen years upstate. Civilian staff for other programs tended to be progressive and sympathetic people who wanted to help those in custody, such as the breezy young Jewish woman who made weekly visits to discuss art techniques and history and encourage the inmates to make art themselves, or the young trans woman from Bushwick, gauges in her ears peeking out from beneath a skateboarding cap, who staffed the barista program. Occasionally, those getting involved in civilian-programming work behind bars had explicitly radical political orientations. Before beginning his incarceration, David was made aware of two fellow anarchists working in one of the programs at Rikers. After his release, he met two anarchist librarians who had engaged in work there in a civilian capacity. But no matter how benevolent their intentions, civilians have no illusions about who is calling the shots. In Buser's orientation, she was told to always defer to the COs: "Remember," the instructor emphasized, "you are guests in *their* house!"[60]

3

A Day in the Life

Every morning, the lights come on at Rikers Island and thousands of human lives play out within the confines of its walls. Life behind bars is a sad approximation of daily life on the outside; inmates eat their meals, groom themselves, catch up on the latest news, go to work, go shopping, attend religious services, seek medical care, socialize, navigate conflicts and feuds, try to keep up with their loved ones on the outside, and chase diversions through television, radio, and the printed word. At the end of the day, the lights go off and they go to sleep, just to do it all again the next day. Though nobody would mistake it for freedom, some semblance of life, however limited, goes on.

We do not believe it possible to speak with authority on the "typical" daily experience of a city-time inmate, and do not claim to attempt that here. Instead, to illustrate what kind of routine can be carved out of the chaos of jail life, we offer this sketch of a typical day for David while he was incarcerated in the 12-Lower dormitory in C-76. Set in the weeks and months before the closure of that building and the onset of COVID-19 caused considerable disruption in whatever normalcy could be said to define city time, it is at once a portrait of daily life at Rikers as we have come to understand it, and a document of that facility in what was perhaps the final stretch of its use as the primary site for caging city-time inmates, dating back to the mid-1960s.

Lights On

The overhead lights turn on all at once. Growling fluorescent tubes suddenly wash a room the size of a basketball court in pale bluish light. "Chow! Chow! Get up for chow!" the woman in blue at the front of the room urges loudly, if somewhat disinterestedly. According to the round plastic clock hanging on the inside of the plexiglass wall behind her, it's 5:30 a.m., near the end of her shift, and she has just spent the past several hours watching people sleep. Now, the room begins to come alive, its residents fighting their way out from under plain white sheets, some sluggishly, some effortlessly, as if they have done it a thousand times before. Most are clad in T-shirts or tank tops and gym shorts, all white, but some wear pants (forest green) and a few, only underwear or long johns—though these are sure to put on shorts or pants before they leave their bunks. We often heard it threatened by COs that appearing before a female officer in only his underwear could earn an inmate a serious disciplinary infraction, though we never encountered this infraction actually being issued. Perhaps more importantly, it might also draw the ire of other inmates who deem it "gay."

Out of sixty numbered beds, all but a handful are occupied. Most of the fifty-odd occupants get up when the lights come on, but perhaps ten do not. They stay in bed, despite the lights, the shouting, and the growing ambient drone of chatter and movement, either because they have jobs that do not start in the morning, because they are taking a day off from work, or—for a small number—because they don't work at all.

The other forty-odd men, who either work jobs that start early in the morning, as most do, or simply figure it makes more sense to get up and eat breakfast than to try to sleep through all the commotion, trickle briskly but groggily into the day room and line up along the wall. There is always a low-key sense of urgency when chow is delivered to the dorm: no one wants to be last, as those who are last tend to get smaller portions. Sometimes there is enough time to make a cup of coffee to go with breakfast, but today there is not. Though it only takes a minute at the hot pot, preparing oneself a cup of coffee will cost an inmate his place in line.

The gang members, who run the house, mostly position themselves at the front of the line, though a few showcase their humility by lining up in the order they arrive. The food, spooned out by a fellow gang member in a disposable plastic apron and hairnet (the COs insist on this point, because their superiors insist on it), is lukewarm grits, a carton of milk, and a pear. Even those gang members who don't rush to the front of the line receive larger portions, as do some of their "neutral" (not-gang-affiliated) friends. The plain steel tables, dotted with rows of built-in round steel stools, are scattered with loaves of crumbly bread wrapped in white wax paper. As they sit down to eat, the inmates rip these open and leave them sitting out for their fellow diners to take as they will. There are two spreads for the bread available on each tray: margarine, doled out to the tune of two pats each, and a small mound of grape jelly. Jelly is a hot commodity here: if it can be stored somehow, it can be used later for peanut butter and jelly sandwiches, or even some variations of cooking, like jailhouse barbecue sauce. To this end, a couple of skinny, scrappy guys with faded tattoos chug their milks, rinse their cartons out, and, after spooning their own jelly into them, go table to table soliciting it from others.

Having eaten, David returns to his bunk and grabs his green plastic mug and a packet of instant coffee crystals, but it is already too late: by the time he reaches the hot pot and pulls the plastic tap, only a dribble of warm water comes out. He asks the CO on the floor to unlock the padlocked plexiglass case holding so he can take the hotpot into the bathroom and refill it beneath the tap. She is one of the dorm's "steady officers," meaning that this is her regular post, and she is usually pretty accommodating, but not now. "In a minute," she mumbles, swarmed by inmates thrusting their wristbands at her. "We're giving out razors right now." Razors are only available Monday to Saturday from 6:00 a.m. to 10:00 a.m. To get one, a person must hand his DOC-issued ID band, which he needs to go anywhere outside the dorm, to the CO on duty. This CO, after verifying that the ID band does indeed belong to the person handing it over, in turn pushes it through an immovable metal slot in the wall behind the CO, just below the giant sheet of plexiglass that forms the upper half. On the other side, another CO sets the ID band aside and replaces it in the slot with a yellow safety razor, snapped up by the waiting inmate. David figures he might as well shave, too, since there will not be any hot water for another half hour at best. He goes back to his bunk, grabs his ID band, and gets in line.

In the bathroom, bleary-eyed men scrape needlessly dull razors across their cheeks, cursing as they accidentally pierce the skin, the bald guys craning their heads around as far as humanly possible, crouching and squinting into the greasy, scratched-up plate-metal mirrors as they try to shave the backs of their own heads, others brushing their teeth with absurdly tiny green toothbrushes, their handles no larger than a thumbprint, and spitting into one of the two long, white, trough-like sinks. A few are showering, and a small cluster of clothed men pass a homemade contraband cigarette back and forth in the tiled corner beside them, just beyond the water's reach. Still others are pissing or shitting in the stalls barely three feet from the sinks. "Yo, you stink, bro!" one guy calls out, drooling frothy toothpaste down his chin. "Throw some water on that!" A flush rings out from behind a knotted bedsheet, daintily draped across one of the open-face toilet stalls. In the next stall over, a nineteen-year-old tucks his head as far below the sheet as he can manage, but the sound of crinkling magazine paper gives him away. "Yo, this nigga cashin' out right now!" someone chuckles, and the room howls a half-amused, half-disgusted response: he is not defecating; he is masturbating. A cold gust of wind blows through the louvered window, stuck open for as long as anyone can remember.

By the time David shaves and brushes his teeth, someone else has convinced the floor officer to let him refill the hot pot. David gauges how long it will be before he can make a treasured cup of instant coffee by pressing his fingers to the pot's metal surface, just above the tap: twenty minutes, maybe more. He decides to get suited up for the day while he waits: two pairs of long johns, two thermal shirts, two pairs of socks (his, fortunately, are wool, mailed in to him by his friends; most have to make do with cheap cotton ones), and then a pair of green canvas pants and a green jersey sweatshirt. To top it off, he winds a scrap of a thermal shirt around his neck, conveniently dismembered by pulling it across a sharp notch worked into the metal frame of his bed years prior by an unknown inmate with an unknown implement. It is cold outside, and this is the closest thing he has to a scarf.

Dressed for the day, he decides to grab an open phone. You never know when the work detail COs are going to arrive, and it has not been long enough for the water to heat up yet. So he calls his mother, as he does every morning, and though he tries to fill the whole fifteen minutes he is permitted with conversation, they only talk for about five. It is early for both of them, and sometimes he feels as though he is running out of things to say. Day to day in jail, there is not that much that changes—at least, not that can be explained to an outsider over the phone.

Walkin' Out!

It is 6:20, and the water is finally hot. Unfortunately, the work detail COs have also just arrived. "S-O-D!" the one in the front calls out as the Bubble CO unlocks the inner gate for him, and he strides, carefree, into the room, plopping his heft down in the plastic chair at the front. "S-O-Deeee!" The COs for SOD (Special Operations Division, the outdoor cleanup crew) keep adding "walkin' out!" to their cries of "S-O-D!," but David is no newbie. He has been here for a couple of months now, and he knows they will not actually walk out for another five or ten minutes. If he had enough time, he might have lain in bed in the few minutes before they arrived, listening to WNYC and sipping his instant coffee. He might even have stayed there until they actually started to leave. But chow was late today—usually it shows up closer to 5:00—so there is not enough time: a splash of hot water, just enough to dilute the heaping plastic spoonful of coffee crystals, and enough cold tap water to make it tepid. He tests it a couple times as he gathers his book, snack, and ID band for the shift, then shoots the dregs back like an espresso when it becomes clear they are serious about walking out.

The inner gate clangs open ("S-O-D, let's *go!*") and he files out, along with a dozen others who wait in the narrow hall between the inner and outer gates of the dorm until the former is closed and the SOD COs have completed a head count. There is shit talking, play fighting, and plenty of staring off into space. The Bubble CO steps out of the Bubble again, this time to unlock the outer gate. David and the dozen others pour into a small corner of the main hallway, partitioned off by a wall of bars, and filled with perhaps twenty other incarcerated workers, collected from different housing units and preparing to go to their jobs. Some work with David on SOD; others work in the bakery or on the construction crew. Inmates from the various work details and housing units take advantage of the short window of time to interact: greetings, rumors, notes, and drugs are exchanged. "S-O-D!" comes the call again, and the metal door next to the one David and the others just exited swings open after a muffled jingling of keys resounds from the inside. SOD's ranks have swollen to perhaps twenty in total with the workers from other units; all twenty file in.

This, too, is a dorm, but it is kept empty on purpose. It seems the architects of this particular jail building did not think to add a changing room for inmates going to work outside jobs, who are required by policy to swap their greens for orange jumpsuits before they do. And so, on the empty bed frames are rows of black work boots and cuboid pouches of yellow vinyl, each with a name tag. Each worker grabs his pouch and a pair of boots, and shuffles into what would be the day room to change. Dressed in orange-and-white-striped jumpsuits, with flimsy, ancient orange bomber jackets and thin knit-cotton caps, also orange, David proceeds into the final holding area, another section of hallway partitioned by bars, where a grumpy old CO behind plexiglass forces each inmate to hold his ID band up to the pane so she can check him off her list. Finally, one of the SOD COs gives the order with a nod, and an inmate pushes open the red metal door in the rear wall—unlocked all along but known to all as untouchable without permission—and fresh air pours in. It is cold, and the light outside is an unwelcoming shade of grayish blue, but it feels undeniably good to get out of the building.

The SOD workers climb into a freezing white bus strewn with stinking trash and wait. It is early; talk and jokes to pass the time are sparse. One of the COs finally shows up and takes the wheel. They rumble across the island to a desolate parking lot in the shadow of a pointed road-salt storage dome, hemmed in by razor wire and shipping containers, and wait some more. Some men roam the parking lot; others exercise with the rusting barbells, dumbbells, and weight machines abandoned there. After an hour or so, the COs divide them up into groups of four or five and lead them off in different directions in different vehicles. Some teams enter the various office buildings and trailers used by the DOC administration and take out the trash, sweeping and mopping the floors. On normal days, the other teams might pick up trash around the island, or do yard work, but today they are salting the roads. It snowed last night; one of the SOD COs even appeared in the dorm at 1:00 a.m., threatening to fire everybody if he did not get three volunteers. More snow is forecast for later today, and hence, more salt.

Dropped off hours later at the same red door they exited, David and the others wait in line for perhaps a half hour as they step one by one into a small room with an x-ray scanner and a CO. They each strip and squat in front of the CO, and hand him most of their clothing. He runs this through the machine, passing it to them on the other end. They hurriedly get dressed, just enough to cover themselves, and limp down the hall to the abandoned day room in the empty dorm, holding up their jumpsuits with one hand. After changing back into their greens, they wait again to exit, then wait to enter their dorm next door. When the Bubble CO unlocks the outer gate, allowing David and the small cluster of returning SOD workers who are either not back in the dorm already or still changing clothes to step back in, they all turn without a word to face the wall and stand with their hands up against it. After locking the outer gate, the CO performs a perfunctory pat frisk, and then unlocks the inner one.

Inside, David arrives just in time for lunch, and before some of the other work crews return, meaning he gets a decent-sized (and relatively hot!) portion. It is meatloaf with boiled cabbage today: not his favorite, but it is one of the dishes soggy enough to soften the dry, tasteless bread. After scarfing down as much as he can stomach, he jumps in the shower. He has figured out that after work is the best time to take one, as the dorm is comparatively empty, and he usually needs it. There is no one else in the shower or waiting to take one, so David can take his time a bit, and even enjoy some semblance of privacy.

Personal Time

David lies down to take a nap. The dorm often stays noisy until midnight and sometimes until 2:00 a.m., long after the 9:00 p.m. lights-out, and he has found that the dorm's relative emptiness in the early afternoon also offers a great time to make up for lost sleep. On average, he has been getting about five hours a night lately, but he hears that in dorms where inmates are not required to work—dorms that are not "working dorms" like his—people often sleep all day long. He can believe it: the handful of guys in his dorm who don't work, or only work a couple of days a week, tend to sleep a lot.

But today, he doesn't get to catch up on lost sleep. The Bubble CO calls out his last name and three others, followed by "get ready!" There is a moment of confusion as they all ask what, exactly, they are supposed to get ready for, then a moment of excitement when the CO responds "V-I!" David has a visit, and the escort CO will arrive between five minutes and an hour from now. Those whose names were called start putting on clothes or gathering their small collection of personal hygiene products. They comb their hair, rub lotion on their hands, or smear deodorant onto their underarms. This is usually about the time mail arrives; David hopes the mailroom CO shows up before the escort CO does. Otherwise he will have to wait another day for his mail.

One guy jumps in the shower, but the escort CO arrives before he finishes. They have a shouting match through the door of the bathroom. Someone trying to sleep with a towel over his eye urges them both to shut the fuck up. The guy in the shower wants the escort CO to wait a classic New York "two minutes" for him to towel off and throw on clothes; the escort CO says he is going to leave now and come back in half an hour. COs are averse to any deference to inmates, no matter how petty. When it comes to managing time—the very essence of a facility for sentenced prisoners—it is imperative to COs that they remain in control of how the day unfolds. So while the escort CO does not have anywhere to be, he does not want to wait even two minutes. The incarcerated man, on the other hand, has nowhere else he *can* be, and so the prospect of an additional, arbitrary thirty-minute wait to see his loved one matters enormously.

As the escort insists they leave, David and the two others try to help out the guy in the shower by dragging their heels. They buy him just enough time to slip through the inner gate before the Bubble officer closes it. After a brief pat frisk, he joins them in walking down the hall ahead of the escort. He is not really a friend of David's—in fact, David doesn't really even like the guy much—but after a couple months of city time, solidarity with other inmates, especially in the face of hostility from staff, is already an engrained response. And then, it feels indisputably satisfying to thwart the designs of the institution and its stooges as often as one can afford to.

The hall is entirely straight, incredibly long, and pretty much deserted. Its every surface is scraped, scratched, cracked, or patched with an odd assortment of materials and colors: blue, cream, and burgundy tiles, mutilated safety glass, the paint on the bars and the walls chipped to reveal decades of neutral tones beneath. Much like the iron buttresses on New York City subway platforms, cracks in the paint reveal generations of accreted colors—a veritable history of decades of half-hearted attempts to spruce up a place of great misery and gloom. Occasionally, a mural appears, advertising the name of the building in block letters as if it is a high school gym and one is supposed to cheer for the home team. Other murals depict jail life or extol the virtues of education. Some evoke the uncanny and often perplexing lexicon of self-help behind bars, such as "Poise, Self-Assurance, Ambidexterity" and "Positive anything is better than negative nothing."

Footsteps and the jangling of keys on the belt of the CO behind the trio in green are the only sounds echoing in the endless blue-white tunnel. A metal door swings open as they cross the open space and an inmate in greens steps out, returning to his dorm. The guy in front gives him a quick pound. "Yo, I took care of that thing for you," he says, even as the CO urges them to return to their respective sides of the hall. "Gentlemen, keep it moving, please!"

Each returns to his right-hand side. "Yo, Big T still in your house?" one calls out to the other as they do.

"Yeah."

"Tell him I said what's up with that!"

"I got you."

And they continue, making sure to "clear the mags," or pass through the regularly spaced metal detectors. The mags seem to beep randomly, even when no one is around. Even if they do beep when someone walks through them, it is a total crapshoot as to whether the nearest CO will care. The one following David to his visit does not seem to.

When they reach the opposite end of the hall, a distance of perhaps four city blocks, another mural greets them, this one depicting a male inmate happily reuniting with a woman and child. The artist has somehow neglected to give any color to the man's irises, giving the mural an eerie effect that overrides its cheesiness. They deposit their ID bands with the CO at the corner, and under another CO's disinterested watch, strip and change into a gray jumpsuit and a pair of rubbery flip-flops. They wait on tiny painted plywood benches until their names are called. Another CO quickly runs down the "dancefloor" rules: no candy, no jewelry, no headgear or religious wear, no communicating with other inmates, and no overly obscene physical contact—or, in his words, "You can grab some ass, but you can't grab no titties." The visiting floor, an old gym littered with single-piece plastic tables and chairs, is busy today. David sees many inmates he knows, and he greets the few he makes eye contact with by giving a slight nod, all he can get away with as the COs look on. His visit goes well; it feels good to get a hug and talk with someone he knows about something other than the ins and outs of daily life in jail—though of course, that figures in their conversation, too. It is hard to avoid when they ask him how he has been, or what's new with him.

Back at the dorm, there has been a search. David is glad he was on a visit at the time. Even though his bed did not really get searched, he almost certainly would have been put through the whole rigamarole of being taken into the bathroom in a group of four or five and forced to strip and squat before a row of men in blue, then marched to the day room to wait in silence until his bed number was called, and subsequently forced to watch as the COs utterly trashed his meager belongings, only to return to the day room and wait in silence until everyone received the same treatment.

This one is not bad: only a handful of people have had their beds trashed. Those unlucky few are still grumbling as they try to reorganize their belongings, dumped into piles atop and around their beds by the search team. Though David's bed is largely untouched, his second mattress is missing. Officially, the jail only allows one thin mattress per person, which is barely enough to insulate between the bony parts of one's body and the metal bed frame. Doubling mattresses up makes lying in bed almost bearable. David sighs. It is back to sleeping on a paltry three inches of foam until he manages to inherit another one, and who knows when that will be. Actually, wait—isn't BK going home in two weeks or so? The two of them are cool, even if they are not exactly best friends. Sometimes they work out together at the yard, and occasionally they cook together in the evening. I should see if his mattress has been claimed by anyone yet, David thinks to himself.

There are only two hours left until dinner now. There is too much noise and activity to take a nap, so David lies in his bed and tries to read. In the day room, people are busy gambling for commissary goods at dominos, slapping them loudly down on the metal table with each move as they do, and cackling raucously when they win. The air is filled with fish tales of gangbanging, drug dealing, magnificent feats of criminality or sexual prowess, and life in other jails or prisons. Several guys are making their afternoon phone calls. One alternates between sweet-talking the woman on the other end in a low voice and screaming out streams of invectives that invariably end with "bitch!" Twice he hangs up the phone in anger, but not too hard, to avoid arousing other inmates' wrath (if he breaks the phone, after all, it will interfere with their ability to call their loved ones, too). Both times, he immediately runs over to another inmate and practically begs to buy a phone call so he can call his girlfriend again. "She just gets under my skin, is all," he explains somewhat sheepishly.

At 3:00 p.m., the COs force everyone from the day room, lock it, and conduct the afternoon count. "Gentlemen, on the count!" rings out, and everyone stops moving, or moves only as much as he can get away with. Moving too much will attract the frustration not only of the CO conducting the head count but all the other inmates: the longer it takes the CO to count, the longer they have to stand still. At 4:00 p.m., the day room is reopened, and at 5:00 p.m. chow arrives.

In this house, they eat meals in the day room. Tonight might well have been Fish Friday, but instead the meal served is "turkey-roni," a portion of soft cavatappi noodles and crumbled turkey-soy mixture in clumpy reddish sauce. David wolfs it down like the others, making sure to wipe his eating area with the communal sponge when he is done. The day room tends to clear out after chow, at least for a bit, and so he takes advantage of the extra space by doing a bit of writing at one of the cold steel tables, even if he has to brush some breadcrumbs and noodles away before he does.

Another One Down

As the sun goes down, an older Black man with a gray pencil mustache kneels on a tiny red rug and prays in the rear corner of the dorm, calling out the nightly Maghrib prayer practiced by Muslims around the world. His voice fills the cavernous room, mingling with the ambient shouts, laughs, slapping down of dominos, and squeaks of rubber soles on tile. When it is fully dark outside, David's neighbor looks around at him and their "section"—those whose bunks are closest to theirs—and says with a self-satisfied sigh the same thing he says every night around this time: "Well, another one down, fellas!" David finds it kind of cheesy, but he cannot deny the feeling of accomplishment that making it through another day in jail, a day less between him and his release date, brings. He mumbles his contribution to the chorus of affirmations that answers.

David makes some more phone calls around 6:30, knowing the phones will start to get busy soon. "Slot time" starts at 7:30, and only those with a fifteen-minute time slot are allowed to use the phones until they cut off at 9:00. David does not have a slot yet, but in this house, slots are not reserved exclusively for gang members. Rather, the gang members assign slots to people who have been in the dorm long enough, so he anticipates getting one as long as he avoids a random transfer to another dorm by the powers that be. In fact, one of the shotcallers approached him the other day and told him he could take over Gunna's 7:45 slot when he goes home next week. But for now, he has to get his phone calls in when he can.

He plays a couple of rounds of dominos with his neighbors, the young Dominican (eight months for gun possession), the middle-aged Ecuadorian (three months for his third DUI), and the old Chinese man (four months for stabbing a guy in a road rage incident). The latter, Tom, keeps muttering "Oh shit . . ." as they play, but somehow managing to trounce everyone by the end of every round. Unlike some of the others in their dorm, the four of them do not gamble. There are no piles of commissary foods next to them. This is just to pass the time, the one thing they all have way too damn much of.

Around 7:00, a CO appears at the inner gate, where a small crowd of methadone users, ID bands in hand and shoes on their feet, has already gathered. "KEEP!" he calls in a loud voice. "Walkin' out! KEEP, walkin' out!" They follow him readily down the hall to get their nightly dose of "KEEP"—an acronym for Key Extended Entry Program, the island's methadone program.

At 7:30, there is a fight over the phones. Nobody challenges anyone to "play the bathroom," meaning to deliberately take their conflict where the COs—and cameras—are less likely to observe. It is an impromptu fight, right there on the floor, between a guy who just arrived in the dorm today. He does not look as though he just arrived in jail, however: he is wearing a sweatshirt and pants, not a jumpsuit, a pair of work boots, not Patakis, and he has a mini-afro grown in beneath a head of long dreadlocks—all sure signs that he has been in for a while. Seems as though he refused to honor slot time, trying to be a tough guy, and got punched in the face for it. Now he and the other guy are squaring off, and the floor CO is grabbing her can of mace, half-heartedly shouting "Stop fighting, stop fighting," as per DOC use-of-force policy, and before they know it, she is aiming it at both of them.

There is an outcry from the entire dorm before she squeezes the trigger, but it is too late. Inmates curse and groan and rush to open every available window, furiously turning tiny metal dials built into the windowsill to ease up the small rectangular panels that can be twisted to furnish slits of outside air. Everyone who can wraps an extra T-shirt, towel, or scrap of bed linen around his face and rushes to a window. The two guys who got maced are no longer trying to punch each other—they are wincing, grunting, and simply trying to stay upright. The others have cut their phone conversations short. "Every man to a bed!" the floor officer calls to a room full of coughing men, coughing herself as she repeats her order again and again.

The Turtles arrive within minutes. They barge down the narrow hall, suited up in a hodgepodge of football and riot-cop gear. Most are just regular COs David has seen around the building, outfitted and mobilized to respond to the altercation. Even beneath their helmets and all their padding, he recognizes a few. They file in like a phalanx, two blocking the only exit with riot shields and batons as the others corner and handcuff the two combatants, each now glued to a spigot in the bathroom, trying desperately to flush his face with water. Things return to normal seconds after their departure. The men leave their beds, and the phones are swarmed again. If not for the lingering smell of mace, it might well be any other night in the Six.

A dispute among some of the guys arises as to whether the windows should be left open to continue airing out the mace, or closed because it is getting cold in the dorm. It is decided that they will be left open a little longer, then mostly closed. The "methheads" have returned to the dorm high on methadone, and now loll, eyes glazed, in plastic chairs facing the TV in the day room, or atop their beds, some even already beneath their covers with towels over their eyes.

Around 8:00, the nightly ritual of cooking "crackhead soup" begins. The usual groups form. David bends over his "bucket," a plain blue Rubbermaid storage bin, and, peeling off the lid, considers what he might contribute. In addition to his paperwork and extra clothing, he has a surplus of coffee, peanut butter, oatmeal, chili-flavored ramen noodles, and packets of tuna, salmon, and mackerel. David, a couple of his neighbors, and the Trinidadian guy with the cane from another section all chip in noodles and fish, among other ingredients purchased from commissary or foraged from the kitchen. Thankfully, the hotpot does not run out of water before lights out tonight. There are not many people cooking, which is unusual at this time of night. Perhaps the smell of mace has put them off chili-flavored ramen, the only type that commissary has sold for months. Requiring little more than a trash bag and hot water, their food is ready in less than fifteen minutes. David eats his nighttime meal in the last few minutes before lights out, then washes his bowl—the bottom half of a plastic two-liter soda bottle—with a bar of DOC-issued Corcraft hand soap and a scrap of a pink dishrag stolen from his job at SOD.

Rikers after Dark

As 9:00 p.m. approaches, guys start drifting away from the phones as their calls run out. At 9:00 p.m., the last two reluctantly hang up their phones. One offers up a heavy sigh ("Damn, man!"), the other smiles sadly for a moment and then gets drawn into a conversation about jailhouse exploits of the past. The CO in the Bubble switches all the lights off, too, as 9:00 p.m. to 5:00 a.m. is lights out. But a chorus of pleas, groans, and invectives from the men in green and white convinces him to cut a few back on for a little while. It is often easier for a CO to acquiesce to inmates' demands for minor rule bending than to remain obstinate to the letter, a fact incarcerated men learn quickly.

Smoking picks up at night, and most of it takes place in the dorm simply because it is harder for the COs to see the smoke in the dark. The smell is also slightly more diffuse than when the act is performed in the bathroom, which is effectively attached to the Bubble. The smokers crouch down among the bunks and beneath the windows along the wall, passing their rollies between them. Anything smokable is so scarce that smoking alone is all but unheard of. Any CO who smells burning tobacco, K2, or—occasionally—weed and actually cares will have to stand up and walk the length of the main aisle, looking left and right for the culprits. Even then, the intrepid CO is unlikely to catch anyone in the act, as any smokers will doubtless be alerted to the officer's approach by other inmates' subtle calls of "walkin' walkin' walkin'!" before they make it more than a few steps, affording them enough time to stub and stash their smokes.

Noise, too, picks up at night. Guys post up in front of the inner gate or in the back corners of the dorm and test out their raps on their friends and neighbors. Serving time on Rikers Island is a universal theme. Even though many men change into their gym shorts or long johns and go to their beds, a rolling volley of jokes and jibes rings out across the room, friends and rivals finding creative ways to insult and belittle each other, often met with raucous laughter from the room.

The floor officer is part of the nighttime drama too, and though she tries to keep up a disinterested facade, she, too, often cracks up after a particularly ridiculous quip. Young and attractive, she becomes the center of attention within minutes of the Bubble CO's shutting off the remaining few lights, leaving only the faint glow from the Bubble, the bathroom, and the searchlights outside. The (mostly younger) men who are courageous enough to perform their flirtations in front of everyone mill lazily around her like sharks, engaging her in a sort of crowdsourced banter. Most are starved for female attention and the validation it brings. The CO, faced with a choice between sheer, stone-faced boredom and playfully accepting their overtures, chooses the latter. Tonight, she makes little effort to conceal her enjoyment of the whole charade.

Many of the guys who do not participate in the evening antics are already in bed, their sheet and gray wool blanket drawn up to their chins, their earphones in their ears and their radios turned up to drown out the sounds around them. David takes a book and makes his exit to the shower: the lights in the bathroom stay on all night, and the small metal bench in the corner of the shower almost affords him a little privacy. In his first weeks, before he adjusted to the nighttime noise, he sometimes wondered if it might actually push him past the brink of sanity. Now, he is able to tune it out. He puts his earphones in and turns some music on low. As he reads, others sometimes float in and steal drags on homemade joints or cigarettes. A few string the knotted white sheets across the faceless toilet stalls and shit. One complains that he cannot go with David sitting there. David brushes him off with a dry retort. David's dispassion is partly a performance, partly a result of desensitization to the suffering of others, especially when it stems from enforced proximity to dozens of other people.

A captain bangs through the inner gate around 10:00 p.m. and "walks the dorm," making his rounds of the main aisle and the bathroom. Most captains don't care if David reads in the shower, but this one does. "You're supposed to be on your bed after lights out," he thunders authoritatively. David has already learned that there is no sense fighting it. He wordlessly closes his book, marking the page with a scrap of notebook paper, and returns to his bed. The captain walks up and down Broadway, not caring that he wakes people with his keys, radio, and flashlight. As soon as he scribbles something in the CO's logbook at the front of the dorm and leaves, David returns to the shower and opens his book back up. The floor CO doesn't care. If she did, David would just reply that he had to shit, and that would almost certainly provide her with sufficient plausible deniability.

By midnight, the noise has mostly died down, even if the smell of mace still lingers faintly in the air in the main space of the dorm. The floor officer, no longer the center of attention, stares out at the darkened room with a bored look. A couple of guys are scheming something in hushed tones from their bunks. A new arrival with some form of severe mental illness sits upright, staring at the wall and muttering rapidly to himself. The room is peppered with sporadic bursts of guys rapping along to the music on their radios, indifferent to those trying to sleep around them. Someone screams out something in his sleep, and those still awake give up a collective giggle. The consensus rolls in: "This nigga buggin' . . ."

It is impossible to tell if many men are asleep or not, as most simply lie in bed, tinny music emanating from the plastic plugs in their ears. The phone in the Bubble rings, and the CO who answers pays no mind to those trying to sleep either, laughing and making loud small talk to her colleague on the other end. "Yo, shut the fuck up!" one man yells in the dark, followed by another. Meanwhile, searchlights atop the corners of the jailhouse send slices of pale light across the grid of metal bunks. David's first bed was directly in the path of the searchlight's glare; when his neighbor went home a month ago, David took his bed, allowing him the luxury of sleeping without pulling the covers over his head.

David strips down to his long johns and lies on his too-thin single mattress. At least, he thinks to himself, they did not take my extra blanket. One blanket simply does not suffice on cold nights like this. Though the *Inmate Handbook* states that every inmate has a right to "sufficient blankets to provide comfort and warmth," getting the COs to give you more than one is a Herculean feat.[1] He turns his radio to static—white noise is better than the residual din of the room—and, pulling the covers up to his chin, is pleasantly surprised to find himself drifting off to sleep with relative ease. He was not able to make up for lost sleep this afternoon, after all.

4

Doing Time

There is an expression city-time inmates often hear: "Do your time, don't let your time do you." There is little to do in Rikers in comparison to state facilities, and finding creative ways to stave off the ever-encroaching boredom and cabin fever quickly becomes a priority. The men serving city time must decide how to relate to a part of their life that is decidedly not their own, but that they must nonetheless live through. This means filling the day with habits, activities, and relationships that make the time tolerable, or at least make it go by quickly.

Daily life for the men in green is therefore filled with minute rituals and activities that serve at once to make the day more comfortable or enjoyable, and help claim a tiny bit of autonomy in a system designed to eliminate it. Early prison ethnographer Hans Reimer, who experienced incarceration, argued that prisoners' behavior in a carceral setting is "outlined by traditions, a social hierarchy, mores, attitudes, and a mythology" produced and maintained by the captive population, not the institution alone.[1] More recently, Michael Walker noted "the set of endurance strategies residents used to manage the psychic, biological, and emotional realities endemic to jail living."[2] Daily reality may be structured by the institution, but it is ultimately shaped by the prisoner. This means that alongside the institution's definition of an inmate's daily activities, including work, meals, and other regular occurrences, blossoms a set of survival skills and daily practices, and a rich folk knowledge through which they are transmitted, including the inmate's relationship to time itself.

Folk Knowledge

We use the term "folk knowledge" to refer to techniques for making daily life easier or more fulfilling during city time. These jailhouse "life hacks" are necessarily passed down orally from one inmate to the next;

even if this collective knowledge could somehow be compiled into a physical format, it would be all but impossible to circulate it among the incarcerated due to the authoritarian nature of the penal institution. Folk knowledge techniques are often highly dependent on the specific physical environment an inmate finds himself in; they encompass every aspect of life, from sleeping to eating to bathing to exercise. In application, folk knowledge techniques often qualify as "affordances," a term coined by psychologist James Gibson to describe what a physical environment offers a person in terms of unofficial use, and the relation between the person and the space based on that use.[3] As one inmate put it to Jarrod, "This place turns you into MacGyver!"[4] Similarly, David took it as high praise when another inmate said of his improvisations, "He be doin' mad jail shit like he been here before." We include a few pieces of folk knowledge below, but these are only a sliver of the countless ways in which modifying their physical environment helps the men at Rikers to pass the time, and pass it better.

Clotheslines

While every housing unit David was in had some system of clotheslines set in place by the inmates, the clothesline system in 12-Lower in the Six was generally much more robust than that in Mod 4 in the Four. This was a direct result of the physical layout of the dorms in the Six. There, an aisle separated every second row of beds. Between the head and foot ends of the beds in each double row there were about eighteen inches of empty space, perfect for hanging a clothesline.

Most of the bunks in 12-Lower also had a vertical component to their frames that the beds in Mod 4 did not: a simple extension of each of the legs of the bunk to a point about two feet above the layer of the metal mattress platform, joined by a horizontal crossbar that ran parallel to the head or foot end of the frame. This configuration allowed the men to tie lengths of breakaway twine or scraps of bedsheets ("lines") between the horizontal crossbars at the foot end of one bunk and the head end of another, forming two parallel lines across the eighteen inches between the two bunks, high enough to hang pants or a T-shirt on without it touching the floor. If these lines were pulled sufficiently taut, smaller lengths of breakaway twine or lines could then be tied across

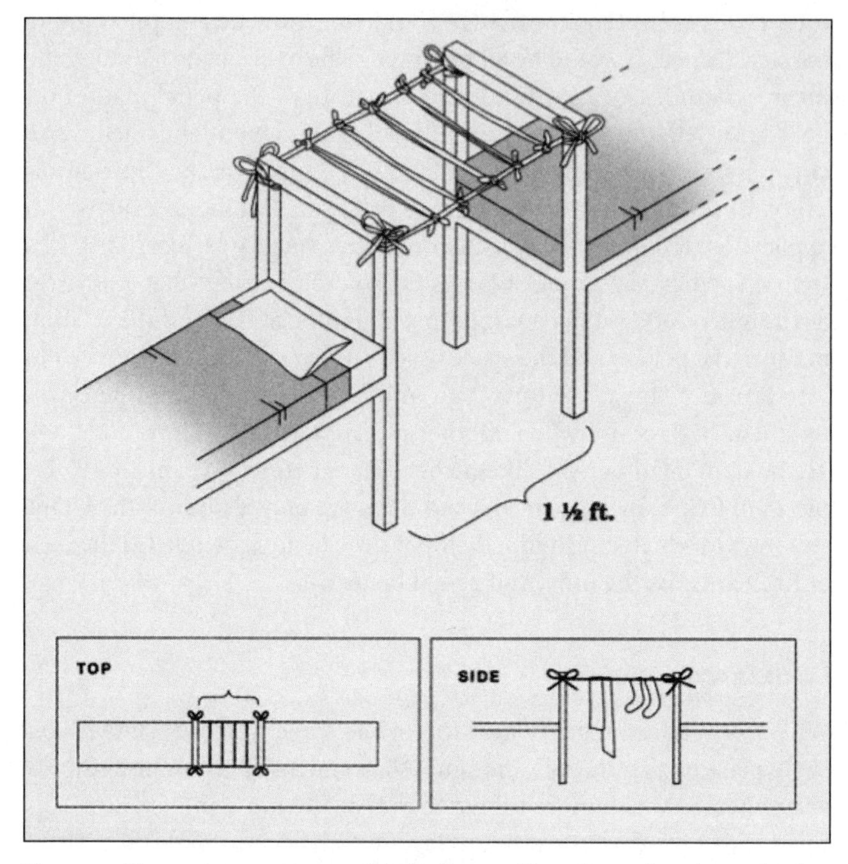

Figure 4.1: The most common type of clothesline used in 12-Lower, based on a sketch by David. Illustration by Chloé Maës, 2023.

them perpendicularly, so that the end result was a sort of flexible, improvised variation on the cheap wire-frame clothes-drying racks often sold in the outside world.

Though most "clotheslines" had about five or six lines, they came in a surprising number of shapes, and there were an equally surprising number of ways to fashion them. There was an element of craftsmanship, too: the ability to string a taut line was highly sought after, as it would not droop to the floor when laundry was placed on it. The greatest success in this was achieved by either twisting the line tight before tying it off or tying some sort of sliding knot and then drawing it tight.

Jarrod was held in one dorm where a particular captain would routinely sweep through and cut clotheslines down. This was triply provocative, as it represented a CO's incursion into an inmate's jealously guarded personal area, for reasons that were pitifully trifling, and, of course, left the string inoperable. The threat of a cut string led to the men improvising clotheslines that were connected to the bed on one end, and were effectively a lasso on the other. If this particular captain, or a search team heralding a shakedown, appeared at the gate, the inmate could easily remove the rope and save the clothesline for another day.

Toothpaste Glue

Toothpaste is widely used as an adhesive on Rikers. Tape and glue are not permitted, so any posting of signs notifying newcomers of the social conventions in the housing unit (which toilets to use, phone or hygiene protocols, etc.) is accomplished using toothpaste. Likewise, many men use toothpaste to decorate the area around their bunks with pictures of their loved ones, their personal interests, or simply pictures of naked or seminaked women. It is also used to glue and stash weapons, drugs, and other contraband, like pens, in the various nooks and crannies available to the inmates. When David was incarcerated, he always had a number of pens glued to various parts of his bedframe with toothpaste. Jarrod observed a cruel prank, in which one inmate stole the suggestive photographs of another's wife and posted them up all over the bathroom using toothpaste, announced by incredulous cries of, "Oooh, they violated that man!" Fortunately, their rightful owner had been transferred out of the house already, preventing what might otherwise have been a dangerous encounter between the two men.

Showerheads

In 12-Lower, the showers generally had good pressure and wide, if uncontrollable, spray. Though each metal push button needed to be pressed every ten to fifteen seconds to keep the shower running, these could be wedged in place with the flat end of a plastic spoon to keep them on.

The showers in Mod 4, it was generally agreed, were a downgrade. There were eight showerheads instead of three, and, unlike in 12-Lower, the physical layout afforded the inmates the ability to string bedsheets up as curtains, giving them a small degree of privacy. But the push buttons were a slightly different shape that could not be wedged in place, and the temperature and pressure of each showerhead was anybody's guess. Worse, even when the pressure was good, the water shot out of the wall in a handful of densely clustered streams that had an uncomfortable pins-and-needles feel when on the skin. To remedy this, men in Mod 4 often constructed improvised showerheads.

The first step was to procure a bottle. Though a number of different bottles could be used, including the commissary-purchased Maximum Security roll-on deodorant and Suave shampoo, the best was Sebex dandruff shampoo, available by prescription only. This bottle was rinsed out and then sawed in half by two inmates, one holding it steady, the other moving a length of twine or strip of bedsheet back and forth over the bottle's surface until the friction weakened the plastic. (This same technique was used by many inmates to make "bowls" out of empty two-liter bottles; the rubber bowls available in commissary were often deemed too small.) The bottom half of the bottle and its screw-on cap were discarded, leaving only the top half and an open neck.

The showerheads in Mod 4 were all-metal and had a peculiar shape that prevented tampering with or hanging things from them: each resembled a half-globe set into a flat, square metal plate at a forty-five-degree angle, which was itself set into the wall. The water shot out of the flat underside of this half-globe. Attaching the open end of the half-bottle to the underside of the half-globe had a funneling effect on the water, so that rather than striking the bather's body in painful jets, it gushed out of the plastic Sebex nozzle in a messy cascade, making for a much more enjoyable shower experience. But because tape is contraband on Rikers Island, attaching the half-bottle was no small feat. Small pieces of tape could occasionally be harvested and recycled from the odd piece of mail, but this was far from a reliable source of adhesives. The standard procedure for showerhead attachment was to solicit a number of Suave shampoo bottles, perhaps four or five, from other inmates in the dorm.

These bottles had two labels each, one on the front and one on the back, each label perhaps three inches long by two inches wide. Waterproof and highly adhesive, these labels could be carefully peeled from the shampoo bottle and then sliced in two lengthwise to create manageably sized strips of tape. The slicing was usually done on one of the many small but sharp edges found on various surfaces in the dorm—in one of David's dorms in Mod 4, for example, it was the jagged, long-broken corner of the wall-mounted plexiglass case protecting the cleaning product dispenser from inmate hands. These strips were then usually arranged in a fan-like shape from the half-bottle on one end to the metal plate of the showerhead on the other, with a number of competing cross-weaving techniques.

It was unclear where it originated, but this technique seemed to be in use in other buildings on the island, too. Often confiscated or simply torn from the wall during a search, the showerhead was a priority for postsearch cleanup, as testified to by calls of "Yo, who got a Sebex?" or "Who got a shampoo bottle for the shower?"

Bed Corsets

The beds on Rikers Island are, perhaps unsurprisingly, notoriously hard and uncomfortable. The mattresses are green vinyl filled with layers of cotton batting; though about three inches thick when uncompressed, they quickly reduce to the width of a yoga mat when supporting a person's weight, and provide about as much comfort, especially atop the unforgiving metal platforms of the bunks.

The most common strategy for making one's modest personal space more bearable for sleep was to procure supplemental mattresses. Among sentenced men, it was very common for people to ask friends or acquaintances if they might "claim" their mattress when they went home. (The practice of surreptitiously handing off one's mattress, after being called for release, without the floor officer noticing, is itself an important skill, and part of the island's folk knowledge.) There are other ways to create extra padding under one's mattress, such as with one's extra clothing, old newspapers, or, in David's case, his letters. The most common alternative was to place folded extra blankets beneath one's mattress. Blankets, though still possibly subject to confiscation on searches, are a lower priority for searches and other whimsical bouts of rule enforcement than mattresses, possibly because of the entry in the *Inmate Handbook* stating that, while inmates are entitled to only one mattress, they are entitled to as many blankets as necessary "to provide comfort and warmth."[5] Though this is by no means true in practice, it can occasionally be leveraged in one's defense.

The "bed corset" was actually one of the rarer techniques for making one's bed more comfortable, but it was a piece of folk knowledge that seemed common across all buildings on Rikers, and even across jails throughout the region and the country—other inmates reported having seen bed corsets in jails and prisons elsewhere in New York, as well as in New Jersey, Mississippi, and ICE detention facilities as far away as Louisiana and Texas. "Bed corset" is our term; strangely, neither of us ever heard a name for this, besides occasionally "wrapping your bed."

There are no fitted sheets on Rikers; inmates must learn to tie a loose sheet around their mattress, a practice often taught to new arrivals by more seasoned residents. This compresses the head and foot ends inward, giving them a bit more spring, but leaves the center of the mattress pooling outward, and just as uncomfortable as before. The bed corset, which mimics this compression effect on the rest of the mattress, is made by flipping the mattress over and using a pencil to punch a line of holes along the edges of the sheet. Then, often using the pencil as a guide, a "line" of fabric, stripped from another bedsheet, is carefully worked through the holes in a zigzag pattern. Tying a knot in the far end of the line serves to anchor it; pulling the line tight and tying it off at the other end yields a scrunched-up, convex mattress that, if still not exactly luxurious, has considerably more spring.

Milk Fridges

Milk is the most common illicitly obtained source of supplemental protein for men on Rikers. But keeping it cold in the dorm—which, of course, made it much more enjoyable and extended its shelf life—posed a particular challenge, especially outside of the winter months, when the tiny cartons could be left near one's window, or even outside it, between the pane and the bars, and kept cold by the ambient temperature outside.

There were usually a handful of milk fridges in David's dorm, perhaps four or five, and they were generally shared among inmates. Some fridge owners charged others "rent," claiming consumption rights for a carton or two in exchange for allowing them to keep their stash cold.

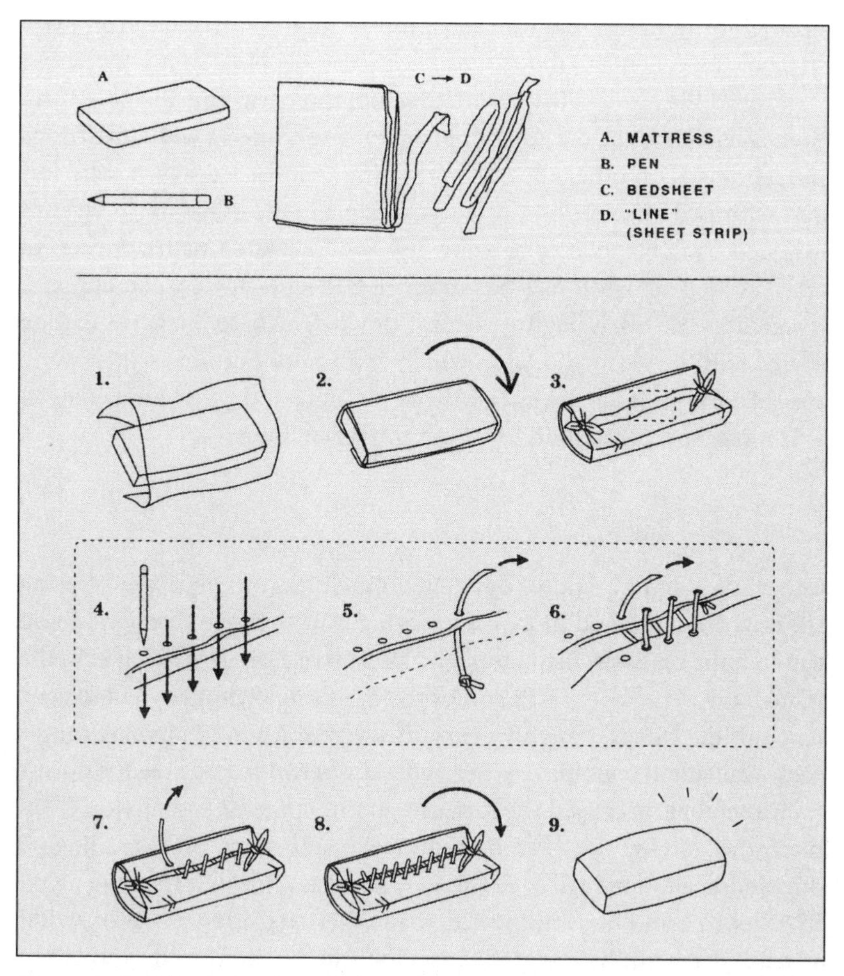

Figure 4.2: Step-by-step instructions for making the "bed corset," based on a sketch by David. Illustration by Chloé Maës, 2023.

The most common strategy for men in Mod 4 to create a "milk fridge" involved extra "blue buckets." The blue bucket was filled with ice, preferably poured over the cartons, as if filling up a cooler for a picnic or barbecue. But ice, too, was technically contraband, and had to be finagled from the institution. Kitchen and mess hall workers often brought back entire trash bags of the stuff for their personal milk fridges.

Fridges often leaked or gave off condensation; this liquid could be a source of conflict if it ran into another's personal space and got his belongings wet. To avoid this, most milk fridge owners placed an extra sheet or towel beneath theirs.

Beyond the basic blue bucket/ice setup, there was considerable variation. David conducted a number of ad hoc experiments with milk fridge models based on others he saw and found that the ice stayed solid longest with two blue buckets, one stacked inside the other, and a layer of crinkled trash bag plastic between the two to create smaller pockets of air. A folded-up trash bag was likewise laid atop the ice, and an extra towel atop the trash bag to weigh it down. The blue bucket was then sealed with its plastic lid, atop which extra books or newspapers were placed to keep it closed as tightly as possible and provide insulation. This method kept ice solid for about thirty-six hours.

Knowing the Ropes

Other types of folk knowledge relied much less on physically altering the environment, and more on knowing how to move through it, and through the invisible, incomprehensible web of rules governing it. In the main hallways of both C-76 and C-74, for example, inmates had to walk through the "mags" roughly every fifty yards. Although pocket radios were available at commissary and generally permitted outside the dorms, their metal parts caused the mags to go off. Some COs didn't care, but many did, forcing the offending inmate to stop, hand off his radio and jumbled headphone wires to the CO, and pass through the mag again. In order to avoid this annoyance, many men perfected a sort of swing-swipe move with their arm, flinging their hand, radio held in it, out in front of them at the last second before passing through the mag. Others used a sort of discreet, shuffling jump-step to break their contact with the ground at the moment they passed through the mag. Both of these techniques were commonly known to COs, but rarely acknowledged, even when performed more or less openly.

Sometimes, even an inmate's release date is not accurately communicated to him by the institution: because the DOC does not release prisoners on weekends, prisoners whose release dates fall on Saturday, Sunday, or even a holiday Monday are released on Friday. David almost never heard this information transmitted via the COs; it was all but exclusively passed on through inmate folk knowledge.

Just about anything an inmate can expect to get away with, or the potential consequences of rule breaking (such as bringing contraband back to the dorm), form the basis of a whole—and essential—set of folk knowledge among men on Rikers. This includes, for example, step-by-step guidelines for navigating the arbitrary application and enforcement of the rules, like how to defend one's actions before the "bing court," where inmates are summoned when issued an infraction. "Jailhouse lawyering" is probably the most clearly defined of these skill sets. Despite not knowing how to navigate bing court, and never having had any firsthand experience of it, David came to be called a jailhouse lawyer simply because he was often the person in the dorm with the most experience filling out forms and dealing with bureaucracy. His jailhouse lawyering usually consisted in helping people file grievances, petitions for early release, appeals, claims of civil rights violations, and so on, as well as trying to decipher chunks of legalese and translate them into layperson's terms, sometimes in Spanish.

In the case of sickness or injury, inmates also often came forward to offer advice on how to get the medical treatment they needed, or simply to offer support. When David injured his shoulder, a number of men volunteered physical therapy exercises they had used for past shoulder injuries of their own. On another occasion, when David was stricken with gastrointestinal illness, other inmates were constantly checking in to see if he was alright.

These types of knowledge give the men stuck in Rikers a greater sense of control and familiarity with their hostile habitat. They likewise often speak about how affordances make it feel, strangely, somewhat homier. By contrast, the daily sight of plain dingy walls, the abrasive sounds of beeping radios and slamming doors, and so on, serve as an unending reminder of captivity. The more the men are confronted with the fact that the space was not made with them or their comfort in mind, the more depressing it is. "I don't even go to the yard. You know why?" one inmate told David. "Because when I go out and I see all that barbed wire out there, that's when I feel like I'm really in jail." A number of other men expressed the same sentiment. A minimal and lackluster effort to counteract this effect seems to have been made by the DOC in the form of the murals occasionally punctuating the long institutional hallways. But by and large, every inch of available space screams, "You're an inmate!"

Getting High, Getting Brolic, and Other Games

Getting high, especially on K2, is a pillar of many daily routines for those incarcerated in Rikers, and may well dictate their daily routine. (Substance abuse is explored in greater detail later.) For some, working out is equally important, as it provides a sense of control over one's time and body, a sense of progress and accomplishment in relation to a goal, a sense of security and social importance in the form of physical strength, and, of course, a rush of endorphins. Outside of a few jobs that afford access to weightlifting equipment, there are no weights on Rikers. Because many men wish to build muscle during their city time, and because the yard is, generally speaking, the only place with a pull-up bar, which makes it much easier to work out the back and biceps, some men construct weights of their own. Intricate dumbbells are crafted by filling empty two-liter bottles with water, lashing them together with strips torn from bedsheets, and inserting a tightly rolled magazine in the center as a handle. These are greatly sought after, though they are a bit unwieldy, rarely exceed thirty-two pounds, and are almost certain to be confiscated on a search.

Another, simpler and more search-resistant option is to procure an extra pillowcase or trash bag and fill it with books, allowing the resistance of external weight. Yet another is to take a few extra plastic day room chairs, if the day room is empty enough, and stack them together to perform curls with. Some men detach the inch-thick rubber gaskets from the insides of the lids of the Cambro drink coolers, if one that still has its gasket can be found. These have some flexibility but are highly durable, and can be used as resistance bands, with people sometimes looping them together to create longer, chain-like bands. On rare occasions, men will even use each other's body weight to increase the difficulty of moves like push-ups.[6]

But the vast bulk of the exercise done on Rikers is pure calisthenics, and it takes many forms. Some guys work out both at the yard and in the dorm, but many work out only in the dorm, often because they find it easier to incorporate a dorm workout into their daily routine. The variations on the traditional push-up are far too numerous to get into here, but they border on infinite, and many inmates perform hundreds every day. A favorite style is "*n*-down," as in "thirty-down," in which a pair or group of exercisers performs thirty push-ups as quickly as possible, then twenty-nine, then twenty-eight, and so on down to one. Decks of playing cards are also used in exercise, sometimes with a "counter" standing by a group of workers-out, flipping over cards from the deck one at a time, the exercisers performing the number of push-ups on the card until they have made it through the deck. Another card-based exercise is to simply throw one card at a time on the floor in front of yourself, or have another person do it for you, and perform a squat, push-up, or burpee as you pick up the card, again until every card has been used. Working out until you urinate blood (exercise-induced hematuria) is a not-uncommon war story at Rikers, often recounted with an odd touch of pride. These stories often featured a version of the card-pickup technique.

Pull-ups, too, come in a whole gamut of different styles. The yard is, generally speaking, the only place with a pull-up bar, which is a highly social and performative site for those who work out. Even if they simply want to exercise and are not looking to showcase their prowess, inmates are likely to get commentary, positive and negative, from the others. The pull-up bar is also a place where one can earn a bit of social status: while anyone who works out a lot is likely to enjoy a degree of respect for it, only an inmate who "gets that money" on the pull-up bar may achieve the title of "bartender."

Game playing is another staple of passing the time behind bars, as it provides an element of excitement and unpredictability, as well as a challenge to prove oneself. For those who gamble, it is even an opportunity to win big in commissary goods. The most common card game by far is spades, followed by rummy. Dominos is also very common, the loud slap of the pieces on the metal day room tables filling the air on a typical day in many dorms. Shooting dice, especially the game known as "trips," is also popular, if less common: dice are not available for sale, and must therefore be crafted from soap and toilet paper, another folk knowledge technique that volumes could well be written about. Though there seemed to be a slight prevalence of Latino men in rounds of dominos, all games, dominos included, regularly transcended racial and ethnic categories.

Some dorms also had time-worn board games in the day room, usually chess, checkers, and Scrabble. During David's time, other dorms had entire video game consoles, in David's experience PlayStation 4 (PS4). Inmates would play these games together or separately for hours on end, chasing the accelerated passage of time they brought. A number of fist-fights broke out over the PS4 during David's time. One guy, known to wake up when the day room opened at 6:00 a.m. every day specifically in order to play PS4 for several hours before the rest of the dorm woke up, was known simply as "Playstation." One of the dorms reserved for the best-behaved adolescent detainees in C-74, known as the "honor dorm," was replete with not only PlayStation but Xbox consoles, a foos-ball table, a mini-basketball/Skee-Ball console, and other ways to try to pacify "the kids" by making their sense of time disappear.

TV

As in the free world, one of the most reliable ways to pass city time is by staring at the television. During our time, when disagreements about what to watch arose, they were often settled by pointing to tradition or common practice, sometimes invoking that it had always been that way, or was done that way "up north" in the state system. Beyond that, the TV is generally up for grabs, though an inmate with some clout in the dorm may essentially order another to hand over the remote or change the channel at basically any time. The TV use in the dorm varies on the basis of several factors, including the number of people present, the existent hierarchy, if any, and the number of TVs. In 12-Lower in C-76, there was only one TV, and a fairly rigid Crip hierarchy. If any Crips were present in the day room, their decision about what to watch was final, and the remote, off-limits. If there were no Crips and few people present, an inmate might well pick up the remote and watch whatever he pleased, but if the day room was crowded, he might have to verbally defend his right to control the TV.

In Mod 4 in C-74, there were three TVs: a large one on one wall of the day room and two smaller ones on the opposite wall. The two smaller ones had no audio, but inmates who had radios could tune in to preset radio frequencies, one bandwidth for each television, to hear it. This removed a great deal of frustration about deciding what to watch. In general, there was one designated "Spanish TV," but TV watching was not at all dominated by racial, ethnic, or even gang affiliation.

Though shotcallers or other respected inmates might have certain seats or places they claimed as their own, or certain shows they insisted on watching at certain times, the viewing environment was generally free-form. The Mod 4 day room also had a number of plastic chairs that could be moved around at will, so the seating arrangements and their occupations were always changing. The only hard rule common to all housing units was absolutely not to turn down the volume or change the channel without asking. That could be grounds for confrontation.

City-time inmates watch a great deal of TV, and much of it is the sort that only airs midday, making for an often-incongruous match of viewer and viewing material. *The Real*, a vacuous daytime talk show with an all-female cast, can reliably be found playing during its midafternoon slot. A large part of the attraction to the show, besides there not being much else on at that hour, seems to be the allure of attractive young women, primped and coiffed, under steady cameras angles that allow the captive viewers to drink up their appearance more than they might be able to for a woman in a movie or TV show, with its higher number of cuts and scene changes. Female meteorologists are generally appreciated for much the same reason; unlike news anchors, meteorologists generally present their segments standing, with wider shots often affording a glimpse of their waist or sometimes lower. Telenovelas, which make up for their higher number of edits with hypersexualization, are also popular, primarily but not only among Spanish speakers, as was Telemundo's *Exatlon*, a reality sports and obstacle-course competition starring fit young people in tiny color-coded outfits. For those seeking intellectual stimulation, the undisputed favorite was *Jeopardy!*

David was surprised to find that many of the inmates, despite professing to detest law enforcement, were avid devotees of cop shows. Perhaps it makes sense; the commission of a crime gives shape and stakes to the narrative from the get-go. The protagonists, who have the right to go pretty much anywhere they please, and assault people largely with impunity, then embark on an action-packed quest to make things right by locking up the bad guys, often while dealing with their inner or interpersonal turmoil along the way. City-time inmates gobble up shows like *Law and Order*, *NCIS*, and even the hokey copaganda series *Blue Bloods*. Some even have favorite characters. One inmate, who referred to all cops and COs as "pigs," could often be caught rushing to catch a seat in the day room to watch "my boy Hank Voight," as he referred to his favorite tough-guy cop on *Chicago P.D.*

In C-74, there was also a circulating pillowcase of DVDs, mostly pirated, that the COs provided. It was a literal grab bag, heavy on the action movies and thrillers. David did the math at one point and found that Dwayne "the Rock" Johnson featured in approximately 80 percent of them. Other favorites during his bid included Quentin Tarantino's *Django Unchained*, Oliver Stone's *Savages*, and Kevin Connolly's *Gotti*. Because of the high turnover rate in jail, there was always a new arrival who had not seen the movies that others might well have grown tired of, and who thought nothing of popping them into the DVD player.

When an important sporting event is still on after light outs, inmates expect extra time in the day room to watch it, as a customary right—nowhere written down, but demanded vociferously. Jarrod witnessed an incident in which a captain visiting the house refused this request. It raised a clamor. "All over the state they let you watch the game!" one man shouted. "Worldwide!" another insisted. "Worldwide!" the first repeated. Allowing extra viewing time for special occasions after lights out was a common measure of a CO's coolness. Once, a CO who seemed to regret having been particularly thorny throughout her shift acquiesced to the men in David's dorm's request to finish watching James Cameron's *Titanic* because they were "sensitive guys."

Reading

Books, which come in through the mail, visiting packages (during our time), or sometimes even COs, carry immeasurable escapist and time-passing value in jail, and enormous social capital as a result.[7] Inmates ask others to give them books when they are finished reading them or go home, and men like David, who generally had a large private collection of books, often lend them out to others, which builds goodwill and establishes trust, as lending implies an eventual giving back. Most housing units have an ad hoc library of books inmates have already read, or books left behind after release. In 12-Lower, the library occupied a roughly two-foot section of the narrow shelf along one of the day room walls. In Mod 4, the extra books were kept on an empty bed, when there was an empty bed to be had. Such libraries are frequently wrecked or even confiscated by search teams, who often simply shove all the books into a trash bag and throw them into a dumpster.

Many of the books read at Rikers are pulp urban fiction, which generally features graphic tales of drug dealing, violence, sex, and 'hood politics. The popular title *Taboo* even takes place on Rikers. A similar bloc of reading material is grocery-store novels, usually detective tales or legal thrillers by authors like John Grisham, Tom Clancy, and Dean Koontz. Other popular books include *The Art of War* or self-help books with an individualistic bent, like *Rich Dad, Poor Dad* or *The 48 Laws of Power*. Conspiracy-theory schlock like *Behold the Pale Horse* can also be found with some regularity. Books about the Mafia, recounting the lives of old-school New York mob characters, for example, or other organized crime figures, like Pablo Escobar, are also widely read. Crips can often be spotted toting founder Stanley "Tookie" Williams's book *Blue Rage, Black Redemption*. Histories of the Black Power movement and autobiographies of Black Power figures like Malcolm X, Assata Shakur, and Huey Newton are widely read, and not only among Black inmates. The Bible and the Koran also circulate, but are hardly dominant in the reading scene; the Gideons pocket Bible (the New Testament, Psalms, and Proverbs) distributed by the Christian chaplains, in particular, sees much more use as a source of rolling papers than as reading material.

Many inmates like to stay abreast of the news, and two copies of the *New York Daily News* and one copy of *El Diario* are supposed to be distributed to every housing unit daily. But in reality, their appearance is far from daily or regular, and unless an unedited version can be smuggled back by a mailroom worker, any story referring to a person on Rikers Island, or making police, COs, or the prison-industrial complex look bad, is ripped out. Many COs read the *New York Post* and throw the paper, intact, into the trash when they are done, meaning that salvaged copies are an irregular but sought-after source of news for inmates. David had a subscription to the *New York Times* and often gave his papers to others, although they no longer contained breaking news—the institutional mail services generally delivered them between four days and four weeks after publication.

David also noticed many nonnative English speakers using grammar books to help them learn or improve their English, and a smattering of native English speakers with books to help them learn or improve a second language, usually Spanish. Popular magazine publications during his time included *Men's Health*, *Men's Journal*, *GQ*, *Sports Illustrated*, and *Maxim*, as well as *National Geographic*, *Popular Mechanics*, various magazines on cars and auto repair, and pornography, both soft- and hard-core, known as "girls" and widely shared. David also saw a number of low-budget magazines that seemed to have incarcerated urban men as their target audience, showcasing an odd mix of softcore pornography shot in locales like the roofs of New York public housing projects, erotic art, hip hop lyrics and lifestyle news, fashion news, depictions of street life, and nods to incarceration.

A less common form of reading comes in irregular delivery of mail. Mail call effects a visceral demarcation between men with substantive support on the outside and those without it. In a 2013 essay, C-76 inmate Pakij Kent Ochjaroem theorizes that it is a generational issue. "Coming in and out of the jail/prison system in the past decade has made me notice that a simple piece of mail/letter is very rare. . . . Usually the only people I see getting letters would be old timers, people with age. And this is most likely because they already have a network of people who put pen to paper. As far as the new generation growing up, being spoiled by texting, emailing, and all those social networking sites, they don't seem to know what it's like to put pen to paper."[8] This is an interesting theory, and many younger inmates do not in fact know how to address an envelope. But while the age gap may be a factor, we found it to be more the case that inmates who did not receive any mail were either locked up for a very short time, had not notified their loved ones they were even inside, or else had burned virtually all of their bridges on their path to city time.

Folklore

"The mythology of a prison community," observed Hans Reimer in 1937, "acts as a strong educative force which, in effect, tends to ensure the behavior of neophytes. . . . The story grows, the characters become actual mythological heroes and their virtues, as the prison community would define them, are brilliantly described."[9] Rikers folklore does what all folklore does: provides a sense of shared place and identity to a group moving through time together. These stories ground incarcerated people in a community with a common history. They shape city time, giving it some sense of positive value, or at the very least, a definition imposed from within the prisoner community, rather than from without.

Part of folklore is a basic institutional history. Rikers Island has been consistently functioning and inhabited by inmates, twenty-four hours a day, seven days a week, since 1903. Since there have been no moments we are aware of in which the entire jail population was released all at once, this means that somebody serving city time on Rikers Island at this moment has done time with somebody who did time with somebody who did time with somebody, and so on, all the way back to 1903. Life in city time is effectively one eternal "now," a present whose past is much more recent than time experienced on the outside.

Referring to unauthorized written inmate communications as "kites," for example, is documented at least as far back as the early 1930s, in the field work conducted by sociologist Donald Clemmer at the Illinois State Penitentiary.[10] Such slang has survived decades of use on Rikers, while New York City street slang changes practically monthly. Even consciousness of change on Rikers becomes reinscribed as a sort of continuity, as stories of "Old Rikers," when inmates were allowed to smoke, beds could be unbolted from the floor to barricade doors, and many COs were afraid to even leave the Bubble to patrol the dormitories for fear of attack, circulate widely, bridging the experiences of older inmates, however embellished, with city time today.

There is a folklore leitmotif, not specific to Rikers but very common there, of the inmate who blows it at the end of his bid, and ends up getting significantly more time. In this story, a guy two weeks away from his release date gets caught with contraband, for example, or hooking up with a social worker, or loses his temper and assaults a CO, and ends up getting years added to his sentence. These tragic stories of "getting caught up" were clearly a way of expressing a perfectly logical fear of a very real phenomenon; all inmates know that the rule is arbitrary, and that the game they must play is rigged against them. They also had basis in reality. David served time with a man who had gone upstate for his first sentence at twenty years old, expecting to serve two years, and got into a knife fight his first week. His two years became eleven and a half; he did not see the street again until his early thirties.

Most things that could arguably be defined as Rikers-specific folklore revolved around the alleged glory of fights, riots (especially among old-timers) and stick-ups past, heists from workplaces like the kitchen, or successful smuggling operations on the visiting floor. Some folk tales centered on sex with DOC staff: there was a female captain in the Six who was widely rumored to have had sex with Lil Wayne during his eight months in custody ("That's that bitch Weezy fucked!"). A female CO in another building was rumored by several guys to fellate inmates in a private space. Guys who had been upstate would often recount these sorts of stories as well, especially about female social workers. Former Rikers CO Gary Heyward classified these sexual tall tales among prisoners with the evocative appellation "lying on your dick." Incidentally, Heyward's own bawdy accounts of copious sex with female COs, and the outrageous claim that he acted as a pimp in a sex ring frequented by prisoners, has done more to add to the island's sexual folklore than a small army of prisoners lying on their dicks.[11]

Exaggeration of past acts, especially one's own, is part of how folklore is generated and transmitted. Former CO C. René West describes how academy instructors "talked about their history in the jails, where they worked, how much time they had on the job and the battles they encountered with the inmates, what they called war stories. Some of these war stories you would feel were being exaggerated, because the story didn't fit the personality of the individual telling the tale. The real tough instructors didn't have to brag about their battles," West concludes.[12] In another instance, the commonly accepted (and entirely fabricated) origin story of the "Brad H" designation for mentally ill patients, to be discussed later, is a piece of Rikers-specific folklore.

A palpable folklore surrounds the history of sexual assault in the sentenced men's facilities at Rikers. On Jarrod's first day, he and another inmate were approached in the cafeteria by an older man who spoke, wide-eyed, about how the inmates there used to masturbate each other under the table. It was a clear overture. The duo declined to get involved, and the man moved on to another table. Jarrod's compatriot, who had been at Rikers before, named the elephant in the room: "That was some gay shit!"

He then explained, as part of Jarrod's social intake, that this used to be common practice, but that today, any kind of sexual behavior was highly taboo in the Six. A widespread and vocal homophobia shared throughout the institution by inmates and COs alike blended relatively seamlessly into a prohibition on sexual assault. Lurid tales of the "booty bandits" of yesteryear abounded. The showers, in particular, were not safe in those days. Nowadays, Jarrod was told time and again, there was a kind of social contract prohibiting sexual assault. Its most visible manifestation was the wearing of underwear in the shower, part of a general prohibition of nakedness. This ban, conflating consensual gay sex, rape, and nudity, was couched in the folklore of inmates' overcoming sexual predation, which Jarrod and David did not in fact observe at Rikers—though this is surely not to say that it does not exist.

One story in particular stands out as a piece of distinctly C-76 folklore. David heard it several times from several different sources who had spent time there, while those who had never been to the Six, even if they were veterans, had never heard the story at all. The story goes that at some point in the '80s or '90s, depending on who was telling it, there were two East Asian men serving city time in the Six. According to some, they were Chinese, to others, Japanese, and in some versions they were also brothers, but all agreed that they were immigrants involved in organized crime. Exactly what organization was also fluid: sometimes they were Triads, sometimes Tongs, sometimes even Yakuza. This was "back in the days" when people were "wildin' out" in the Six. But these two were martial arts experts; nobody could touch them. They even "fucked up the Turtles," the emergency response units in riot gear and padding. Finally, they were transferred to another dorm (since they could not be moved by force, this may imply some sort of all-too-common trickery by DOC staff). But this dorm was full of Bloods, who had been tipped off about the two men's arrival and who were waiting, weapons in hand. The two men gave as well as they got, and dealt serious damage to the onslaught of attackers, but in the end they were overpowered, and by some accounts even killed. Even former CO Heyward recounts being told this story—"the story of these famous Chinese brothers that kicked everybody's ass, including the warden's"—on the first day of DOC academy![13]

The prevalence of this story, despite its vagueness on certain details, leads us to believe it may well be based on a kernel of truth. As with most folk tales and jailhouse stories, it is all but impossible to separate fact from fiction. But the practical lesson is clear enough: it is useless to try to fight the COs head-on, since even the toughest men in the island's history could not succeed. This story functions as a practice of care; it is at once a salve for the sting of complying with the insults and degradations of the COs and assistance to other inmates in doing the same. It also demonstrates that the COs' folk tales run parallel to—and sometimes even overlap with—the inmates'.

Folklore among COs can have even clearer utilitarian functions. "One female officer sleeping in a dormitory with over 50 male inmates," writes West, "was said to have woken up with semen all over her uniform, and she had no idea who ejaculated on her." The story served its purposes. "Whether true or false," West continues, "it was enough for me to keep the coffee coming."[14] Heyward, for his part, simply repeats the story as fact.[15] In all likelihood, this has happened somewhere, if not at Rikers. After all, if there is a sexual practice the human mind can conceptualize, someone has probably done it. As a folk tale, however, it strikes the perfect thematic blend of caution, schadenfreude, and prurient smut that keeps tabloid newspapers in business all over the world. And from the vantage of COs and their superiors, what better story to dissuade rookies from sleeping on the job?

West recounts another grave warning circulating among staff: if a prisoner dies during the night shift, and the CO is sleeping, it can mean the end of the latter's career. As West puts it, "That inmate's body had better not be cold, or you will be left holding the bag." A story from the academy dramatized the imperative to avoid getting stuck with a cold corpse. "We were told that one officer put a dead inmate on a heater to try to warm his body after a suicide in an attempt to change the time of death. . . . But the burns on his skin were a dead giveaway to the coroner. . . . He was ultimately fired."[16]

Time Strategies

Goffman found among prisoners "a strong feeling that time spent in the establishment is time wasted or destroyed or taken from one's life; it is time that must be written off." This helps explain "removal activities" that primarily function to remove incarcerated people from the reality of their situation.[17] To achieve this consistently, and make time go by faster, the importance of establishing a routine is widely acknowledged among jailhouse old heads, especially those who have served time in prison. But this is easier said than done: because the institutional schedule is in constant flux, an inmate's carefully crafted routine might fall to pieces shortly after its construction. David, for example, estimates that he had no less than a dozen different routines during his time behind bars; he was repeatedly forced to adapt his schedule, which included large chunks of time devoted to reading, writing, and translating, to changes in programming, like yard time, or work. Despite this, he generally held himself to the schedule he set, as he found that time moved faster, and that he had a greater sense of control, accomplishment, and even anticipation for the next day to begin.

Many inmates organized their routines around things like their jobs, any programs they were participating in, institutional meals or personal ones, drug use, working out in the dorm or at the yard, a general preference for staying up late or getting up early, and so on. For some, factors included "slot time," usually beginning after 7:00 p.m., when the phones were only available to certain people with fifteen-minute "slots," or their favorite TV show (David once took a 7:30 p.m. slot instead of a 7:00 p.m. one so he could watch *Jeopardy!* in the evening). Work, in particular, features prominently in the routines of those who do not sleep the day away. Some men work two or even three jobs despite only getting paid for one, and paltry wages at that. In philosophical terms, *doing* city time means developing a relationship to time itself, as inmates grapple with the ethical predicament that the time they spend behind bars is decidedly not their own, but time they must live nonetheless. This means deciding how to conceptualize the days, weeks, and months separating the inmates from freedom, and how best to inhabit this unfree time until its conclusion.

Daily activities, large and small, are guided by an overall orientation to the passage of city time. Rikers city-time inmate Marcos Perez captured this obsessive fixation that incarcerated people risk developing toward time in a poem he penned while at C-76:

> How far is happiness for me you
> ask? Well, in my current position
> would be two weeks; four days
> from now; or 392 hours or 23,520

minutes or 1,411,200 seconds from now
would bring me ultimate happiness
because it will be the day I
get to go home and be with my
loved ones and get away from
this abuse they call jail!!![18]

As we experienced, these numbers can be deceiving; time may be measurable by objective instruments, but it is subjectively lived by human beings, and comparable stretches of time can seem vastly longer or shorter depending on the activities one engages in and how one relates to their duration. And time is just different when experienced in a cage.

The political prisoner Victor Serge recounts, "The contrast between the vacant, empty prison time and the intense rhythm of normal life is so violent that it will take a long and painful period of adaptation to slow down the pulse of life, to deaden the will, to stifle, blot out, obliterate every unsettling image from my mind."[19] The old saying "a watched pot never boils" captures the almost boundless interiority of even small portions of time, when a person is too attentive to its passage and single-mindedly focused on its end. The enforced idleness and discomfort of the pens, for instance, may be experienced as longer than exponentially more time in the comparative ease of the dormitory, to say nothing of a pleasant day on the outside. This is perhaps especially true of city time. We found it nearly universally agreed, by those with experience, that city time passes more slowly than normal prison time. "I did eleven years upstate, and this six months is going slower than that eleven years," one inmate told David. Another, who was serving only a few months of city time but had done eight and a half years upstate in his youth, told David after his release, "I don't know *how* you did all that time on the island."

When human beings are kept in cages for a determinant amount of time, their release date can become an all-encompassing fixation that crowds out all other thoughts and has the tragic effect of making the intervening time seem almost endless. Avoiding this hell-within-a-hell presents practical problems for inmates. How often, for instance, should they tabulate the remaining days before their release? This question is often discussed and debated. One day a younger man in Jarrod's dorm began talking at great length about the number of days he had left—counting, recounting, asking for a third-party verification of his math, and seeming unable to mentally process any other topic. An older man with experience in the state system cautioned against thinking too hard about the days ahead. "Upstate, I didn't look at the calendar," he remarked. "I looked at the season." It was a popular sentiment; other OG inmates joined in, sharing their own beliefs that fixating on the amount of time remaining in one's sentence was a great way to make it go by as slowly as possible.

When David hung up a calendar his friends had sent him, his neighbors quickly asked him to put it away. In another dorm David was confined to, one inmate with a fair amount of status in the social hierarchy kept a paper calendar glued to the wall with toothpaste, crossing out each day with a big X as it passed. No one criticized him, but when he went home, the first thing the man who moved into his bunk did was peel it off the wall. "Yo, that's the stupidest fuckin' thing you could do right there," another commented, looking on. "Put a goddamn calendar on the wall." Instead of fixating on the amount of time until release, bearers of this folk knowledge encourage inmates to consider each day as the possibility for reasonable comfort and small enjoyments, and to simply live one's life thusly for the duration of one's stay. In a study of state prisoners, convict criminologist John Irwin described this pragmatic approach as "doing time."[20]

Even for those able to cultivate a practical relationship to time sufficient to make it go by without considerable hardship or obsessive thinking, the months, weeks, and days leading up to release pose a particular challenge. We observed—and experienced—a mounting disgust and frustration at the environment felt by the inmate as his release date approached. Dreaming of all the things they will do once released, inmates cannot help but compare their dismal surroundings with the much more enjoyable world outside. Day in and day out, every waking moment, they are confronted with the reality that they are still in jail, even as their image of the outside world, and themselves inhabiting it, comes into sharper focus. Many begin sleeping the days away, or disobeying COs in little ways, where before they had kept their head down. Others pick fights; David once prevented a friend, only two weeks from freedom, from picking a fight with a guy he had had no prior issues with, over a video game he never played.

Even for those who have remained incredibly patient during their bid, the conventional wisdom of not counting the days becomes increasingly difficult, if not impossible, the closer one's release date gets. While inmates generally differed on whether it was helpful or harmful to "count your days," many in Mod 4 celebrated the thirty-fifth day before their release date, when they could start "counting the wall": the bunk numbers up to thirty-five are painted prominently on the wall in Mod 4. Inmates "counting the wall" often used this visual representation to track their progress, pointing at the bed with the same number as the number of days they had left and gleefully exclaiming, "I'm right there, bro!"

David's last few weeks took on a surreal quality, and he found it increasingly difficult to focus on things that had previously carried him through his time, like reading, writing, and translation. He started picking up shifts at the job he had quit months prior, and jumping at opportunities to go to institutional movie events, which, for the most part, he had previously waved off.

It is generally agreed that one's last day drags on eternally. Victor Serge called the final hours of his incarceration "perhaps the most endless of my life."[21] David's last day went more quickly than anticipated, but there was an unexpected two-hour delay between his being told to get ready to be escorted to the intake pens for release and the actual arrival of the escort CO. David spent this time trying to read a book, but the words seemed to blur on the page, his mouth dry, his pulse racing, the second hand on the clock mired in unseen molasses.

A central fixture of how inmates relate to their impending release is what Goffman calls "the release binge fantasy," the frequently discussed plans for great excesses in the outside world, often framed as making up for lost time or rewarding oneself.[22] These fantasies can take different forms. Future sex with women is a major theme in city-time discussions, which, statistically speaking, include a number of men who do not actually enjoy it or plan to do it upon release. Groups of boosters, or professional shoplifters, often compare notes on the best places to expropriate the most valuable goods, with minimum risk, upon release. After a stretch of city time comparing notes with other boosters, akin to professional development training, they prepare to return to the outside world, energized and ready to get back to work.

But the main theme of release binge fantasies is getting high. Inmates discourse endlessly on how high they will get—and stay—upon release, "like hungry men who can talk about nothing but food," in the words of seasoned detainee and self-identified "junky" William S. Burroughs.[23] While the discussion is typically framed around marijuana, at least in larger discussion circles where hard drug users are looked down upon, weed surely functions for some as a metonym for drugs like crack and heroin. And in many cases, the binge is not a fantasy: as former Rikers health official Homer Venters writes, the likelihood of a drug-addicted person overdosing increases significantly following that person's release from jail.[24]

Those who do not overdose are likely to reimmerse themselves in a familiar cycle of drug use, petty crime, and, ultimately, spending more time on Rikers.[25] David personally witnessed multiple inmates with addiction problems be released, only to return months later for possession or other drug-related crimes. Jarrod heard anecdotes of COs telling released inmates that their jail job would be waiting for them when they were ultimately rearrested. It is tragic confirmation that many of these men are, as a common cliché in the system runs, serving "life sentences on the installment plan."

5

Work

"Tell him I come for him in the morning," John Lam tells David, handing him a dented hotel pan of steamed cabbage as they work their afternoon shift in the kitchen. David has just confirmed the arrival, a day prior, of a Chinese immigrant, like Lam, in his dorm.

"OK, I'll tell him," David replies. "But why, exactly, are you coming for him in the morning?"

"So he can come to work!" says Lam, as if it is the most obvious thing in the world.

David has the brief urge to ask Lam how he can be so sure that a man he has never met does, in fact, want a job. But he has also been locked up for over three months by this point, and he is able to suppress the thought before voicing it aloud. He quickly realizes why Lam is so confident the man will want to work, especially if he can do it while mingling with Lam, who probably speaks the same language. It is the same reason Lam volunteers to work the morning shift, too, despite the policy limiting inmate pay to one job's wages per week: working passes the time. And as someone who served over a decade in prison in his youth, Lam ought to know.

This is a widely accepted truism among inmates, but Lam voiced it so often, and in his distinctive dialect, that it became adopted as a catch phrase oft repeated by the other men on David's crew. When you work multiple jobs, Lam always said, "Time go fast!"

Official Work

Like the vast majority of incarcerated workers in the United States, Rikers inmates with jobs do not manufacture commodities for the market, but instead labor to reproduce the institution by working in the commissary, cafeteria, laundry, clinic, law library, car wash for corrections buses (and unofficially, the COs' cars), or general building maintenance, including painting, construction, and janitorial services. Until 2021, city-time inmates also buried the city's unclaimed and indigent dead in New York's potter's field on nearby Hart Island, a longtime DOC property and former home of the city workhouse.[1]

Their wages varied considerably. The "suicide prevention aid" or "SPA" job paid very well by Rikers standards, and mostly entailed reading a book in a high-security cell block, occasionally making the rounds to spot people trying to kill themselves, and reporting them if they are caught in the act. "SPA is the highest paying job an inmate can get," recounts Lil Wayne, who briefly held this position. "The job is basically to monitor the tier for an eight-hour shift, and if someone wants to hang up (meaning to kill themselves), to not negotiate with them or try to talk them out of it, but just to alert an officer." This discovery came with a bonus. "You get paid $50 if you stop the person from actually hanging themselves, and $25 if you find them hung up. Yeah, it's that real."[2]

Another piece-rate position, the coveted "spill cleanup" job, paid seventy-five dollars per pool of blood mopped during David's time. "Piss and shit is only fifty dollars," one inmate who worked in that position once told him, downcast. There are also a number of oddly specific jobs on the DOC books that no one had ever heard of, including "glazier," "potato peeler," and "inmate musical entertainer." The latter, the policy stipulates, is strictly limited to inmates who rehearse their musical performances twenty hours a week or more, "subject to the Commanding Officer's approval."[3]

David and Jarrod never saw postings for these jobs. The far more common work revolved around cooking, cleaning, laundry, and other essential functions of sustaining a large captive population. Inmates with these jobs often had strong opinions about why they were the best assignments, or coveted better ones for clearly defined reasons.

The most basic janitorial upkeep of city-time dorms, where upwards of sixty men live in one open room, is maintained by "house detail" or "house gang" inmates who work in their own dormitory. Accordingly, the house detail becomes responsible for enforcing, quite often with unvarnished aggression, the rules of hygiene and cleanliness on those around them. These inmates are much more likely than the COs to call out slovenly behavior or the transgression of hygiene rules, and since their workplace is also their living quarters, they are almost always on the lookout. This is an official waged position, but sometimes house detail work is done for free, akin to an audition, as a means of appealing to the COs to get on the rolls officially.

This level of enthusiasm is not limited to house detail. It is not uncommon for inmates in the hallway or mess hall to make a quick break away from the CO escorting them to give their name and number to an official they believe can get them a coveted job. This often works; David and Jarrod both encountered industrious men who learned the "who's who" of Rikers COs with the alacrity of high-society social climbers, and used this knowledge to secure work. Though the DOC claims to implement an intricate "Inmate Work Application" policy, there was no sign of this during either of our sentences; all jobs were either randomly assigned from above, or obtained by either word of mouth or informal appeals to well-positioned COs.[4]

Since the introduction of the Inmate Wage Incentive Plan in 1960, Rikers inmates have been compensated for their work.[5] During both Jarrod's and David's time, jobs paid a rate of forty dollars a week, or one dollar an hour. It was common practice for some work-detail COs to pay their employees overtime as a means of making their job more attractive, thereby buying more stable labor from their incarcerated employees, as inmates who did not want to lose their comparatively well-paid jobs were unlikely to quit or cause trouble at work. The DOC overtime policy, if not the pay, is actually better than the time-and-a-half policy implemented for those in the outside world according to the Fair Labor Standards Act: overtime on Rikers is double the regular wages for any amount of time beyond the usual hours. This means a forty dollars/week job yielded eighty dollars/week if the worker stayed late, went in on a day off, or had the good fortune to work for a CO who always paid overtime.[6]

There were a small number of jobs that broke the eighty-dollar ceiling. These were usually in high demand. The most coveted job for those who cared about pay was, during David's sentence, West Facility. This is the name of the island's medical center, and inmates who worked there made just over three hundred dollars a week if they worked double shifts, or six- to seven-day weeks. Though all jobs were based on a forty-hour scale, some jobs had shifts as short as an hour per day. Others entailed well over forty hours a week, but all seemed to involve a great deal of downtime, and most wages, pitiful as they were, did not therefore reflect time spent actually working.

In August 2020, in the final months of David's sentence and amid the supposed financial hardships the city faced under COVID-19, inmate wages were universally slashed to ten dollars/week, or about twenty-five cents an hour.[7] This unannounced and unqualified pay cut was especially devastating for those who had been working comparatively well-paid jobs. West Facility workers, for instance, saw their wages plummet from three hundred dollars to ten dollars literally overnight. Despite some work-detail COs' continuing to implement their across-the-board overtime practice, this now amounted to a mere twenty dollars/week, and a full-blown labor dispute erupted, with a wave of resignations by inmate-workers. A quarter an hour seems to have remained the going rate until October 2021, when a new directive, issued under Commissioner Vincent Schiraldi's brief tenure, established "low," "medium," and "high" inmate pay rates at $.55, $1.00, and $1.45 per hour, respectively.[8] To the best of our knowledge, these are the current pay rates for those inmates who work on Rikers Island.

Not all inmates on Rikers work. Pretrial detainees are formally innocent in the eyes of the law and cannot be legally compelled to work, though they often volunteer to, just to pass the time and make some money. City-time inmates, on the other hand, are subject to state-imposed labor, and face the threat of institutional sanctions like loss of good time should they fail to comply.[9] But it would be a mistake to assume that people serving city time there are forced to perform hard labor. While the conditions in DOC facilities tend to be poor as a result of the department's general indifference to the well-being of those in its custody, and some jobs might occasionally qualify as physically difficult, most are anything but. Nobody picks oakum or breaks rocks on Rikers, and there are no commodities produced for sale by private corporations. Nor does the City of New York make any money off its inmates; instead, it saves money here and there by paying below minimum wage to incarcerated people for jobs that would otherwise be done by civilians making much more.

Far from the modern heir to a southern plantation, Rikers has the feeling of a New Deal–era jobs program with more workers than work, geared more toward keeping redundant laborers busy than accomplishing any profitable or even important tasks. Rarely does there seem to be any engaging, productive work that needs doing, and when there is, there are almost always too many people clamoring to do it. On his job with the island's outdoor cleanup crew, for example, David often found himself milling around awkwardly with three other men as they watched a fifth man change the bag in an institutional trash can. That same job included COs chauffeuring their incarcerated staff around the island for hours at a time just to look busy for any DOC superiors who might see them.

Among the most bizarre vestiges of life in the outside world one finds on Rikers is the freedom inmates have to quit their jobs and get others. Mass actions in which numerous inmate-workers quit at once constitute a collective power that both David and Jarrod observed. Ironically, however, this can also just reveal how few workers are actually needed in the first place. After the August 2020 pay dispute, in which a large number of people quit their jobs in protest, a friend remarked to David that the kitchen was running much more smoothly with six workers instead of thirty. DOC guidelines state that sentenced inmates are supposed to be rotated to new work details every ninety days, but neither David, Jarrod, nor anyone they served time with had ever heard of this happening.[10] On the other hand, most jobs can be switched, or simply quit, with a quitting inmate having little trouble finding employment elsewhere. The SOD COs were notorious for trying to get any worker who quit or got fired blacklisted from other jobs, with varying degrees of success. David knew a guy who got fired for calling them "racist-ass white boys," but got hired at the bakery the following day.

The same is true for many inmates who get fired for allegedly disrespecting a CO on the job, or being caught in violation of an unignorable rule at work, like passing contraband. Since sentenced inmates are required to work, the incarcerated labor market is wildly different from its counterpart in the outside world: nobody will have any trouble finding employment, unless his paperwork somehow slips through the administrative cracks, or he does something so egregious as to get himself blacklisted. The impetus not to quit or get fired, then, is fairly low.

Thanks to the generosity of activists on the outside, Jarrod had enough money for commissary and did not need to seek work. He was, however, housed for a time in a "work house," or "working dorm," where the majority of the inmates spent much of the day working outside of the dormitory. Here, and throughout his stay at Rikers, he met only one man who had been assigned a job that he did not want, and who was weighing whether to refuse. This meant possibly risking losing "good time," prolonging his stay, and being moved from a relatively calm and peaceful dormitory into what could be a more hectic and violent one. Jarrod was released before the drama was resolved, but this man was probably just fine. "Box time," losing good time, or transfer are certainly serious threats for inmates trying to get out in one piece as quickly as possible. But by all accounts, these penalties are rarely imposed. Those who quit their jobs and did not get another were not penalized. And every other inmate Jarrod spoke with wanted either a job, a second job, or a better one. Except one.

Jarrod bunked next to a Russian immigrant who lived by the strict code of Russian criminal culture—indicated by the tattoo of a wolf on his hand, symbolizing the rejection of lawful authority. He regularly expressed to Jarrod his disgust and bewilderment that American prisoners so willingly "worked for the police." In his world, he explained, a respectable criminal would never assist the state in any way. He recounted being tortured in Russia for refusing to cooperate, and removed two sets of complete dentures to demonstrate that his teeth had been pulled out, one by one, during interrogation. By the time Jarrod took a bed next to him at Rikers, he had flown under the radar for months without being assigned work. He insisted that if ordered to work, he would have to refuse. Otherwise, word might get around in his social circles on the outside that he had become nothing short of a police collaborator, ruining his life. This man had particular disdain for inmate-workers who openly identified with gang culture. One day, he watched, his face full of pure contempt, as a group of openly gang-affiliated inmates gleefully departed for their job at the car wash. "Look at these 'gangsters,'" he spat, putting the word in air quotes, "washing the policeman's car."

The Perks

Wages are, of course, important to many inmates serving city time. The so-called chow at Rikers covers only the barest subsistence, and most inmates need to purchase commissary food simply to stave off hunger, even if they eat all the food that is provided to them, which few can stomach. They also need extra money for hygiene products, stamps, and other basic commodities. During Jarrod's time, even phone calls cost money. Court fees can be deducted directly from the inmates' commissary account without notice, months before they are due, leaving one completely broke. This happened to Jarrod, who discovered that his commissary funds had been wiped out shortly before he was scheduled to go, leaving no time to replace them. Inmates can also save the money they make, or send it to dependents on the outside, which can be used to support families or simply keep up rent, car payments, and the like. The money they make from work is certainly put to use—but even the most enthusiastic inmate-workers realize that they are being exploited for far below minimum wage.

Every jail job has a number of other perks, which tend to feature in the incarcerated population's estimation of the job's worth. Perks of the jobs may be intangible, like getting outside with SOD, or tangible, like extra food. For many, especially after the August 2020 pay reduction, the perks mattered more than the pay itself. Many jobs give their incarcerated workers a few cartons of milk and single-serving packages of cereal to take back to the dorm at the end of their shift. Working in the kitchen afforded David access to not only milk and cereal but a virtually unlimited supply of fresh fruit, spices, sugar, and other edible goods inaccessible under normal circumstances. Working at the car wash gets inmates access to powdered bleach, which can be used to brighten their white clothing ("whites"), or sell to others. Working at Intake affords access to discarded street clothes from new arrivals, which can likewise be worn by the procurer or sold to those looking to inject some variety into their jail wardrobes. These sorts of transactions feed into an entire parallel jailhouse marketplace, which includes the circulation of items acquired on the job, but also takes on a seemingly endless stream of innovative permutations, forming a very particular gig economy. It is an economy that constitutes a veritable lifeline for many. Just like on the outside, inmates are forced to find creative ways to make ends meet when the jobs just do not pay enough.

Beyond the predictable commodities, like tobacco, it is just as common for a tightly rationed product as banal as jelly or matzo bread to be wildly popular. When Jarrod was first approached with a hushed offer of jelly, he assumed it was the name of an illicit street drug he had not heard before. But it was ordinary jelly, which the man had smuggled from his kitchen job—though, considering the excitement that surrounded its appearance in the dorm, it might as well have been a designer drug. Similarly, matzo bread is only accessible with a kosher dining card, or backdoor kitchen access. By virtue of their sheer rarity, the bland and flavorless crackers are a hot commodity at Rikers. When David was still inside, Jarrod recounted to him over the phone how a photograph of Harvey Weinstein had been leaked from Rikers showing the disgraced producer dining with an entire box of matzo at his side. David responded, in grave earnestness, "He is a very rich man."

Other items seemed to circulate solely through this sort of gray market, such as the "two-piece" uniforms. Though inmates are given ill-fitting, uncomfortable jumpsuits upon arrival, there are shirts and pants of the same color, which mark the wearer as someone who knows his way around the place, circulating through back channels. We saw no legitimate means through which to secure these garments, and their informal circulation occurred unhampered by any authorities. Access to rare items confers an advantage in informal economies, social hierarchies, or simply friendship. While some inmates were unabashed entrepreneurs, David and Jarrod were both surprised by the degree to which items, including precious commodities like jelly, were freely given away by men who had secured access to them through their jobs.

Sometimes inmates prefer to work even when there are no clear perks of any kind. Jarrod encountered a house duty inmate who cleaned the dormitory's bathroom for free, when he was not on the schedule, just for something to do. The Russian career criminal remarked that in prisons back home, this work would place the man at the bottom of the prison hierarchy, with "the untouchables," shunned by everyone outside this wretched caste. But to the Americans and others at Rikers, it lacked any stigma or even appearance of abnormality; cleaning the bathroom was simply better than sitting around, doing nothing. With food and shelter guaranteed, there is almost nothing to do all day besides watch garbage TV, listen to the same increasingly boring war stories from those around you, play repetitive games, or steal some reading over the incessant shouting. In any case, if someone wants to make a few extra bucks, there are plenty of ways to do it that do not involve working for the institution.

Unofficial Work

In a facility packed with men who support themselves off informal economies on the outside, official DOC employment is, of course, not the only game in town. During Jarrod's time, the most common way to make a little extra money was selling phone calls. Surplus phone time was exchanged for packets of ramen, coffee, and other common items. Jarrod freely traded his phone time and used that of others, as did just about everyone, despite the fact that the DOC boasted of a program called Voice Verify that prevented inmates from using each other's phone time. During intake, Jarrod and David were forced to record themselves repeating bizarre phrases, such as "Like the moon and the stars in the sky" and "So you really think you can dance like that?" These recordings supposedly created a composite of speakers' vocal pattern, preventing anyone else from using their phone time. The free exchange of phone time that thrived in defiance of this safeguard suggested to us that the program did little else but inject a bit more surreality into the intake process. Nonetheless, we have little doubt that the contractor who sold this worthless software to DOC was paid handsomely; at Rikers, as in the rest of the city, penny-ante hustles are for the lowly prisoners, while the big con jobs are typically reserved for respectable, law-abiding citizens.

In May 2019, a few months before David began his sentence, phone calls at Rikers became available free of charge, after a concerted effort by activist organizations, public defenders, and prisoners' families. Inmates now get two free phone calls every three hours.[11] Guys who make few or no calls still often sell theirs to "phone junkies" for a buck or so apiece. A similar practice arose with regard to stamps after in-person visits were suspended due to the COVID-19 pandemic. To compensate for the lack of visits, the DOC began issuing three free stamps per week to every inmate who asked for them, which those who sent few or no letters would hoard and resell. The guy in the bed next to David's would sell him three fifty-cent stamps for a dollar—a good deal for him, too, as one dollar equals two packets of instant coffee or ramen noodles. This is, in fact, the handy common denominator of all small-scale transactions: inmates pay each other by exchanging commissary goods based on their institutional purchasing price. Larger transactions are handled differently, but we won't discuss that here for a number of reasons known to those who engage in them.

Artistically inclined inmates will often take commissions for sketches or other artwork. In David's time, there was a poor white Oklahoman who spent all day fashioning cross necklaces to sell from the various types and colors of fabric he had somehow managed to acquire. Another man, a Bronx-born Puerto Rican with a "buck-fifty" (giant facial scar) offered a nice, close shave for only a dollar. He would also turn your pants into shorts if you wanted, or sew pockets into them, for a nominal fee. David was often paid in commissary products—or his preference, regular pens, as opposed to the soft plastic commissary pens—for helping others with paperwork like grievances and lawsuits, writing short stories and love poems, or teaching English lessons. Some guys even paid others to fill out their commissary order forms and keep them under budget.

Enforced scarcity drives the jail economy in city time. Out-of-stock commissary items can be resold for triple or quadruple their price. Whole onions, when they can be pilfered from the kitchen, go for up to three dollars apiece, a price many are willing to pay even if they do not have a coveted plastic knife, also stolen from the kitchen, to slice them with. Even more valuable are successful batches of "hooch" (jail-brewed liquor), which are bottled and sold at a premium. David met one guy who claimed to have fashioned and sold two shanks for seventy-five dollars each, and he probably was not the only one in the shank-manufacturing business.

The most lucrative sector of the illicit Rikers economy is by far the sale of K2, usually called "deuce" or "plane." Because it is colorless, odorless, and tasteless, all but impossible to detect, and legally available in liquid format on the outside, it is often sprayed onto a sheet of paper and mailed in as a letter. In reality, the amounts of K2 smuggled in this way are probably too small to be for anything but personal use. All major drug distribution was rumored to depend on inside help, a claim we find believable based on DOC staff's proven track record of smuggling contraband into Rikers, which continues up to the present.[12] In May 2021, for example, nine DOC employees, including seven COs, were charged with introducing contraband, including K2, into various facilities from 2019 to 2021.[13] One of them was one of David's former steady officers in Mod 4; in November 2022, he was sentenced to twenty-seven months in federal prison for smuggling K2, cigarettes, and a weapon into RNDC at approximately the same time David was there.[14]

"Deuce" is positively rampant in jails and prisons around the country, and even beyond, notably in Britain.[15] A small bottle of this stuff can be used to make several sheets of K2-dosed paper, and costs $450 on the outside.[16] Inside, a single sheet of paper goes for up to one thousand dollars wholesale. A small torn-off square of a K2-soaked sheet, about the size of a postage stamp and appropriately called "a stamp," goes for twenty to fifty dollars, depending on a number of market factors like supply, demand, and quality, meaning that a single sheet can have a retail value of up to forty-five hundred dollars in jail if sold by the stamp. There are even rumored to be guys who will deliberately get themselves locked up for a few months just to make a killing selling deuce.

The only thing that comes close to deuce in terms of profitability is tobacco, the use of which is at least as widespread despite a blanket prohibition policy on the island since 2003, when it was banned on Rikers along with all New York's restaurants and bars.[17] This created a massive black market for "'bacco." On the odd occasion when COs smuggle and sell whole packs of cigarettes to inmates, they go for up to a thousand dollars apiece. One inmate David didn't know once tried to sell him a pack of Newports for three hundred dollars; David declined. Other inmates later informed him that *a price that low* was indicative of a scam.[18]

Much more common is repurposed tobacco. This is king of all job perks for those willing to put in the work and take on the risks. Without going into too much detail, all outside jobs afford access—some more than others—to discarded cigarette (and occasionally cigar) butts. Some guys will pick these up and empty them into a scrap of plastic, then smuggle them back into the building. If caught, enterprising tobacconists will almost certainly be fired and possibly charged with smuggling or possession of contraband. But if they make it inside, as they usually do, they can sell their product at a premium. A "finger" of street tobacco, literally a torn-off finger of a plastic glove, goes for fifty dollars. A single "stick" (a homemade cigarette rolled in a page from a pocket Bible and barely thicker than a match) costs ten to twenty dollars.

"You Gotta Get outta the Dorm"

In both David's and Jarrod's times, inmates allowed to work outside the facility walls were dressed in a jumpsuit with bright orange and white stripes, indicating "outside clearance." This signifies that they are allowed outside the jail. For some inmates, orange stripes are a source of pride, kept starched and impeccably clean, especially compared to the grubby greens of the dormitory homebody. This clear marking of the relatively privileged outside-clearance workers cuts to the core of the real incentives for inmate-workers: escape from the boredom and brutality of life in the dorms, mobility across the facility and outside of it, and, more generally, an increased control over daily life yielding a heightened sense of self. In his study of a French short-stay prison, sociologist Didier Fassin describes how, for prisoners, "working means having a certain status, not feeling idle and useless, establishing habits conducive to re-entry into society, [and] coming closer to a normal life outside prison. Having a job and also being paid," he concludes, "allows them to regain a form of dignity."[19]

Jarrod spoke to one man who worked as a painter, well over forty hours per week, for $112. He did not even bother keeping track of his hours. Like many, he would half-heartedly boast about the money, but it seemed as though he did not believe his own bluster, and that he knew deep down that his pay was nothing to brag about. His compensation was of a different sort: as a worker with outside clearance, he was able to leave the chaotic dorms for a good part of the day and night. He sometimes traveled across the seemingly remote and endless bridge leading off the island into a vanishing point of flashing sirens—an occasion about which most inmates must content themselves to fantasize for the tenure of their incarceration. He was also able to eat food from the outside, the topic of endless hours of strained reminiscences over sparse plates of bland prison fare. He could relate to his coworkers not as fellow victims of their debased condition but as part of a cooperative project. And the impatient, aggravated way he related to his free time on days off from work underscored the principal motivations for him and many inmate-workers: escaping boredom, making time go by faster, and getting out of the dormitories for as long as possible.

Another man with outside clearance worked all day and well into the night in the kitchen at another jail. He rolled his eyes at the money—he had enough support on the outside to do without it. So why did he look forward to his job? He was not in jail, he told Jarrod, when he was there. A chef by training, he worked at his own pace in the kitchen, under his own direction, and could get lost in the work. The COs at his work site treated him as more of a colleague than a captive, even helping him correct a clerical error that had extended his sentence beyond his release date. He also had freedom to prepare his own food, and even eat food from outside. And for a few hours each day he had downtime to watch TV alone, or otherwise enjoy the indescribably rare privilege of solitude, far from the imposed stupidity of dormitory life. Back at Rikers, he winced at the constant shrieking of the house COs, the inter-inmate hostilities, and the countless indignities built into even the smoothest day of city time. He was happy to rise before the sun and get away from it all.

Goffman argues that the time experienced by those held in what he termed "total institutions" was a gaping void of "dead and heavy-hanging time" that needed to be filled at all costs. "Every total institution can be seen as a kind of dead sea in which little islands of vivid, encapturing activity appear," he wrote, portraying the "dead time" as a constant, unvarying burden.[20] While our experience strongly supports Goffman's former claim, that time weighs on inmates in a distinctive and oppressive way, demanding to be passed by any means necessary, we just as strongly dispute the latter claim. Life behind bars can often have an element of timelessness to it, but it is anything but unvarying. As we have argued, time is a malleable substance, and the inmate must learn to command it, or else be hopelessly dominated by it. A particularly busy day, for example, can seem to fly by if filled with activities that occupy his attention, freeing him from a sole fixation on the constant weight of the sentence yet to be served. Hence, the vast majority of Rikers inmates seek to keep themselves busy. One of the simplest ways to stay consistently busy is to work.

This is the thesis of a 2010 report by French sociologist Fabrice Guilbaud entitled "Working in Prison: Time as Experienced by Inmate-Workers," based on his study in a number of French jails and prisons. Guilbaud, while positioning himself largely within Goffman's theoretical framework, contests his notion that time takes on a uniformity for those behind bars. Instead, Guilbaud focuses on the subjectivity experienced by prisoners when they go to work, both in the passage of time and in the roles they perform in relation to each other and to the institution. His study was conducted in a number of different French penal institutions, but his observations on how inmates in short-term jail facilities (*maisons d'arrêt*) talk about work could well have been taken directly from Rikers.[21] "Once work life is mentioned . . . inmates respond with two refrains, virtual *leitmotive*. The first—'Time goes faster [when you're working]'—is almost always accompanied by the spatial corollary: 'It gets you out of the cell.' In the interviews, these *leitmotive* usually get mentioned one right after the other. And for the inmates it was quite obvious that the two went together—like a diptych."[22]

Guilbaud notes that work also affords prisoners a certain structure to their day: work time allows prisoners to define their "leisure" time by virtue of opposition to it. The observation by critical theorist Theodor Adorno that "free time" is never truly free under capitalism, because it is simply defined by the absence of wage labor, is doubly true for the incarcerated.[23] But, as David and Jarrod consistently observed, a city-time inmate seeks not to enjoy time as much as to annihilate it. All activities, by and large, no matter the comparative pleasure or satisfaction they bring, are ultimately about forcing the time to pass.

Work is the most effective of city time's removal activities, or ways of removing oneself from the painfully slow passage of "dead" institutional time.[24] Separate and apart from its pitiful remuneration, then, work during city time is one of the most popular ways of staving off the acute cabin fever that creeps into the mind of any confined person. "You gotta get outta the dorm" is a frequently invoked truism among city-time inmates at Rikers. Working consistently presents this opportunity.

6

Special Occasions

Most city-time inmates fall into a daily rhythm, however precariously, of doing time. Lights on at 5:00 a.m., routine work schedules, the day room emptied and locked from 7:00 a.m. to 8:00 a.m. and 3:00 p.m. to 4:00 p.m. for headcounts, regular and predictable meals, methadone calls, the nightly cooking of the bag meal, and lights off at 9:00 p.m., sometimes before the sun has even set.[1] These events harmonize to produce a kind of normalcy in a place that is anything but ordinary. Other events recur less regularly—and in the case of searches, without warning—but they, too, characterize daily life for those serving city time. Some of these occasions, like visits, provide liminal spaces between the world of city time and the outside, with slackened relations between COs and inmates. Others, like searches, reinscribe these roles with great fanfare and the threat of violence. Such special occasions are worth examining in detail.

Commissary

Shopping at the jail commissary, known simply as "commissary," is an essential resource for most city-time inmates. The weekly shopping trip allows the men to supplement the scanty and often disgusting food served by the institution—though commissary food costs money, and really is not that much better. Commissary changed beginning in April 2022, when the DOC signed a no-bid contract with a new private vendor, Keefe, which uses a digital commissary ordering system and seems to offer a wider variety of products, but also engages in serious price gouging.[2] As of December 2023, Keefe's contract is still in effect.[3] But the way commissary functioned during the authors' time on Rikers, described below, was the way it had functioned for decades.

The commissary at C-76 was a small room with three rectangular glass panels and six benches where inmates sat and waited their turn

COMMISSARY PRICE LIST

ITEMS	COST/QTY		ITEMS	COST/QTY		ITEMS	COST/QT	
TOPPINGS-Limit (10)	Cost	Qty	BEVERAGES	Cost	Qty	PERSONAL HYGIENE	Cost	Q
Yellow Tuna Steak (10)	$2.23		Wyler's Lemonade	$1.24		Irish Spring Soap	$1.04	
Bumblebee Tuna (10)	$2.02					Dove soap	$1.86	
Salmon Flakes (10)	$1.75					Lubriderm Lotion	$3.95	
Mackerel (10)	$1.09	1				Suave shampoo	$1.97	
Sardines (10)	$1.30					Deodorant	$0.60	
Beef Crumbles (10)	$2.70					Close-Up Toothpaste	$1.92	
Chicken (10)	$3.37		Regal coffee	$0.54		Shower Slippers	$0.87	
			Bottled Water (3)	$0.99	3	**Select Size**	S/M/L/XL/2	
Beef Sticks (20)	$0.55		Bromley's Hot Te	$2.72	1			
SOUPS/SIDES-Limit (24)								
Ramen Spicy Veg. Soup	$0.45	2	COOKIES			ACCESSORIES		
			Iced Oatmeal (5)	$2.06		Winn Radio	$12.00	
Low Sodium Ramen Chili soup (24)	$0.45		Chocolate Chip (5)	$1.97		*Must Return Old Batteries*		
Refried Pinto Beans	$1.07		Coconut Crunch (5)	$1.97		AA Batteries (2)	$0.23	
						AAA Batteries (4)	$0.23	2
Oatmeal	$2.45					Headphones	$2.26	
Tortilla Wraps	$3.31		Applesauce Oatmeal	$0.74		Pen	$0.23	
CHIPS-Limit (5)			Lemon	$0.74		Writing Pad	$1.95	
						English Word Puzzle	$2.02	
			CONDIMENTS			UNO Playing Cards	$7.61	
			Coffee Creamers (50)	$0.09		Aviator Playing Cards	$2.06	
			Mayonnaise (50)	$0.08		Pinochle Playing Cards	$2.88	
Regal Cheddar Chips	$0.55		Sweet Mate Sugar	$0.88				
			Halls	$0.83		Forever Envelope	$0.62	
Regal Sour Cream	$0.55		Fireballs	$0.60		Forever Stamp	$0.50	7
Kettle Chips (MOON)	$0.55	1	Trail Mix	$0.44	10	Greeting Cards	$1.01	
			Cheddar Cheese Block	$2.20		*Specify Card*		
CAKES-Limit (5)			Peanut Butter $2.63	~~$1.75~~	3			
			Corn	$1.03				
Chocolate Danish	$1.12					**Items are Subject To Change**		
Cinnamon Danish	$1.12							
Fudge Surprise	$1.12							

Figure 6.1: A 2020 commissary order form from RNDC, which replaced in-person commissary visits during the pandemic. Unavailable items were blacked out, but these changed weekly, and were rarely accurate. Courtesy of the authors.

to be called. Each window had a clerk, an opening to place the order, and an opening to receive items. Most of the commissary workers were inmates, save for a CO who oversaw them. Typically, an entire dorm went at once. While the date was preordained, the time was often announced on the spot, making any activities outside the dormitory risky on commissary day, except for work assignments, which compensated for missed commissary by having their own designated time. Those who missed commissary for other reasons might be able to go on a special trip, but this was at the COs' discretion—hardly a variable worth staking a week's worth of supplies on.

Shopping at commissary was fast-paced and disorienting for the newcomer. Supply lists were rare, so inmates had to have a running knowledge of what commodities were available, and be able to quickly improvise should their desired items not be in stock. Unavailable items changed weekly, as did the seemingly random purchasing limits on things. Some items could only be ordered at certain points in the process, and trying to order them early could prompt a haranguing from staff. As in the dormitory, inmate names were shouted, often mispronounced, in a loud and crowded room, so some did not even realize they were being called, only to be upbraided and rushed through their order. It was a chaotic and stressful environment somewhere between bidding at an auction house and purchasing counterfeit luxury goods on Canal Street. All the while, savvy commissary workers plied the shopper for a "tip," meaning an item purchased and given to them as a gift. These overtures were often unabashed strong-arm tactics, largely tolerated by the COs, who simply asked the shoppers to confirm their consent. Finally, the order was served up in a large brown paper bag.

Popular commissary items included instant ramen noodles, pouches of beef, chicken, and fish, peanut butter, instant coffee, sugar packets, and a variety of snacks high in carbohydrates and sugar with little nutritional value. The commissary also sold useful items like reusable bowls, writing utensils, envelopes, stamps, playing cards, shower slippers, soap, and deodorant. The first major purchase most inmates made was a small handheld radio, made out of clear plastic to prevent stashing contraband inside, and onto which the commissary employees carved the inmates' number directly upon purchase. The junk food available at the commissary was roughly the same as that found in the aisles of a gas station or the sparse bodegas that dot the otherwise barren food deserts where many Rikers inmates live, just as visiting the commissary itself was reminiscent of a trip to the liquor store in poor neighborhoods.

A common mistake of new arrivals with outside financial support is to splurge at commissary. City-time folk wisdom cautions against this; it singles the inmate out as someone who not only is a good mark for extortion (or at least consistent mooching) but also doesn't know the ropes. Acting on this advice, David and Jarrod kept their initial commissary orders simple: a radio, some writing utensils, envelopes, stamps, some basic food like ramen noodles. Jarrod does not have much use for snacks but was anxious to support his coffee addiction with as many bags of single-serving instant coffee as he could get his hands on. He also procured large quantities of oatmeal and peanut butter, which he mixed into a paste and ate throughout the day. David also purchased a great deal of peanut butter, oatmeal, and coffee, as well as pouches of tuna, salmon, "jack mack" (mackerel), ground beef, chicken, cheese, ramen noodles, beef or turkey "ey-yo's" (jerky sticks), bottled water, the odd packet of chips, and a few coveted snack items to use as trading capital with other inmates, such as Fudge Surprises or cinnamon Danishes.

In-Person Visits

"Open mouth," drones the CO, "show hands." Inmates file by, flashing their palms and opening wide, to demonstrate that they are not holding any contraband as they enter the visitation area. At C-76, visits take place in a large disused gymnasium commonly called "the dancehall" or "the dancefloor." It features clusters of the same plastic chairs found throughout the facility. There is a small area for children to play in, and a cage in the corner where inmates denied contact visits can shout to their loved ones through holes drilled in plexiglass. Otherwise, inmates are able to sit close to their friends and family, though COs patrol the floor to prevent overly sexual touching or the transfer of contraband.

We heard regular previsit warnings, like the following de facto guidelines Jarrod received for visiting an intimate partner: "Kiss, squeeze the booty once, don't play with the titties, don't try to fingerbang, and if you a homo, no grabbing the wiener. If I see you making out too much

I'll pull you off the floor to inspect your mouth, the clock will keep running, and it will take me as long as it takes. That's my way of being a dick."

"As any visitor can attest," writes former Rikers writing teacher Jennifer Wynn, "penetrating Rikers Island is a punishing experience."[4] Before COVID-19, in-person visits were allowed throughout the week, though eligibility varied for inmates based on where their last name falls in the alphabet. For example, some weeks, inmates with last names beginning with the letters A through L are allowed visits on Thursday and Sunday, and those beginning with the letters M through Z, on Wednesday and Saturday, with Friday open to all, and the visiting area closed Monday and Tuesday. But this was constantly changing, and visitors had to stay on top of the schedule.

Visits are one hour long, and allowed from roughly 1:00 p.m. to 9:00 p.m. on weekdays and 8:00 a.m. to 4:00 p.m. on weekends. Visitors are required to complete registration one hour before closing. They can apply for two-hour visits if they have traveled a considerable distance (in Rikers folk wisdom, this means anywhere outside the five boroughs), but this is up to the COs and if granted, long visits can still be terminated at their discretion. Detainees awaiting trial in Rikers are entitled to three visits per week, while sentenced inmates serving city time are allowed two. All prisoners' visits are limited to one per day and can include up to three visitors. During our sentences, visitors could bring permitted personal items like socks, underwear, or books, and inmates received them from COs at the end of their visit.

Visits, often called "V-Is," represent a key lifeline to the outside world, and are often a precious thread holding together families and romantic partnerships. Yet just as visits bridge the inmate to the outside world, they insert the outsider into the social world of the jail. The process is accordingly arduous for the visitor. Even getting to the foot of the Rikers Island bridge can take upwards of two hours via public transportation from neighborhoods like Flatbush and East New York, which account for a disproportionate share of Rikers prisoners. From there, visitors must pay a fare to be ferried across the bridge by the Q100 bus, their only way across. Intake in the island's visitor's center, and then again at the jail itself, is akin to going through an airline checkpoint multiple times in a row, including an invasive search long criticized by visitors as targeting women for unwarranted strip searches. In 2019 a federal judge concurred, and ordered the city to pay $12.5 million to complainants in a class action lawsuit.[5]

This treatment is symptomatic of a process in which an inmate's loved ones are treated with all the verbal abuse and disrespect COs mete out to inmates themselves, a fact observed by both David's and Jarrod's visitors. Interestingly, when David was moved to C-74, a number of visitors commented that the COs were more polite than those in C-76; one prominent theory ran that the adolescent prisoners who were a majority there, known for their recalcitrance and willingness to fight when disrespected, forced the COs to be nicer.

In both facilities, however, visitors are menaced and humiliated as potential smugglers of contraband. In the Rikers visitation zine "Visiting Day," Queens zinester and artist Maud Pryor describes her bus being boarded by a CO with a drug-sniffing dog. When a visitor objected to the dog coming too close to him, he was singled out for a special search in retaliation.[6] Inside, the walls are plastered with stomach-churning photographs of gaping face wounds, in full view of children, meant to supposedly shame would-be weapons smugglers. The Correction Officers Benevolent Association has long insisted that contraband comes primarily through the visiting areas and should be blamed on the inmates and their families.[7] COs, however, are routinely apprehended smuggling all manner of contraband into Rikers. The ease with which Rikers COs can smuggle contraband—and the widespread nature of the practice—was documented in a dramatic fashion by former CO Gary Heyward's 2015 memoir *Corruption Officer*, which details Heyward's own adventures in smuggling that culminated in his 2006 arrest.

Corroborating much of Heyward's account a decade later, the New York City Department of Investigation tested the island's security protocol in 2016, demonstrating the ease with which COs could smuggle high volumes of contraband, including drugs, alcohol, and a razor blade. A 2018 follow-up found the island had not done much to fix the deficiencies outlined in 2016.[8] And if, as COBA insists, the visitation area is in fact the primary source of contraband, it remains difficult to explain how, during David's time, when visits were suspended due to COVID-19, the amount of contraband circulating on Rikers actually *increased*.[9]

These facts do not matter in the visitation process, as the visitor suffers a presupposition of guilt.

Similarly, the process of interminable waiting, punctuated by sudden shouted commands to hurry up, that characterizes incarcerated life, also defines a visitation process that can take as long as five hours, *after* crossing the bridge, for visitors to even lay eyes on their loved one. A visitor can therefore lose the equivalent of a full workday for an hour-long visit.[10] Political prisoner Carlo de Fornado, who served city time at New York City's Blackwell's Island penal colony in 1910, described a process uncannily similar: "Visitors who have to support themselves with their daily work find that all kinds of difficulties are put in their way. They have to get a card at the commissioner's office at 20th Street, then they must take a special boat, and when they arrive at the prison they are forced to wait an hour before they are searched. Thus nearly a whole day, from nine in the morning till two in the afternoon, is given just to see the object of all the trouble, and then, separated by a thick screen of wire, they are allowed only fifteen minutes."[11] Today, the visits are longer, well-behaved inmates (and visitors) may sit face to face, a special bus has replaced the special boat, and the requisite card can be secured on site. Yet, the enduring similarities bespeak the unchanging social position of inmates and their loved ones in New York City.

Like most events on Rikers, our experience of the visitation process at C-76 began for the inmate with the belligerent shouting of his name through the deafening dormitory. He was notified to "Get ready for V-I!"—which could signify anywhere from a few minutes to over an hour before the escort CO arrives. Most took this as a cue to begin making themselves presentable. The escort CO usually arrived in a huff and expressed frustration that the inmates were not immediately ready to walk out. Berated and threatened with being left behind, the assembled inmates were herded down the labyrinthine building's hallways into a dingy basement in the southernmost corner of the facility. They dropped their DOC IDs with the COs at a battered desk as collateral, and proceeded to the designated changing area, where cubbies contained gray jumpsuits and sandals. This room, like the entire visiting area, was painted institutional gray.

Visitation jumpsuits can run absurdly large, giving the visitor the impression their loved one has wasted away. The tan plastic sandals with their ornate Mediterranean design are the same ones used at a

Figure 6.2: Artists Nate McDonough and Maud Pryor confront the incomprehensible order while visiting Jarrod in "Visiting Day." Illustration by Nate McDonough, 2017.

number of New York's no-frills Russian bathhouses. Across from the three open-faced changing stalls in C-76 was another battered desk, this one flanked by trash barrels full of used jumpsuits, staffed by a single CO. After changing, the inmate was herded into a narrow hallway consisting of a thirteen-foot bench, illuminated by faint daylight through a narrow, basement-level barred window overtaken with ivy. After waiting for upwards of an hour, the inmate passed through the portal to the dancehall, a sloped hallway ascending from the basement level to the ground floor. This area was manned by COs at individual booths, like voting booths but without the privacy curtain, where inmates were strip searched after visits. Those at the door likewise checked each inmate's hands and mouth before he entered or exited.

The visitation room—a gymnasium that seems, like much of the old Rikers buildings, to simply be jerry-rigged onto the facility—was a liminal space between jail and the streets. The COs, who spend all day talking to both the inmates with visits and the inmate-workers who do all the actual labor, are often friendlier and less formal than other COs. One CO in particular, a heavyset Latino in his forties who regularly manned the portal area during Jarrod's time, went above and beyond in treating the inmates like friends, however obnoxiously. He playfully represented Queens in the common New York practice of neighborhood nationalism, gossiped about women showing their breasts in the dancehall, and claimed to know who among the inmates had "fat and ugly girlfriends."

"Some women actually engage in fistfights in an effort to visit a man in jail," recounts former Rikers CO C. René West. "An ex-girlfriend, wife, or current baby's mother sometimes go to war in the registration booth. We handle matters on a first-come-first-served basis. If the ex-girlfriend registered to visit the inmate before the wife or current girlfriend, the later visitor would be denied access. Many women would wait until the visit was completed to see who took their visiting time. Sometimes they would go to blows . . . and both would end up arrested for assault."[12] During our city time, this story was told time and again, especially by COs and inmates stationed in the visiting area.

The post-visit strip search consists of the inmate presenting himself naked, first frontally, then turning around and spreading his ass, though David found that as the visit COs got to know him, they were less stringent, sometimes not following this procedure at all. Like the intake

CO, the overseeing CO generally performs his displeasure at the sight of penises and male anuses. "My favorite part of the day," the Latino CO mentioned above once wryly remarked to Jarrod, "the strip search." Jarrod was once waiting to be called for his visit while inmates in the visiting area discussed a CO, newly stationed there, who had previously worked in the state system and brought a rigor to searches that no other CO observed. Inmates may give overzealous strip-search COs like him sarcastic nicknames such as "the cock and balls crew" or "the bootyman," since, like the COs, male inmates at Rikers seem to agree that enthusiastic body searches are a sign of homosexuality. "He made me run my fingers across my asshole, balls, and lips!" one scandalized inmate recounted. "In what order?" another replied, to gales of laughter.

Post-visit strip searches, like the monitored pre-visit clothing change, are justified as preventing smuggling. Visits are monitored for this reason, too. Surely some low-level smuggling occurs, but only the most masterful duo could accomplish the transfer of substantial contraband on a visit. Far from being a complex criminal operation, this kind of smuggling is actually quite pathetic. Not only do smuggling visitors risk criminal charges, but as the vast majority of visitors to male inmates at Rikers are women, and many bring children with them, the matter can also become a case for Child Protective Services.

On one occasion, Jarrod was in transit to the visiting area when an alarm sounded, forcing the inmates to wait in the hallway for what seemed like hours. When he finally moved ahead, he heard that a tall, heavyset inmate visiting with his partner and children had returned with a bag of "white powder" in his mouth, which was detected during the strip search. He panicked, and decided to run. "Motherfucker forgot he was in the can!" one CO remarked. He came bounding through the processing area "looking like the Fridge, that old football player," another CO put it. Seeing him coming, a slim CO standing in his path simply stepped aside. A few seconds later, an overweight CO from the dancehall stumbled in, out of breath, and gasped, "Hit the button!" At this, the inmates erupted in laughter, and some impersonated him by wheezing, "Hit the button!"

They also teased the CO who had let him pass, but he was unapologetic. "I'm a punter," he said. "I don't tackle." Asked why he didn't trip the man, he replied, "So he could slip, hit his head on the table, and die?"

Of course the escapee did not get very far; he was running deeper into a building filled with locked doors. The whole incident was largely treated as a joke by the inmates and low-level COs in the visiting area.

Meanwhile, a small group of captains arrived on the scene and began interrogating the CO who had stepped aside, asking how the inmate got through. He played dumb, saying very little. The captains quickly gave up, and had an even more difficult time getting anything out of the inmates. One white prisoner who had seen the whole thing told them flatly, "I've been getting locked up since '96 and giving statements is not on my resume." Befitting its position between the cell block and the streets, this kind of tenuous solidarity sometimes appeared between inmates and COs in the visiting area—though it was soon replaced by the rote ritual of "Open mouth, show hands."

Video Visits

Video visits replaced in-person visits when the COVID-19 pandemic struck in March 2020. A much smaller video visit program called TeleStory, operated in partnership with New York City's public library systems, had existed before then, though few inmates seemed to know or care.[13] David was made aware of the program by his defense committee. He was all too happy to receive visits this way, as TeleStory video visits did not count against the total of two in-person visits per week permitted to sentenced men. On all but one of these occasions, David was the only inmate present in C-74's video visiting room. Many inmates were familiar with the room itself, but only because the video booths there were also used for occasional video court appearances.

Instead of going to the C-74 visiting floor, inmates receiving TeleStory visits were led down a corridor off the North side main hall to a black metal door with an image of a camcorder and the words "Video Court" painted on it. Behind the door was a holding pen, a cluttered COs' desk, and four gray soundproof booths. Each booth contained a plastic chair and a gray metal-frame monitor mounted to the wall, with a heavy black phone receiver, identical to those in the dorms (and to pay phones in the outside world). Two of the booths had what appeared to be analog clocks hanging above the screens. Upon closer inspection, these "clocks" revealed themselves to be thermometers, which was hardly useful, as it invariably became very hot inside the booths during the course of the visit, even in winter, and their creeping needles only reminded the inmate that it was in fact very hot.

Unlike for in-person visits, David was never forced to change clothes for TeleStory visits, and was even allowed to bring small things like a snack or a book into the booth with him. Approximately two minutes before the visit was scheduled to start, David would be ushered into a preselected booth, and the CO on duty would lock him in. At the scheduled time, the screen would light up with the words "incoming call," and the phone would begin to ring. If the inmate missed the call or inadvertently hung up, there was no way to try again; the opportunity was simply lost. These video visits lasted one hour, and had to be scheduled in advance at a local New York City library branch, where visitors would then go on the day of the visit and conduct the visit from one of the library's study or conference rooms.

In-person visits were summarily ended on March 16, 2020, due to COVID-19, and libraries closed shortly thereafter; no visits whatsoever took place for over a month. When visits resumed, they were video only. But unlike the pre–COVID-19 TeleStory visits, postpandemic video visits were administered directly by the DOC, and took place on the C-74 visiting floor, where plexiglass cases containing computer monitors had been bolted to the wooden counter at which inmates and their loved ones usually sat.[14] The screens were placed six feet apart, in strict compliance with social-distancing protocols, but with no thought given to real-world considerations: for some, the only place an inmate could sit and actually be seen by his visitor was the empty space between the ends of two of the long benches running the counter's length. Similarly, the plexiglass boxes had only a few two-inch holes drilled across the bottom at odd intervals to facilitate communication, making it very difficult to actually hold a conversation.

On one occasion, it was so hard to speak with his visitor that David simply asked to be taken back to the dorm, ending his visit early. After three months of pressure from inmates and visitors alike, the DOC finally installed cheap USB phone handsets, which drastically improved the experience for both parties. But there were still technical difficulties galore, from the DOC's Internet connection to computers not being turned on at the time of the visit, which often led to delayed starts.

This was a source of frustration for many, because video visits were prescheduled to cut off at a certain time. The visiting-floor COs would usually promise to call one of their superiors and ask to get time added to the visit, but this rarely happened.

Many of David's friends in the activist community were also reluctant to install software from the DOC on their computer, which was required for video visits. Those willing to do so faced a pile of daunting hurdles afterward. The DOC required visitors to sign up online, giving three different days and times, ranked in order of preference. But David's visitors all told him that the time slots they chose seemed to have little to no impact on when the actual video visit was scheduled. The COs who managed visiting schedules were supposed to call and email the visitor in advance and confirm, but sometimes simply failed to do either, instead calling mere minutes before the visit, or in some cases not at all. When visitors were scheduled for a time they had not requested and during which they were unavailable, or were never told of their scheduled visit time, it could be quite frustrating for them, and also for David, who would spend what seemed like an eternity staring expectantly at the screen. After his release, David signed up for a video visit with a friend he had made in Rikers, and simply never heard back from the DOC.

Inmates were required to change into gray jumpsuits for postpandemic video visits, just as for in-person visits, ostensibly to prevent them from passing contraband or assaulting each other. They then waited in front of a screensaver depicting a range of rocky, snow-capped mountains, a maddening evocation of untrammeled freedom, while the words "1 of 1 in call" glowed on the screen until, finally, their visitor's face appeared. Most men considered these visits, with their lack of physical contact, to be inferior to in-person visits, which did not resume again for over a year.[15] Yet for all their disadvantages, postpandemic video visits presented some benefits: people could visit from the comfort of their own homes without having to make the trek to Rikers or the library, and they did not even have to be in New York. David was visited by friends from out of state and even as far away as France and Brazil. David was also able to visit with Jarrod, who was by this point located in Chicago, on a regular basis and for much longer than a phone call, holding many discussions that eventually turned into this book.

Searches

Searches are unpredictable and chaotic. They are reviled and unavoidable. "A search can happen at any moment in the cell blocks and dormitories," observed Pierre Raphaël, a Rikers chaplain in the 1980s. "A dozen guards suddenly appear in the hall and, at a captain's orders, strip search every prisoner, going through their clothes and cells with a fine-tooth comb, sometimes accompanied by drug dogs."[16]

Not much has changed since then. Searches could happen as rarely as once a month or even less—during the first wave of COVID-19, David's dorm suffered no searches for three months straight. He also met one inmate who claimed not to have suffered a single search in six months on "the Boat," or the Vernon C. Bains Center. On the other hand, searches might happen as often as twice a week, virtually any time of the day, including the early morning or the middle of the night. A search that occurred after the 9:00 p.m. lights out was rare and was likely to be all but a formality, in which a small team of COs, overseen by a captain, lackadaisically shone their flashlights around the day room, scribbled some things on a clipboard, and left, often without even waking anyone up. Searches occurring right at 6:00 a.m., when the institutional day had just begun, or around 8:00 p.m., in the last hour before lights out, were likewise few and far between. But when exactly the next one would occur was anybody's guess.

There was usually no warning preceding a search, so inmates tended to keep certain things stashed away when not in use. This practice was hardly limited to things the inmates knew to be contraband, like drugs and weapons, as there was no rhyme or reason at all to what the COs confiscated on searches. Many times, David had items confiscated that were entirely permissible according to the *Inmate Handbook*, and that had been approved by the mail room or the visiting floor, and had survived several previous searches. For example, a self-defense manual he was mailed in his first month was confiscated during a search in his last month. Permissible items as innocuous as T-shirts, gym shorts, and medical supplies were regularly confiscated with no reason given.

When there was warning before a search, it almost always came from other inmates returning from work or a visit, who had seen the search team treading ominously down the main hall of the facility, distinguishable by their lockstep marching in two tight lines, with a handful of "Turtles" in the front. Rumors of searches were common and spread like wildfire, but often served no practical purpose, as the DOC defied all attempts at guessing which housing units it chose to strike and when. Even a search in the unit next door or across the hall was not a surefire sign that one's dorm would be next.

Searches may be conducted by either a team of COs assembled from those normally posted to the building (a "building search") or, more rarely, by the Special Search Team, or SST. SST COs, identifiable by their crisp navy blue, almost black uniforms, complete with matching baseball caps, generally took their jobs (and themselves) much more seriously. As a result, their searches were generally much more vigorous, though this was not necessarily true in every case. On one occasion, the SST officer searching David's bed told him "I got you, bro," in a reassuring tone, and, though he confiscated a number of things, also chose to strategically overlook many more, including David's cherished pens and workout gloves. And though the same officer confiscated David's milk fridge, he actually allowed him to take the milk cartons out of it first. Conversely, a search carried out by the building search team was not necessarily more lax—to the contrary, it could be prosecuted with great zeal. It often depended on the captain or captains overseeing the search, and even the individual officer searching one's bed.

Yet the basics of a search are always the same, regardless of who carries it out: inmates are ordered to sit on their beds in silence, then taken into the bathroom in groups of four or five and strip searched. They are then marched to the day room, still in silence, until their bunk number is called, at which point they are escorted from the day room only to stand beside their bed and watch as an officer or two rifles unceremoniously through everything they own, dumping it across the bed frame and floor. Inmates are often forced to clasp their hands, stick their elbows out perpendicular to their bodies, and hold the flabby mattresses that the COs, after removing them from their bunks, drape over their arms. These mattresses, though painfully thin to sleep on, can quickly become tiresome to hold, especially for older inmates. Inmates were sometimes berated for not properly maintaining this difficult and humiliating posture.

Of course, nothing occurs with any great degree of reliability on Rikers. The bathroom strip search may be compounded with a urine test, replaced with a simple pat frisk, or forgone altogether. Similarly, the COs may simply trash the dorm unobserved once the inmates are in the day room, instead of calling them out to stand by their beds. In these cases, the inmates simply emerge from the day room at the end of the search, groaning and sighing at the apocalyptic scene before them, with everyone's stuff strewn about as if a band of unruly children had been given free rein to play in the dorm for an afternoon. An inmate returning to the house after missing a search might well find his mattress missing. This meant another inmate had taken it, having lost his second mattress during the search, and knowing that the COs would have to provide the victim a new one. David also observed that those in the dorm who worked on the building's sanitation crew, collecting the trash bags from the various housing units, were an asset in the postsearch recovery period: as they handled the dorms' trash bags, they were often able to recover things that had been confiscated on the search and thrown away by the COs. On multiple occasions, David was able to recover his workout gloves, a prized possession for any inmate who exercises regularly, through these channels.

Searches are far from limited to the institutional imperative to locate and confiscate contraband. In common practice, they are used as a tool of punishment, control, and even personal vendetta, from which the inmates are consistently forced to recover.

Transfers

Though they are perhaps less immediately dramatic than searches, it is impossible to understate how disruptive transfers can be to inmates clinging to the barest sense of security and predictability in a chaotic and tumultuous setting. Michael Walker recounts transfers as "rips in the fabric of one's sense of self in the social world," which uproot the inmate from a hard-won sense of normalcy.[17] For this reason, transfers are often used as punishment.

Transfers almost always come out of nowhere. Abruptly and seemingly at random, the city-time inmate is hurriedly instructed to "pack up." This comes with no further information, beyond the occasional insistence that he will be leaving in ten or fifteen minutes, which can just as well mean ten or fifteen hours. The first time this happened to Jarrod he took the words literally, and packed up all his belongings as if he was leaving immediately, exchanging emotional farewells with a handful of confidants. Hours went by, and slowly he unpacked the items he needed and returned to his daily business, attempting to banish the thought that soon his tenuous social ties and daily routine would be severed and that he would be plunged into a completely new environment with unknown dangers and challenges. As soon as the transfer COs arrived, however, packing up and leaving became a matter of urgency—how could inmates not be prepared with so much advance notice?

In one transfer Jarrod experienced, the COs absentmindedly shuffled men one at a time to different houses, crisscrossing the halls confusedly, as everyone lost patience. The inmates carried all their belongings bundled up in sheets. Experienced inmates instructed everyone not to set them down on the floor, because that was grimy, and hence taboo. This prohibition was weakened, however, by the passage of time. After a half hour of bearing these heavy bundles, letting them down suddenly did not seem like such a big deal, and one inmate after another let theirs sink to the floor. Meanwhile, one man who claimed to be on his fifty-sixth visit to the island greeted every passing CO by name, and was received warmly in turn. As each man was assigned a house, he called out the details: it was a Blood house, or "a work house, lots of OTs [old-timers]," and so forth.

Transfer includes many unknowns, not least of which is the time one can spend in Intake between houses, which may be no time at all or a matter of hours, but may also last for days—or, in rare cases, weeks. It is often unclear, as with many things on Rikers, whether any of this stems from a desire to punish on the part of the staff, or simply from their disorganization and incompetence. David, for example, was transferred twice during his year in custody, Jarrod twice in his month. The first time for David was his transfer from C-76 to C-74. David and a dozen others were told to pack up in ten minutes, then waited four hours. Just as chow was served and they were sitting down to eat dinner, they were rushed from the dorm into an intake pen, dragging their belongings bundled in sheets, blankets, or trash bags across the filthy jailhouse floor, which one CO explained was "policy." They spent about three hours in the pens, then were handcuffed in pairs and loaded onto a bus that drove across the street, where they waited for three or four more hours before being processed into C-74 at a painfully slow rate. The COs themselves were also complaining that the backup was due to no reason other than disorganization. All told, it took the DOC thirteen hours to transfer the men to the building across the street.

Holidays

Holidays cut both ways on Rikers. For some, they are cause for celebration: in addition to the festive occasion itself, the arrival of a holiday is a concrete sign of the advancement of time, and hence the arrival of the cherished release date. These men are happy to observe the holiday. For others, the holidays are a pale copy of what they should be in the outside world, and only remind them of the fact that they are separated from their loved ones—and the freedom to enjoy themselves—by razor wire and paperwork.

The COs sometimes encourage holiday observances by bringing dollar-store decorations and enlisting incarcerated volunteers to help them spruce up the unit. On Halloween, for example, only a week after David's arrival, one of the steady officers put bags of candy corn out on the day room tables. Many inmates were happy to partake, grateful for anything that broke up the monotonous stream of chow and commissary consumables. One guy, however, refused to touch the stuff. "If you got a criminal gene in your body," he declared matter-of-factly, "you don't eat candy corn."

Christmas decorations were a much more involved affair. One of the steady officers convinced a small army of inmates to help her decorate 12-Lower during David's time there. Within minutes, snowflakes and Christmas trees were dangling from the backs of the numerous security cameras, the cinder block columns bisecting the room were covered in wrapping paper with skiing Santa Clauses and penguins wearing scarves and sunglasses, and a decorative vinyl sheet patterned with candy cane–toting snowmen adorned the wall of the day room. These decorations remained up through the New Year's celebration, which was observed by many of the residents of 12-Lower by drinking hooch and smoking spliffs in the lead-up to midnight. Many of the spliffs were the standard tobacco-and-K2 admixture, but David also smelled an unusually high amount of marijuana smoke on New Year's Eve. In fact, one of the shot-callers even offered him, a relative newbie and non–gang member, a hit of his joint, explaining that it was "real sticky."

For most of these holidays, the observance boils down to the meal—often institutional, but augmented by enterprising jailhouse chefs—and the verbal acknowledgment between inmates, such as "Happy Halloween, niggas!" to use the language of one of David's acquaintances. But even lesser holidays are unlikely to escape the inmates' attention, attuned as they are to the passing of time, despite all their efforts to forget it. "Damn, bro, I can't believe this shit," one man complained to David as he prepared to make a phone call on Leap Day 2020. "One extra day every four fuckin' years, and we gotta be locked up for it."

Programs

According to most COs and inmates David spoke to, C-76 had a relatively high number of programs compared to the other buildings on Rikers, with C-74 not far behind. There were short-term courses in fields as diverse as scaffolding and flagging certifications, creative writing, debate, acting, anger management, culinary skills, which offered inmates a chance to break up the monotony of jailhouse cuisine, and barista training, which likewise offered a much-welcomed alternative to the instant coffee sold at commissary.

At C-76, the most coveted program by far was "the dog program," in which inmates were taught the basics of dog training and grooming, and paired with dogs to apply their training knowledge. Once trained, these dogs were given up for adoption. Beyond the allure of canine companionship, the dog program entitled participants to a dorm of their own, known colloquially as a sort of "honor dorm," where there were rarely more than ten people at a time. Inmates lived alongside their dogs, and the phones, showers, and day room were available at all hours. A similar live-in policy applied for a Christian religious study program, in which participants moved to a "chill" dorm with a routine focused on prayer and Bible study for about two weeks. At C-74, inmates could even work toward their commercial driver's license (CDL) with the help of six giant truck-driving simulation modules, often referred to by inmates as "Cruisin' USA," in reference to the arcade racing game of the same name.

These were located in C-74's "Peace Center," a former dorm in the basement that had been converted into a sort of recreation and educational space, with the odd quotation celebrating peace painted on the walls in flowing calligraphy. Inmates generally jumped at the opportunity to take a trip to the Peace Center, which, besides the CDL training modules, contained a number of classrooms, a horticulture room, a handful of light exercise equipment, ping pong tables, video game consoles, a small movie theater, a recording studio, and a sound editing room. The studio, much to the consternation of David's fellow inmates, was reserved exclusively for the adolescent detainees, but the movie theater was often offered to David's dorm. There, they would watch bootlegged versions of the latest action films, illegally downloaded by the COs, on a projector screen with two small, tinny speakers on either side. The Peace Center even had a popcorn machine, which was sometimes functional. On those occasions, a CO would offer the incarcerated spectators red-and-white-striped cardboard sleeves of popcorn as the movie began, in a surreal, if only skin-deep, reversal of the normal power dynamic.

COs at C-74 whose duties brought them in contact with the Peace Center liked to point out this symbolically powerful but substantively meaningless gesture of offering inmates popcorn as an indication of how far the city had come in terms of progressive penology. Similarly, they were wont to boast of the Peace Center's $2 million price tag, as if this figure was statistically significant given the DOC's bloated annual budget, by far the most expensive of any jail system in the country. In fiscal year 2020, for example, the year that formed the bulk of David's time inside, New York City spent $2.559 billion on the Department of Correction.[18] The total cost of keeping one inmate on Rikers for one year in the same fiscal period was nearly $500,000.[19] The following year, this number rose past $550,000, meaning that it would take the release of only four inmates serving sentences equal in length to David's to save the DOC more money than the Peace Center cost to build.[20]

Other programs sent representatives of nonprofit associations directly into the housing units to work with the inmates there. For example, the Fortune Society, in partnership with the Osborne Association, runs the Individualized Corrections Achievement Network, I-CAN. According to the Fortune Society, this program, launched in 2013, "facilitates skill-building workshops and provides discharge preparation services for individuals during incarceration."[21] An undated DOC document touts I-CAN as "an innovative evidence-based reentry initiative designed to reduce recidivism among incarcerated men and women," drawing on "national best practices to provide individuals in DOC custody with the tools and support needed to ensure a successful return to the community."[22]

In reality, this program, often known simply as "Fortune Society" among inmates, did little more than engage the men in occasional conversation. The representatives, meaning well but perceiving the program's inadequacy to effect real change, often ended up simply swapping jail stories, as they were typically formerly incarcerated themselves. Many tried to mix in their best attempts at offering life advice on things like good parenting, credit cards, or anger management. They also provided weekly handouts on the same themes, which also included instructional material and worksheets to help inmates get their lives in order and move forward upon release, along with contact information for nonprofit organizations they could contact if they wanted further assistance.

These handouts were often mocked as cheesy, unrealistic, and unrelatable, and were hopelessly out of touch by any objective measure. One handout, bearing the title "Look Great Feel Great," presented a list of forty-seven foods and drinks inmates could consume to stay healthy, of which a grand total of five were sold at commissary. They were also filled with inspirational quotations and pure time-killing material like word searches, crosswords, mazes, "find the difference," and "I spy" images, pages to which most men flipped immediately upon reception. David's personal favorite was a ten-page packet of crudely photocopied pages reading "Irrational Beliefs That Lead to Criminal Behavior" at the top. At the bottom of every page appeared the words, "It is illegal to duplicate this page in any manner."

Nonprofit representatives would constantly urge anyone who happened into the day room to sign the clipboard they had brought, in order to keep their program-participant numbers high. David, for example, who often worked on writing or translation projects in the day room, was one day granted an I-CAN certificate "in recognition of [his] dedicated participation in Wellness-Self management."[23] David has no idea what he did to earn this certification, other than sign the Fortune Society representative's clipboard, at the latter's repeated insistence, so he could work in peace. A steady number of names on the clipboard—and "graduates"—after all, ensures a steady stream of funding. Other similar programs, such as the one run by the STRIVE Network, functioned in much the same way; indeed, to the inmates, they were all but indistinguishable.

The one thing all these programs had in common was that they were hardly taken seriously by either the staff or the inmates. Their relative popularity seemed to be due more to their enabling inmates to escape the monotony of the dorm than to any practical expectation of personal improvement. In the outside world, the vast majority of the men at Rikers would likely have scoffed at all of them. A few guys who had spent time in the upstate prison system and taken vocational training courses there claimed to have found work or even careers with these certifications upon release. In contrast, despite the high number of Rikers veterans David met, very few reported ever having found work because of programs they had taken at Rikers. The OSHA certification course, for example, provided those who completed it successfully with a document attesting to their completion of thirty hours of training. Successful completion took much less time and effort: one man told David that the entire program consisted of a single hour, through which half the students slept. Unfortunately, another repeat offender told David that many employers in the industries for which such certificates earned at Rikers might be applicable knew which certificates had been earned in jail and used that knowledge as a basis of discrimination. They were therefore more likely to hire a person who had no training at all over someone who had ten vocational certificates he had earned at Rikers.

Live from New York

Many inmate programs make only sporadic appearances. One program worker, for example, came to David's dorm only twice, several months apart, and showed the inmates creative ways to work out with the furniture in the day room. Others seem to be one-time affairs, such as when Jarrod's house was invited to a comedy show in the C-76 gymnasium.

The gym did not appear to see much use in those days. Jarrod almost always saw it empty, with the exception of a staff meeting and a basketball game among six inmates, remarked upon for its rarity. The crowd amassed for the comedy show was small, consisting of Jarrod's house and another adult house on the left, and a juvenile house on the right, divided by a wide aisle. Unlike in C-74, the juvenile population was carefully segregated from the adults in C-76; this was the closest Jarrod saw groups of adults and juveniles together. Around ten COs and captains lurked in the back of the room. A DJ blasted hip hop and dance music, far too loud, in jarring contrast to a world ordinarily without audible music.

The event's emcee, a Black comedian, opened with some icebreakers by singling out audience members and roasting them. He performed an impression of the oldest inmate present, a man in his seventies, trying to get away from the police but unable to run fast enough. Soon he turned to Jarrod, making the usual joke that a white person who has overcome the structural racism in New York's punishment system sufficient to be locked up in Rikers must have done something awful. He repeatedly joked that Jarrod was a "people-eating motherfucker" like Hannibal Lecter, along with some vaguely homophobic jabs and the claim that Jarrod had broken the law to spite his parents. Jarrod of course had no illusions, going to this show, that he was not going to get totally roasted.

The host concluded his opening act with a plea to the adolescents to turn their lives around and listen to the OTs, before yielding the stage to the featured comics. One comic from the South Bronx named Destiny got the most laughs. He evoked vivid scenes from the street, using queued music to impersonate a bodega door swinging open and shut as someone begged for change outside. He also acted out the difference between South Asian and African store owners stopping a shoplifter. He had been locked up at Rikers before, and joked about gang-run pay phones. Addressing the adolescents, he also impersonated a junkie uncle trying to give a young person advice as he nodded out. They went wild, including some who had reclined all the way back in their seats and remained emotionless up until then. The other comedians offered similar material. A white comic from East New York impersonated Jamaicans, to roars and applause from the mostly Black audience.

After the three comics had finished, the host delivered another plea to the adolescents, mentioning that he hoped Rikers would close, and that it was designed to prevent their success. He nonetheless encouraged the inmates to respect the staff, whom he said he had grown up being taught to hate, before realizing they were from the same neighborhood as their captives, only "they got a job and y'all didn't." He said the older generation had failed them, and encouraged them to listen to the words of Louis Farrakhan.

As the attendees from Jarrod's house returned to the dormitory, everyone was laughing and joking in the entrance hallway, recounting their favorite moments from the show. A Black female CO stood on the other side of the gate, in silence, refusing to open it and staring angrily at the men. Eventually, someone asked her what she was waiting for. She replied, "Y'all need to remember which side of the aisle is yours," pointing to a few guys who were not standing against the wall, and who were instead carrying on joyfully, having forgotten the basic protocol separating inmates from staff at Rikers. "Y'all get too excited," she said. "It's just a comedy show in a jail gymnasium."

"Thanks, CO, for spoiling the dream," one man replied. "For a minute, I was in New York."

7

Food

"Chow! Chow! Chow! Walkin' out for chow!" The blue-suited CO's voice rings out over a sea of listless figures in shapeless forest green. There is not often a rush for the door when chow is called, but today is different.

"Bird day, fellas!" calls an inmate in David's dormitory, grabbing his wristband, a wad of toilet paper, and an empty plastic mop bag. "Y'all better get that bird!" A similar scene plays out across the dorm, men stuffing wads of single-ply toilet tissue and recycled plastic bags into their waistbands for want of pockets. A line quickly forms, and the inmates are escorted down a maze of halls to the mess hall. This procession, reminiscent of middle school, is one of the countless ways men serving city time are infantilized by the conditions of their captivity. "The only thing missing," a neighbor remarked to Jarrod, "is 'Now hold hands.'"

In the mess hall, there is even a sense of excitement in the air. Some broadcast their anticipation by cartoonishly rubbing their hands together and stamping their feet. "Let me get a extra bird, bro!" some try to persuade the inmate serving food from the other side of the thin metal slot. Others bend down and peek through the slot, pointing out which piece of meat they want ("Let me get that black-ass bird!") before the mess hall CO barks, "Sir! Pick ya head up!" Most of the gang members, having pushed their way to the front of the line, are given larger portions, or even two trays. For everyone else, whether they get an extra bird depends on whether they know the inmate serving food, how much food is left, and a number of other factors.

The men sit down and dig into their chicken, pausing occasionally to wipe their fingers on their wads of toilet paper. Many are quick to negotiate custody of unwanted birds before they even take their first bites: those who do not care for the chicken, or prefer to eat food they have purchased in commissary, usually give theirs away rather than dump them in the trash. Jarrod, who keeps a vegan diet, exchanged his chicken for everything else on another's tray—a trade all parties considered a great deal—when he was too hungry to simply give it away.

The lucky ones who manage to procure extra pieces of meat slip them into their plastic bags and tuck them back into their waistlines to be eaten later—if they can be successfully smuggled back into the dorm. As he sits down to dine, one guy calls out a familiar joke to a friend across the mess hall: "Enjoy that Rikers Island seagull, son!"

Chow

Institutional meals on Rikers are not called "food." From the highest levels of DOC administration to the freshest new arrival among the incarcerated, meals are referred to as "chow." This seems to be the standard term for meals behind bars across location, jurisdiction, and security level. The word is also used this way in the military, and sometimes among the general public. But mostly, "chow" applies to animals.[1] An inmate who spoke only Spanish once asked David, "What does 'chow' mean?" as they put on their shoes to go to the mess hall. David, with his limited Spanish proficiency, had to keep his answer simple: "Food for dogs."

Beyond the word's implicit comparison of inmates to animals, the kennel-like living conditions make associating "chow" with "dogfood" unavoidable. Hence, every meal is a point at which the degraded status of those in green uniforms is reinforced. During Jarrod's time, the label on an antiquated handheld camera positioned in a plexiglass enclosed box and trained on the dining hall made this comparison even more bluntly; it simply said "feeding." This was common terminology among COs. David arrived late to lunch one day and was asked by a captain, "Are you here for the feeding?"

Blandness and mushiness are chow's two near-universal qualities. "Just chew and swallow, that's what I tell myself every time," one man cheerfully commented to David as they sat down to eat a meal at some point early in his bid. "Just chew and swallow." It was advice David found useful long after the man went home: everything the inmates eat at chow comes from a can, box, or bag, and has the taste and texture to match.

The mess hall at C-76 is a large rectangular room with much of the same drab institutional tile found throughout the facility. Like the dormitories, it juts out from the skeleton of the building, connected on only one end. Large panes of windows running alongside the perpendicular walls facilitate a generous view of the island's industrial landscape, offset by a prisoner-painted mural depicting a tropical paradise. Inmates enter on the right side of the room and wait in line, hemmed in by a metal railing, along the wall. The scene is very much like a public school cafeteria, with many of the same dynamics: entitled inmates cut in line or clamor for extra food (and other perks, like halal or kosher meals), as annoyed COs roll their eyes and attempt to keep things moving, peppering the men with condescending remarks.

At the mess hall's far end, metal-framed slots, through which inmates are handed their meals, connect the dining area to the kitchen, where they are prepared. At the center of this serving area, an insulated Cambro dispenses sugar-water into the green cups inmates have brought with them from the house. The dining area consists of two neat rows of eight steel tables, with sixteen seats apiece, all firmly bolted together and affixed to the floor, separated by an aisle splitting the room in half. Inmates are marched to designated tables and seated in the order they came in, and their movements are closely watched and regulated. After meals, they are marched out of the left-hand side of the room and hand in their trays, which are washed in a walled-off dishwashing area separating the entrance from the exit.

Meals in this cafeteria last for less than ten minutes. Given that the populations of dormitory houses are, theoretically at least, curated to avoid conflict, COs work to keep houses separate as much as they can, or at least give the appearance of doing so to their supervisors, who are never far from the potentially combustible combination of men one finds in the dining area. It is a lively time, as inmates must eat what they can, acquire additional food through trades or gifts, and prepare to smuggle certain items to the dormitory, all in a window of time so short that it seems calculated to make eating the full meal all but impossible. Haste is therefore the most distinctive characteristic of mealtime for those who dine in the mess hall. Units with in-house dining can take their time a bit; the inmates serving chow have an hour or so to pack the trays and pans back into the rolling plastic food cart after its arrival. But in the mess hall, the COs are always in a rush to feed all the housing units, and return to doing nothing as soon as possible.

The floor officer from the unit, who accompanies the inmates to the mess hall at chow time, usually posts up at the back of the room, chatting with one of the mess hall officers until the next housing unit begins arriving. Then the floor officer bellows, "Let's go, gentlemen, chow time's over!" This often occurs just as those last in line are sitting down with their trays, and is always met with groans and complaints that there has not been enough time to eat. Technically, food is not supposed to leave the cafeteria, but the practice of bringing back items like fruit and bread is tolerated, so long as inmates are not so obvious about it in the hallway as to deprive the COs of plausible deniability. Like most de facto policies, inmates become aware of this conditional tolerance when it is revoked; every so often, we witnessed a passing captain confiscate a trivial item like an apple or box of cereal in the hallway, raising murmurs that customary rights were being stepped on. The COs themselves, understandably enough, couldn't really care less either way.

Many inmates swap or give away portions of their meals during chow, usually holding the entire tray out for his fellow prisoner to take from directly. But reaching over people, coughing, laughing, or talking too loudly over their food is taboo. It is also standard practice for some incarcerated diners to bring the small ramen seasoning packets to chow in order to give some flavor to the otherwise bland and tasteless food. Though "chili" and "chicken" flavor are hardly novelties, a dash of either can make the difference between an institutional dish being palatable and borderline inedible. As a single person is unlikely to use an entire packet for one meal, he usually offers it to those nearby. Even total strangers will often pass the packet wordlessly around their table. Plain old table salt, on the other hand, is extremely rare and valuable. David once paid another inmate a dollar apiece in commissary items for two of the tiny single-serving paper salt packets sometimes found in prepackaged plastic utensil sets, a fraction of a gram each. Another man who had managed to steal an entire salt shaker from the COs' mess hall once whispered David over to his bunk and showed off his stash with greater concern for discretion than many inmates had with their bangers, for fear others might steal it or hound him for it when they wanted to cook.

Lunch is generally served between 10:30 a.m. and 1:00 p.m., and dinner between 4:00 p.m. and 7:00 p.m., with little to no regularity from one day to the next. Both meals are mandatory for all inmates. Even those registered as Muslim are forced to go to the mess hall and scan in during their Ramadan fast. Understood to stem from the DOC's obsession with avoiding legal liability, the practice of getting a paper or electronic record of every inmate attending meals is so sacred that refusing to comply with it is actually a tool that can be leveraged in protest. During the first wave of COVID-19, David's unit and the neighboring unit "stuck it up," refusing to go to chow, and actually won concessions in basic protective equipment and the quarantining of sick prisoners, who until that point had been left in the general-population dormitory.

Breakfast is served sometime between 5:00 and 6:00 a.m. and, unlike lunch and dinner, is not mandatory. In 12-Lower, most men woke up and ate breakfast chow before heading out to work, and many of those who did not have to leave for work chose to get up anyway, because sleeping with all the commotion and the overhead lights on was all but impossible. Getting up for breakfast in 12-Lower was also more appealing because it was a dorm with "in-house dining" (a term that deceptively evokes the luxury of, say, breakfast in bed), meaning all the meals were eaten in the day room. Inmates there never went to the mess hall at all. Rather, chow was delivered three times a day in a rolling insulated plastic food wagon. In-house dining is the policy for higher-security dorms and cellblocks on Rikers. 12-Lower was low security, but had in-house dining because it was a "working dorm." The inmates' heterogenous work hours made it difficult for the DOC to get them all to the mess hall, especially without interacting with inmates from other housing units. Jarrod's houses at C-76, on the other hand, all went to the dining hall for breakfast (except for a few days when chow was never called), and breakfast was much less popular.

The same was true in Mod 4, where many inmates did not work in the morning and meals were served in the mess hall. The vast majority of men slept through the predawn call for chow, often little more than a whisper on the CO's part. There, the lights were rarely turned on when breakfast was called, and actually procuring the meal entailed hurriedly putting on greens (the gym shorts and T-shirts most people sleep in are unacceptable attire outside the housing units) and shoes, walking down the main hallway, a distance roughly equivalent to a long city block, and finally packing into the mess hall, usually already echoing with shouted commentary, conversations, and arguments between COs and inmates.

Given these disincentives, it was common for only five or even fewer of these units' inmates to attend breakfast.

Breakfast at Rikers is always the same: hot or cold cereal, one small pink carton of 2 percent milk—or, with a little luck, two—a piece of fruit, and the ubiquitous inedible bread, with two small pats of margarine on wax paper. Hot cereal consisted of oatmeal or grits. Cold cereal, at least during our time, could only mean Total Raisin Bran, Honey Nut Cheerios, or Cinnamon Chex, all served in the sort of tear-off single-serving plastic containers often seen in hotel continental breakfast spreads. Sundays are the most popular breakfast days, as they include a small prepackaged muffin (corn, bran, or blueberry flavored).

The most distinctly Rikers part of every meal is the bread: bone dry and utterly tasteless, it crumbles at the slightest touch. The dough is so poorly mixed that it is not uncommon to find a loaf with pockets of flour inside, or one where all the various components are still visible, like stratified rock, in each slice. "Shit be lookin' like Cinnamon Toast Crunch," one inmate once grumbled. The bakery inmate-workers are not shy about recounting the grisly details of the conditions there ("They got a whole squirrel living in one of them machines!"). The presliced loaves are served in unmarked white wax paper, which inmates tear open by hand and leave sitting on the table for others to take as they will. This wax paper often bears holes chewed by mice and rats, or a light crust of dried bird droppings. This is the only type of bread on the island, and it is the only thing served with every single meal.

Chicken is served twice a week at Rikers, on Thursdays and Saturdays. Few things on the island are as sure or as constant as "bird day." Each tray comes with a small portion of breast and a wing attached. The meat is often dry and overcooked, or cold and undercooked. More than a few bouts of diarrhea have been suffered the following day. Yet chicken, known as "bird," is the only identifiable, nonprocessed meat the inmates are offered, and is therefore wildly popular. Many look enthusiastically forward to the next bird day, and remind their co-incarcerees nonstop from the early morning until chow is called, "It's bird day!" Day in and day out, there is not much to look forward to, and so inmates learn to appreciate the little things.

Chicken may be served for lunch or dinner on bird day. A chicken meal is always followed or preceded by "cop-out," a cold meal that few people eat, let alone enjoy. Cop-out may be turkey or baloney cold cuts, pasta salad, tuna salad, or egg salad, but it is always cold and rarely eaten by any but the hungriest of inmates. If there is chicken for lunch, there will surely be cop-out for dinner, and vice versa. This pairing is one of the only constants on the menu; on only a handful of occasions did David observe a second hot meal served on bird day. For all the excitement that chicken entails among the incarcerated, then, there is an equal but opposite lack of enthusiasm at the prospect of its cold-meal counterpart, a reminder that inside, few good things come without cost; bird day is also cop-out day.

Meals vary substantially for the rest of the week. "Cop-out Sunday," when both lunch and dinner are cold meals, is a much-derided weekly occurrence. "Meatless Mondays," implemented in New York City's public schools and city jails in late 2019, earned comparable criticism, despite the fact that most prisoners also found the meat thoroughly unappetizing.[2] There is Taco Tuesday, though this is sporadic, and tacos may be served on other days. Fish Friday, likewise, is not every Friday, nor is fish served only on Fridays. The fact that the institution tries but fails to organize meals along these themes only reinforces the inmates' perception that it is hopelessly incompetent and disorganized. Similarly, the same dinner or lunch is sometimes served two or three days in a row, provoking vocal complaints among the incarcerated diners.

Complaints abound, for myriad other reasons, too. The plastic silverware at Rikers is limited to forks and spoons, and the wrong utensil is often the only one available, leaving inmates to try eating cereal with a fork, or spaghetti with a spoon. Meals are often late, early, or cold. Because the food is prepared by incarcerated workers or civilian cooks, and distributed by COs and incarcerated workers—none of whom care much about its quality—it differs considerably from one batch to the next. One pan of fish patties might be cold, hard, and burned to a crisp, while another is warm and soggy. Undermixing, especially with salt, is a common issue, and one that strikes with all the unpredictability of a search. Multiple times during his bid, David witnessed an inmate begin choking and spluttering after a bite of his food revealed itself, too late, to be massively oversalted, often giving rise to knowing jeers and laughter among the other diners. This was particularly ironic, as the chow is usually drastically undersalted. The lack of salt and sugar in chow was rumored to stem from the DOC's abovementioned obsession with avoiding lawsuits, after having lost several to former inmates who had developed conditions like diabetes, high blood pressure, and other health problems.

This policy seemed only halfway implemented at commissary, where the universal staples were potato chips and ramen noodles, but only sugar-free drinks—like sodas loaded with aspartame and stevia, and "juice packets" of dissolvable lemonade- and raspberry-flavored crystals—were sold. The only real sweets were Atomic Fireballs, small, cinnamon-flavored globes of hard candy. By contrast, commissary also sold eight different varieties of cookies, including the popular Fudge Surprise, a cake-like puck of dough filled with processed chocolate. Prepackaged Danishes were another of the sweetest and most popular items. Though these were nominally available in cinnamon, raspberry, and chocolate flavors, C-74's commissary usually stocked only the least-popular raspberry Danish. In C-76, where a handwritten sign reading "No raspberry danish EVER!!!" hung on the commissary plexiglass, only cinnamon Danishes were available, and rarely at that.

Between the chow and "commo food," and an enforced hypersedentary lifestyle, even the most committed of fitness enthusiasts soon finds himself girdled with an unexpected layer of fat across the midsection. David met several men, mostly hard-drug addicts, who entered rail thin and left only months later with a hanging paunch, and many others who complained that their blood pressure had shot up over the time they had been inside.

There are worse things in the food. Unsanitary conditions are the law of the land on Rikers, and the chow is no exception. David heard consistent reports from both inmates and COs of mold, roaches, and even decomposing mice ending up on inmates' trays. On several occasions, he observed others open food purchased at commissary only to find it moldy or spoiled. In addition to his job in the kitchen, where he observed pitifully low sanitary standards, David worked briefly in the mess hall in C-74. There, he once saw a rat as big as a small house cat scurrying along the baseboards. "Oh, he lives here," one of the other workers explained.

Jarrod was surprised to learn that Rikers recognized veganism. After a week of trading meat for vegetables, Jarrod was called in to the nutritionist's office, a tiny, decrepit room with an old metal desk, two chairs, and two massive green filing cabinets stacked high with five-hundred-count reams of typing paper. The African doctor approved Jarrod's vegan diet, and told him to expect a new ID card with a special insignia. A few days later, Jarrod received this card, entitling him to soy milk in the morning and "vegan entrees" with his other meals, which largely consisted of extra portions of beans and large heaps of bread and greens. Between these meals and a thick paste made of peanut butter and oatmeal from commissary, Jarrod managed to stave off hunger, and get enough calories to stay in shape.

Others were not as fortunate. One elderly man David knew, with numerous health issues, including diabetes and severe lactose intolerance, was regularly heard berating COs in the mess hall and housing unit because he had not received his required meals. The DOC's system for indicating inmate dietary restrictions was laughably disorganized. One inmate David knew received a blue "fish allergy" card on two different occasions; he was not allergic to fish and had not requested the card. In addition to matzo, those registered as Jewish can request "kosher meals," prepackaged in black plastic trays, but these are not always available. Muslims are likewise entitled to halal fare, served on the same trays as regular chow, but whether these were actually halal was anybody's guess: working in the kitchen, David observed practically no distinction whatsoever between halal and regular chow meals or serving utensils.

Redistribution

Of the three cereals served at breakfast, the Cheerios packets were the largest, but also the least flavorful and therefore the least prized. Total was slightly more sought after, and Cinnamon Chex was virtually worth its weight in gold; COs often gave inmates who worked in the kitchen boxes of Chex to take back to their dorm at the end of the shift. Even the most hardened street toughs would hurriedly flock to a CO distributing Chex like pigeons to breadcrumbs, grabbing as many single-serving packets as they could take. Milk, one of the only ways to get supplemental protein, was also always in extremely high demand. It was common to see inmate-workers returning from their jobs in the mess hall or kitchen with a couple of cartons, or sometimes even entire trash bags full of milk cartons and ice. If they made it back to the dorm without having this contraband confiscated, they usually put their haul into a milk fridge, drinking it or giving it away at will. Often bombarded with other inmates' pleas for milk as they entered the dorm, bearers commonly deflected the charge of greediness by shelling out a carton or two, if they had enough to spare.

The kitchen also stocked Pearl brand soy milk. Jarrod received this in small disposable soup cups with his morning breakfast, and found that being able to mix with his coffee throughout the day was good motivation to get out of bed. David often stole entire thirty-two-ounce cartons of soy milk, finding it to be an excellent alternative to dairy milk, which only came in eight-ounce cartons. Not only did soy milk have a comparable protein content, but most others were uninterested in it, and it seemed easy enough to ward off those who might be by simply taking very public swigs from the carton's spout, claiming the whole thing for himself.

Kitchen and mess hall inmate-workers get special perks beyond access to milk. Chief among these are larger portions and sometimes better food, which is usually consumed on the job site but can occasionally be brought back into the housing unit and consumed later or given to others. The civilian cooks and kitchen COs often facilitate the inmates-workers' access to more extra portions and tastier fare, sometimes giving it to them directly, but more often simply looking the other way. They may do this because they have established a rapport with an inmate, as a way of buying reliable, complaint-free labor, or sheerly because it takes much less effort and costs them nothing to acquiesce to inmates' requests for things like spices, milk, and racks of leftover chow. This food can drastically improve an inmate's experience. Once, on hot dog day, a kitchen CO gifted David and the other inmate-workers a bag of real hot dog buns. For guys accustomed to the standard crumbly Rikers Island bread, the experience of eating a hot dog with an actual bun was a luxury akin to eating "street food."

Popular dishes available to kitchen workers include grilled cheese sandwiches and egg sandwiches (discreet use of C-74's commercial kitchen equipment was generally tolerated), and sometimes food from the CO mess hall. The CO mess hall serves fare largely derived from the same basic ingredients as the chow, but generally much more flavorful and appetizing, including things like fresh salad and curried chicken. Entire sheets of the carrot cake served to inmates on Thanksgiving and Christmas make regular appearances there, and occasionally end up in incarcerated kitchen workers' hands. On bird day, there is sure to be a surplus of chicken in the kitchen; guys who work there only occasionally to pass the time, as a second or third job, are sure to go to work then. During the shift's downtime, they sit around stuffing themselves with one piece of chicken after another. The same goes for hot dog, hamburger, and beef patty days. The beef patties served on Rikers are real Tower Isles patties, and though they are poorly cooked, are probably the only thing that rivals bird day for popularity. Sundays likewise bring the near-guarantee of a muffin windfall, sometimes substantial, for kitchen or mess hall workers.

It is considered in poor taste to sell things that are too easily available, even if they are technically contraband and must be stolen. While stolen things could be charged for if they were sufficiently rare, like muffins, soy milk, onions, or spices (paprika, garlic powder, black pepper, or salt, when it could be found), people are generally not expected to pay for things like chicken, milk cartons, or cereal packets. Occasionally, an inmate who has "nothing in his bucket," meaning little commissary food to supplement the mess hall fare, will sell things like this to get by, but when he does so he will invariably present the request for payment as a bit of a favor. "Help me out with a soup," for example, may be asked in return for a single piece of chicken, carton of milk, or packet of cereal. Usually, these were given away to one's section or friends with no payment expected in return. Sometimes a worker who had brought back a substantial haul from the kitchen would call out to the whole dorm that he had extra food available for free, or announce that he was leaving it in the day room, if it was perishables like chicken, burgers, or milk.

Giving things away was not without its benefits for the giver, either—it served to build social capital for an inmate and decrease his chances of coming into conflict with others, and to increase his chances of being supported by others if he did come into conflict with another inmate or COs. This was a factor in David's habit of offering the extra fruit and milk he stole from the kitchen to others upon entering the dorm, and seemed to be a factor for others, too.

In addition to stealing things to bring back to the dorm to give away or sell, inmates also stole just for the sheer pleasure of subverting the institution by stealing and redistributing its goods. In one case, David was awakened by his neighbor returning from the night shift in the kitchen around 4:00 a.m. "Want some chicken?" he said, throwing a mop bag full of warm chicken onto David's stomach. David politely declined. "Shit's warm!" his neighbor insisted. David declined again. "Want some mayonnaise?" he asked, scooping chicken off his stomach and plopping a mop bag full of mayonnaise onto him instead. "I don't really like mayonnaise," David groggily replied. "Yeah, me neither," his neighbor responded. "I just like to fuck with 'em."

This language, "fucking with them," was a common formulation of the attitude that stealing from the institution was not only morally acceptable but bordered on a sort of duty for some. One fellow kitchen worker referred to his and David's daily practice of stealing food from the walk-in refrigerators as "holding it down for thievery."

Holiday Fare

The specialty meals served on Christmas, Thanksgiving, and July Fourth are a double-edged sword. For some, they offer a welcome break from the standard fare; the holiday meals are indisputably better, if only marginally, than regular chow. But for others, these holiday meals seem a sad mockery of what should be, bringing their captivity into stark relief. The Thanksgiving Day presentation of a single slice of reconstituted turkey breast wrapped in soggy deli paper, real meat though it may be, recalls for many the image of family gathered around the table to devour a turkey, both real and whole. Christmas dinner is largely the same: the standard Rikers Island stuffing (a year-round staple made from recycled bread scraps), a tiny, gluey wad of cranberry sauce, a slice of soggy roast beef, and a spongy cube of frosted carrot cake. On July Fourth, David was served hot dogs with baked beans and sauerkraut. This meal in particular seemed to do more psychological harm than good. Hot dogs were not a specialty meal, but rather one available year-round. Though it was actually one of the more popular meals, the fact that most inmates were already well acquainted with it meant that there was no novelty factor at play. No one was excited about the hot dogs. They served only as a rubbery, soy-based reminder that the men in greens were not out grilling, drinking beers, and shooting off fireworks with friends and family as they might normally be.

However, holidays also offered unique opportunities for food sharing and community building among the incarcerated. On Christmas Day and New Year's Day, for example, a man who had served time in state prison led a team of self-appointed inmate-cooks in creating a sort of holiday "cake" from cinnamon Danishes, peanut butter, sugar, and coffee creamer, among other things. These ingredients were thoroughly mixed and then pressed flat on a table in the day room. The mixture was placed between two halves of a fresh plastic garbage bag, with books placed on top, and the cooks then pressing down on the books. The resulting loaf, which resembled a brownie with a light-brown coloration, was about an inch thick. It was cut into small portions and shared widely among the inmates, freely offered by those who made it. This dish, David was told, was not a Riker's Island invention but rather had been imported from the state prison system, an edible testament to the constant circulation of people and knowledge between state time and city time.

Similarly, a jailhouse version of the Dominican drink *morir soñando* (literally "to die dreaming") frequently made an appearance at holidays, and at odd moments whenever there happened to be a surplus of oranges. *Morir soñando* is similar in taste to a Creamsicle or Dreamsicle. Though it has its origins in the Dominican Republic, it is popular not just among New York's sizable Dominican immigrant population but among other Latin national and ethnic groups as well. The guy who most frequently made *morir soñando* during David's time inside was from a Bronx Puerto Rican family.

Outside, the drink is made from milk or evaporated milk, sugar, and orange juice. Inside, orange juice is never served, but the strange fluctuations in the availability of fruit on Rikers mean that there are often enormous surpluses of bananas, apples, oranges, and other fruit that can be stolen from the kitchen or mess hall and smuggled back into the dorm. Large amounts of fruit can also be acquired simply by asking others if they are going to eat their fruit while dining: many are entirely uninterested in it and will give it away at the first request.

Once a few dozen oranges have been acquired, they must be squeezed into a clean, empty white bucket in the dorm—no small feat for this many oranges, as each must be peeled and squeezed entirely by hand. Even if one of the juicers has a banger, he is unlikely to use it for this purpose and risk giving himself away to the authorities, or another inmate who might snitch him out. Next, the juice crafters will dump in countless packets of white sugar. Sugar is available only at breakfast, and each tray comes with only two packets, but kitchen and mess hall workers can acquire more, and are often asked to do so. To the sugar, several dozen individual packets of nondairy coffee creamer, less than half a fluid ounce each, are added. These must be purchased in commissary; someone planning to make a batch of *morir soñando* will often buy as many creamers as possible the week before, or trade other inmates for them, as a single batch of the drink requires thirty packets or more. The resulting mixture is thoroughly stirred (by hand, using a stolen food service glove), scooped up in a clean green cup, and served over ice. Like the holiday cake, this drink was usually freely offered and widely shared among the dorm's residents.

"Crackhead Soup"

Both the holiday cake and *morir soñando* are excellent examples of the diverse and often ingenious fare that constitutes extra-institutional inmate cuisine. The things that can be bought in commissary or stolen from the institution are combined in a dizzying variety of snacks, drinks, and dishes. Despite this, there was really only one dish that could be regularly cooked and shared among inmates. Though occasionally referred to as "crackhead soup," the dish more commonly went nameless, referred to by the process of cooking, as in "I'm cooking, you want in on this?" David once asked a man exactly *what* he was about to begin cooking. "I'm, you know . . . cooking," was his response. Such dishes were similar enough to perhaps not warrant distinctive names. For instance, the only starches that could be purchased at commissary and used as a meal base were ramen noodles and boil-in-bag rice. Any starches that could be pilfered from the kitchen or mess hall, like regular rice or noodles or dehydrated potatoes, were useless to inmates cooking in the housing units because all cooking there depends on hot water from the hot pot.

Each unit's hot pot, a large metal urn equipped with a plastic tap, keeps the water inside at a constant temperature between 120 and 190 degrees Fahrenheit. This temperature differs greatly between housing units. If inmates deem their hot pot's temperature too low, and the COs are unwilling to fix it, they may steal the hot pot, smash open the bottom with a DOC-issued wooden walking cane, and recalibrate the thermostat themselves. David witnessed this twice.

The Parade brand boil-in-bag rice available at commissary was rarely used because it was so difficult to cook. According to the label, it is intended to be boiled for twenty minutes. As the water in the hot pot never reaches a boil, cooking it in the dorm requires an inmate to put the rice in his plastic cup, cover it with hot water, cover the cup with a book (usually inserting a piece of plastic like a stolen food service glove between the top of the cup and the book for sanitary reasons), and then let it sit for about forty minutes. Even if he has managed to acquire an extra cup, and can therefore cook rice without becoming unable to drink anything for the duration, he is likely to be discouraged by the long wait time and high amount of equipment required compared to ramen noodles. Noodles, known as "soups," take only a few minutes to cook, and when made as crackhead soup require only a clean plastic trash bag. But of course, even ramen requires hot water. The hot pot often runs dry, and reheating the water takes at least thirty minutes, not including the time it takes to convince a CO to unlock its plexiglass case and let the inmates refill it. After becoming impatient waiting for the hot pot, Jarrod once began simply snacking away on chunks of hard uncooked ramen. A neighbor, regularly homeless on the outside, expressed disgust at this spartan meal and tried to convince Jarrod to be kinder to himself, saying, "It's not that bad, bro!"

Crackhead soup is a nightly ritual. As the sun sets and inmates settle in for lights out, many prepare their real dinner, from which they derive the calories, protein, and satisfaction that chow fails to provide. Crackhead soup can be made a number of different ways using ingredients like fish, chicken (either commissary-bought packets or shredded chow chicken), corn, cheese, beef or turkey sticks, and chips. Ground beef, available in packets from commissary, was occasionally used, but most men seemed disgusted by the stuff, preferring chicken or fish instead. Contributions were solicited by one or two cooks; the usual buy-in price was two soups and one or two packets of fish. The fish could usually be of any variety, but if the cooks did not like, for example, sardines, they would let the potential contributors know. Men with nothing in their buckets were sometimes accepted at a lower buy-in cost, such as "one soup and one fish," if the cooks were sympathetic, but if they suspected their generosity was being abused, they usually called the freeloader out and cut him off from future meals unless he could pay the full price.

The key component of crackhead soup is a simple clear plastic trash bag. Though formally contraband, trash bags are used widely throughout the jail and are not guarded with any particular zeal, so they can be pocketed from a number of jobs and even acquired by simply asking a sympathetic CO. Their ready availability makes them a staple of the preparation of many jailhouse meals, attested to by the occasional reference to crackhead soup and similar dishes as "bag meals." The trash bag is sawed down to a manageable size by cutting it in half horizontally with a "knife" (piece of string) or the edge of a bedframe. If the meal is on the smaller side, for perhaps two or three people, the bag may sometimes be cut in half again, this time vertically, leaving two intact but separate bottom corners.

The ramen noodles are then crumbled, either by slapping them loudly against the floor—many inmate-cooks pride themselves on being able to break a packet of noodles up completely with a single slap—or crushing them between the fingers in the packaging. The fish or chicken is then dumped atop them, followed by other ingredients, like corn, cheese, or shredded beef or turkey sticks. Crushed potato chips are an essential component of cooking, as they add otherwise-unavailable salt, flavor, and crunch. The ramen seasoning packets are emptied atop the whole pile, which is thoroughly mixed by hand with a stolen clear plastic food service glove.

Filling the bag with enough hot water to cover the mixture is usually a two-person job, with one person holding the bag with both hands while the other controls the hot-pot tap. A large batch requires a substantial amount of water, and even a full hot pot will only withstand three or four average batches of crackhead soup. This sometimes leads to conflict over accusations of people emptying the hot pot without replacing the water inside, especially given the half-hour reheating wait time.

The bag is then tied shut in a simple overhand knot, or with a stolen twist-tie, wrapped in a wool blanket or towel, and left to stew in its own heat for five to ten minutes. It is then moved, to an empty bed frame or to the day room, opened, and distributed by hand to the tune of two handfuls per diner, the server often reusing the same clear plastic glove previously used to stir the mixture. Though this was by far the most common way of "cooking," rumors of ingesting rat poison and/or getting cancer from heating the trash bags, occasionally encouraged by DOC staff, spurred many inmates to develop alternative ways of making their crackhead soup, such as using stolen plastic food service aprons or plastic food containers pilfered from COs or civilian kitchen workers, or else cooking out of a spare white bucket kept clean for that purpose.

There are many different variations on crackhead soup, and some take great pride in their recipes, occasionally offering tastes to others to showcase their talent. Jarrod befriended one such man who had worked as a chef on the outside and vaunted his endless, if subtle, variations on the jailhouse dishes. And crackhead soup is of course not just a Rikers thing. Ethnographer Michael Walker recalls an identical process in California jails, where it is called a "spread."[3] Other common extra-institutional dishes, similar to crackhead soup and to each other, are the "burrito," which is not really a burrito, and the "egg roll," which is not really an egg roll. Both entail cooking the ramen noodles in their original packaging and consuming them the same way, and offer a texture different from the ubiquitous mush, but in different ways. The egg roll has a gummy, chewy consistency; the burrito includes crushed chips added right before eating for extra crunch.

Former Rikers CO C. René West compares the ingenuity of the inmate cuisine she observed at Rikers to the practice of slaves cooking nourishing "soul food" from the parts of the animal that the master discarded.[4] This is a profound observation.

Drinks

In units with in-house dining like 12-Lower, it is easy to accompany one's meal with a drink, as meals are eaten in the day room, and inmates' green cups are therefore on hand. In David's experience, few men brought their cups to the C-74 mess hall; most meals there were eaten without anything to wash them down. Some inmates brought empty water bottles, as the mess hall's Cambro coolers occasionally dispensed drinks more exciting than water (apple juice or "[pink] juice"), which they could load up on and bring back to the dorm.

Cambros, recall, are insulated beverage dispensers, a food service staple for the incarcerated. They are about a foot wide and two feet tall, made of hard-shell plastic, with a detachable lid at the top and a small black plastic tap at the bottom.[5] During David's time in C-76, they were usually filled with ice water, but occasionally contained apple juice (a sticky, funny-tasting artificial liquid that left a lingering smell in one's cup) or, more rarely, "juice," a pink, "fruit"-flavored Kool Aid–like substance. In the heat of the summer months, which David spent in C-74, Cambros were universally loaded with ice alone; throughout the day, inmates would fill their plastic cups with ice and chill their drinks this way. To avoid dipping the cups they drank from into the communal ice, they used a clear plastic food service glove, stolen by a kitchen or mess hall inmate-worker and volunteered for that purpose. Using this glove, left pinched beneath the Cambro's lid, was an absolute requirement—dipping one's cup directly into the ice was strongly condemned.

Housing units with in-house dining are supposed to receive a Cambro atop the rolling insulated food carts, commonly referred to as "food wagons," that bear their meals. David's job in C-74's kitchen consisted mainly of loading and delivering food wagons to the various higher-security housing units, which did not go to the mess hall for chow. There were never enough Cambros for each house. Which houses actually received Cambros was decided either purely randomly or following fierce debate, with some inmate-workers advocating for their housing unit to receive Cambros at the others' expense. When David was in 12-Lower in C-76, Cambros sometimes failed to appear with the food wagons, leaving only the empty Cambro from the previous meal sitting on the day room table, to the great consternation of those who tried to drink from it.

Housing units that went to the mess hall for chow, like Mod 4 in C-74, seemed to have no official channel for getting a new Cambro or refilling the Cambro they had. Usually, someone volunteered to carry the house Cambro from the day room to the mess hall—a distance roughly equivalent to a long city block—and refill it with ice or ice water, but who exactly this responsibility fell to was entirely open. It was not uncommon for an inmate to grab the Cambro and passive-aggressively announce to the dorm that he was doing everybody a favor, so as not to have his good deed go unappreciated. At other times, one or a few inmates would do this without asking for a word of thanks. A Cambro in a mess-hall dorm that had been in the unit for a while must also suddenly be deemed "nasty" by public opinion. To avoid drinking from it any longer, the dorm residents would ask one of their number who worked in the kitchen if he would swap it out for a new one when he went to work. But this actually accomplished little in terms of sanitation. In fact, after he started working in the kitchen, David stopped drinking from the Cambros altogether, because he discovered that the Cambros and their lids were often left lying around on the floor, were often used to stash things ranging from milk cartons to soup to various types of contraband, and were almost never washed.

Some C-74 inmates, despite their familiarity with the unsanitary kitchen conditions, still preferred to drink from the Cambros because the water they contained was dispensed from an apparatus with a highly visible commercial-grade water filter in it, a fact reported back to the dorms by the kitchen workers. The only other option was to drink the tap water. Though New York City traditionally prides itself on having "some of the best tap water in the world," that rule does not extend to Rikers Island.[6] While David did not notice any funny odor or taste, others often complained that they did, and on perhaps a half-dozen occasions during his year in jail, the tap water suddenly ran brown or even black for hours at a time. Even after the DOC contractors managed to restore the tap water to a normal color, this was enough to sap all confidence in the plumbing on Rikers.

Yet inmates often have little choice but to drink from the tap. Bottles of water are sold at commissary, but buyers are limited to only three bottles a week. About halfway through David's year, the water bottles sold decreased in size from .75 liters to .5 liters, but the number of bottles inmates were able to purchase stayed the same. When pressed on the subject, the commissary COs repeatedly assured inmates, "We're trying to get that fixed," without ever actually getting it fixed. Some inmates, if they have enough money, circumvented the three-bottle weekly limit by approaching others who did not generally buy bottled water and offering to trade them commissary goods of their choosing if they did. One shotcaller in 12-Lower managed to accumulate a massive reserve of bottled water in this way, perhaps twenty-five or thirty bottles, and claimed never to drink tap water. But even he could not avoid it for everything: the water in the hot pot came from the tap, and of course he had to brush his teeth.

In addition to the questionable tap water, the hot pots also dispensed plastic. There was a common practice among inmates of heating up Danishes and Fudge Surprises by placing them atop the hot pot's domed black plastic lid, provided they could convince a CO to give them access to it for such a trivial reason. They insisted that warming their pastries up made them much more enjoyable, and it is hard to begrudge anyone small pleasures in such circumstances. But most objects slid off the convex shape of the hot pot lid, so the usual move was to flip it upside down before placing the pastry atop it. The outside of the lid, unlike the underside, was clearly not designed to be repeatedly steamed, and it gradually degraded and crumbled away into the water below. Unless their hot pot was brand new, those who used it were therefore invariably consuming tiny bits of plastic, sometimes large enough to be visible or discovered when bitten down upon.

None of the various plastic bottles available through commissary had mouths wide enough to accommodate the ice cubes on Rikers. Bottles with lids keep ice or iced drinks cold longer than cups—not significantly, but enough to matter to someone who has limited access to creature comforts. The much greater portability of a bottled drink also meant that bottles with mouths wide enough to fit ice cubes were in high demand in summer by inmates who wanted to take cold drinks to the yard or hot work environments like the kitchen. All of these bottles were stolen from COs or civilian staff, or fished out of the trash, washed out, and recycled. Of course, any bottle not purchased at commissary will likely be confiscated on a search, despite the fact that COs are generally well aware of this practice of stealing or salvaging bottles to keep drinks cold.

There is no reason why wide-mouthed bottles are not sold—they just aren't, and so the cycle of stealing-reusing-losing bottles continues. Guys who would never dumpster dive in the outside world thought nothing of this practice; on the contrary, a bottle that could fit ice cubes was a status symbol. Stolen or salvaged bottles that stood out less, like Gatorade bottles, or clear Kedem brand grape juice bottles—one of the more common ones, as the kitchen has pallets of the stuff—could easily be taken to work or the yard without attracting too much attention from the COs. Bottles that more readily caught the eye were a liability, and were not generally taken out of the dorms. One guy during David's time managed to acquire a much-praised hot pink thermos, perhaps a liter in volume, but left it sitting in plain sight on the empty bunk next to his. It was so obvious that a passing CO confiscated it right there in the dorm, where small-level contraband was usually left untouched unless there was a search.

Any beverage that breaks up the monotony of jail life, like cold soda from the COs' mess hall, or real coffee, is hugely popular. Lil Wayne, for example, describes officiating a mock wedding at C-76, where contraband Gatorade was distributed to mark the occasion. "We even had a reception, [to] which everyone brought something for the couple," he writes. When one inmate "brought 12 Gatorades, it went down in this bitch. We were all like OOOOH SHIT . . . It's going dooowwwn!"[7]

Feast and Famine

Scarcity of seemingly random, various food items followed no clear logic, beside consistency. For most of David's sentence, there were only two ramen noodle flavors available at commissary: chicken and chili. When, towards the end of his sentence, commissary began offering "Spicy Vegetable" flavor, it caused a veritable craze among the captive shoppers. During his time in C-76, commissary was "sold out" of chicken-flavored ramen for a month and a half straight, leaving chili ramen the only option for dorm cooking, and giving rise to an epidemic of heartburn and disgust.

These bouts of scarcity can drive the prices of goods up substantially on the unofficial market. David heard multiple reports from several sources of a time shortly before his arrival in C-76 when commissary was out of coffee for two weeks, and single packets of the stuff, usually about fifty cents, were being sold between inmates for four dollars apiece. According to both COs and inmates, especially those who work in the island's warehouse, these shortages are never due to an actual lack of a specific item on Rikers. Rather, they are due to a poor communication and delivery system run by people disinterested in their customers' opinions, and therefore in restocking things with any great rush. Hence, in the time when C-76 had only chili ramen, mountains of chicken ramen were likely being consumed in other facilities on the island.

The foodstuffs that are technically contraband but generally readily available, such as cereal, milk, and fruit, also seem to be in constant and unpredictable flux. Milk is usually available in great quantities, but from time to time the kitchen COs and civilian staff will complain that they do not have enough on hand for institutional meals, and stop their practice of giving cartons to the inmate-workers. Cereal packets are always available, but what type of cereal is anyone's guess: it may be nothing but the unpopular Cheerios for days or weeks at a time.

Fruit, in particular, goes through bizarre cycles of scarcity and surplus. These are usually, but not always, based on what fruits are cheapest for the institution to buy depending on market factors like growing season. When David arrived in October, the fruit served with chow was almost exclusively pears. As time went on, pears disappeared from the trays, and then reappeared as he neared the end of his sentence a year later. The same dynamic was true for other fruits like apples, oranges, plums, and apricots. It was common knowledge among Rikers veterans, for example, that bananas were never found there in the fall. At other times of year, however, they were virtually the only fruit available. Rikers veterans also reported, perplexingly, that there were never any apples in C-95, at any time of year, for reasons unknown.

In fact, there are often enormous surpluses of many types of food on Rikers, much of it inevitably going to waste. Up to four pallets of fruit at a time often sat unattended in the kitchen, slowly going bad no matter how fast COs, civilian cooks, and inmate-workers could take them. In 12-Lower, and in the C-74 kitchen, David witnessed untold amounts of untouched ripe fruit, unopened packets of cereal, and cartons of fresh milk dumped directly into the trash cans every day for "security reasons." This was in keeping with the general attitude of DOC staff, who used and wasted as much as they pleased. Like most things at Rikers, the books are opaque and therefore inscrutable to the outside world, and the correction budget, they all rest assured, will keep going up, regardless of what happens on Rikers Island.

One of the unintended benefits of this wastefulness for those inmates who worked in the kitchen was access to fresh-squeezed orange juice. Boxes upon boxes of soon-expiring oranges were sometimes offered to them by the civilian cooks, or simply taken on the inmates' own initiative. When this happened, a small crowd of impromptu juicers was sure to form. The most common tactic was to slide an orange along the bottom edge of the commercial food preparation tables, cutting the peel enough to then pry the fruit open with one's fingers and squeeze it into an empty half pan, each inmate with his own pan. This would continue until each was satisfied with the amount of raw juice in his pan. The raw juice, a slurry with pulp and pips, needed to be strained before drinking. The most common way to do this was to slowly pour the juice through a plastic fork. Alternatively, kitchen workers could steal quart-sized wide-mouth spice bottles with sifter holes in the lids. After dumping the spice in the trash and washing the bottles out, they poured the raw juice in, then screwed the lid on and poured it back into their half pan through the holes.

Many times in the hot summer weather, groups of inmate kitchen workers could be found sitting wordlessly atop scattered milk crates, staring off into space and savoring a refreshing drink that might well cost more than they would be willing to pay in the outside world.

8

Hygiene

Excited banter cuts through the excruciating noise of Jarrod's bustling dormitory at peak capacity. Voices rise, tones harden, and harsh words are exchanged. The spectacle earns just about everyone's attention; this is more interesting than the TV!

"That's nasty!" one inmate yells.

"You really gonna do that in front of everyone?" adds another.

"And then touch the phone!" rejoins the first.

A middle-aged Eastern European man, who has largely kept to himself, stands in the spotlight, accused of publicly scratching his ass, inside his pants, while waiting in line for the phone. Initially he tries to defuse the conflict by brushing it off, but as the chorus of opprobrium grows louder, he becomes angry and digs in his heels.

"I scratch my ass, you scratch your ass!" he proclaims, waving off the outrage. "You put tobacco up your ass and out of it we smoke!"

His righteous anger, combined with the absurdity of the situation, throws cold water on the dormitory's collective outrage. Amid murmurs of "He nasty!" the conflict mutates into a collective joke. But this man is lucky; the hygiene rules that structure city time are no laughing matter. Denied privacy, subjected to a crushing forced scarcity, confined to a tiny space, and disallowed most of the decisions that characterize adult life on the outside, the inmate is left with very little to control beyond the cleanliness of his surroundings. This terrain of self-determination, no matter how meager, is jealously guarded with all the zeal of a paranoid suburban homeowner.

The social nature of everything in the dormitories for city-time men means that even the most intimate of functions is not private. On the contrary, bodily functions are highly social. The inmate's loss of privacy is itself painful, as is one's unavoidable proximity to scores of strange bodies within an enclosed space that one cannot freely leave. These factors are compounded by foul odors, grotesque sights, and other irritations that can be typically avoided in the outside world. This amounts to a constant and grating reminder that one is not free to remove oneself from the often-disgusting environment of city time. As Lil Wayne tersely observes in his C-76 diary, "Someone is always shitting!"[1]

This dangerous concentration of frustration and disgust can escalate the most mundane conflicts about bodily comportment into violence. Thus, attentive discretion is key, and cleaning up after oneself is highly important, though both are far from universally practiced. In this context, observing commonly held standards of hygiene is not just a means of keeping oneself clean and healthy but more importantly of avoiding trouble with fellow inmates.

Collective Hygiene

There are collective efforts, organized or not, to maintain a sanitary living environment. The common practice in the Six was for everyone to clean their section on Sunday, a day off for most institutional jobs. Indeed, "everybody cleans on Sunday" was a sort of mantra in 12-Lower. In the Four, this practice came and went depending on who was in the dorm and how many people there were, but seemed to be acknowledged as tradition even when it was not practiced. Alison Spedding, an anthropologist imprisoned in a women's jail in Bolivia, observed a similar pattern, which she attributes to the "intent to impose order in a context of impotence and social disaggregation. At times it seems to extend to an attempt to scrub away the stigma of being a prisoner."[2]

The precise terrain one must keep clean depends on the political geography of the dormitory house. One's section consists of his bunk, the bunks closest to his, and the surrounding area. Exactly where a section begins and ends is very fluid, and depends largely on social interactions. For example, a group of three Spanish-speaking inmates who get along well and have bunks next to each other might consider themselves a section, but not the person next to them if he does not also speak Spanish. But the physical layout of the space also plays a role: if the three friends would have to go out of their way not to clean the area around the fourth guy's bed, this might be perceived as a slight, and so they may include him in their section cleaning just to make things easier for everyone.

Generally speaking, an inmate sweeps and mops his "bunk" or his "bed," which usually refers not to the bed frame or mattress but to the space immediately around and underneath the bed itself. He, or someone else in his section, then sweeps and mops the small aisles in between the rows of beds, and maybe even the adjacent section of Broadway. Many inmates also clean their bed or section throughout the week, often borrowing the broom or mop from one of the "house gang" crew as they clean in the evening.

Though there were only two mops and two brooms during David's time in 12-Lower, inmates were extremely polite and efficient about sharing them so that everyone could clean. In an atmosphere that often seems designed to simulate a Hobbesian war of all against all, there was a powerful collective sense that keeping the facility clean was in everybody's interest. Collective cleaning time can have the excitement and conviviality of cooperative labor toward a shared objective, and gives inmates a chance to momentarily escape the crushing powerlessness of their situation and work in common to create a result in which they can recognize themselves.

The majority of Broadway, as well as the other common spaces like the day room, bathroom, and phone areas, are usually cleaned by the "house gang," a group of three or four inmates who are paid by the DOC to keep the housing unit clean. In theory, this means cleaning the common areas every night, and many house gang workers take pride in cleaning regularly and thoroughly. Some, however, only clean occasionally, and on one occasion all the members of the house gang in Mod 4 stopped cleaning for two months in protest after the DOC suddenly stopped paying them.

Members of the house gang also make it known, by shouting it out to the whole dorm, if spaces like the day room, toilets, or showers are left in states of disarray they consider unacceptable. Sometimes, if the others persisted in leaving a certain part of the dorm a mess, the house gang would refuse to clean it any more. Some house gang workers spent their days in protracted agitation about the cleanliness of the dorm, or lack thereof. In an extreme case, one angry house gang member berated Jarrod's dorm: "I don't know who it is that is taking the towels for cleaning the bathroom to clean your ass, but whoever it is, I'm gonna catch you!" The outside observer might think an announcement like this would elicit giggles. But such matters are of the utmost seriousness.

Despite all these practices, the living environment was always one of extreme filth, with dust, leaks, pests, wrappers and bits of food, wads of toilet paper, and worse perpetually strewn around the unit. In this light, collective cleaning took on a quality of staving off the worst; even if scrubbed to the point of shining, the dorm would soon be filthy again. Any possible respite from the squalor is embraced. "I learned how to make air freshener with a nasal-spray bottle, shampoo, and water," recounts Lil Wayne in his C-76 diary. "It actually works."[3] David, who also learned this method, was similarly surprised at its effectiveness.

The phones, as the only thing nearly everyone in the unit physically holds and breathes into, are often the subject of strictly regulated hygiene measures. In 12-Lower, hand-drawn signs bearing an image of the Disney character Goofy, tricked out with a cocked baseball hat, enormous chain necklace, and other bling, declared, "WASH YO TEETH B4 USING PHONES!!!!" These sorts of signs declaring hygiene standards are common, especially in the bathroom, where they might indicate which toilets can be urinated in and which can be defecated in, or urge inmates not to clog the sinks with trash or bits of food. One housing unit David delivered chow to as part of his kitchen job had a sign posted on the front gate: "For dirt bags this is a clean house!"

The common convention of sheathing phones in socks, though an individual practice, can also be seen as a collective hygiene measure. It consists of writing one's name on a clean sock and using it to cover the phone's mouthpiece when in use, so as to limit exposure to others' germs. Those who do this, of course, equally limit the degree of others' exposure to their own germs. Though this practice predates COVID-19, it exploded in popularity after the pandemic began; those who had previously scoffed at the efficacy of a cheap cotton sock as a sanitary barrier, like David, started using them.

Lastly, the practice of reclaiming some small amount of privacy by hanging extra bedsheets can be seen as a collective hygiene measure in that it allows inmates to clean themselves without worrying about others looking on as they do. For example, in 12-Lower, the sheets had to be knotted in a certain way if they were to hang over the front of the stall properly. The layout of the toilet stalls in Mod 4 required an intricate set of makeshift rigging over which privacy sheets were draped, which had to be reconstructed after nearly every search. Similar practices were used to give privacy in the shower, too, when possible.

Shit, Piss, and Scarcity

The inmates' environment of enforced scarcity also contributes significantly to how and when they are able to clean themselves and their surroundings. The DOC supplies only four hygiene products (soap, toilet paper, toothpaste, and toothbrushes), all with great irregularity. Though provided with this minimum of personal hygiene products, inmates are largely robbed of the sense of autonomy and dignity that caring for oneself provides.

Corcraft soap, the standard-issue DOC soap, is essentially the Dr. Bronner's of Rikers Island. An all-purpose caustic white bar only one ounce in size, it is highly astringent and good for cleaning hands, underarms, laundry, dishes, or even the floor.[4] For some, it is prized as a facial cleanser; they will occasionally rub it into a foamy mask, leaving it on for up to twenty minutes at a time. Those who swear by its benefits may even take some home with them when they leave. This seems to have been the popular opinion of Corcraft for some time: the 1994 HBO documentary *Lock-Up: The Prisoners of Rikers Island* shows a number of incarcerated women in "Rosie's" (the Rose M. Singer Center) grating a bar of Corcraft across a metal air vent cover and explaining, "It takes stains off your skin. Your complexion—it lightens your complexion. That soap is pretty good. . . . A lotta people, they sleep with it on they face."[5]

The soap is known colloquially simply by its brand name, "Corcraft," as the only marking it bears is this word stamped into its surface. Corcraft is a public corporation owned by the state prison system, which oversees the production of commodities for state and municipal agencies by inmate-workers serving state time. While New York State prisoners do not labor for private corporations, many of the commodities in state prisons and at Rikers are produced by their labor.[6] The ubiquitous greens, for example, also bear a Corcraft logo.

In addition to bars of Corcraft hand soap, inmates are given thumb-sized green "security" toothbrushes, travel-sized tubes of mint toothpaste, and variously sized wads of single-ply toilet paper. Consensus holds that they are supposed to be available to the inmates at any time, but this is rarely the case, and the policy on how to access them changes considerably from one housing unit to the next. The most common technique we encountered was for the steady officers to periodically restock a "white bucket" with these items and leave it somewhere near the Bubble at the front of the dorm for inmates to take as they needed. But this bucket is often empty, or devoid of at least one of these items, and convincing one of the steady officers to refill it depended largely on the individual officer and the particular mood the officer might be in.

One or all four of the items might be unavailable for hours or days on end. Though cinnamon-flavored Close-Up toothpaste and Irish Spring and Dove hand soaps could be bought at commissary, there were no official alternatives for procuring toilet paper or toothbrushes. On one occasion during David's sentence, inmates were not given fresh toothbrushes for a week straight. In jail, this is significant, as the near impossibility of storing one's toothbrush in a sealed container or on a sanitary surface means it begins collecting ambient dust and grime immediately after its first use. Some inmates carefully slide the toothbrush back into its disposable plastic sleeve, but these often tear upon opening, so most don't hold onto their toothbrushes for more than a day or two.

Faced with this hygiene-product insecurity, most inmates take what they can, when they can. If the "house bucket" is full of soap, for example, someone might grab a whole handful rather than one bar, stashing some for later. This creates a feedback loop in which the COs are reluctant to restock the house bucket because they feel that people are abusing their access to it, and the inmates, never knowing when it will be restocked, are therefore further encouraged to seize as much of each product as possible when it is available. Once, when David brought it to the steady officers' attention that there had been no hand soap in the house bucket for two days, the floor officer blamed the other inmates for taking too much, even as the Bubble officer berated David for not having taken extra hand soap himself and set it aside earlier.

The housing units in which a different distribution policy had been developed to counteract this problem fared little better. The most obvious alternative was to keep everything in the Bubble, forcing inmates to ask for a product every time they needed it. But even this arrangement failed to prevent staff from perpetually running out of basic necessities for no reason other than poor communication with the COs who handled restocking, and their near-universal indifference to the inmates' well-being. In 12-Lower in C-76, a hand-sized slot had been rudely cut into the plexiglass wall of the Bubble, through which one could reach to tear some of the standard single-ply toilet paper from a roll hanging from a mopstick mounted on the wall. This single roll of toilet paper, incredibly, was supposed to serve the entire sixty-bed dorm. This would be a ridiculous arrangement even if toilet paper was only used when defecating, but this is far from the case: as the only disposable paper cleaning product available, toilet paper is also widely used as a tissue, napkin, paper towel, or improvised toilet seat, greatly increasing demand for it.

No matter how much toilet paper an inmate may or may not have, his toilet practices are not his own. Shitting, like everything in jail, is a social affair. One of the first things new arrivals learn is that they must flush the toilet multiple times as they defecate in order to minimize the smell of their feces. The bathroom is a shared space, and no one wants it to smell any worse than it must, especially given that the phones, where inmates might spend twenty minutes or more talking to friends or loved ones, are usually placed right outside the bathroom (in Mod 4, two of the five phones were actually inside it). If others think someone's bowel movement smells too strongly, they will not hesitate to make their opinion known, usually with injunctions like "Yo, courtesy!"—a reference to the expected "courtesy flushes"—or perhaps "Throw some water on that!"

Since the toilets do not have seats, an inmate who needs to shit must sit directly on the rim of the toilet, spotted with dried drops of urine splashback, unless he takes it upon himself to alter his shitting environment. Some guys wipe the rim down with a wad of toilet paper before sitting on it. In Mod 4, where the layout made the cleaning supply closet more accessible than in C-76, an inmate with a good rapport with a steady officer might ask the officer to unlock the closet so he could take out the bleach-based cleaning spray, technically reserved for the house gang, and clean the toilet with that. Other inmates create a multilayered lining of toilet paper, sometimes referred to as a "nest," or sit atop an extra pair of the flip-flop sandals available at commissary for eighty-seven cents, their straps removed, and dedicated for that purpose. (On the final day of Jarrod's time, he learned that many men in his dormitory did this. His amused neighbors could not believe he had been directly sitting on the seat that whole time.) Possible social censure accompanies nearly every step of the process; an inmate might be scolded or threatened by others for clogging the toilet too frequently or leaving his nest behind.

The dormitory toilet stalls have slightly different designs between the Four and the Six, but what they all have in common is that they are only about four feet tall, and are completely open in the front. An inmate who wants some privacy while shitting, as most do, will hang an extra bedsheet on the front of the stall when he uses the toilet. These toilet sheets stay in the bathroom at all times, and depend on some level of cooperation. This is a rule that most first-timers discover by breaking it. It was not uncommon in C-76's intake dormitory, in particular, to hear comments like "Yo, cover yourself when you shit!" as inmates fresh off the streets are instructed in the facility's de facto policies.

Beyond its practical purpose, the sheet-curtain also has a symbolic value. Initially, Jarrod did not want to touch the sheet, presuming it was covered in some mixture of bodily fluids, including semen. He discovered that his jumpsuit, when lowered down to the waist, provided more than enough cover of his genitals—which he assumed was the point of the sheet. But no sooner did he try this method than he was berated as "wild nasty," an unenviable designation, for appearing uncovered. David occasionally witnessed inmates shield themselves on the toilet solely by placing a plastic chair in front of themselves instead; they were likewise denounced as "nasty." An inmate quickly learns that the sheet is not simply for privacy, but functions as a performative barricade communicating to other inmates that he is not complicit in the indignity of their enforced proximity, and therefore not deserving of the anger and scorn these conditions evoke.

Urination is also governed by its own rules. All housing units seem to set aside a number of toilets, usually those closest to the bathroom entrance, for urination only. Sometimes this is declared by a makeshift sign ("These toilets for pee-ing only!!!"), and sometimes simply by social convention. In 12-Lower, there were two urinals built into the wall next to six full toilets in booths. Because two urinals hardly sufficed for sixty men, the first two full toilets were also set aside for urinating only. Shitting on one of these would earn an inmate instant ridicule and disgust.

Conversely, urinating into a toilet reserved for defecation could lead to serious repercussions, especially in a dorm where these practices were tightly regulated by a rigid hierarchy—again, no toilet seats means urine inevitably splashes up onto the same rim of the toilet that inmates sit on.

"The toilet is for shit and the urinal for piss," a house leader announced while Jarrod was in the 1-Upper intake dormitory. "You think the police [COs] clean the bathroom? They don't—we do!" On the other hand, in a dorm in Mod 4 with a less rigid hierarchy, David sometimes saw inmates with some social clout urinate in these toilets when no others were available, with only minor disapproval voiced by those nearby.

The mopstick toilet paper dispenser in 12-Lower invariably ran empty several times a day. When asked to replace it, the CO in the Bubble often claimed to be busy (a claim that was true only periodically at best), forcing the inmate to linger awkwardly on "the bridge," the very public four-square-foot space between the Bubble and the day room entrance, holding his bowel movement until the CO deigned to put a new roll of paper on the mopstick. On a few occasions, David even witnessed the CO in the Bubble actually take a full toilet paper roll off the mopstick for several hours as an act of collective punishment for a few inmates' having smoked weed, K2, or tobacco. A person who needed to defecate during this time, if he had no stashed toilet paper of his own, would be forced, somewhat embarrassingly, to solicit it from those around him.

When toilet paper was available on the mopstick-dispenser in 12-Lower, an inmate had to take as much as he thought he might need for his particular bowel movement on the spot. Taking too little could leave him stranded on the toilet without enough paper on hand; taking too much could elicit crude commentary about his toilet habits, and mild ridicule, from the other inmates in the dorm, such as, "'Bout to blow it up in there, huh?"

New arrivals therefore quickly learned that they were better off stashing toilet paper in anticipation of their next trip to the toilet, rather than relying on the benevolence of the COs at the time they had to shit. Thus, when inmates saw a roll of toilet paper on the mopstick in 12-Lower, they were likely to subtly pull off reams of the stuff ahead of time, carefully folding it and placing it aside for later use. This, of course, fueled the same sort of endless cycle David observed in housing units that used the "house bucket" strategy of dispensing hygiene products. Inmates, out of sheer necessity, take what they can when they can; COs decry their supposed abuse of the system and drag their heels providing replacements, further prompting inmates to take as much as possible the next time. This cycle, in all its iterations across the various housing units, constantly gives rise to a great deal of conflict, resentment, and threats between the inmates and COs.

Another solution was to steal entire rolls of toilet paper when the opportunity presented itself. The dorms in the Six, for example, were so arranged that the staff bathroom was found next to the cleaning supply closet along the short, narrow hall between the inner and outer gates. Both the door to the staff bathroom and the door to the cleaning supply closet were usually kept locked, but on rare occasions the COs would fail to lock them properly, and inmates passing by would manage to duck inside and grab a roll or two of toilet paper. Though David once nearly received a "ticket" (disciplinary infraction) for this, attempts at toilet-paper theft usually went unpunished; if caught, inmates simply replaced the roll and moved on. Most inmates knew which COs would pretend not to notice, or wouldn't care if they did, and only took the risk when they could get away with it.

Much more widespread was the introduction of rolls of toilet paper into the dorm by inmate-workers returning from their shifts. Inmates working jobs that entail restocking the DOC staff bathrooms, like the SOD and sanitation details, have access to rolls of toilet paper, and most COs don't stop them from bringing them back to the dorm. They often keep these for themselves, but also give out rolls to their friends or neighbors. When he worked on SOD, David frequently gave out extra rolls of toilet paper to those in his section and those with whom he had a good rapport in order to build social capital.

In 12-Lower, when the sporadic delivery of hygiene products occurred, a CO appeared dragging a trash bag full of toilet paper, Corcraft, and other necessities, into the dorm. There was always a rush to grab rolls of toilet paper before the bag was locked in the supply closet at the back of the day room. In the short distance from the inner gate to the back of the day room, this CO was usually mobbed by savvy inmates hounding the CO, "Yo, lemme get a roll!" Not wanting to deal with the fallout from denying their requests, the CO usually acquiesced. Though it means nothing to the CO, an entire roll of toilet paper is a luxury for inmates. It is also contraband that may well be confiscated on a search, but it makes daily life a great deal more comfortable as long as they can hold onto it.

Razor Blades and Fingernails

Few items are as anxiously prohibited in a jail as a razor blade, yet shaving remains an essential component of many men's daily personal hygiene routines. Yellow safety razors are coveted objects, and only offered from 6:00 a.m. to 10:00 a.m., Monday to Saturday. The bald guys who shave their heads—the ones who wake up, in any case—are usually the first to swarm the Bubble in the early morning. Though each inmate is technically allowed one razor per day, there are almost never enough razors in the Bubble for the entire dorm, and they tend to run out quickly. Hence, those who are committed to getting a razor must get up as early as possible in hopes of procuring one.

But even an early bird may not get a razor, as the DOC sometimes fails to deliver them for days or even weeks at a time. Those who do procure one have a long road ahead, as the razors are incredibly dull. Their dullness has nothing to do with safety, as they are still plenty sharp for slicing flesh, and people sometimes make them into bangers. Rather, it seems to be a function of sheer cheapness, like the spotty ink in the commissary pens. Despite shaving cream, shaving soap, shaving brushes, styptic pencils, and aftershave being listed in the *Inmate Handbook* as available in commissary, this was not our reality.[7] We found nothing to put between razor and skin except hand lotion or the ubiquitous, astringent Corcraft. The razor's efficiency can be improved ever so slightly by pulling the blade across a towel before use to smooth out the tiny burrs on the edge, but this doesn't help much. Some guys place one end of the razor's head in their mouth with the blade facing outward, and bite down hard on the plastic casing to crack it open and remove it, which they claim makes the razor easier to shave (or make a banger) with.

On a practical level, this means many of those who shave experience painful pulling at their stubble, not to mention nicks and scrapes, as they drag the blade across their jaws or scalps. Dripping blood, these cuts can be a source of conflict with others who, afraid of contracting some disease, let it be known exactly how they feel about another guy bleeding all over the communal sinks. Many of those who shave their scalps spend a good part of the morning with scraps of single-ply institutional toilet paper sticking out from their heads at odd angles, blotted to their skin with dried blood.

Scalp shavers face particular difficulty, as, due to the razors' dullness, it takes two or three to shave a person's entire head. This presents a problem, as each inmate must give the CO in the Bubble his ID band as collateral for his allotted daily razor. The solution is to solicit razors from others who are not shaving that day, asking them to turn in their ID bands and then hand their razors over. This request is usually presented as a favor; David never saw any inmate in need of multiple razors offer to compensate another for his, despite the obvious risks of checking out a blade and leaving it in someone else's hands. Though a man who lends a razor to another must have a working trust that he will not use it to slash someone—a very rare occurrence among sentenced inmates, in any event—there is always the risk that he will lose it. This, in turn, opens up the possibility of someone else finding it and using it to make a banger, an eventuality that could spell trouble for the person in whose name the razor was originally checked out.

Then there was the issue of shaving the back of one's head. Some solicit others to do this for them, despite the stigma against having another man groom them, which some inmates deem "gay." Others simply go at it themselves, often leaving their heads bleeding, scraped-up messes; these guys accept perpetually mutilated scalps as the price of some shred of bodily control. All of this adds up to mean that shaving is simply not worth the trouble for many inmates, and they give it up, growing scraggly, irregular beards during their time inside. Such was the case with David; after little more than a month of painfully struggling to shave every two or three days, he simply abandoned it.

Trimming one's nails, like shaving, was an unnecessarily Herculean feat. It is easy to forget how often fingernails, in particular, must be cut, until one is deprived of the means to clip them at will. This is one of the myriad freedoms that free adults take for granted, and that inmates become acutely aware of no longer possessing. Watching our nails grow against our will was doubly frustrating, as long nails became at once a source of physical discomfort and a constant visual reminder of our lack of basic bodily autonomy. Most inmates' nails remained long and talon-like, which made nicks and scratches, especially on the face, a common side effect of fistfights. A frustrated neighbor once gestured to his fingernails, remarking to Jarrod, "Why don't they want to confiscate these dangerous weapons?"

Inmates in lower-security units were afforded occasional trips to the barbershop and could trim their nails there, if they happened to be in the dorm when the barbershop was called. At the barbershop, there was one small and one large set of nail clippers in a small plastic container of blue Barbicide disinfectant liquid. Those who wished to trim their nails had to take turns using the clippers, dunking them in disinfectant between users. Fingernails were clipped over an open trash can, but toenails were clipped sitting down on the same barbershop bench where everyone waited to get their hair cut. The common practice was to take one's feet from one's shoes and then place them atop the shoes to avoid contact with the floor. Barefoot contact with the floor anywhere in the jail was universally scorned and considered the sure sign someone was a mentally ill "bugout." People wore shoes, boots, or sandals in the dorms, but never went barefoot. For unknown reasons, the COs stationed to the barbershop always insisted that inmates leave their toenail clippings where they fell, meaning that barbershop visits often ended with tiny piles of toenail detritus in a neat line at the bottom of the bench.

During the COVID-19 pandemic, David witnessed firsthand how hard it must be for those incarcerated in higher-security units, who are not afforded trips to the barbershop, to trim their nails. Barbershop visits were shut down for several months, and the only way to trim one's nails was to badger a steady officer or captain, who usually made empty promises to provide a pair of clippers. On one occasion, after repeatedly being asked over several days by inmates who had not been able to trim their nails in weeks and were growing understandably irate at her failure to follow through, a captain stormed into the dorm, harangued the entire unit while waving a pair of toenail clippers in the air, then threw them on the floor and petulantly stormed out. She left no sanitizing materials to accompany the clippers.

In fact, the clippers that were brought into the dorms during this period were rarely accompanied by any sanitizing product. If anything, it was likely to be a handful of single-use alcohol-based disinfecting towelettes—hardly enough for everyone to use one. These clippers, captains confessed when pressured, made the rounds of the entire jail this way. Given the lack of sanitary conditions and the difficulty involved, David took to filing his fingernails down on the grout between the tiles on the wall in the kitchen when he went to work there, and he was not the only one. Even then, trimming one's toenails remained a problem, and left him at the mercy of the DOC. It was rumored that if all else failed, an inmate could claim his toenails had gone untrimmed so long they were causing him pain, and visit the clinic to have them clipped by the medical staff there.

"Who Got Next?"

In the C-76 dormitory houses, inmates were free to shower on their own schedule throughout the day, except when the showers were turned off as a punitive measure during lockdowns, as both Jarrod and David experienced on multiple occasions. All three C-76 dormitories Jarrod was held in had open communal showers that could be viewed from the Bubble and, obliquely, through translucent plexiglass and metal grating, from the hallway leading into the house. The dormitory showers we encountered had metal buttons set in metal plates, mounted on the wall at about waist height below each showerhead. This button had to be continually pressed in order for an inmate to shower, in most cases, about every ten to fifteen seconds. In 12-Lower, the tip of a plastic spoon could be jimmied between the button and the plate to keep it depressed, and thus keep the shower running. In Mod 4, the buttons were slightly different, rendering this impossible.

Factors like water temperature, pressure, and duration vary enormously from one showerhead to the next. In Mod 4-Lower South, David conducted a test of all eight showers for water temperature, pressure, and duration, and found considerable differences on all three points: duration ranged from ten seconds to over a minute, for example. Further complicating matters, these variables are in constant flux; one's favorite showerhead might become a scalding spray or freezing drizzle from one week or even day to the next. While cleaning the Mod 4–Lower South showers one day a few months after David's experiment, an inmate accidentally pressed one of the buttons. The shower stayed on continuously, twenty-four hours a day, for three months straight, and possibly longer—it was still running when David was released in October 2020.

In 12-Lower, the physical design of the bathroom did not allow inmates to hang bedsheets for privacy, but Mod 4's layout made it possible to string a line across the top of the entrance to the showers and hang extra sheets over it. This practice was tolerated by steady officers and most captains, but a search team would almost invariably tear the bedsheets down. In David's experiences, the Mod 4 dorms ran a "one-at-a-time" policy in the shower except when the dorm was at its most crowded, or "maxed out." As with the phones, there was never a physical line for the shower; as everyone was already confined to the same room, one's place in line was tracked verbally instead.

If he doesn't hear any showers running as he approaches the bedsheet-curtains, an inmate may simply call out, "Anybody in the shower?" If he hears water, the common practice is to instead call out, "Who got next [in the shower]?" He then finds the inmate named as next in line and asks him who is next after him, continuing to follow the line in this fashion until he comes to the last guy and informs him that he is now last in line. A similar, if simpler, practice played out during David's time in 12-Lower, where, due to the high level of crowding and the lack of bedsheet-curtains, guys generally showered two or three at a time. A person who needed to shower would poke his head into the showering area and ask one of the showering men, "Who got next?"

Most inmates carry what they need into the showers in their white buckets. White buckets are used by most men to store their hygiene items when not showering, so it is crucial to get an extra one in order to avoid having to dump their hygiene items onto their beds while showering, possibly exposing them to ambient dirt or theft. Extra white buckets are almost certain to be taken on a search. When there is a long line for the shower, a line of white buckets with towels, shampoo, soap, and so on usually appears on nearby surfaces, such as the small metal bench in the shower in 12-Lower, or the rarely used water fountain/sinks in Mod 4.

In addition to showering in their underwear, most inmates wore sandals in the shower. Though the prohibition on naked showering was a bit more relaxed in Mod 4, with its curtains and one-at-a-time policy, nearly all inmates there still showered in their underwear. Toweling off, removing one's wet underwear, and changing into dry clothes while wearing sandals and a towel was a feat of pure acrobatics. Jarrod typically walked back to his bed shirtless and clad in a towel, and performed this maneuver under the sheets.

A majority of the inmates seemed to shower every day, or every other day, and many made it loudly known that they felt others should do the same. Not showering frequently enough could get someone threatened with a forced shower, clothes and all, or a pack-up by the dorm hierarchy, though threats generally sufficed, and we never saw either of these actually enforced. An inmate who took little to no care of his personal hygiene, his clothes, or his section was likely to be given a disparaging nickname, or referred to as a "bum," "slob," or "Viking." The latter term seemed to be primarily used in the upstate prison system, but was also used and recognized by some city-time inmates.

This practice was echoed by some of the COs. Jarrod encountered one Black female CO who would regularly berate the men in the dormitory, "Your asses stink!" and demand everyone shower more. Methods of enforcement among inmates and COs alike range from passive aggression—yelling out "stinky ass feet!" or "someone shitted themselves!" to nobody in particular—to direct confrontation. Jarrod had been used to hanging out in punk rock and activist circles where natural body odors are accepted, and had not worn deodorant in years. At Rikers, he was quietly pulled aside on multiple occasions and warned that his body odor was not socially acceptable, and that he had better get some deodorant. Deciding he would go along to get along, he picked some up at commissary. The habit stuck.

Such softer methods of enforcement evince a more nuanced and compassionate application of the island's de facto hygiene standards. On one occasion, a new arrival in 1-Upper came off the streets smelling terrible, landed right in the bed next to Jarrod's, and immediately went to sleep. One of the shotcallers walked by, commenting to Jarrod, "You in a bad spot!" but assuring him that the situation would be handled. He returned with a towel, gently woke the sleeping man, and, whispering so that virtually nobody could hear, told him that he needed to shower. The man uncovered his face, and at once they recognized each other—they had been locked up together before. At this moment, in what was apparently a planned intervention, another shotcaller arrived, and was assured by his compatriot that the new arrival was alright. To help him save face, the two shotcallers even took his side against imaginary plaintiffs who had raised the case against him. "Niggas need to mind their own business!" the man grumbled on his way to the shower.

The showers were often unpredictable and dirty, sometimes smelled of urine or feces, and attracted insects like gnats and large cockroaches. Yet we found that their jets of water, when they were warm and had good pressure, offered a brief escape from the harsh and squalid world of city time. For David, this was particularly true in Mod 4, where the inmates' bedsheet-curtains and one-at-a-time policy afforded him real, if tenuous, privacy. Jarrod showered multiple times per day as a meditative activity, feeling comfortable enough to briefly close his eyes, breathe slowly, and put the place out of his mind. And though popular culture had made him averse to any sort of social interaction in a jail shower, Jarrod often found himself pleasantly conversing with other inmates about his tattoos. As far as he could tell, these exchanges were not overtures to sexual assault.

Laundry

The same imperatives that govern bodily hygiene also relate to uniforms and bedclothes. The terms "bum" or "slob" are also used for those who fail to wash their clothes or sheets often enough. Though clothes-washing services are nominally provided twice weekly at Rikers, they are, like everything, far from regular or dependable.[8] The appearance of a CO clamoring "Laundry, gentlemen, laundry!" at the entrance to the unit is at best a weekly occurrence, and the hours can change substantially from one week to the next. David sometimes observed COs briefly calling laundry pickup at 6:00 or 7:00 a.m., when few inmates were awake, and leaving without waiting for a response. At other times, the laundry crew ran out of "net bags," the mesh bags used to keep each individual's load separate, and simply stopped accepting dirty clothing.

The quality of the actual laundering is unpredictable, too. Many are reluctant to turn their clothing in to the institutional laundry services at all, given that white clothes ("whites") often come back with strange brown stains, a diffuse yellowish tint, or a mildewy smell. Greens sometimes come back bleached a couple of shades lighter; the institutional green sweatshirts were especially susceptible to bleaching and shrinkage. Those who had slightly nicer clothing articles, like luxury-brand plain white T-shirts instead of the ubiquitous Hanes and Fruit of the Loom, often worried that the laundry inmate-workers would steal them, or claimed they already had. There was also widespread revulsion at the idea of commingling the fabrics that one slept on and wore on one's body with all the dirty laundry of an entire jail building, and all its attendant blood, urine, feces, semen, sweat, and general environmental filth.

Nor are inmates guaranteed to get the same clothing back. A new arrival may not want to give up his reasonably well-fitting jumpsuit for fear of receiving a cartoonishly large one. For more established inmates, any contraband article of clothing that has somehow managed to make its way into their hands is likely to be as highly prized by its owner as it is to be confiscated if submitted to the institutional laundry service. All of this adds up to mean that most inmates wash their own laundry by hand with Corcraft soap, daily or near-daily, in their white buckets—yet another reason to procure a second white bucket as soon as possible. These unofficial laundry practices are much more reliable, and inmates may even perform them for each other, bucking the traditional carceral taboo against washing others' clothing. When an elderly prisoner in David's dorm had surgery, leaving him too weak to wash his clothes, other inmates did it for him because the institution could not be trusted to. A neighbor of Jarrod's in 12-Lower even ran a small business washing uniforms: one dollar for pants and shirts, and two dollars for jumpsuits.

All of this in-house clothes washing necessitates a lot of in-house clothes drying. Inmates quickly dominate any available dormitory real estate to dry their wet clothes. There are a wide variety of techniques for stringing clotheslines, but nearly all involve the dormitory's metal bed frames. Though sloppily coated with a layer of thick black or gray paint, the surfaces of the bed frames are so rough and irregular that a white piece of fabric, if it comes in contact with the frame while wet, will come away with faint rust spots. Entire methodologies for avoiding rust spots when drying laundry exist, as someone who wears whites with rust spots will necessarily be branded a bum or a slob. The most common is to lay a strip of plastic from a clear plastic trash bag beneath the drying laundry, preventing it from touching the bed frame directly.

Bedclothes are the only item generally not washed by hand. Too large to be draped across any of the makeshift clotheslines without touching the floor, they are always given to the institutional linen service. Linen service, different from laundry service but just as irregular, is usually announced by a CO repeatedly shouting "One sheet, one towel!"—or, rarely, "Two sheets, one towel!"—at the door to the dorm, causing a scramble to tear one's sheets from one's bed. This rush is especially pronounced when word spreads that the sheets are brand new, discernible by their factory-pressed crispness and eliciting remarks of "Them shits crispy!" When this happened in Mod 4, a few inmates who already had clean sheets on their beds might run into the bathroom, each grabbing one of the dirty bedsheet-curtains around the toilets and shower, and perform a sort of public service by exchanging them for new ones.

The standard bed setup requires two sheets: one tied around the mattress, and one atop the inmate beneath his gray wool blanket as he slept, meaning one fresh sheet a week still leaves him with a dirty one either atop or beneath him. But inmates tend to accumulate extra sheets by inheriting them when others go home, or via certain jobs like the laundry, linen, or sanitation crews. In this way, some manage to have fresh sheets every week, especially if the linen service actually comes as often as it is supposed to.

The DOC claims in the *Inmate Handbook* to issue everyone one washcloth, one pillowcase, two sheets, and two towels.[9] But in our experience, sheets and towels were usually given out one at a time, and washcloths and pillowcases were so rare that a layperson might well think the linen service was giving out free K2 on the odd occasion they were distributed. Pillowcases were likely to be claimed, inherited, and reused by inmates when a friend or acquaintance went home, either for their intended purpose or as a bag to hold books or water bottles, creating makeshift dumbbells for exercise. Washcloths, on the other hand, were almost never claimed, inherited, or recycled: besides their intended use, it was widely accepted that washcloths were the most common place for inmates to ejaculate when they managed to steal a moment's relative privacy and masturbate in the shower, toilet stall, or even under their covers after lights out. Leaving semen behind, as with any bodily detritus, could cause enormous problems for an inmate.

Washcloths were small enough to be discreetly carried into the bathroom in one's white bucket or pocket, and unobtrusively washed in one's white bucket when soiled. When hung out to dry in the very public dorm, the unfalsifiable claim that a washcloth had simply been used for washing was enough to ward off any speculation.

9

Clothing

Within the very limited set of garments available for city-time inmates, a culture of fashion nonetheless thrives, complete with the ruthless judgment of its transgressors. Rikers Island is, after all, still New York City. A person might be branded a bum or a slob for wearing his white shirts or underwear too long after they became stained from normal wear and tear. Inmates are expected to call their family and ask to be sent new clothing when needed, unless they are too poor to afford it, or have no one on the outside to call. Likewise, fresh greens without stains or tears are highly valued, especially if they look brand new. During David's time, pants with pockets were particularly coveted, as the DOC had recently begun phasing them out. Pants with pockets were never submitted to the laundry service, as inmates assumed they would be confiscated and replaced with a new but pocketless pair. There were no shorts with pockets, save those inmates had somehow managed to sew pockets into, or the odd pair of pants with pockets that had been cut off at the knee.

The DOC issues inmates two types of shirts: a simple, scrub-like V-neck T-shirt with no pocket and flared sleeves, made of heavy cotton canvas, and a lighter-weight button-down with a plain collar and breast pocket. A visitor once commented to David on a pre-COVID-19 TeleStory video visit that the latter was "very 1950s auto mechanic." The button-downs are preferred by most, as they look less ridiculous and they have a precious pocket. Of course, wearing any shirt-and-pants combination is an accomplishment at Rikers, given the green jumpsuits, or "one-pieces," that are issued upon arrival. These ill-fitting garments, which bear the letters "DOC" across the back, tug at one's body in odd ways as one moves, and make any sort of physical activity, like exercise, practically impossible. At best, they can be modified into uncomfortable pants by rolling the top half down to the waist and tying the loose fabric into a knot. One man Jarrod encountered found a good use for the jumpsuits, removing the strip of Velcro that held them shut down the front to fashion a sleek and practical belt for oversized pants.

Inmates were always quick to exchange their one-pieces, universally scorned as uncomfortable, undignified, and the mark of a new arrival, for a pair of pants and a shirt. Doing this through official channels, however, was all but unheard of: institutional clothing was rarely distributed by DOC officials, leaving those who needed it to turn to the inmate marketplace. By far the most common way of procuring new clothing was to buy it from someone who had a surplus, or to claim and inherit it when someone went home. "I just bought a pair of pants for a bag of Sun Chips," a fellow first-timer, who arrived at about the same time as David, lamented to him during their first week. "We in jail *for real*!" David himself first upgraded to a pair of pants by fishing them out of the day room trash can after another inmate went home and dumped his extra belongings. As they were a size XL and David is usually a medium, he was skeptical they would fit, but quickly found out that clothing sizes run quite small at Rikers.

Green cotton sweatshirts and canvas shorts are both seasonal. Sweatshirts, generally referred to as "sweaters," are issued in early October. In David's experience, a CO simply appeared at the gate one day and began yelling, "Sweaters, gentlemen, sweaters!" An inmate who misses this unscheduled appearance is out of luck for the entire season. Try as he might to acquire a sweater through official channels, he is highly unlikely to succeed. His best bet is to ask someone with an approaching release date to inherit his sweater when he leaves. Shorts are issued in early May, in a similarly haphazard fashion.

Sweaters are supposed to be collected by the COs when shorts are issued. They never are, but after early May, an inmate's sweater may well be confiscated on a search, in keeping with the DOC's practice of arbitrary confiscation. If he petitions to have it returned, either through formal means like filing a grievance or calling 311, or informal ones like asking one of his steady officers or captains, he is certain to be denied and told that his sweater should have been turned in when shorts were issued. The same is true for shorts: they are supposed to be collected when sweaters are issued in October. They are never collected in any organized way, but an individual might find that his shorts have been randomly confiscated between October and May, with no real recourse to get them back.

DOC staff often go to great lengths to control how or where city-time inmates can wear their clothes. Many captains and some rank-and-file COs will call out an inmate who is wearing shorts in the hallway outside of the approved May–October time frame, for example, sending him back to his housing unit to change into a pair of pants. If chastised for walking in the main hall with his shirt unbuttoned, an inmate may suck his teeth and fasten a single button, paying lip service to the policy while almost flouting it. These rules were enforced with particular zeal in C-76. In C-74, these rules were generally enforced for so-called Greens, but many DOC staff did not even try with Tans, who had no good time to lose and were likely to give defiant and sometimes vulgar responses. As a result, Tans could often be seen walking unmolested along one side of the hall in white T-shirts, tank tops, or DOC-issued knit caps (also forbidden in the main hall), while Greens, walking along the other side, were upbraided for not having enough buttons fastened.

During Jarrod's time, inmates were required to carry plastic ID cards bearing their name, photo, and book and case number everywhere they went. By David's time, ID wristbands had been introduced that included the person's name, sentencing status, New York State ID number, book and case number, religion, and mugshot beside a barcode. The ID bands were scanned upon one's entering and leaving the dorm, and upon arriving at one's destination, such as the mess hall, yard, commissary, or visiting floor. Inmates were required to wear these whenever they left the dorm, and some wore them all the time, even while sleeping. But just as many seemed to conveniently forget their ID bands every time they left the dorm for the sheer pleasure of forcing the COs to frustratedly enter the book and case number into the system by hand. Rarely did those waiting in line behind someone who had left his ID band in the dorm complain about the hold-up; they, too, enjoyed hindering the institution's pretensions at total control.

Knowing how to decipher the designs and insignia of DOC staff uniforms can be enormously valuable for inmates, and those who don't know how to interpret them will often ask others who do. Whereas a new arrival will likely be able to do little more than distinguish rank-and-file officers from white shirts, an inmate who has been in long enough can tell how long a CO has been on the job or whether a CO has had prior military service, for example, just by the CO's uniform.

Experienced inmates can likewise distinguish between the various white shirts, such as captains and deps, simply by glancing at their collar, and can identify the loathed Special Search Team all the way from the far end of the main hall, a distance of roughly four city blocks.[1]

Street Clothes

A limited number of articles of clothing can be sent to an inmate by friends or family. These garments must follow strict guidelines, which are of course enforced with great irregularity. For example, the DOC permits gym shorts, provided they are pocketless. Though not allowed outside the dormitory, gym shorts are much more comfortable for sleeping or lounging around than the stiff canvas green shorts. Most inmates who have been in for any significant amount of time have acquired a pair by mail, trade, or inheritance. Some gym shorts with pockets do manage to make it inside, past the DOC's various security screening processes, where they are highly valued despite the fact that they may be seized on a search. David had a pair of gym shorts with pockets that lasted six months and several searches before being randomly confiscated. A week later, he received another pair of gym shorts in the mail, also bearing forbidden pockets, only to have them confiscated two days later.

All undergarments, socks, T-shirts, tank tops, thermal shirts, long johns, knit caps, and gym shorts are supposed to be white, gray, or tan (or black, depending on which CO you ask), but various other colors do occasionally make it through security. All of these articles (in the sanctioned colors, of course) can be acquired through the institution by asking to go to the "Clothes Box," a sort of free secondhand clothes store in every building for inmates who don't have enough clothing. Going to the Clothes Box is generally avoided, however—it is frowned on as a sign of poverty, and given the thriving trade among inmates in an environment where people are perpetually going home and abandoning their possessions, it is not often necessary.

The only clothing item sold at commissary was simple white foam flip-flops, or "slippers," which could be purchased for eighty-seven cents. Though they were listed as "shower slippers," and people did indeed shower in them, most guys liked to wear them during the long periods of time when they were confined to the dorm, as they were more comfortable than the institutional sneakers, and easier to slip on and off. On more than one occasion Jarrod lined up to go to chow before realizing he was still wearing his shower slippers, and had to rush back to his bed to change. This is in direct contrast to most Tan (pretrial detainee) units, and especially adolescent Tan units, where inmates generally wear sneakers or boots in case conflict arises. Rarely, if a Green has a beef with another inmate in his dorm, he might keep his shoes or boots on, even sleeping in them in case he is attacked at night.

To call the slippers more comfortable than the institutional sneakers, however, is not saying much, and some guys lash an extra set of slipper soles onto their flip-flops in order to double the amount of foam between their feet and the floor. Anyone who has been in for longer than a few weeks is likely to have two sets of slippers, so that he can change out of his wet footwear once he has finished showering. The practice of stealing the sandals from the visitation floor is also extremely common; "VI slippers" are composed of comparatively thick, cushy rubber, making for a much more comfortable experience in the dorm. VI slippers are treasured, and never worn in the shower, but will almost certainly be taken on the next search. Extra pairs of regular shower slippers, on the other hand, are rarely confiscated on searches, even though inmates are technically limited to one pair each.

Certain work details also provide rare articles of clothing: SOD workers can often get thermal shirts, long johns, socks, knit caps, and work boots by asking the supervising officer on their work detail, for example. Unlike most of the clothing from the Clothes Box, these were usually still in their plastic packaging, and therefore acceptable. When the weather turned cold in mid-November, one of the SOD COs even purchased insulated orange Cabela's hunting gloves for the workers out of pocket, as the DOC only supplies the sort of cheap rubberized knit-cotton work gloves found at dollar stores and construction sites.

Though useless for insulating one's hands against the cold, these thin gloves are in extremely high demand for working out. This practice also has a social element: no one wants to be the "nasty" guy who works out with no gloves. There is technically a blanket prohibition on work gloves in the dorms, and they will almost certainly be confiscated on a search. But because the SOD and sanitation jobs and certain programs and classes afford access to them, they are always present to some degree. Some work-detail COs even instructed their workers to take their gloves back to their dorms, for lack of anywhere else to store them, simply supplying them with new pairs when they were confiscated.

Air Patakis

Shoes, unlike clothes, run large on Rikers. David, who is usually a size 13, found himself wearing size 11 work boots and tennis shoes. Like work gloves, the black work boots given out by some work details are technically not allowed in the housing units, but are smuggled back in so often that they are always present in the dorms. Work boots were generally confiscated on searches in the Six, but not in the Four, where there was sometimes such a surplus of brand-new boots, still in their plastic packaging, that inmates gave them away to others, or sold them for very cheap. Anyone who has been in for any significant length of time is likely to have a pair, even if he doesn't have a job that requires them, or even a job at all. Cheap, clunky, and terribly uncomfortable, the boots are so poorly made that the black tint inside rubs off onto inmates' white socks with every use, and the faux-leather upper begins to flake off after only a week. But boots are generally accepted as the best thing to wear if one has to fight, as they have more grip, ankle stability, and weight than the standard-issue black-canvas tennis shoes. Many inmates buy into this hype, wearing boots more to appear ready for a fight than because of any pressing need to defend themselves.

The standard-issue black-canvas tennis shoes, given to every inmate upon his arrival, are essentially the New York State carceral apparatus's knockoff version of the Chuck Taylor All-Star. Comically thin and flimsy, with a simple waffle pattern on the sole, they lack any support at the arch or ankle, and bear only three plain Velcro strips for fastening. They are colloquially referred to as "Patakis" or "Air Patakis" in sarcastic homage to Governor George Pataki, whose policies, alongside Rudy Giuliani's during his tenure as mayor of New York City, led to a massive increase in the state's incarcerated population. Whether Patakis had actually been invented during Pataki's tenure, no one seemed to know or care. Air Patakis are so painful to run or exercise in that some inmates actually prefer to wear their work boots to the yard. WNYC reported in 2011 that an "improved" Air Pataki was in the works, but the Rikers old heads we met claimed that the sneakers hadn't changed a bit in decades, save for the addition of Velcro straps.[2]

There is a rare modified version of the Pataki with thick translucent tan soles, issued to inmates with severe mental health issues. Though usually housed in Bellevue's criminal psych ward, they may circulate in and out of the general population at Rikers during their detention or sentence. A guy wearing these souped-up Patakis, with much better arch support and, of course, the draw of being a novelty item, is generally regarded with a dose of suspicion, because they also imply that the wearer is a so-called bugout. He may just have bought them from another inmate, but then again, he might be "MO *for real*," meaning a prisoner with serious mental health issues.

DOC policy also allows for three models of Puma brand sneakers, in black or white only, to be sent in to an inmate. David almost never witnessed shoes other than Patakis or work boots in the Six, and rarely came across guys wearing Pumas there. In keeping with the Six's reputation as being by far the most tightly controlled space on Rikers Island, inmates there had to go to the clinic and get a doctor's written approval to request that a pair of Pumas be sent in to them. In the Four, on the other hand, he found that any inmate was allowed to have Pumas sent to him, and quickly took advantage of this variance to upgrade his footwear. Pumas generally had to be sent in from outside; unlike most other items, guys generally did not give away their Pumas when they left. Yet they were fairly common in the Four. Anyone who was still wearing only Patakis or work boots after several months there was generally suspected to be a drug addict, mentally ill, and/or extremely poor. While these are of course all very common characteristics of prisoners throughout Rikers, inmate culture places a very high premium on not appearing to be any of them.

David also witnessed significant trade in shoes other than Patakis, Pumas, or work boots in the Four. These seemed to make their way in from the outside world via new arrestees. New arrestees, especially if they were detained and not sentenced, might "stick it up" when being processed through Intake and refuse to hand over their shoes. Or, if they did, an enterprising inmate-worker stationed at Intake might pull them from the trash can or the corner of the bullpen, smuggle them back to the housing unit, and wear them or resell them for a fraction of their street value, but an enormous profit in jail. A number of COs were rumored to do the same. Flashy street shoes ran a very high risk of being confiscated on a search, especially given the possibility that a CO might take them with the specific intention of reselling them elsewhere in the building. But to an astonishing number of inmates, the benefit of having stylish footwear, and the jailhouse prestige they brought, were worth the high price and the near certainty of their being confiscated within a few months at best.

There is a long history of contraband clothing being used to both recapture identity and signal status. In a 1962 paper, John Irwin and Donald R. Cressey detail their social function in California prisons, and the name given to contraband couture: "bonaroo," from red "bonnet rouge" caps once worn by trustees in French prisons to distinguish themselves from the ordinary inmates. As these scholars emphasized, a prisoner being able to procure these items, and to get away with wearing them in the presence of COs without their immediate seizure, made them a status symbol.[3]

Jail Fashion

Those who don't have Pumas or fancy street shoes can still add some swag to their footwear by carefully removing the outer layer of black canvas on their Air Patakis' Velcro straps. Patakis are made from recycled fabrics of all colors, patterns, weights, and textures. With a banger, a sharp-edged surface, or even just a pen and a little persistence, an inmate can easily pick apart the shoddy sewing and pull back the black canvas on the uppermost side of the straps, exposing the fabric beneath.

This practice was more common in the tightly regulated space of C-76, where David watched numerous inmates modify their footwear in this way out of sheer boredom and a desire to wear something other than what they had been issued—which was also, of course, an implicit thumbing of the nose at the DOC. The moment the underlying fabric was revealed was always one of excitement, like unwrapping a tiny gift. From safety green to shiny silver to camouflage, the interiors of the Pataki Velcro straps brought a satisfying element of variety to the environment.

On one occasion, David even witnessed a guy tear the interior strip of fabric out and sell it to another who was irresistibly attracted to its design.

Other jail fashion trends during David's time included splashing one's greens with bleach, available via certain jobs, for a sort of splattered, single-tone tie-dye effect, and distressing one's pants in parallel horizontal lines above the knee, mimicking the popular style of "biker" jeans, with layered ribbing around the knees, in the outside world. This distressed-pants look was rare among Greens, but common among adolescent Tans in C-74. Distressed pants, like cutoff shorts, begged the question of *how* the pants were cut, implying that the wearer perhaps possessed a banger. While this effect could be achieved without a banger, by pulling the garment along the rough edge of a surface in the dorm, and any clothing item might have been purchased or inherited from another inmate, these modifications served an effective double function as fashion statement and mild warning to others, signaling the possibility that the wearer was armed.

On Rikers, religious wear, since it technically cannot be confiscated, is often adopted by nonreligious or only nominally religious inmates as a way of expressing personal style, or establishing some control over their appearance. Rosary beads, for example, are often worn by nonpracticing Catholics, Protestants, and those who seem to have no religious persuasion at all. Rosaries can easily be obtained from the Catholic chaplains, but a person need not be registered as Catholic, or even speak to the chaplain, to acquire one: others generally leave them behind when they are released, so there are always plenty in circulation. Kufis, too, some with very ornate patterning, are worn by non-Muslims or those who are only nominally Muslim, especially in spaces where inmates socialize with those from other housing units, like the hallways, mess hall, and yard. The same held true for yarmulkes.

This is not to say that these religious ornaments were never worn in good faith by people who actually subscribed to the belief systems they represented, but that they had much wider use among the nonreligious for purely stylistic reasons. Sometimes these religious trappings, adopted as secular style, also took on gang significance. For example, in 12-Lower, rosary beads were carefully taken apart, colored blue with stolen paint, and sold to the Crips who ran the dorm by two non-gang-affiliated

Latinos. Their business extended well beyond gang-affiliated clientele, too: often, carefully restringing a line of plastic beads in a more intricate pattern was enough to sell a necklace. Some inmates who had managed to acquire a needle, or something they could use as a needle, even ran businesses repairing torn clothes, taking pant legs in, or even sewing pockets into the pocketless DOC shorts. Though these sorts of services, which might broadly be labeled "jewelry making" or "tailoring," were not always present in the dorms, they could be found semiregularly.

Transitional Objects

There are other accessories that come from the outside world or else provide a connection to it in a setting otherwise defined by persistent emphasis on one's captivity. These can be classed as what psychoanalyst Donald Winnicott terms "transitional objects," items from a previous age or social environment that ease one's transition into a new, often intimidating setting.[4] Jewelry, especially small pieces like piercings, wedding rings, and even necklaces and bracelets, all make it into Rikers from the outside world. None of these are technically permitted except wedding rings, which are supposed to have a value of $150 or less.[5] How exactly the DOC plans to implement on-the-spot wedding-band appraisals for every new arrival is left to the imagination. In practice, in our experience, those wearing wedding bands upon arrival generally kept them, no matter the value.

The same held true for glasses: though they were supposed to be generic, plastic, verified by the clinic, and, according to some COs, have a value of fifty dollars or less, all sorts of makes and models could be found, including luxury brands and metal frames.[6] Glasses could also be obtained through the institution if one was willing to make an eye-exam trip to West Facility—a dreaded all-day affair that entailed spending several hours in the pens on both ends of a bus ride in shackles, followed by a three-week wait to actually receive them.

Permitted personal items like wedding bands, and unpermitted ones, like purely ornamental jewelry, often provided a valuable sense of identity and connection to the outside world for inmates. As the initial intake process strips a new arrival of his identity and replaces it with a new one, defined partly by the institution and partly by his place in the inmate social world, having a reminder of who he was in the outside world can be enormously important for his sense of self.

Unpermitted jewelry was much more common in the Four than in the Six. In the tightly regimented environment of the Six, whose captive population rarely misbehaved for fear of losing good time, there was an expectation and an acceptance that these things would be lost in Intake. COs in the Six knew that the sentenced men in their custody wanted to go home as soon as possible, and were therefore unlikely to "stick it up" for their personal items during the intake process. Thus, while the COs in other buildings might not even bother to ask a new arrival to surrender these items, the COs in the Six not only asked but expected new arrivals to comply, which they generally did.

In other buildings, this was hardly the case. In the Four, David witnessed a much greater number of pieces of unpermitted outside jewelry, and when he asked the wearers how they had managed to bring the items through Intake, they usually responded that they had refused to comply ("stuck it up"), or that the intake COs had not even asked about them. Unpermitted jewelry in the Four, especially items retained by sticking it up, was much more common among Tans than Greens, in keeping with Tans' comparative readiness to buck the rules and Greens' general conformity. But David noticed that even sentenced inmates in the Four tended to have more unpermitted jewelry, in contrast to the Six, where he hardly saw any at all unless it had been crafted inside the jail itself. This is the case because the more lax rule-enforcement standards of COs who worked in a building with mostly Tans, like the Four, naturally tend to trickle down to Greens as well. A sentenced inmate who was processed through Intake in the Four, then, might never be asked about his earrings or bracelet, while in the Six these items would almost certainly be taken.

The most valuable articles of clothing by far are those that manage to make their way in from the street, bringing some variety to the dorm. Besides outside workers' orange jumpsuits, the green uniforms of city-time inmates, and the tan ones of pretrial detainees, the only clothing colors on Rikers are white, black, and gray. Anything that differs even mildly is an automatic eye catcher: T-shirts with logos, intricately patterned or brightly colored gym shorts, sweatpants, or durags. Even socks or underwear can be status symbols, as the use of clotheslines in the dorm means that inmates generally see all of each other's laundry.

It is not only bright or patterned garments that are valued, either: for example, David once paid another inmate two dollars for a plain black knit cap salvaged from the corner of an intake pen. The institution only issues orange knit caps to sentenced men (detainees are sometimes given brown ones), and even those are only given to inmates with outside job details. Though some COs told David that his black cap was permitted, and it survived several months of searches, other COs told him that it was technically contraband. Its official status notwithstanding, David's cap was very rare, and he was constantly hounded by other inmates asking him if they could have it when he went home. People paid good money for things like this, sometimes for comfort, and sometimes for the sheer pleasure of feeling more stylish, wealthy, or socially important than others. Declaring yourself an individual, distinct from others who have been similarly dehumanized and ascribed a string of digits after their name, is itself rewarding in this environment.

Unpermitted personal items from the street like these might also be transitional objects for inmates; they might have deep personal significance, or give the possessor a badly needed sense of connection to his home, his loved ones, or simply the outside world at large. They might also be used to denote gang affiliation; David met Bloods who had somehow managed to bring in red articles of clothing, like durags and sweatpants, and Crips who had somehow managed to bring in blue ones. Even unpermitted articles of clothing that do have strong personal significance or advertise gang allegiance, however, often end up passed down or resold when the possessor goes home, with the exception of socks and underwear. And of course, anything unpermitted, no matter how important it may be to an inmate, is liable to be randomly snatched on the next random search.

Hairstyles

One of the only benefits of spending time incarcerated on Rikers is the price of haircuts: a mere two dollars. It is common practice to tip the barber another one or two dollars in commissary goods, and considered rude not to. Trips to the barber are a supposedly weekly, but actually highly irregular affair. Many look forward to them, not only as an opportunity to get cleaned up but as an excuse to leave the dorm and interact with the barbers, who are generally inmates from other housing units. But with the low price comes high risk—haircuts on Rikers are a notorious gamble, and an inmate never knows if he is going to get what he requested or something totally different.

There are no scissors on Rikers; if it can't be done with a buzzer, it can't be done at all. Many men with dreads, braids, cornrows, or other more intricate hairdos never make trips to the barbershop at all, knowing they will not get enough time there, or refusing on principle to have another man do their hair. Many Black men for whom this is true develop a characteristic mini-afro beneath their dreads or braids, from which it is possible to estimate how long they have been incarcerated.

A lot of inmates, whatever their hairstyle, simply choose to let their hair grow. They will get a cut when they are back on the street, they say. But just as many make great efforts to go to the barbershop as often as possible, as control over their appearance—specifically, how neat they appear—gives them a broader sense of self-respect and control over their lives in a place where these things are hard to come by. Many also insist on getting a haircut in the days before their release date—they want to look good for their "girl" when they come home, they often explain.

Some inmates also buck the homophobic practice of refusing to let another man touch their hair and take advantage of the island's many amateur aestheticians. They may simply be maintaining an intricate hairstyle, or if they have long enough hair, they may decide to get one while inside. Anything that can be done with no equipment beyond a comb, such as dreadlocks, braids, twists, cornrows, or Bantu knots, can be performed by one inmate on another, as long as the inmate is willing to sit still in the dorm, in the yard, or even during downtime at work. David sometimes saw some men getting their hair worked on in the kitchen. Jarrod encountered a man who gave elaborate haircuts using only the dull inmate razor, staring intently at his subjects' heads and slowly whittling away with the patience and poise of a sculptor. For these men, even the risk of being slandered as "gay" does not outweigh the benefit of having some control over their appearance and feeling good about how they look.

10

Substance Abuse and Mental Health

"Last day, baby!" David's neighbor exclaims gleefully as he rifles through his bucket, pulling out a towering stack of ramen noodles and fish packets. "Last day! Chasing the bag all day today."

"You cooking?" David asks, confused, jutting his chin over the top of an open book toward his neighbor's pile of commissary food. It is 11:00 a.m., and though the man just woke up a few minutes ago, an odd time to prepare a meal. In all probability, they will be calling chow any minute. It is also quite a lot of food for one person, and David has never seen the guy share a meal with anyone.

"Hell no!" he responds. "I'm chasing the bag!" he chirps again happily, before scurrying off and throwing the edible currency down on another inmate's bed.

"The bag" is a catch-all Rikers slang term for drugs. "Chasing the bag," then, means "looking for drugs" or "trying to get high." David's neighbor, having bought into a soon-to-be-rolled K2 joint with his commissary items, was well on his way to spending his final hours in jail as high as he could afford to be.

Substance abuse is extremely common among the city-time population, both while free and while at Rikers. We both would have had an easy time getting our hands on some drugs, though neither of us used that method to pass our time. Substance abuse is a source of recreation, a removal activity, and a time strategy in itself, though a costly one. But just as on the outside, it also can go hand in hand with mental illness, as people experiencing severe emotional distress find few outlets to relieve their suffering besides temporary, chemical-induced escape.

Paper Plane

K2 is a proprietary eponym for so-called synthetic marijuana, a potent chemical concoction marketed as replicating the effects of marijuana.

The drug is largely composed of synthetic cannabinoids, which can resemble compounds found in marijuana, and its initial effects seem to be similar in a number of ways.[1] After smoking, users often appear hazy and happy or even giddy, albeit slightly confused. Some lie in bed, staring off into space, or find a chair in the day room where they can sit and watch TV, perhaps snacking on cookies or chips from commissary. David soon learned to identify when one of his neighbors was high on K2 by the way his hair looked: when high, he would sit on the edge of his bed, smiling vacantly at the wall and combing it into a sort of clumsy mohawk with his fingers.

The preferred mixer for K2 consumption is black tea. Not the Bromley's Earl Grey or English Breakfast available at commissary, though these will do in a pinch, but the DOC-issued Golden Tip tea in its bland white paper packets. This is available only from the mess hall or kitchen, and therefore only obtainable by theft. Theft of teabags is so low on the DOC's list of enforcement priorities, however, that it never brings any punishment. If caught, a guy with something like tea, fruit, or milk on his person can generally expect to have his goods confiscated, but it is unheard of for an inmate to be issued a ticket for this sort of trafficking.

Once the tea is procured and smuggled back into the dorm, the K2 smokers will rip a page from a pocket Bible, tear a corner from the bag of Golden Tip, and sprinkle it onto the middle of the page. They then place tiny square pieces of K2-soaked paper (and the stubs of their old K2 spliffs) atop the tea in a neat little line, and roll it up like a joint or cigarette, sealing the gumless paper with a healthy dose of saliva.

Lighting this creation is another multistep process. First, the smokers will need a battery—either of the two varieties available in commissary, AA or AAA, will do, as long as the battery is relatively fresh. The coating of the battery is scratched off somewhere along the length of the cylinder to allow access to the metal casing and cathode beneath, usually by rubbing it against a wall or metal bed frame. Next is a piece of wire. The most common way to obtain one of these is to take the twist ties from a newly opened box of trash bags; certain jobs afford access to these. Headphone wires also work, though these are valuable if they are still functional. Lastly, the smokers need a wick—something to catch the battery's charge and ignite. This is usually a strand of loose cotton yarn from a mop head. The mop must be unused: while smokers do not shy away from things that have been trafficked via "boofing" (carrying in the rectum), or soaked in another person's saliva, lighting their cigarette with a strand from a dirty mop is entirely taboo.

To achieve ignition, one end of the wire is touched to the bare spot on the battery and the other to the negative end. The cotton wick, pinched between either one of them, will absorb enough of the current to burst into flames. Dangling it from its nonburning end, the smokers will then light their plane and puff. The smoking of a K2 joint is thus invariably accompanied by the smell of burning Bible paper, burning cotton, and burning tea. Depending on how lenient the CO on duty is, some houses can reek of this smell all day.

The sheer ingenuity of this technique is not lost on inmates. As Jarrod sat for hours in the intake pen, the meandering discussion turned to a spirited debate of whether the pyramids were built by Egyptians or aliens from outer space. One inmate, a History Channel enthusiast, was pushing hard for the latter hypothesis, claiming that humans could not have possibly transported and arranged the massive stones. Several men took offense on humanity's behalf and defended the Egyptians. Meanwhile, a new arrival asked if anyone minded if he lit up some K2. Nobody objected, and he produced his DIY lighter kit and got to work.

"Look at all of us sitting here with nothing to do," argued one inmate. "People did that stuff when they worked together and used their heads, my dude."

An older inmate agreed. "Think about lighting a cigarette with a battery and wire," he said, gesturing toward the K2 smoker. "How the fuck you gonna think of that? But somebody did!"

This is a common scene, as the use of K2 is positively rampant inside Rikers, even if the number of users and the frequency of use in a given dorm vary greatly depending on a number of factors. David spent time in dorms where there was no K2 at all for weeks at a time; in other dorms, he was one of only two or three people who abstained, out of a total of two dozen inmates or more. While those who smoke K2 in the outside world generally smoke it for its incredibly cheap and accessible high, those incarcerated smoke it not because it is affordable (in jail, it's not) but because it is perhaps the ideal drug to smuggle inside. A colorless, odorless, tasteless liquid, K2 is all but impossible to detect, and does not show up in the urinalysis drug tests DOC uses. Any sheet of paper can be saturated with K2 and mailed in as a letter (or carried in by COs). As long as a letter does not raise the mail CO's suspicions, it will then make it into the housing units, where it will be smoked or resold by the recipient.

K2 smoking in Rikers is a highly social event. Of course, it is impossible to hide most behavior in the jail environment, and smoking K2 alone could invite unwanted attention in the form of bullies demanding a cut, so-called sneak thieves looking for a valuable score, or simply other K2 users who feel snubbed. But K2 users seem to prefer the company of others when smoking for the sheer pleasure of getting intoxicated together. It is not uncommon for a new arrival to the dorm to be offered to partake in a K2 joint as a welcoming gift. The same way one might invite a friend out for drinks or over for a joint, K2 smokers will notify those regular members of their smoking circle when they are preparing to withdraw into the bathroom and light up. As one of the most common nicknames for K2 is "paper plane" or simply "plane," one of their favorite jokes before smoking is to notify another smoker with some variation of "Yo, you got a flight to catch, bro!" Similarly, a K2 smoker who wants to know when his cohorts next plan to smoke may politely inquire, "What time does the flight depart?" Other nicknames for the drug include "deuce" and "spice." Those who have deuce to smoke will usually solicit a buy-in payment from others who wish to smoke but don't have any K2 of their own, paid, of course, in the form of commissary items.

Many plane users compare its effects to those of marijuana, and its most stalwart advocates insist it is "the same thing." Though the euphoria may feel similar to some, many of the effects are much different. Rikers plane users, for example, accept the occasional K2-induced seizure as a simple fact of life. Referred to as "getting stuck" (as in a "frozen" movie or video game) or "catching an epi" (epileptic seizure), these episodes can have serious consequences, including sending the sufferer to the clinic and, once it is discovered that he was smoking deuce, a punitive search of the housing unit in the following days. To avoid "making the house hot" and bringing down a retributive search, the other smokers will usually sit the "stuck" person down on a toilet, as their smoking almost invariably occurs in the bathroom, and wait for him to ride it out. Despite the serious risks, plane smokers often joke about these drug-induced seizures. "You gotta put two stamps in it, you really tryna feel that epi," David once overheard one smoker tell another as he rolled a K2 joint. (A "stamp" is a postage-stamp-sized piece of K2-soaked paper.)

Different batches of K2 seem to produce wildly different effects, too. Sometimes the smokers will stumble out of the bathroom doubled over in fits of giggly laughter, or screaming at each other, or dancing to music that doesn't exist. Some wave to imagined strangers in the distance, or even hold entire conversations with them. Some become intensely paranoid, whipping their heads over their shoulders with wild eyes and furrowed brows. Some tremble uncontrollably, vomit, withdraw into themselves, pass out, or wield invisible instruments.

Over time, the effects of regular K2 use become more pronounced. Users become lethargic, irritable, and short-tempered, with a perpetual brain fog, reduced to "zombies" who amble between snacking, sleeping, hallucinating, and bursts of outrage. David spent five months living with an inmate named Mike who at first only dabbled in occasional plane use but soon began smoking it several times a day. Once a quick-witted practical joker with an infectious laugh, in a matter of weeks he became cagey, dull, selfish, and unable to string together complex thoughts. His laugh was reduced to a husky chuckle, his penchant for pranks transformed into threatening outbursts at those he imagined had disrespected him—and always, he wanted to know when the next K2 joint would be smoked.

"He's a zombie, bro," another inmate, who had known Mike for the same length of time, once commented. "He's weak. It's not like old jail. You s'posta be on yo' shit all the time. How can you be on yo' shit if you passed out on the toilet? You s'posta be a soldier, bro, s'posta keep yo' head on a swivel. These niggas smokin' deuce every day . . ." He sighed. "I'll smoke the sticky, but not that shit." His criticism, that smoking K2 emasculates users by rendering them unfit to defend themselves, is a common one among nonsmokers of the drug. Interestingly enough, the common description of serious K2 users as "zombies" mirrors a common cultural practice on the outside, described by scholar Travis Linnemann, by which drug users are represented as the living dead—and hence, subject to rightful disposal by US police.[2]

Just as those who smoke deuce in jail are frowned upon by some of their incarcerated peers, those who smoke it on the outside are looked down upon by most, including many who smoke it themselves in jail. The latter claim to smoke K2 only because it is available to them, and because they are in dire need of escaping, if only mentally, the confines of their incarceration and its attendant boredom. They would use marijuana (or crack, or heroin, or alcohol) instead if they could get it, they claim, sometimes deriding those who smoke plane in the outside world as "baseheads," an old term analogous to "crackhead."

Hooch and Other Drugs

Marijuana was the only other drug from the outside world that we observed in Rikers, and its appearance was fairly rare. Its sporadic presence was usually announced by the telltale smell of its smoke wafting through the dorm, usually met with under-the-breath commentary among the inmates: "Someone got that sticky, huh?" Like K2 and other illicit substances, the presence of marijuana in Rikers begs the question of how it gets in there in the first place.

Though small numbers of staff can smuggle in disproportionate amounts of contraband, it doesn't only come through the COs' entrance.[3] On two occasions, David witnessed a new inmate arrive in the dorm and tell the house hierarchy that he had marijuana in his "suitcase," or rectum. In both cases the bearer was immediately told to "make something happen" and escorted into the bathroom. There he sat on a toilet and pushed out the package, surrounded by those belonging to (or tolerated by) the inmate hierarchy and eager to smoke. Some urged the arrivant to hurry up, lest they attract the attention of the floor officer, or worse, a captain making rounds.

Once excreted, the weed was then rolled up in a Bible page and hastily smoked, each participant getting only perhaps two drags before it was gone. It was unclear in either case if the bearer had been compensated for his weed. It would make little sense for him to try to keep it to himself even if not being compensated, as any attempt to smoke it would immediately give him away due to the smell. Thus, it may well have been more worthwhile for him to build some social capital by offering his weed to those in charge. It was also unclear in either case if all the weed had been smoked in one go, or if a portion had been kept for later enjoyment. Keeping a portion, of course, entailed hiding it somewhere where it would not be discovered by a search, a significantly more difficult feat than stashing plane, given marijuana's strong odor.

At his going-away party two days before he turned himself in, David was gifted an eighth of high-grade marijuana by a stranger who had learned of his case, and revealed that he had been previously incarcerated on Rikers Island himself. When David protested that he could not consume the entire eighth before he turned himself in, the generous man responded, "Do what you can." David took this as a suggestion that he smoke what he could in two days and leave the rest. But after his arrival on Rikers, David ran into a guy he recognized from their neighborhood, and who, as it happened, actually knew the man who had given David the marijuana at his going-away party. When David relayed this story to him, he insisted that his friend's comment, "do what you can," had been an invocation to David to smuggle the remaining weed into jail in his rectum. A number of other inmates who were present at the time unanimously agreed. David, for his part, did not consider his failure to do so a missed opportunity.

Weed, besides being more detectable, is significantly more prized than plane, and therefore significantly more expensive. A single gram, which might cost fifteen dollars on the outside, is several orders of magnitude more expensive, perhaps as much as a hundred dollars depending on internal market factors. Smoking weed at Rikers also requires dedication. The smell is a dead giveaway to COs, and other inmates, no matter how much tobacco is added to the mix—usually a lot. This means risking exposure to shakedowns from other inmates and invasive dorm searches. The Bible paper burns very quickly, immolating a very pricey piece of plant in half the usual time. Inmates are also subjected to random drug testing, which can result in box time and the loss of good time, prolonging their sentence.

In short, smoking weed at Rikers means making a big commitment to that particular high. Jarrod met a few people who managed to smoke regularly, especially in the intake dormitory, which was closest to the street. But the average smoker was more occasional, holding on to small amounts over time and breaking it out for special occasions, like friends' departures or holidays. On New Year's Eve, for example, David observed several joints being smoked in addition to the widespread consumption of "hooch," or homemade alcohol.

Hooch is usually an opaque yellow-orange or red-orange slurry with a trademark funky vinegar smell and tart, grapefruit-like taste. It is made primarily from oranges but often sweetened with stolen white sugar, or the sugar-free powdered juice packets sold at commissary. Hooch is also sometimes made more potent by the addition of any number of prescription drugs from the clinic, when available. Hooch is available only intermittently, as it takes two to three weeks to make, during which time it may be confiscated on a search, or, if stashed somewhere outside the dorm, such as the hooch maker's workplace, discovered and enjoyed by other inmates. Ready batches of hooch also tend to disappear quickly, as people are eager for its intoxicating effects. The ever-present fear of losing one's hooch to a random search also drives rapid consumption; a batch may be consumed in only a day or two. Though it is often shared with friends free of charge, it is usually sold by the bottle at a premium to those further socially removed from those who produce it.

Hooch is usually consumed during the daytime. Inmates have nowhere to go and little to occupy their minds, and it is all but impossible to enjoy any sort of secondary activity while imbibing—like watching TV—after lights out, when the dorm is dark and the day room closed. This, coupled with the greater likelihood of creating conflict by getting drunk and belligerent while others are trying to sleep at night, means most hooch drinkers do so in broad daylight, often starting as soon as they wake up in the morning and shuffling through the day in a drunken haze until they fall asleep midafternoon. Their consumption is often oddly public: hooch is usually kept in reused clear plastic bottles, and is therefore very easy to identify with its distinct cloudy, yellowish color. But most COs and even some captains choose to ignore the drink's consumption completely. On several occasions, David witnessed men talking on the phone, sipping from bottles of hooch as they did, even as a captain made rounds in the dorm. The inmates know which DOC staff actually care about hooch, and simply keep it out of their sight.

There is widespread trafficking and recreational use of what seemed like all the drugs available through legitimate channels in jail, including prescription medications and drugs designed for managing withdrawal from other drugs. In the intake dorm, Jarrod noticed a much higher volume of pills than in the residence dorms, including stray pills on the floor. A recreational pill user remarked to him, "I'm finding pills all over the place. I wish I had my phone to look up what they are!" Other inmates regularly approached David with pills they had found and asked him to identify them because he "looked smart."

Most pills had to be obtained by a visit to the clinic. But this was no small feat. David was surprised to find that, contrary to the conventional wisdom that carceral authorities are glad to keep inmates as tranquilized as possible with prescription drugs, most city-time inmates decried the doctors' extreme reluctance to prescribe anything at all—a claim that was generally confirmed by his personal experience. The walls of the clinic at C-76 bore paper signs ordering patients not to even ask their doctors for prescription painkillers or muscle relaxers, or a note recommending they be allowed a second mattress or more comfortable shoes. The COs in 12-Lower would occasionally give inmates ibuprofen from their stash in the Bubble, but even that medication usually required a trip to the clinic and convincing a doctor.

When inmates criticize this tight-fisted approach, the responses by the DOC or Correctional Health Services (CHS) staff tend to rely on the argument that inmates will abuse any drug they can get their hands on, and should therefore be kept away from all drugs unless absolutely necessary. Drug use is certainly rampant in jail, and some men will indeed abuse any drug they can get their hands on. Some even crush up and snort ibuprofen or melatonin tablets (commonly prescribed as a sleep aid). Though a few claim to experience a brief rush from this, most admit to being addicted to the behavior itself of snorting powder up their nose, and to snort pills with no intoxicating effects purely for that reason. In general, however, these behaviors are comparatively rare, and the institution's reticence to distribute medicine causes a great deal of preventable suffering.

A handful of people in the dorm at any given moment seemed to be prescribed the most coveted drugs. There is Remeron, or "Rems," an antidepression medicine that makes people sleepy as a side effect, in high demand on the jail market as a sleep aid. Rarely, a patient may be prescribed Xanax for anxiety, or muscle relaxants for severe or chronic muscular pain—both likewise frequently circulated on the jailhouse market.

The exception to the DOC's general prescription reluctance is opioid maintenance drugs intended for habitual heroin users, which are extremely easy to come by. A newly incarcerated person need only claim to use heroin during the intake process, and that person can choose between a prescription for methadone or a prescription for Suboxone, at a strength also of their choosing. Methadone is, confusingly, sometimes known as "meth" among inmates. Further complicating matters, methadone users are occasionally referred to as "methheads"—this despite the fact that there are also methamphetamine addicts on Rikers, if comparatively few.

Methadone has been available in the DOC system to anyone who asks for it since 1971, and seems to serve the tranquilizing or disciplinary function mentioned above. It would be difficult for any modern observer, sitting in a dormitory where dozens of men sleep through the day, to conclude otherwise. Prison scholar Jennifer Wynn argues that the Key Extended Entry Program, or KEEP, is a medical failure that simply keeps inmates pacified and nourishes addictions they return to on the streets.[4] It may surprise contemporary readers that KEEP was actually an early victory for the public health movement advocating so-called methadone detoxification as an alternative to brutal cold-turkey withdrawal in designated areas of the city jails, where large numbers of inmates experiencing withdrawal were quarantined together. While methadone had been approved by the City Council in 1969, the DOC dragged its feet in implementing the program, and it was only the city-wide jail rebellion of 1970 that forced the department to act.[5]

Today, KEEP combines "methadone maintenance" (as opposed to detoxification) doses with social-work options for the inmate upon release.[6] Methadone itself is commonly called "KEEP" by both COs and inmates in the Six. In the other buildings on the island, it is called "DOT," for "Directly Observed Treatment," as methadone is supposed to be swallowed in front of a clinician. Twice a day, once early in the morning and once in the evening, escort COs arrive at the dorm gate and call out "KEEP!" or "D-O-T!" Those taking methadone usually mill around in a loose line by the door well in anticipation of this moment, and rush down the hall as soon as the gate is opened. Others stay in bed until the call, and promptly return to bed when they come back from the clinic, no matter the time of day.

A delay in the calling of methadone treatment can give rise to downright riotous behavior among those to whom it has been prescribed, including banging on or kicking the gate or the Bubble, or even screaming at the steady officer. Fistfights over who is first in line are not uncommon, despite the fact that the drug seems to be administered in a semirandom fashion. Once they arrive in the clinic, KEEP users are packed into a holding cage, and then called out individually—sometimes in the order in which they arrived in the clinic, sometimes not—to receive their dose. After they have taken their methadone, patients become lethargic and spacey, often quite literally nodding out, eyes fluttering, mouths hanging open, as they read a book or watch TV. Because methadone also causes difficulty urinating, these inmates can often be found passed out standing up at the toilet at night.

Methadone in Rikers is served as a clear, syrupy liquid. Though the administering clinician is supposed to "directly observe" each patient's consumption, a small number of methadone recipients are able to hold the liquid in their mouths without being detected. Once out of sight, they produce a small plastic bag or glove and spit the methadone out into it. The "juice" is then resold to another inmate, who drinks this admixture of methadone and saliva to get high.

Some of those who buy juice are already on methadone themselves, but want to take more at will throughout the day, or feel their prescription is not high enough. Inmates have a surprising amount of freedom to choose the concentration of methadone they want, from as low as 5 milligrams up to 220 milligrams. For a heavy heroin user, for example, even 220 milligrams might be enough to stave off the worst effects of withdrawal, but not quite enough to get him his coveted high.

Other juice buyers may be addicts who hid their addiction from the court and jail system, for whatever reason, during their arrest and intake process, or who were never asked about their addiction, or else nonaddicts who occasionally want to get high recreationally or to help themselves fall asleep. It is even rumored that some savvy inmates who do not use heroin will claim to use it during the intake process in order to get a methadone prescription and make money reselling it to others. David met one man who claimed not to have ever used heroin, and to have gotten addicted to methadone in jail because he had faked a heroin addiction in order to get a softer plea deal. (Many inmates talk about receiving significantly better plea deals if they claim to be struggling with drug addiction.) Mandated treatment had been a part of his deal, and so he had ended up in the clinic, a nurse watching him expectantly, a line of impatient addicts behind him, and a cup of methadone syrup in his hand.

The other option for opioid addiction treatment is Suboxone (a combination of buprenorphine and naloxone), also known as "Subs" or more commonly, "Chinita." Inmates have a choice between Suboxone film strips and tablets, and, unlike with methadone, are given their medicine to take on their own schedule. Many prefer the tablets because they can be crushed up and snorted. Though Suboxone is designed to counter this sort of abuse, many still claim to experience an energetic, upbeat high, much less disorienting and sedating than taking Suboxone orally as intended.[7] Though these users claim not to feel strung out or jittery, they talk and move at a disorientingly fast pace, and seem to have trouble staying focused, as if they have consumed an enormous amount of coffee in a short amount of time.

It is common knowledge on Rikers that Suboxone is also designed to induce nausea in people simultaneously using heroin or anything resembling it at the chemical level, including methadone. If combined with other opioids, Suboxone will provoke precipitated withdrawal, including nausea, vomiting, and even flu-like symptoms.[8] Yet some inmates insist on risking this in their quest for intoxication. The result is occasional violent vomiting in the bathroom. Nonetheless, Subuxone remains in demand, and takes on the quality of an illicitly traded drug. Furtive calls of "Chinita" were not uncommon in spaces where inmates from different housing units congregated like the yard or the mess hall, akin to a walk through Washington Square Park, where drugs are sold in the open, despite close proximity to the cops.

Married

In short, the inconveniences visited upon incarcerated drug users by the institution do little to discourage their use. On one occasion, David witnessed a group of K2 smokers come perilously close to being caught in the act by a CO making his required rounds throughout the dorm and bathroom. The owner of the joint quickly snuffed the glowing tip out with his fingertips and swallowed the half-joint that remained. Once the CO left, he hunched over a toilet and forced himself to vomit it back up in order to roll it into a new joint.

Neither random drug tests nor the very real possibility of losing all of one's good time in one swoop for failing one is enough to discourage the rampant drug use on Rikers. As mentioned above, K2 does not show up in the DOC's urinalysis tests, and therefore does not present this risk for those who use it. And then, too, drug tests are administered infrequently, with highly irregular variation between housing units.

Only once in twelve months did David experience a random drug test, though he heard of or witnessed them happening in other housing units on multiple occasions. Around 9:00 a.m., a number of COs swept into the dorm and ordered everyone into the bathroom, handing each an iCup urine test kit as he entered. One inmate refused; the COs thoroughly trashed his bed and unceremoniously removed him from the dorm, sending his belongings a few hours later. Where he was going, DOC staff would not say, but it was assumed he was being transferred to the Beacon for box time. Jarrod met an inmate serving two consecutive one-year "bullet" sentences who refused to give up smoking weed, despite having previously run afoul of drug tests, and losing his job and good time as a result. Given how long he was being held, he considered the consequences of drug tests a risk worth taking for the temporary escapes from city time he enjoyed while high.

Those addicted to hard drugs like crack or heroin on the outside, almost without exception, have one goal upon their release: to get high. Most will unabashedly admit as much. How high one plans to get upon release is among the most common conversation topics. Some boast or compare notes about how long they have been using their drug of choice, or how much they had been using before they were incarcerated. "Y'all just datin' crack," one guy once announced to a small group of fellow crack users, all younger than himself. "I'm married to this bitch." One protested, "I'm married, too, bro!" A small number of addicts claim to want to get clean for good, but even some of these plan to get high "just for a little bit" after their release, begging the question of whether they are likely to be able to kick the habit at all.

Even those who want to kick seem largely unable to imagine what life might be like for them if they were not using hard drugs, making quick, illegal cash to support their habit, and drifting in and out of jail. For them, it is all a package deal, and the prospect of a year or less on Rikers is just something that comes with the territory. "This is what I choose to deal with," one heroin addict in David's dormitory said, gesturing at the scene around him, "because I choose to get high." While this may have been a simple matter of personal preference in some cases, many inmates were clearly leaning on street drugs to regulate serious issues with mental health.

MO in GP

When Jarrod was in 12-Lower, one new inmate's arrival generated almost immediate animosity. He was an unkempt, middle-aged Black man who demonstrated obvious symptoms of severe mental distress. The man sat on his bed all day, seemingly impervious to his surroundings, rocking back and forth in a frenzy as he rifled through a deck of cards, inspecting each one, and rarely taking his eyes off this work. When he did arise from the bed, he would wander through the house at random, ignoring the taboo on entering other inmates' sections or sleeping areas without a clear purpose. Compounding this transgression, he failed to observe the de facto hygiene rules governing the institution. As his behavior raised hackles, he remained seemingly oblivious to the danger he was placing himself in. When confronted by others, he did not respond in a coherent way, being to all appearances miles away.

Physician Homer Venters, who oversaw healthcare on Rikers Island from 2008 to 2019, including five years as chief medical officer of Correctional Health Services, argues that since the 1960s, "multiple policy misadventures of the war on drugs and dismantling of the nation's mental health service have transformed jails and prisons into the de facto mental health service for the poor and especially for minorities."[9] Venters recounts how even during his time, quite late in this history of so-called deinstitutionalization, the number of inmates requiring some kind of mental health service increased from one-third to one-half, and the percentage of inmates with serious mental illness more than doubled, from 5 to 11 percent—all as the overall jail population decreased.[10] This statistic is backed up by the 2022 New York City Mayor's Management Report for the Department of Correction, which shows that 50 percent of all city prisoners had some sort of mental health diagnosis in fiscal year 2022, and likewise shows a five-year average of about 47 percent.[11] This is a steady increase from 2010 and 2016, when the figures were reported at 29 percent and 42 percent, respectively.[12] One can only imagine by how much those numbers would increase were all the undiagnosed cases accounted for.

Someone with mental health issues is colloquially known at Rikers as "MO," for "Mental Observation," the terms used in internal DOC paperwork to flag someone as having mental health issues. The arrival of an inmate who, for mental health reasons, is clearly at odds with the social rules structuring house life becomes something of a reality television show, to which dozens of viewers can tune in throughout the day. It also provides fodder for discussion, debate, and speculation about what might happen, akin to the punditry one finds on sports radio.

In the case of the new arrival to Jarrod's dormitory, many inmates noted the unfairness of it all; the jail administrators had placed someone with diminished mental capacities in general population, where it was only a matter of time before he would be beaten up for blatantly transgressing inmate rules. But just as a judge on the outside had not refrained from passing his sentence, nobody seemed to dispute the eventual necessity of violence. It was coming. What else could be done with someone who refused to respect the modicum of privacy inmates eke out for themselves in a world of forced togetherness?

The only solution was to get this man out of the house, and out of general population ("GP") altogether, if possible. As tensions grew, Jarrod and two other inmates approached the CO in the Bubble, a young Black woman. They told her that there was a man who had clear mental health issues and needed to be taken out of GP for his own safety. Initially she stuck to the default posture of Rikers COs when inmates question an administrative decision, dismissing them with a wave; it was not her job to classify inmates, after all. But they persisted.

"You don't understand," Jarrod said at last, looking her directly in the eyes. "I am a psychologist"—this was a bit of a stretch; he was a first-year graduate student in environmental psychology—"and this man is demonstrating clear symptoms of schizophrenia. He is in danger here." This line worked; the CO, likely fearing liability, dropped her defenses and agreed to report the matter to her superiors. Soon after, the inmate was transferred out.

Mental health issues are often a source of conflict not only between inmates but between inmates and COs as well. This is especially true given the high-stress environment, in which things change inexplicably and at a moment's notice, and in which even the most well-adjusted inmates have trouble knowing and following the rules. A 2016 *New York Times* investigation, for example, published in the wake of a four-month study of Rikers by the paper, concluded that "brutal attacks by correction officers on inmates—particularly those with mental health issues—are common occurrences inside Rikers. . . . What emerges is a damning portrait of COs on Rikers Island, who are poorly equipped to deal with mental illness and instead repeatedly respond with overwhelming force to even minor provocations."[13]

Regular reports of DOC staff responding to mental health crises with brutality were still quite common during David's time there. These responses might consist of repeatedly targeting an inmate for strip searches, or trashing his bunk, or confining him to the dismal "why-me pen" in Intake, or even pepper spraying or bludgeoning them while handcuffed or confined to a holding cell. Older inmates recounted even more gruesome stories of conflict between COs and inmates. One man told David of an MO inmate who, in a desperate bid to finally get taken to the clinic for his medication, took out a razor he'd been concealing and sliced himself across the face. When the emergency response team arrived, they tased him, clubbed him, handcuffed him, and then dragged him out by the cuffs, leaving a trail of blood behind.

Brad H. and Bugouts

A person may be flagged as MO for anything from mild depression to severe schizophrenia and debilitating bipolar episodes. In the argot of city time, MOs can be divided into these two categories depending on how seriously their mental illness presents. Those with observable symptoms, who are clearly intellectually disabled or are otherwise a little "off," are generally considered "bugouts," as in, "That dude's crazy, man, don't listen to him, he's a fuckin' bugout." More severe cases are dubbed "MO *for real*." One fellow inmate once demonstrated this distinction to David, in describing another guy he had been incarcerated with on a prior bid: "I mean *really* MO, like Tasmanian fuckin' Devil," he said, illustrating the point with his best Looney Tunes Tasmanian Devil impression, complete with outstretched arms, wild eyes, and lolling tongue.

Generally, an inmate with no obvious symptoms, who might have a mild condition like depression, or who might have begun therapy behind bars solely to gain access to medications like antidepressants, painkillers, or sleeping pills, will not be referred to as a bugout or MO, and will take offense if he is. If asked whether he is MO, he will usually answer truthfully—lying is frowned upon as indicative of general dishonesty, and is likely to be discovered eventually—but in a way that downplays the significance of his MO status.

"Yeah, these mothafuckas put me MO, I ain't even never been to Mental Health!" one told David. Some don't even know their MO status, or at least claim not to, until released. One guy, who had the same release date as David, found out as David was being taken to the pens at 2:30 a.m. that he had been flagged as MO, and would therefore have to wait until the morning to be released. For inmates like this, it is generally accepted that they are not "really crazy," but are rather victims of the island's absurd bureaucracy—an entirely reasonable assumption, given the apparent randomness with which this opaque entity regulates every aspect of daily life.

Even men who admit their need for mental health treatment often struggle to be taken seriously by COs. As assistant Rikers Island Mental Health Unit chief Mary E. Buser has documented, incarcerated people demonstrating symptoms of mental illness are widely considered "malingerers," or fakers, by the COs, and even many civilian workers alike. "For the most part," she recalls, "DOC was of the view that the mentally ill were faking it. They made their own frank assessments, which they were only too happy to share. To us, the mentally ill are patients; to them, they are inmates. To us, they are sick and often misunderstood; to DOC they are manipulators who are always trying to 'get over.'"[14]

Among inmates, visits to therapy are generally brushed aside as unmanly and unneeded. One of the periodic shouts punctuating the commotion of the dorm is the cry of an inmate's last name followed by "Mental Health! Walkin' out!" Inmates respond with near invariability, "Refuse!" or variants like "I ain't goin'!" or "That's a dub," meaning no, or simply, "Fuck that shit!" The COs tasked with escorting them to the mental health clinic have no horse in the race; having called out the required words, they have done their duty. They simply turn and leave the unit. Little to no effort to actually get decent mental health services to inmates in real life—as distinct from the fantastical world of DOC paperwork—is ever made.

When an inmate died in David's unit, a DOC mental health professional showed up in the dormitory a week later, and made an announcement offering mental health treatment for anyone who felt traumatized by the man's death. She walked down the aisles, asking each inmate individually if he wanted to schedule a visit with a therapist. Every single inmate, one by one, declined. This particular mental health worker actually seemed to care, and seemed genuinely disappointed that no one wanted treatment. But given the eminently social and public nature of everything in the dormitories, no one would admit to the therapist that he needed help, even if he was able to admit it to himself—all eyes were on each individual as he responded.

This was common; mental health treatment is looked upon with extreme skepticism by inmates. Even if an inmate refuses a visit to the mental health office, his summons alone is usually met with derision, either in a playful, mocking tone by those he is closest to or with evident scorn, if he is not high on the totem pole. "Retarded-ass nigga!" is a common remark, or, alternatively, "Yo, get this nigga outta here! This nigga MO!"

An inmate flagged as MO may also be referred to as "seven-thirty." According to most inmates on Rikers, this designation is supposedly derived from the name of the internal DOC document that designates a person as having specific needs related to his mental health. Our research indicates that it is more likely derived from Article 730 of New York Criminal Procedure Law, which governs a number of the intersections of mental health and the punishment system, including the lengthy psychological evaluation process by which a defendant is determined to be "incapacitated" (not competent to stand trial).[15]

Much more commonly, inmates with mental health issues are referred to as "Brad H." Both "seven-thirty" and "Brad H.," like "MO," have been adopted from the institutional language about mental illness, and become staples of the inmate lexicon. Rikers folklore holds that Brad H., a Rikers inmate with severe mental illness, was dumped on the streets of Queens in the middle of the night, with nothing more than subway fare, as is common practice. He then supposedly proceeded to the Jackson Heights–Roosevelt Avenue subway station, where he physically and sexually assaulted a woman before pushing her onto the tracks, where she was hit and killed by a train.

The reality is much less gruesome: Brad H. was the lead plaintiff in a 1999 class-action lawsuit against the city for its treatment of people with mental illnesses, specifically as it related to the practice of discharge from DOC custody. In the nearly two decades since the final ruling in 2003, the city has repeatedly demonstrated its inability to fulfill its end of the bargain (prescription medicines, appointments for mental health or substance abuse treatment, referrals for housing and Medicaid, and in some cases, food stamps and transportation, among other services), to the point that the terms of the original settlement have now been upgraded and extended several times. The DOC's discharge planning practices are currently supervised by the federal *Nunez* monitor.[16]

The terms "Brad H." and "MO" seemed to be used interchangeably for the most part, but in a broad sense, the former was applied more generally, and might refer to someone simply taking anxiety medication, while the latter, though also applied quite freely, could be used to denote more serious mental health conditions (no one ever said "Brad H. for real," for example).

Inmates designated Brad H. receive an official form letter stating that they fall under the jurisdiction of the landmark case *Brad H. v. the City of New York*, and are therefore entitled to mental health care while incarcerated and after release. Those who don't throw this form directly into the trash generally keep it as a safeguard against any changes in the DOC's electronic system—like everything, liable to happen at a moment's notice and without good reason or explanation—that would prevent them from receiving any prescriptions or treatments they rely on.

The most significant aspect of being Brad H. for many, however, is that it extends their stay on Rikers Island for anywhere from one to twelve hours, depending on how unlucky they are. Brad H. inmates, ever since the lawsuit of that name, can no longer be dumped on the street in the middle of the night like everybody else; they must wait until the morning to be dumped on the street. "Morning," when it comes to discharge from Rikers Island, may be any time from 6:00 a.m. to 2:00 p.m.

Not wishing to add *any* time to their stay, even a matter of hours, is a factor in many inmates' decisions not to seek mental health support.

We're All Mad Here

Being too MO will almost certainly get an inmate "packed up" by the others in the unit. This means the inmate is instructed to pack up his belongings and inform the CO that he no longer feels safe in the dormitory. The CO must comply and transfer him out, or both can expect violence—and, for the CO, the attendant liability. David once witnessed the arrival of a man who seemed friendly, collected, and easy enough to get along with; he was generally welcomed into the dorm. But within minutes of his arrival, he smoked a bit of K2 and began "wildin'": he suddenly did a 360-degree spin in the middle of the dorm, then started dancing while laughing and talking to himself, staring off into space. He was immediately packed up by the gang hierarchy. At another point in David's incarceration, an MO inmate was packed up after stunted social interactions, masturbating as a well-liked female CO walked by, and, finally, urinating in the shower while wearing all his clothes.

Though most city-time men might look down on these kinds of inmates, they still find themselves navigating scarcity and proximity together, and the stigma around such prisoners did not extend to accepting gifts from them upon their departure. "Nigga was a psychopath for real," an inmate in David's house recalled. "Talkin' to himself all day long. He gave me a pair of socks, though. And his blanket."

David also met MO inmates who enjoyed some social status, such as Bugout Sam, who was loud, raucous, and extremely aggressive toward COs, often threatening to kill them outright. Overt threatening of DOC staff is commonly frowned upon, as it can cause unnecessary problems for the entire unit. But Bugout Sam was also a Crip. The Crips have comparatively little real estate in the Six Building, and are generally at greater risk of harassment than other gangs. His fellow Crips knew that if they packed him up, they would be as good as disowning him, and maybe putting him at risk of serious violence from members of rival gangs. So Bugout Sam was tolerated, despite his disruptive presence; it probably helped that he arrived with only a week left until his release date. By contrast, a Blood who was obviously MO was packed up by a neutral inmate with whom he had a beef, and three other Bloods stood by and let it happen, breaking gang solidarity. In talking with each other, they all cited the guy's MO status as their reason.

On the other hand, being MO is sometimes seen as a harmless and even charming quirk. In a crazy world full of crazy people, after all, a crazy person who makes you laugh is not such bad company. One MO inmate David met early in his sentence was generally referred to as "Prime Minister," as he availed himself of anyone who would listen—and many who would not—to claim that he was in fact the white rapper of the same stage name from the 1980s hip hop trio Third Base. This was not true: a cursory online investigation shows that the two men bore little resemblance to each other, and the real Prime Minister from Third Base to be a free man. Yet the city-time Prime Minister insisted that he had had a glorious career in the early rap days—and more importantly, that Eminem had stolen his rhyme book.

"Eminem stole my rhyme book!" he would blurt out suddenly, his face a mask of genuine concern. "I was crossing Central Park and I ran into Eminem and it was a red leather book. It had my rhymes in it. I showed it to Eminem; he said can I borrow this and I said OK and he took it and he never gave it back!" While some eventually grew tired of this story, and told him to "chill on that shit," most responded with a chuckle, finding it good for breaking up the dreariness and monotony of the day.

Fufi was another MO inmate David met with a number of eccentric personality traits, including talking and singing to himself, the inability to focus for any lengthy period of time, mood swings and violent outbursts, and childlike behavior such as playing pranks and even sucking his thumb. He spoke very little English, but had no qualms about approaching any inmate or CO and striking up a rapid-fire conversation in the heavily accented Spanish of rural Puerto Rico, whether or not they understood Spanish at all. Fufi was mostly tolerated by the other inmates because his antics were considered entertaining, because he had an infectious laugh and upbeat personality, and because he generally volunteered to clean the common spaces with the house gang. He was accepted even despite his violent outbursts, which often included serious threats, menacing with improvised weapons, and language that was generally regarded as necessitating a fight, such as "pussy" or "suck my dick."

Treatment Centers without Treatment

The idea of a small administrative "mental health" department in a vast brutal bureaucracy whose main function seems to be meting out daily trauma to its residents would be laughable if it were not so sad. Add to this the facts that the mental health services, like the medical services and the DOC at large, are badly disorganized and rarely function smoothly, and that mental health treatment is universally shunned by the incarcerated, and it becomes clear that no one's mental health could possibly improve at Rikers under even the best of circumstances. This is significant in a place where approximately half the population has been diagnosed with some type of mental illness for the past five years.[17]

In *Rikers: An Oral History*, Eve Kessler, former director of DOC public affairs, recalls how DOC commissioner Joseph Ponte "said publicly many times that Rikers was the largest mental hospital on the East Coast."[18] But the truth is, in fact, much worse: according to a September 2016 report from the nonprofit Treatment Advocacy Center, Rikers Island holds more mentally ill people than any psychiatric hospital in the country. This is in keeping with the national trend of jails and prisons displacing psychiatric facilities, in the wake of massive defunding of mental health services, as the largest institutional repositories for mentally ill people. These de facto mental illness treatment centers do not actually offer any treatment at all.

This is one of the central points of disability and abolition scholar Liat Ben-Moshe's critique of the notion, commonplace today, that prisons are the new asylums. "To be regarded as a mental health facility," she writes, "and not a warehouse for all kinds of indigent populations, carceral spaces need to actually provide mental health treatment." Instead, jails and prisons are "places of disablement that create and exacerbate mental ill health." Ben-Moshe is careful to insist that "a return to the asylum," which she posits as merely another point on the spectrum of incarceration, is not the answer, arguing instead that the notion of treatment behind bars is itself an oxymoron.[19]

We are inclined to agree. Rikers is a place where people with serious medical needs like substance dependency and mental illness are made to suffer quite pointlessly, at great risk to their already tenuous health. To be sure, both of us found that the experience of city time did little for our mental health, to say the least. Thankfully, neither of us suffered from severe mental health issues. But many prisoners do nationwide: the same Treatment Advocacy Center report estimates that fully 20 percent of those incarcerated in America's jails are afflicted by severe mental illness—or, as the guys on Rikers might say, "MO *for real*."[20]

11

Interpersonal Relationships

"What Ack say?"

"He say he got it from Walid."

"What he say?"

"He say he got it gambling."

"They do both be gambling a lot," says one shotcaller. "But I don't think Ack would steal."

No one speaks up for Walid.

During David's time, an inmate called Ack purchased a bowl from another, Chapín, and paid him in packets of tuna. This was a transaction so quotidian it would normally have been unremarkable. But Chapín, whose bed sat quite close to Ack's, had been periodically complaining of food missing from his bucket for some time, the sure sign of a sneak thief at work. To discourage the thief, and recuperate his items if stolen, he had begun carefully writing a number on the bottom of each of his commissary food items in black ballpoint pen. One of the packets of tuna that Ack paid him with had a "5" carefully written on the silvery bottom of the packaging.

Chapín called Ack out on this shortly after the sale. Ack, sputtering, vehemently denied it, and tore the lid off his bucket to show how full it was. "Why would I steal?" he said, "when my bucket is full? Why would I pay you with that same tuna if I stole it?"

Chapín challenged Ack to explain where he got the tuna. Ack said he got it from Walid, whose bed sat between them. Walid also denied the theft, and opened his bucket to prove that he was also jail-wealthy enough not to need to steal.

One of the men who had gathered around to watch the conflict then brought it to the attention of the shotcallers, who were playing Spades in the day room.

"We can't let this shit go," one announced. "It'll just get worse." There was no talk of how punishing the wrong man might embolden the actual thief by giving others a false sense of security, nor of the moral issues of punishing an innocent person.

Another shotcaller entered the day room.

"Yo, somebody stealin' out niggas' buckets," said one of the card players.

"Who?" he asked.

"Walid," said one of the card players definitively, as if he knew.

The shotcaller's face darkened, and he rushed angrily over to Walid, loudly and aggressively confronting him about the stolen tuna. Walid kept his cool. "All that proves," he said, "is that someone stole it from Chapín and lost it gambling to me."

But it didn't matter. The decision had been made, based on rumor and personal preference alone. One of the shotcallers threw an empty trash bag at Walid. The rank-and-file gang members were now lurking in the background, crossing their arms, their mere presence a threat of force.

"One way or another, bro," a shotcaller said, pounding a meaty fist into a fleshy palm to accentuate his words, "you got to go."

Walid sighed and grabbed the bag. He knew he had no choice but to pack up.

Hell Is Other People

As we have seen, the majority of the rules inmates must follow are not written in any book, and most transgressions one can commit are not in violation of any institutional statute. Instead, a complex and often ad hoc inmate code structures social life in countless ways, which may be invisible to the new arrival but which must be discerned and observed quickly to avoid dangerous conflict—even if inmates privately resist internalizing them. As rapper Lil Wayne puts it in his C-76 diary, "It's crazy how jail can make doing what you wouldn't regularly do make sense. I'll have to be mindful not to get lost in this opposite world."[1]

While these codes are nuanced and contingent on a number of local variables, like the power structure of the dormitory and the give and take between inmates and COs, they serve two distinct, and sometimes contradictory functions. First, the customs governing city-time houses are designed to create a kind of "surface order," the outward appearance of a smoothly run jail.[2] This enables a number of transgressions like smoking and contraband exchange to occur, without constituting a direct affront to the power of the COs. Second, and often to the contrary, some inmate customs, especially derived from the codes of gang life, call for violence that breaks this surface order and risks bringing unwanted CO attention down on the dormitory, including invasive searches that turn up all manner of contraband.

Gangs, for instance, explicitly mandate solidarity among members, creating a code that compels men, who might otherwise be reluctant, into dangerous situations to either back up a comrade under assault or else avenge an attack from the past. Beyond gang codes, the ordinary codes of masculinity force inmates to avenge any affronts to their manliness, however slight, which can lead to violence. Thus, while disturbances that could potentially bring scrutiny and collective penalties down on all inmates are generally frowned upon, the same system of de facto rules that discourages this behavior sometimes commands it.

Similarly, those at the top of the hierarchy, the shotcallers, who have "secured a measure of relief from degradation," in the words of sociologist Richard Cloward, may be pushed into calling for or even ordering revolt if they feel the institution is failing to respect the arrangement that affords them a modicum of decency.[3] Such was the case when David's dorm organized a strike, along with the neighboring dorm, to protest unsafe conditions under COVID-19. While the strike was organized nonhierarchically in David's dorm, the action was initiated in the neighboring unit by those at the top of the gang hierarchy. Without their support, organizing would have been difficult, and potentially dangerous.

Beneath any organized or even coherent structure of de facto or de jure rules we saw at Rikers lay the simple reality of adult men forced to share space, with little to no privacy and few means of escape from enforced proximity to dozens of other people in the same situation. As sociologist Loïc Wacquant observed of the Men's Central Jail in Los Angeles, "Sartre's sentence 'l'enfer, c'est les autres' ['hell is other people'] is truer here than anywhere else."[4] Inmates must negotiate forced exposure to people they might not ordinarily associate with, and may harbor suspicions or hostility toward. Anthropologist and novelist Alison Spedding describes experiencing this "bizarre community which is not a community" while incarcerated at a women's jail in Bolivia. "We spend every day in intimate contact but the only thing we have in common is the repeated cry of 'I want to get out!' ('¡Quiero irme!')"[5] One man incarcerated at Rikers in 2020 put it more bluntly: "We have a common interest to get the fuck up out here as soon as possible."[6]

It is a climate suffused with what ethnographer Michael Walker calls "conflict energy," meaning "charged up intersubjectivity and emotional energy toward potential conflict."[7] In such a setting, the most mundane actions can provoke violence, or more commonly, a general state of constant, grating, simmering annoyance. "I wish this dude would shut the fuck up!" writes Lil Wayne. "Damn! Jailhouse communication is the worst shit ever. . . . And to make matters worse, they repeat everything twice like 'Eh, you, them niggas down there be buggin' . . . them niggas be buggin'! That's my word . . . that's my word, son.' I don't know if it's a jailhouse thing, New York thing, or a New York jailhouse thing, but it's for damn sure an annoying-as-fuck thing!"[8]

A person who has not experienced this degree of forced proximity may have a difficult time grasping how frustrating and humiliating it can be to be deprived of any privacy at all, day in and day out, from the most vulnerable and potentially embarrassing moments of daily life, especially bodily functions like defecation, through banalities like reading the newspaper, daydreaming, or simply wanting to be alone. Both David and Jarrod, for instance, covet sustained silent time for reading and writing, and struggled with their resentment of inmates who casually interrupted this. To avoid unnecessary conflict, and to cultivate necessary social ties, we had to work on masking how utterly apoplectic casual interruptions made us. Life in city-time dormitories is a constant and obligatory social affair, far in excess of what most people experience on the outside. This inescapable presence of others, even at their least offensive, is a ceaseless dull irritation, always threatening to explode. Much attention, then, is paid to the minutiae of interpersonal relations, and how to keep things running as painlessly as possible. Despite the appearance of chaos, the social life of city time is as structured an affair as you can find just about anywhere else.

Phobias

Sentenced men on Rikers spoke commonly of C-76's "mook dorm," 8-Lower. "Mook" in this context is a slur for queer or nonbinary men or trans women; this meaning may be Rikers specific. The mook dorm was reputedly a place for gay and queer men who either requested to be sent there, or who were deemed not to be straight-passing by the institution during intake. There were also a number of trans women there, judging by fleeting contact with residents of 8-Lower that other prisoners reported. There was not a wall of total segregation between those in 8-Lower and the rest of the men in C-76; on his very first day at the yard, for example, David observed a queer couple, led out to the yard with about fifty feet and two guards between them and the other men, who spent their time slowly walking around the dirt track, hand in hand, and admiring the Manhattan skyline through the chain link fences. Though those prisoners in the main body of the yard could be heard making the occasional derisive comment, the couple was largely left alone.

During Jarrod's time, there was a trans woman in general population who became something of a jail celebrity. She was the common subject of sexual taunts, to which she responded with mockery and playful flirtation, adeptly highlighting that these kinds of transphobic remarks often reveal the aggressor to be sexually interested, however ambivalently. Of course, she never should have had to defend herself like this in the first place. While trans prisoners at Rikers are supposed to be afforded housing consistent with their gender identity, this is handled about as incompetently and uncompassionately as everything else. Trans women in particular have a difficult time securing a gender-affirming assignment, exposing them to harassment and assault. Gender-affirming housing is also contingent on good behavior.[9]

Rikers offered some degree of separation for queer and trans prisoners for decades. The 1994 HBO documentary *Lock-Up: The Prisoners of Rikers Island* shows a visibly uncomfortable deputy warden telling the camera, "When I first saw gay inmates housed together, it was a . . . shocking experience." We have no knowledge of what became of the inmates of 8-Lower after EMTC's closure in early 2020, but sadly, queer and trans housing on Rikers has suffered greatly under Mayor Eric Adams, subjecting trans prisoners, in particular, to horrific conditions in general population.[10]

The barrier between outwardly queer and heteronormative-presenting inmates was also permeable in the other direction: avowedly straight men sometimes ended up in 8-Lower. Time spent there left a prisoner with a severe stigma, and would almost certainly follow him even if he was transferred to another unit. Such transfers to 8-Lower seemed to be, like many things, either an act of retribution by DOC staff or the result of sheer incompetence and disinterest. During our time on Rikers there were numerous rumors regarding what went on in 8-Lower; David witnessed a new arrival in his dorm from 8-Lower insisting to anyone who would listen that the dorm had been a "hellhole" and that he had had to fight to defend himself from queer advances every day. This may well have been an exaggeration—he had a point to prove after all—but he also brought stories of witnessing sex acts between the residents of 8-Lower that Rikers veterans seemed to find believable. In *Lock-Up*, the interviewer blurts out, "So can you guys have sex in here [the queer housing unit]?" The two interviewees burst out laughing. "Yeah, you can," they reply.

We saw little of this world apart. But we were immersed in a pervasive attitude of homophobia and transphobia throughout city time's general population. This surely reflects the dominant values in the communities these men call home, but it is intensified by the absence of heterosexual relationships, on which so many men's sense of themselves rests. Political prisoner Mumia Abu-Jamal has called this "state-enforced celibacy."[11] This deprivation constitutes one of the foremost "pains of imprisonment" chronicled by sociologist Gresham Sykes, as the prisoner "is shut off from the world of women which by its very polarity gives the male world much of its meaning."[12] Given that much of what it means to be a man, in the traditional sense, is bound up with relations with women, the absence of women behind bars can install a crisis at the center of masculinity, at the exact moment when its performance becomes paramount for survival. Sykes chronicled the adaptation that masculinity undergoes in this setting, as men overemphasize "the accompaniments of sexuality," those aspects of the masculine performance that are not forbidden by incarceration.[13] And sex with women is only one component of traditional working-class masculinity denied city-time prisoners; virtually every aspect of the humiliating unfreedom of institutional life infantilizes and emasculates prisoners in search of a traditional masculine identity, often under the explicit direction of female guards.

This results in the paradox that male facilities at Rikers are filled with men denied self-sufficiency, self-determination, and heterosexual relationships, who nonetheless perform working-class masculinity with great enthusiasm and ferocity. Everything at Rikers seems bigger, meaner, and chock-fuller of macho bluster than on the outside. Voices seemed to be dropped deeper, chests puffed out further, and sexual successes with women on the outside boasted of more loudly, and improbably, than on the street. Much as in the free world, many men who feel emasculated by their social conditions find meaning in an exaggerated performance of what they believe it means to be a man.

Unfortunately, this is often accompanied by a vocal expression of homophobia and transphobia. Statistically speaking, there are surely lots of men in general population who experience same-sex and trans-amorous desire, and likely a smaller subset who clandestinely act on it. But this is all kept quiet amid a near-constant barrage of homophobic sentiments voiced loudly by inmates and COs alike. We both observed men who spent much of the day ranting about "undercover faggots" or "mooks." Since there were apparently none in sight, we could not help but assume such people were dealing quite publicly with their own conflicted desires; denied the permitted sexual outlets for heterosexual men, they were nonetheless surrounded by the pungent smells and inescapable sights of half-naked people they could conceivably do it with. At the risk of psychoanalyzing these men, the "mook" in question was likely a voice within their own head.

Conflict

Conflict between city-time inmates can be dangerous, and the potential for violence leaves most inmates desiring its speedy redress. It is also highly social in character. If a man feels wronged by another, the first step is usually to call him out where others can see and hear (which is nearly everywhere on Rikers), as Chapín did Ack in the tuna theft incident. This is a way of proving one's willingness to stand up for oneself, and simultaneously of bringing the issue to wider public attention. Confrontation demonstrates how quick-witted, courageous, or collected participants are.

David similarly observed that play fighting, the simulation of a physical confrontation, was socially essential for some city-time inmates, allowing both the participants and the ever-present audience to estimate a prisoner's ability to hold his own. The frequency and acceptability of this varied between individuals and housing units—David experienced much more play fighting in C-76 than in C-74—but it seemed to be characteristic of city time. Tans were rarely seen play fighting, and by all accounts, the practice is not generally tolerated in prison.

When actual fights break out between prisoners, they are often due to a perceived lack of respect. David once witnessed an inmate square off against another, much larger man due to a perceived slight, within an hour of being called to pack up for release. He often saw fights justified by both participants and observers shouting things like "It's what men do!" or "It's what you're supposed to do in jail!" Backing away from a fight, especially after being called a "bitch" or being insulted with "suck my dick," is a surefire way to get labeled a "bitch" or a person who "ain't about shit." These allegations will almost certainly follow inmates between housing units and even buildings.

If an inmate is called a bitch or "invited to another man's dick," he is all but required to challenge the speaker to "play the bathroom"—to go into the bathroom, where there are no cameras, and fight. The consequences of some provocative expressions, "suck my dick" in particular, are dramatized in a scene from former C-74 detainee Russell "Half" Allen's account of his time at Rikers as an adolescent: "Scooby Ru hopped up out of the chair and snatched his shirt off and said, 'I'm talking to you, fuck boy!' 'Fuck boy?! Nigga suck my dick, faggot!' Doe Boi replied. I tried to stop them but it was too late. . . . The 'fuck boy' and the 'suck my dick, faggot' talk couldn't be solved no other way but by fighting."[14] When such language is invoked, a fight between the two men is all but a foregone conclusion.

Inmates often challenge each other to play the bathroom without first rising to the levels of disrespect mentioned above. Other sources of conflict that may lead to playing the bathroom are too numerous and quotidian to count. They include farting, especially after being notified that one's farts are "disrespectful" (a sort of couched threat), doing things perceived as "gay" like "freeballing" (showering naked) or walking around the dorm in one's underwear, or disputing one's place in the line. Physical altercations often have roots in seemingly trivial incidents, including something as simple as a harmless joke or comment interpreted as an insult. Theft or snitching earns an inmate threats and violence; sometimes, simply accusing another inmate of being a "snitch" or a "sneak thief" can result in playing the bathroom. Other inmates in the unit may sometimes discourage two men from playing the bathroom or even physically intervene, as a report of a fight is an almost surefire way to bring down a retaliatory search on the unit.

While more serious injuries do occur, they are rare. Stabbings were almost unheard of in the Six Building; slashings ("shooting" or "getting cut") did happen, but not often. Jarrod experienced a day-long lockdown of the Six after an inmate in another dormitory was slashed, and based on everything he had heard about Rikers in popular culture, was surprised by how gravely everyone received the news. He had expected it to be treated like an everyday occurrence. Fighting, on the other hand, is common and expected, but rarely serious among those serving sentences at C-76. Bloody noses and black eyes are the most common injuries. Facial scratches are common, too, given the virtual talons sprouting from most inmates' fingers. Other injuries sustained as a result of physical conflict, like sprains and fractures, are hard to gauge in terms of frequency, but they, too, certainly do occur.

Gang members in a housing unit usually act with some cohesion, but there are occasionally cases where they break gang solidarity. For example, if a gang member comes into conflict with a non–gang member over something evidently petty and personal, other gang members might well stay out of the conflict altogether rather than step in, as might be expected. In one case David witnessed, gang members offered no resistance to one of their own being packed up by the COs after he, unprovoked, assaulted two people in their sleep. Any objections would not likely have affected the COs' decision, but in most cases gang members will at least make a show of their disagreement. When David had an issue with a young and unruly gang member, he was given the go-ahead by the only other two gang members in the dorm, both older and more seasoned, with whom David had become friendly, to assault the young man if he chose.

In most cases, however, gang members can suffer severe penalties for not showing solidarity with each other when physical confrontation erupts. In one case David observed, a number of rival gang members rushed a young member of the Bloods in the main hall. An older and higher-ranking Blood from the same housing unit was nearby but did not intervene. When they returned to the housing unit, the younger Blood, though much smaller, less experienced, and lower in status, publicly voiced his anger with the older Blood who had left him stranded, challenging him to play the bathroom. Even though the older Blood had no relationship with the younger Blood other than gang affiliation, and was only two weeks away from his release date—close enough to make anyone wary of getting involved in a fight—he was packed up by the other Bloods in the dorm for having refused to fight alongside the younger one.

Pack-Ups and Good Time

The simplest and most common way of resolving a conflict in a housing unit is by "packing someone up" and making the person leave the house. This functions as a sort of banishment. The packed-up inmate is forced to approach the CO posted to the unit, either on the floor or in the Bubble, and say that he cannot live in the housing unit any more. Most COs understand the subtext immediately, but if the inmate is asked why, his answer is invariably something like, "I don't feel safe." These are the magic words for requesting a move: liability for future lawsuits is often DOC's primary concern, and its slumbering bureaucracy can quickly spring to life when faced with the risk of creating any record that could become grist for legal action.

Packing up was usually achieved without violence in C-76. The resident gang members in the unit would often surround the offending person on his bed, not threatening directly, but making their presence known, while one of the shotcallers spoke to him and told him he needed to leave. Sometimes this was done fairly quietly, with everyone involved speaking in reasoned tones. During the tuna theft incident, David witnessed the "big homie" simply throw a plastic bag at Walid, shouting, "Pack yo shit, bro!" Though aggressive, there was no violence used, only the threat of it. Anyone told to pack up understood that resorting to violence would only make it worse; the inmate would inevitably lose a confrontation with all of the gang members in the house, and would thus end up packed up anyway.

Pack-ups are also instigated by the institution in the wake of a physical fight. Once the belligerents have been removed to Intake and a decision has been made by some opaque authority as to which of the two combatants is to be packed up, the phone in the Bubble will ring, and after a moment's conversation, the Bubble officer will call out the order to pack up the personal belongings of the one selected to be moved to another unit. The floor officer will usually solicit volunteers, often simply by calling out, "Who wants to pack up X's stuff?" These volunteers are just as likely to be friends of the deportee as they are to be opportunists looking to skim a little off the top as they stuff his belongings into a trash bag.

Peaceful conflict resolution can sometimes be achieved thanks to the "good time" incentive. Under this system, a city-time inmate's sentence is reduced by one-third upon admission, under the threat of the DOC adding that time back should he break the rules. Fighting is a common way to lose good time; Jarrod befriended a man who had been beaten by another inmate following a verbal dispute, so much that his face bore deep purple bruises and abrasions weeks later. But because he offered some resistance at the onset of this lopsided conflict, he also lost some good time.

Generally, the structure of good time is one of the most effective disciplinary tools at the institution's disposal. Unlike incarcerated people serving long stretches or life sentences, inmates serving city time can typically visualize the end of their sentence. They spend large amounts of their waking time discussing their date of release and postrelease plans, and generally do not want to do anything to jeopardize this fantasy coming true. In the case of potentially violent conflicts, the specter of good-time loss can be deployed as a form of deescalation.

We observed that many inmates who found themselves in potentially violent showdowns did not actually want to use violence or have it visited upon them. Instead, those who came to blows, or approached the threshold where words give way to violence, seemed hemmed in by the pressure to perform their toughness, lest they risk being diminished in the eyes of their peers or penalized by their gang. The anger and frustration attendant to incarceration, amplified by the emasculation it imposes on male inmates, surely plays a role in emotional outbursts of violence behind bars. But only the most irrational inmate acts on impulse alone; the typical man serving city time treats every decision, including whether to fight, with the kind of cold calculation that is necessary for survival in such a hostile environment.

It is therefore not uncommon to see two city-time inmates, toe to toe, squaring off to fight, when all at once one of them declares, "You're not worth my good time." The message is clear: not only is the inmate not walking away from the fight out of cowardice, and therefore not deserving of social sanction, but he is asserting his social standing as so markedly above that of his rival that engaging any further, at the risk of losing his precious freedom, is simply beneath him.

The statement that another inmate is not worth your good time has the advantage of being true; most men we encountered were simply trying to get through their sentence with their good time intact. They are marking the days before their release, and making their lives as comfortable as possible in the interim. The stakes of whatever interpersonal conflicts might arise in the meantime are secondary to the objective of getting out and rebuilding a life on the outside. The striving of many inmates to simply inhabit a generic subject position, docile enough to avoid trouble but tough-seeming enough to save face in the eyes of his peers, was dramatized tersely by an ordinarily diplomatic inmate Jarrod heard remark ominously, "I'm about to break character."

Another way to avoid a fight, once two guys have begun challenging each other, is for a third to step in and force or implore them to back down and keep the peace. This can have the added weight of keeping dormitories free from shakedowns or other undue scrutiny, which concerns everyone, especially shotcallers. Finally, in some cases a challenged person can appeal to his rival's sense of reason, solidarity, or decency: "C'mon man, I wouldn't do that to you," or "You know that's not right." David used this tactic on a number of occasions, generally to positive effect.

Cooperation

While carceral facilities are notorious for conflict between inmates, we witnessed a surprising number and variety of cooperation practices, many of which have already been discussed, like the nightly communal meals, the special holiday dishes given out all but freely, the sharing of communal assets such as laundry lines and milk fridges, and the oral transmission and communal enforcement of intricate inmate-created rules. Here, we will examine cooperation in greater detail. Though far from exhaustive, these examples serve to present a telling snapshot of the rich culture of solidarity among sentenced men at Rikers.

The Phones

Each dorm counts between four and five phones mounted on the wall. Resembling old-school public pay phones, they consist of a hard black plastic receiver and a plain metal box with a hook and a keypad, but no change slot. These phones, for all their simplicity, are the single most important point of contact with the outside world for the overwhelming majority of inmates. As such, they are often the first front in a dormitory power struggle. Accordingly, a great number of rules and regulations regarding their use are created and maintained by the inmate population.

In 12-Lower, for example, the Crips posted signs insisting that everyone brush their teeth before using the phones; verbally, this was extended to washing one's hands as well. They also enforced "slot time," a policy governing the use of the phones in the last sixty to ninety minutes before lights out. Slot time varied from one housing unit to the next. On a couple of occasions, when David was in a dorm far under capacity (ten to fifteen people in an approximately fifty-bed dorm), there was actually no slot time at all. Yet slot time is by and large a given on Rikers. This is one of the most important pieces of social intake information, and the phone protocol is one of the first questions a savvy inmate asks about upon arrival in a new house.

Under slot time, certain inmates are entitled to a fifteen-minute "slot" (inmates receive one fifteen-minute and one six-minute phone call every three hours) at a specific time and phone to which they are granted exclusive access sometime generally between 7:00 or 7:30 and 8:30 p.m. The 8:30 slot, being the final one before the phones are cut off, is generally the most sought after. The last outgoing call can be made at 8:46, but in-progress calls do not cut off until 9:00 p.m. This means that an inmate who uses his fifteen-minute call beginning promptly at 8:30 can quickly dial again and enjoy his six-minute call afterward—or, if he has another inmate willing to dial his ID number and let him use his phone time standing by, even another fifteen-minute call. This novelty is a sort of status marker for the owner of the 8:30 slot.

Slot time is generally respected by everyone—a person can leave his phone untouched for the entire fifteen-minute slot and still expect no one to use it. In 12-Lower, the Crips kept a logbook of the various slots and their owners, serving a highly effective bureaucratic function in the messy world of city time. In another dorm David was confined to, this one lacking a strong hierarchy, the inmates simply posted scraps of paper declaring the slots and their owners above every phone, and modified them ad hoc when someone went home or otherwise left the dorm.

Even before COVID-19, many inmates placed clean socks bearing their names over a phone they intended to use soon or, if they had the social capital to back it up, claiming it for their exclusive use. This practice, often referred to as "planting flags," served a double function as a public hygiene measure and a claiming of turf. Planting flags could sometimes become downright egregious; David briefly lived in a dorm where four of the five phones were claimed for exclusive use by five individual Bloods, leaving only one phone for everybody else, about thirty men. But these rules were not rigid, either; anyone who had a decent amount of respect and goodwill from the other inmates could ask a person who had claimed a phone with a sock if they could use it for a call, and reasonably expect to receive their consent.

There are multiple daily arguments on the phones, when frustrated men yell at their wives or girlfriends, but no matter how worked up they may get, rarely does anyone slam the phone down. Risking a broken phone, after all, means risking a pack-up, as no one wants to lose a point of contact with the outside world.[15]

Passing It On

The no-snitching culture of life behind bars is well known, and Rikers is no exception.[16] In its broadest sense, not snitching simply means not passing any information that might be used against other prisoners to the agents of the institution, whether on purpose or by accident. Conversely, there exists another common but lesser-known shibboleth of inmate loyalty: the passing on of messages to each other, whether verbal or physical. Physical messages are often small notes written on scraps of paper ("kites"). Inmates often ask others, including those they barely know, to pass kites on to their intended recipients if they confirm that they will in fact cross paths with the recipient in their shared housing unit, or elsewhere, such as the yard, mess hall, workplace, or methadone clinic. It is completely taboo to read a kite one is only passing on. As there are practically no private spaces on Rikers, and word travels quickly among inmates, even a quick peek could easily land a person in dire straits. This request for transmission usually takes the form of a quick impromptu conversation ("Yo, is X in your house? Give this to him."), with the kite itself slipping from one hand to another almost at the same time the request is made. Verbal messages are usually vague, along the lines of "Tell X I got that thing for him when he ready" or "X says come to the yard today, he wants to talk to you."

People also ask others, again including those they barely know, to traffic small contraband items, like drugs or tobacco, from one housing unit to the next, but the expectation of participation is much lower. Unless an inmate knows the person he is asking to take on the role of transporter well, or the potential transporter will somehow profit from the operation, it is generally acceptable to refuse. On several occasions, David was asked by near-strangers to carry tobacco or illicit prescription drugs from work to the dorm or vice versa. He politely declined and offered to pass the word on to the intended recipient instead. The two people looking to make the exchange would then find another time and place to meet.

Those requesting delivery of a message or item will inevitably find a way to confirm its delivery, usually by requesting another message be passed through someone. "Ask X if he got that thing." In the event that a message cannot be transmitted directly to the recipient, it can usually be passed on to another person in the same housing unit. Once, a gang member in David's dorm gave him a kite to pass to a gang member in another dorm on his daily meal-distribution route, part of his kitchen job. Having only a few seconds at the door, and not finding the intended recipient there, David instead passed the kite to the inmate who answered the door, a total stranger, and then relayed that man's name and appearance to the sender, who later confirmed that the message had indeed reached its destination.

C-O-D

Another type of message that demonstrates allegiance to the inmates over the jail administration is the verbal warning inmates often shout to each other when a guard or captain approaches. As with the NYPD, all DOC officials with a rank higher than officer are distinguishable by their white, as opposed to blue, shirts. Captains, as the middle managers of the world behind bars, are both the most frequently seen "white shirts" and the DOC officials most likely to actually enforce rules that rank-and-file officers are willing to let slide in exchange for some sort of equilibrium with the captive populations they oversee.

Captains make the rounds of the housing units every hour or so, walking the length of the dorm, checking the secured red metal fire door at the far end, and scribbling a few notes in red ink in the log book before leaving. If the captain spots anything that violates DOC policy (contraband, smoking, etc.), the captain is likely to confiscate it or order the inmates to stop the activity, and may even issue them a ticket. This, of course, depends very much on the individual captain, the captain's mood, the day, and the housing unit, but few inmates want to be caught off guard by the appearance of a captain. Thus, in the few seconds it takes for the Bubble officer to unlock the gate, a captain's white shirt will inevitably be spotted by one of the men in the unit, and cries of "C-O-D!" will ring out from the front of the dorm. According to inmates, "COD" is an abbreviation of "Captain on deck!"

COs posted to the housing units are required to make the rounds hourly, as well, and "walk the unit," in the same manner as the captains. In general, inmates do not announce the approach of a steady officer unless the officer is new, or known to be particularly strict, or if someone is overtly engaging in some unpermitted activity. In this case, to distinguish that the approaching authority figure is a CO and not a captain, the inmates call out, "Walkin'!" This call is sometimes used to denote the approach of captains, too, but was usually reserved for rank-and-file officers, and is commonly heard to alert those smoking a joint or stick together at the back of the bathroom. For example, a person using a sink or a toilet, or one of the phones located at the front of the bathroom may call out "Walkin'! Walkin'!" to give the smokers in the shower the few seconds' notice they need to dispose of the joint or stick they are enjoying.

This practice is common, though far from required, even among nonsmokers such as David. In Mod 4 in C-74, David often placed a plastic chair in the open space at the front of the bathroom to read books late at night, as the bathroom lights stayed on all night. If a CO or captain began to approach the bathroom, David would sometimes, but not always, alert any smokers in the back by calling out, "Walkin'!" He was often thanked by smokers quickly leaving the bathroom as if nothing untoward was happening, who muttered "good lookin'" as they passed, and never once was he criticized for not alerting them. It was a gesture of solidarity, not a requirement.

"You Right There, Bro"

Contrary to popular conceptions of jail as a place where the golden rule is replaced by a cutthroat *homo homini lupus* ethos, sentenced inmates at Rikers are constantly offering each other words of encouragement as their release dates approach. Overhearing snippets of conversation with upbeat phrases like "Four months? You good," "You outta here," and "You right there, bro" happens several times a day. Other common forms of encouragement include expressions like "That's right around the corner," "You got that," and "Hold your head." These communal acts of care are very common, even among men with no particularly close emotional bonds.

City-sentenced Greens, however, generally avoid broaching the topic with pretrial Tans. Besides potentially arousing the jealousy of a man facing—or already sentenced to, and awaiting transfer upstate for—much more time, Greens often find themselves at a loss for words when the situation arises. David once dared to ask a Tan he had found himself working out with a lot in the yard what kind of time he was facing. "That fucking judge . . . ," the man said, staring off into the empty sky. "He gave me life." David, who had just revealed that he had only two months left until his release date, did not know what to say to a man for whom his own rules of passing time simply did not apply.

Gang Affiliation

The gang is the most explicit form of inmate cooperation. Gang members in greens are generally considered "inactive" by their superiors and by other gang members, according to Rikers conventional wisdom, because they have an upcoming release date. As the saying among city-time men goes, "Ain't nobody on that kinda time." Though conflicts do arise between people because of gang affiliation, they are generally fewer in number and less serious in degree than those gang-based conflicts that arise among detainees. Gang members in greens may still be expected to declare and represent their affiliation, but they can likely get away with not having to take risky action based on it. The exception is the Crips: they are the only gang on Rikers that never has to declare their affiliation, as they are small in number and generally targeted by other gangs. Trinitarios, during David's time at Rikers, were also widely disliked by other gangs, due to a gruesome mistaken-identity murder that dominated New York headlines periodically from its occurrence in June 2018. The Bloods, in particular, were rumored to be beefing with the "Trinis."

Repping gang affiliation is usually done through the odd piece of colored clothing or jewelry that somehow makes it through Intake, the mail, or, during our time, in-person visit packages. David watched a red, camouflage-pattern durag change hands several times over an eight-month period, for example—as one Blood went home, he gifted it to another. David encountered a number of gang members who had been able to keep small colored bracelets upon their arrival at Rikers, and used these as identifying marks. Red rosaries were fashioned in the same way for Bloods using the ink sticks from red pens, which, as they had to be stolen from captains or other ranking officials, were particularly valuable. Yellow rosaries were crafted for Latin Kings using the ink sticks from yellow highlighters. Some gang members can also identify each other by tattoos or, sometimes, certain types of ornamental scarring. A person's street name, jail name, or nickname can also reveal his gang allegiance, as can a person's word choice. Slangy greetings that are interchangeable for most people in the street, for example, can betray a person's gang membership in Rikers. A Crip would never say "What's poppin'?" but rather "What's crackin'?" and vice versa for Bloods.

All gangs on Rikers have specific code words that serve as both greetings and identifiers of gang affiliation. These code words are often shouted out windows and as inmates pass each other in the halls, sometimes in chains, in call-and-response style. When shouted in passing, they may serve as an opening for a larger conversation, time permitting, or simply be a way of saying hello. When shouted out a window in the direction of another housing unit—or, for inmates in their cellblocks after lock-in hours, another cell—they are a sign that the person initiating the call wishes to speak to a fellow gang member in the target housing unit, usually to discuss an important matter in a mix of coded and purposefully vague language.

Much of the graffiti covering the walls of Rikers's interior spaces is gang related and symbolic; common themes include crowns, stars, both five- and six-pointed, pitchforks, both right side up and upside down, and numbers, most notably five and six. Many gang members also use hand signals and even entire pidgin languages with contrived and impenetrable vocabularies to signal membership to each other and communicate quickly and confidentially in the common spaces, such as when being led past each other in the hall. David witnessed this exchange on several occasions. Sometimes, gang members may also flash a hand sign across the dorm just to affirm their gang solidarity. These hand signals and invented languages can be incredibly complex.

Gang members generally exchange handshakes and secret words upon arrival in a dorm run by their own gang. The question "You bang?" is posed to most new arrivals. A new arrival can declare his neutrality by simply answering in the negative, describing himself as neutral, or "five-fifty," as in "I'm five-fifty, ya heard?" Like "seven-thirty," this term is rumored to stem from a DOC code used to designate inmates as gang affiliated. Answering dishonestly can be dangerous. One of David's friends had been in a local street crew technically affiliated with the Latin Kings in his adolescence, over fifteen years before they met at Rikers. He had answered "No" in 12-Lower, a Crip dorm, but months later, when asked by a high-ranking Latin King in a neutral dorm, revealed that he had formerly been in a King-affiliated crew. He later explained to David that it could have caused problems for him if he had concealed his prior affiliation in that scenario.

Gangs are not necessarily racially or ethnically homogenous—we met Puerto Rican Crips, Black American and Greek American Latin Kings, and even heard from numerous inmates that there exists an entire subset of Chinese American Bloods. Additionally, David was told on multiple occasions that Muslim inmates generally defend each other at Rikers and in the upstate prison system as well, meaning that, while not a gang, they may perform the self-defense functions of one on the basis of religious identity. Gang identity can also cut across the CO-inmate divide, as many COs are rumored to be gang affiliated.

Despite their sensationally negative portrayal in the media, gangs on Rikers can serve very positive functions, especially as a bulwark against the violence of the DOC's own foot soldiers. Of course, the gangs' power lends itself to that same power's abuse, especially in a stressful, scarce, and dehumanizing environment. Far from a universally benevolent force, gang authority is often used to enforce a system that benefits only the gang members, and the gang hierarchy in particular, at the expense of the other inmates—or worse, metes out brutality with an arbitrariness to rival that of the institution itself.

Dormitory Power Structure

Gang Houses

The DOC began housing inmates by gang affiliation in 2014 in an attempt to decrease the number of gang-involved assaults.[17] Beginning in January 2021, DOC commissioner Louis Molina targeted the policy and set about dismantling it under the guise of protecting inmates from the abuses of gang rule, though this move was likely just as much about preventing the inmates from having any meaningful collective power.[18]

In our experience, many dormitories were run by a fairly rigid gang-based hierarchy that functioned as a sort of proto-state, composed of rank-and-file gang members, shotcallers, and the lead shotcaller, or "big homie." This term is not necessarily restricted to gang members; a big homie is simply the person with the most authority in the house. This authority may be achieved via gang hierarchy or other means.

A gang hierarchy running the dorm eliminates a good deal of ambiguity that might otherwise lead to violence. For example, in a house with no gang hierarchy, a new arrival might claim a phone slot that already belongs to another inmate, forcing him to either submit or challenge the newcomer to play the bathroom. In a gang dorm, slot time may be carefully managed, as in 12-Lower, or less rigorously enforced, as we observed elsewhere, but the gang hierarchy always serves as a last line of enforcement.

Difficult decisions requiring collective power, such as pack-ups, are made quickly and easily with a centralized gang hierarchy, as gang members are expected to line up behind the shotcaller's decision and enforce it physically if necessary. "In a gang house, he would've been cut up and packed up already," a fellow inmate once remarked to David, of a particularly annoying and presumptuous inmate who lived in the same (neutral) dorm as they. In another case, while David was in 12-Lower, the Crips immediately packed up a young Black man for stealing, despite the fact that he was friendly and well-liked by all of them, and that the person he stole from was a white heroin addict, newly arrived and with no real social standing. Both the thief and victim were non–gang members. Gang members often led the charge in standing up for the dorm as a whole when the institution was particularly egregious in its interactions with the inmates. David once witnessed gang members in 12-Lower physically block a CO from leaving the dorm when it appeared that the house would not be taken to commissary as regularly scheduled, demanding the CO call his superiors and request the commissary trip. They were successful.

In another instance, this one related to David on several occasions by multiple different inmates, the Latin Kings who ran a sentenced housing unit in C-95 led what can only be described as a sit-in for racial justice. Fed up with one of the steady officers' constant racist remarks, they convinced everyone to pack their belongings into trash bags, demonstrating their readiness to move to another housing unit, which would be a significant hassle for the COs. They sat on the floor of the unit, demanding that either they all be transferred to another unit, or the CO be rotated to another post. Again, they were successful: Turtles and captains came, and, after discussion, the offending CO was eventually removed. Of course, the gang hierarchy cuts both ways. Though it functions as a proto-state, rarely is there any due process. In the tuna theft incident described previously, for example, Walid was targeted for a pack-up even though there was no more definitive proof against him than there was against Ack.

Ruling gang members will likely take the best beds and may strictly regulate where others can sleep, when they can watch TV or use the video game console, if there is one, or what they may watch or play. If this behavior goes too far, it will likely be deemed "oppressing" by the other inmates. This word seemed to have a special meaning in Rikers. David heard rumors, for example, of a shotcaller in another house who took the remote control to bed with him every night, preventing the others from watching TV in the morning until he woke up, and this was deemed "oppressing." No matter how far the measures taken by the gang hierarchy went, they were likely to present them as their rightful reward for "running the dorm," a jailhouse reflection of power's classic defense of itself: "Without us, there would be chaos."

Gang leaders unity could be deceptive, however. One shotcaller confided in David, after they had both been released, that he had been in near-constant conflict with another shotcaller, but that they generally kept it under wraps to present a united front to the rest of the dorm.

Neutral Houses

Not all dormitories were run by gangs. A dorm with the absence of a gang hierarchy is referred to as a "neutral house" and may have any number of power arrangements among the residents. Most neutral houses still have a big homie, but unlike in a gang house, where the big homie's rule is backed up by the rank-and-file gang members, a neutral house's big homie is more likely to have claimed the title for himself. This step is usually taken when a number of factors are present: the absence of a strong hierarchy, often in the wake of the previous big homie's departure, veteran status (those stepping up to the big homie plate are likely to have been in the dorm for a substantial length of time already), some degree of respect or social capital, and a fairly long time remaining before release date (at least a few months). Neutral big homies seem to claim the title for a number of reasons, some of which are clearly self-serving. Feeling that their seniority entitles them to certain privileges in the dorm—such as an exclusive phone or coveted slot, "dibs" on the best bed in the dorm once the current occupant goes home, or the right to watch their favorite TV show—big homies often claim these for themselves as the just rewards of leadership. But inmates also seemed to claim the position in order to fill a power vacuum, out of fear that the dorm would fail to function smoothly if they didn't.

Neutral big homies generally did not have a crew to back them up if their abuses caused conflict, so they trod more lightly. For instance, David observed that they tended to be less assertive in the perks they claimed for running the dorm, and were much more likely to use "soft power," or negotiation, rather than coercion or intimidation, in times of crisis. Without a group of soldiers to back them up, a neutral big homie has much more reason to take a person aside and speak to him in private, appealing to him as an equal and attempting to change his mind about whatever issue has arisen. It is also likely the case that gang shotcallers risk looking weak to the rank and file if they do not demonstrate an aggressive response to perceived social transgressions, thus perpetuating the threat or use of violence, a dynamic that was absent in David's experience with neutral big homies.

Unlike in a gang, where allegiance to a common purpose is assumed, a consensus must generally be established among the residents of a neutral dorm if they are to take action together. On two occasions, David was part of impromptu, nonhierarchically organized pack-ups in neutral dorms. In both cases, word spread quietly in advance among a significant number of the inmates, who then took the decisive action of removing the belongings of the individual to be packed up from the dorm while he was away at work or chow. Placing all of the inmate's buckets and other belongings "on the bridge" outside the gate (one inmate would ask the Bubble CO to open it for a mundane reason, and then hold it open for the others) served as a clear sign to both him and the COs that he was not welcome.

A neutral big homie's power may also be so subtle as to be almost imperceptible. In one instance, there was a month-long period with no clear leadership in Mod 4-Lower South, following the previous big homie's release. The normal functions of the dorm, such as cleaning, mediating conflict, and even packing people up all continued without much difference. After a month or so, David noticed the inmate with the most seniority in the dorm beginning to claim a phone for himself, and approaching new arrivals to explain the house rules. His role served in some ways as a check on unlimited power. "This is a neutral house," he would explain. "Everybody gets along, we don't want no trouble. Slot time starts at 8:00 p.m."

David considers the month-long interim period without a clear leader to be an example of nonhierarchical organizing in a neutral dorm. A similar situation arose in the wake of the mass release of sentenced men during the first wave of COVID-19.[19] David was left in a forty-eight-bed dorm, previously fully occupied, with only a dozen others. There were a couple of gang members, but no clear leader, and no real disputes. A contributing factor was surely that the living environment of those left behind had flipped from one of scarcity to one of abundance: everyone who was released simply abandoned all their belongings, leaving David and the others with several months' worth of commissary food and hygiene products, extra pillows, blankets and mattresses, and plenty of space, phones, showers, toilets, and TV time for everyone. As with the other nonhierarchical period mentioned above, the normal functions of the dorm continued as usual. When conflict arose, other inmates stepped in to diffuse it.

Though he never witnessed it personally, David also heard rumors from other inmates of neutral houses electing a "mayor." One guy who knew David was interested in the practice once pointed out another inmate from another housing unit in the mess hall, saying that he had been the mayor of a unit they had both been confined to months earlier. David took a seat across from the man and asked him if it was true.

"Yup!" The man answered, happily munching on his bland DOC chow.

"How did you become mayor?" David inquired, hoping for an exposition of jailhouse direct democracy. But the man only chuckled.

"Beatin' motherfuckers' asses," he replied with a smile.

David remains unsure if the man was joking, but if his statement was true, his mayorship can hardly be taken as a shining example of the democratic process.

The fact that a house is neutral does not mean there are no gang members in it (in any case, the relatively high prevalence of gang members on Rikers makes this very unlikely). To the contrary, a neutral house usually has a handful of members of different gangs, sometimes only one or two, but none of whom has numerical superiority or the motivation to rock the boat by trying to take over the dorm.

Tensions and Transitions

Houses may also transition from neutral to gang or gang to neutral, or change hands between gangs. A neutral house usually becomes a gang house due to a critical mass of inmates with the same gang affiliation deciding to take things over. Unless the neutral dorm can quickly and effectively present a united front against their efforts, they are likely to succeed. A gang house becoming a neutral house is rarer but can happen if all the gang members' release dates fall within a short period and no new gang members arrive for a significant period of time after their departure, or if the gang members are otherwise rotated out of the dorm.

In one interesting example, David lived in a dorm with three gang members who claimed to "run the house" but in reality did little more than claim exclusive use of the phones and smoke plane all day. Though the dorm was at half capacity, the DOC moved in nearly two dozen men from another dorm all at once, creating tension over the phones between the two gang members present at the time and the rest of the dorm. The neutral inmates began squaring off against the two gang members, but before physical conflict could arise, the Bubble CO contacted her superiors, who sent a transfer team to pack the two gang members up and move them to another unit. When the third gang member returned from work later that afternoon, he found that the dorm had become a neutral house, and he was in no position to contest it.

A similar anecdote was recounted to David in C-74 by several inmates who had been in 12-Lower after he left. Though the Crips who ran 12-Lower during David's time there had a very generous policy with the phones, sometime after David's departure, a new batch of gang members tried to dominate the phones and invited "anybody who ain't with it" to play the bathroom. They were surprised to find themselves facing off against nearly half the dorm, and quickly dropped the issue, effectively conceding neutral rule on the issue of the phones.

People could also move up in status in a house without necessarily being a member of the hierarchy, for example, by being particularly handy with the terrain (knowing how to best use affordances in that particular dorm), by negotiating well with the COs, or simply by being there the longest, becoming what was sometimes jokingly referred to as the "dorm OG" or "house OG." Any of these could earn someone some respect and make others in the house more inclined to listen to him and let him use the space more freely, enjoy a "prime real estate" bed, a choice slot on the phone, or even a say in what TV show to watch. All inmates naturally acquired some status in a dorm over time if new arrivals consistently deemed them competent enough to ask how something worked.

Race and Ethnicity

Since its early colonial period, the United States has been characterized by a hierarchical division of labor that privileges Euro-Americans over other so-called races. This balance of wealth and power permeates nearly every social institution, and defines daily life, from its most lamentable tragedies to its most banal details.[20] Our socialization as white has explicitly trained us to ignore the effects of white supremacy as it plays out in our lives, and to simply accept the racial hierarchy as the way things ought to be. We have therefore sought to correct this "white blind spot," to whatever extent it is possible for us to escape it, by consulting as many nonwhite perspectives as possible, and premising our race analysis on the likely prospect that we had missed something that was right in front of our faces.[21] Surely, institutional racism decided who was at Rikers, what resources they had behind them, and what they could look forward to when they got out. But on an interpersonal level, regardless of how hard we looked, we found race relations amid city time to be more complex than the rigid segregation for which prisons and jails are rightfully notorious.

White inmates could often be a bit "cliquey," to quote a Black inmate David knew, in where they chose to sleep, but never limited their interactions or friendships to other white people. This was true even of white inmates who had been members of white-supremacist prison gangs on previous bids in state or federal prison. By their telling, joining such a gang was as much a matter of survival in the state system as joining a street gang might be for someone growing up in the 'hood. Though it is easy—and prudent—to be skeptical of anyone claiming to be a fair-weather white supremacist, David did, in fact, sometimes find this explanation believable. Of course, the numerically rare white inmates on Rikers have a vested interest in disavowing white supremacy as a matter of social survival. On the few occasions when David heard racial slurs against people of color, those using them never dared speak them in the presence of the racial or ethnic group they were slandering.

Even the rare out-and-out white supremacist generally did not advertise his beliefs on Rikers. One man with white-supremacist sympathies in David's dorm once revealed a picture of a swastika and another of Adolf Hitler he kept taped to the inside cover of his journal. The fact that he kept them hidden instead of displaying them outright is a testament to the risks displaying such symbols carried. "Those guys generally keep their tats covered here," a Black CO once told David with a look that explained exactly why.

Another inmate once told David a story to the same effect: he had been smoking plane regularly with a group of three other men in C-95. It was in the summer, and the cells were insufferably hot, but they smoked there to avoid detection. Most of the group ended up stripping off their shirts as they rolled and shared one joint of deuce after another, but one member of the group, a Salvadorian, never removed his, and never explained why. One day, overheating and in the throes of a fresh K2 high, he tore off his T-shirt to reveal a giant swastika tattoo on his shoulder. Shocked, the inmate who later told the story to David stopped associating with the Salvadorian. The mere fact that this man chose to keep this tattoo covered for so long, despite the discomfort it caused him, speaks volumes about the reception these sorts of symbols receive at Rikers, as does the storyteller's decision to cut him off, despite being a white man himself.

Some white inmates at Rikers harbored theories about "reverse racism" from inmates of color, and especially staff of color, but these were almost always revealed to be victimhood fantasies. Resentment of white people and their privilege, especially those obviously hailing from more affluent backgrounds, is certainly expressed among some people of color, particularly those from working-class backgrounds. But we found this no more pronounced at Rikers than anywhere else in New York City. Furthermore, on many occasions when white inmates grumbled under their breath about reverse racism from staff, it seemed clear to us that the issue was an interpersonal one, and the racial dimension, if actually a factor and not merely a figment of the white prisoner's imagination, was not the one at the heart of the matter.

White men were also not the only ones to form sections based on racial or ethnic identity. This tendency to coalesce, however, often seemed to be based as much on linguistic ties as on racial, ethnic, or cultural ones. For example, on two different occasions in two different dorms, David witnessed Cantonese-speaking Chinese immigrants take adjoining beds. In the first case, neither spoke much English; their decision to become neighbors seemed mostly about the comfort actually holding a sustained conversation with another person brought. A Korean man and an American-born man of Thai descent were later directed to open beds next to the two Chinese inmates by the gang members who ran the dorm, forming a four-bed section that was known, predictably, as

"Chinatown" or "Canal Street." As soon as more beds opened up in the dorm, the two Cantonese speakers stayed together, but the newcomers moved elsewhere, each to a separate section; they felt no pressure to keep themselves grouped together on the basis of so-called race.

In the second case, one of the Chinese speakers was fluent in both English and Cantonese, while the other spoke very little English. The bilingual man therefore took it upon himself to serve as an interpreter for the other one. This dynamic was often at work among inmates for whom language was a barrier to understanding the strange world around them, most notably the numerous Latino inmates.

Latino inmates' forming sections, when it happened, offered a complex illustration of how race, ethnicity, and language contribute to concepts of group identity in jail. In one dorm, David observed a "Spanish section" consisting of a Mexican immigrant who spoke no English and generally had the features of a person with indigenous Central American ancestry; a Colombian American who spoke both Spanish and English, and was tall with dark European features and olive skin; a white-presenting Puerto Rican who spoke no English; and a Dominican who spoke no English and would likely be identified by most Americans as Black. Another Spanish section consisted of two Ecuadorians who looked as though they were largely of indigenous Central American ancestry, a Black Guatemalan, all of whom spoke some English, but none fluently, and a third-generation Puerto Rican New Yorker with very fair skin, fluent in both languages. In both of these cases, there were other Latinos scattered throughout the dorm, either in sections of their own, in pairs, or by themselves.

All activities beyond forming sections, such as exercising, watching TV, eating together in the mess hall, cooking together, or sharing drugs seemed to follow this same pattern. Inmates might coalesce around others they identified as belonging to their own in-groups, but the boundaries of these groups were extremely porous. Never once, for example, did David see a TV, phone, or pull-up bar reserved for members of one racial or ethnic group.

Perhaps the most shocking facet of racial politics on Rikers is that many white inmates feel entitled to use the n-word as a term of endearment. This word is almost always pronounced with the nonrhotic "R," (ending in "-a," not "-er"), and invariably has the meaning of "friend," "dude," or even just "person." This practice is tolerated to varying degrees by the Black inmates on Rikers. In one dorm where a white section had formed, David observed the white inmates there constantly tagging this term onto the ends of their sentences when addressing each other. Two of David's friends, both Black and sitting at the other end of the dorm, grumbled to each other that they found the practice infuriating, and wanted to confront the men, but did not want to risk losing good time. David surmised that this unwillingness to lose good time played a fundamental role in the ability of white men, especially those who grow up in working-class neighborhoods of color, live in the projects, or are often homeless, to get away with using this word in jail. David confronted one of these men, who defended his words with the classic argument: "I'm from the street. And I have a lot of Black friends."

It was also possible to go too far. David witnessed an Italian American from Staten Island tossing the word around but pronouncing it with the rhotic "R," known colloquially as the "hard R," amiably greeting his neighbors with perhaps the worst slur in the English language. Even though he used it to mean "friend" or "person," this evidently crossed a line. He was promptly called out by a Black Crip, who scolded him, "Yo! I told you twice already—you're white. You can't say that word. If I hear you say it again, I'ma slap the shit out you."

Racial and ethnic tensions like this do arise among sentenced men on Rikers, and they sometimes escalate to violence, but neither of us ever witnessed anything along the lines of the sort of full-scale race-oriented brawl of which Hollywood is so enamored. People often mocked the accents of nonnative English speakers (and of native speakers with odd regionalisms), but the subjects of the insults just as often laughed along with them, or brushed them off. David once witnessed a Puerto Rican and two Mexican Americans squaring off against a Barbadian American because he had dismissively referred to them as "Goya bean motherfuckers." Others intervened, preventing them from coming to blows; in any case, the main issue seemed to be defending their honor, as most inmates feel obligated to do when faced with any insult. This insult's racial or ethnic character merely served as an intensifier.

So what accounts for the remarkably porous racial and ethnic boundaries in these facilities? Our best answer comes from the scholarship of ethnographer Michael Walker, who experienced incarceration in multiple California county jails. Walker describes rigid racial segregation in some housing units, so stringent that food and amenities could not even be shared across these lines. In one of the same facilities, however, he also experienced one housing unit, an honor block, where this was not the case. The difference, Walker argues, did not come from the prisoners, who, like himself, were often the same exact people behaving very differently in these two unique contexts. Instead, in general population, he found that the COs had organized the segregation, separating out prisoners into three sloppy categories (Asian prisoners, for instance, were Black), and delegating each to a de facto representative who mediated power relations and otherwise managed the prisoners of their designated group. This suggested to Walker that the segregation he encountered was imposed by the jail administration, using the time-honored technique of divide and rule.

At Rikers, then, we simply experienced a different regime of dormitory control, rooted in house gangs, shotcallers, and big homies, whom the COs could rely upon to keep some semblance of surface order in multiracial dormitories. This arrangement was surely pernicious to prisoners who caught its bad side, but was nonetheless not based on overt racial segregation. Free of such divisions, city-time prisoners, like those in Walker's honor block, were happy to associate across lines that would be impermeable elsewhere.[22]

Friendship

The most essential social unit in jail, with the exception of gang affiliation, is the friendship group. If philosopher Jacques Derrida's assertion that friendship, at least in the outside world, can be thought of as a sort of pact to mourn each other's deaths, friendship among sentenced men on Rikers Island can be thought of as a pact to celebrate each other's release dates—and to offer the attendant psychological support to make it there.[23]

Beyond that, friendship mostly means some combination of sharing extra resources or food, cooking and working out together, helping each other steal things from the institution, but also sometimes lending each other an ear, or perhaps offering up that extra bed next to you if the dorm starts to get crowded and it looks like a new arrival (i.e., stranger) might otherwise take it. Friends can also stand up for each other in the face of institutional pressure. When David was targeted by a captain for having too many buckets, after people had gifted him their belongings during the mass release of the first wave of COVID-19, three of his friends (an Italian American, a Black Puerto Rican, and an Ecuadorian) agreed to take some of his extra buckets and store them beneath their beds. This act relied not only on David's trust in his friends but on their trust that he would not complicate their lives by accusing them of stealing, or bothering them too frequently to access his buckets.

It is rare but possible that friends have to jump into a fight on another friend's behalf. Indeed, this can be thought of as the lowest form of friendship among Greens on Rikers. One guy even once told David, "We're cool. We're not friends, but I wouldn't let you get jumped or nothin'." On another occasion, an inmate in the dorm yelled to David, "Yo! Come get ya boy, bro! He buggin' on the door!" A friend of David's was making a scene at the gate, shouting threats at a man from the housing unit across the hall with whom he had beef. Because David was known to have an affinity for the man, he was expected to intervene.

City-time inmates find moments of camaraderie where they can, and sharing a story or a joke scratches the social itch, if only temporarily. Other arrangements indicative of a level of friendship include mutual wake-up agreements, such as for breakfast chow or early-morning services like law library, or even the yard. Inmates will generally sit with friends when they dine in the mess hall, and may form workout crews together. Over one two-month period during David's bid, he and a number of others worked out several times a week together in the yard, under the aegis of another inmate who was a CrossFit trainer in the outside world, and whom they jokingly called "Coach." Nothing, however, compares to the pleasure of gifting things to your friends when you leave. Selecting the most useful, most expensive, most unique, or most coveted items from your personal belongings and giving them to someone who has helped you make it through your bid, in order to help him make it through the rest of his, brings a very particular type of satisfaction.

Not everything is always as it seems when it comes to friendships among Greens at Rikers, however. Because of the high turnover, short duration, and enforced proximity, most inmates will just go along to get along rather than resist or refuse a spontaneously forming association with another. But once someone leaves, one or more of their erstwhile friends may well be found slandering him to the others, or even the dorm at large. Many times, David witnessed a person who had been talking and laughing with a now-departed inmate only the day before describe them as "crazy," an "asshole," or worse. Some friendships, however, do last beyond jail. David has a handful of them, and most of the guys he is in touch with are in turn still friends with others they met behind bars. Yet most friendships, even close ones, seem to end when both people have been released. Most guys, it seems, want to put their time on Rikers behind them, and cannot separate friends they made on the island from their unpleasant experience there.

12

Institutional Relationships

"Take that thing off your head," the captain orders dismissively.

"Man, get the fuck outta my goddamn face," his target shoots back without missing a beat.

On his head, he wears a ragged pair of white Hanes briefs, tied up like a durag with the elastic waistband reading "HANES" across the flesh of his forehead. He points at it, explaining, "This here is my motherfuckin' religion." As he calmly, steadily continues past the now-flabbergasted captain, he turns his head over a shoulder to call back, as if for added clarification, "Ain't got time for your bullshit today!"

David and the other inmates on their way to breakfast cannot help but laugh at his brazen ploy. Invoking the specter of a religious-discrimination lawsuit, however unlikely, was enough to make the captain drop the issue entirely, even despite the man's humiliation of him. It is a truth any inmate learns after any significant amount of time: you have to use the institutional rules against the institution itself.

What to Do and How to Do It

"Among themselves," writes incarcerated author Jack Henry Abbott, "guards are human. Among themselves, the prisoners are human. Yet between these two, the relationship is not human. *It is animal.*"[1] Put a bit less dramatically, in the words of former C-76 inmates Neville "Storm" Redd, "I have to get up day after day and look at someone every day having them tellin' me when I can sleep, eat, or shit, and Storm don't like people tellin' him what to do and how to do it."[2] Despite the animosity built into their opposing subject positions, however, city-time inmates and COs are stuck with each other, and the functioning of the jail requires some degree of their cooperation. This means that within what we might call a state of low-intensity social war, some modicum of cooperation must be eked out.

The most stubborn fact of relations between COs and inmates is that underneath the uniforms that aim, quite overtly, to definitively establish and enforce their very different social roles, everyone is a human being. In undertaking their duties, COs demonstrate considerable variance in their individual personalities, levels of sympathy or antipathy toward the inmates, and enforcement of the jail's rules (or lack thereof). But at the end of the day, with no respect to their individuality, the COs have a job to do—one that puts them at odds with the inmate. "For the custodian, control is the central interest," writes sociologist Richard Cloward, "for the inmate, escape from material and social deprivation."[3] We can surmise that even the COs who smuggle contraband or otherwise break the law with select inmates spend most of their time enforcing the institution's rules, in the interest of preserving the appearance of normality, especially if they are concerned with avoiding detection.

Relations between inmates and COs, therefore, assume the paradox inherent in many hierarchical institutions where people interact with each other as both human beings and representatives of the structural position they have been assigned. While these roles may be relaxed when things are going well, any slackening of the jail's rigid inmate-CO division will not last long. When an inmate in Jarrod's dormitory, who had been exchanging flirtations with a female CO, purchased her a sweet treat from commissary as a gift, one of Jarrod's section mates remarked in disgust, "What kind of motherfucker goes to commissary and gets something for a CO? She got a helmet upstairs," he continued, referring to COs' riot gear, "and she gonna put it on and bust your head."

Locked Together

Former Rikers CO Robin K. Miller recounts how the "newly hired correction officers are brainwashed and abusive seeds are planted by academy instructors, programming them to believe that a Rikers Island prisoner . . . is an animal, the enemy, [a] scumbag, and extremely dangerous."[4] COs are instructed in the basic arguments from books like *Games Criminals Play*, which instill within the recruit a sense that every overture from an inmate, ranging from social familiarity to a request for basic assistance, could be part of a complex con designed to seduce the CO into a life of crime. More broadly, CO culture is steeped in an us-versus-them mentality, which enforces solidarity among COs, lest one be considered an "inmate lover"—a term of derision concerningly similar to a segregationist invective against whites who dared cross the color line.[5] This has a socially cohesive function for the CO workforce, but also helps COs dissociate from the injustices they witness, by recourse to, in the words of John Irwin, "the readily available theory that prisoners deserve their fate."[6]

It would, however, be impossible for COs to go about their daily business in overt conflict with the inmates, just as it would be for the inmates to be in constant upheaval against the COs. Thus, some kind of uneasy peace is required. In practical terms, the easiest way for COs to keep a lid on the dormitory is to deputize the lion's share of enforcing compliance to its most powerful inmates, the big homies and shotcallers. C. René West recounts how this power arrangement is called "running the dorm," a term both of us encountered numerous times during our sentences. West reasons that it is impossible for COs to disrupt the de facto prisoner power structure, because they don't spend enough time in the dormitory, and anyway, the prisoners in power are willing to back up their rules with violent force that inspires fear. "I try to do my job fairly," West writes, "but the bottom line is I am going home and I can't change anything in one day."[7]

City time cannot be structured by brute force alone. This means the guard must work with the prisoner to make the institution function, and therefore must engage in reciprocity, making "deals" or "trades" with prisoners, and observing de facto protocols. Early prison ethnographer Gresham Sykes argues, "Despite the guns and the surveillance, the searches and the precautions of the custodians, the actual behavior of the inmate population differs markedly from that which is called for by official commands and decrees. . . . Far from being omnipotent rulers who have crushed all signs of rebellion against their regime, the custodians are engaged in a continuous struggle to maintain order—and it is a struggle in which custodians fail."[8]

Experienced COs know that recognizing the authority of a small inmate elite is bound up in their helping to keep other inmates in line, and enforcing the sustained order of the cell block or dormitory house. Smart COs even take an active role in shaping these dynamics, by choosing who they recognize as worthy of inhabiting them, through the institutional recognition that is often essential for their success. The end result of structural accommodation is a hierarchized and divided body of inmates characterized by privileged actors breaking the rules in exchange for enforcing docility and order where it matters.[9] This arrangement can be quite explicit. Recall, a decade before David served his city time in C-74, the facility was made notorious by the disclosure of "The Program," a systematic and organized extortion racket run through the cooperative effort of powerful adolescent prisoners and COs, resulting in the death of at least one young man.[10] Shortly after David's time, the disclosure of a similar arrangement at Rikers, dubbed the "World Tour," revealed that little had changed despite considerable scrutiny of the deadly practice of CO-sanctioned prisoner violence.[11]

David was incarcerated with a man called Ra during one of Mod 4's neutral and nonhierarchical periods. Ra was addicted to crack and homeless on the outside, but enjoyed some status in jail because he was so familiar with it. He had been coming to Rikers on and off for decades, and had served a couple of years' time upstate, too. Though a big guy with a booming voice, he did not impose himself on others—he was generally pleasant to be around, could take a joke, and cleaned the place regularly for free. Yet he was also the kind of guy who wanted to avoid rocking the boat at all costs; more than anything, he craved stability. The COs seized on this as a chance to divide and conquer the inmates. When one highly combative new arrival once lost his temper at a CO and shouted "Suck my dick!" at him, Ra swooped in, raising his hands in the air, palms out, shouting, "No, no no." Ra remained on the CO's side, even after the CO began casually threatening to bring down a punishing search on the house—a threat everyone knew he was good for. In turn, Ra apologized and told the CO he would talk to the new guy. The next day, a search team did appear, but they only trashed the new guy's bed.

On another occasion, an inmate's expensive new sneakers disappeared after a search. He began filing grievance after grievance and complaining to any captain or dep who would listen, until Ra came back to the dorm one day and announced to everyone that he had just passed the security captain, who oversaw searches, in the hall. "If you don't cut it out with them shoes, he said they coming back with a search and they takin' everybody's shoes." One of David's neighbors later grumbled some biting criticism of Ra: "If we was back in slavery times,

Ra'd be one of them niggas helpin' them chase other niggas down and shit." None of this stopped Ra from adhering, at least in his mind, to some version of the inmate ethos of not snitching. Even this favored the institution; he and David once had a heated discussion about whether calling 311 to file a complaint about the conditions in the jail constituted snitching, with David arguing that you cannot "snitch" on a CO or jail in which you are captive, and Ra adopting the common CO position that this behavior made the inmate a snitch.

But CO cooperation with select inmates is not simply due to a divide-and-rule strategy. In practical terms, there are many times when the COs themselves are unable to function without the knowledge of those in their custody. The most obvious example is labor: during David's time, a large-scale inmate strike left COs pushing mops, brooms, and food carts because there were no inmate-workers to do it. COs who are unfamiliar with a certain housing unit's schedule will often ask the inmates what time a given event, like chow or yard, usually occurs. In Mod 4, the electrical wiring for the overhead lighting, controlled from a single light switch panel located in the Bubble, was hopelessly convoluted and counterintuitive. At lights out, COs unfamiliar with the house would try one switch after another. The lights would go on and off on each side, giving rise to shouts, jeers, and grumblings like, "These motherfuckers stupid." The CO often ended up asking an inmate to enter the Bubble and demonstrate how the control panel worked.

To maintain the balance of power in their favor, and to keep the whole operation cloaked in deniability, it is important to COs that they not seem deferential to the inmates. Preferential treatment is most covert when it assumes the form of selective enforcement of the rules, rather than the overt granting of special privileges. When COs see something they know to be a violation of the rules, they have the choice to take action or to act as if they have not seen it. COs are largely strategic in how they make this decision, and favoring certain inmates is part of the calculation. This pragmatic, relational approach to running carceral facilities has been dubbed "reciprocity."

Reciprocity amounts to the generous use of discretion, creating a constant state of negotiation that asserts the authority of the COs more so than the written rules, especially when the two contradict.[12] "In the authority to choose how to enforce security," write scholars David Correia and Tyler Wall, "is an authority to make law itself."[13] Interestingly, one 1998 study of six long-term prisons in the Northeast discovered that COs were unlikely, if given multiple-choice questions, to describe their management of the jail in this way, but when they were asked open-ended questions, typically described some form of regular reciprocity as part of their approach.[14]

An incident from one of Jarrod's dormitory houses is instructive on this account. Inmates smoked all day in 10-Upper, which stank of the unmistakable odor of Bible paper in a way the COs could not have missed. Given that the house was otherwise quiet, and enforcing smoking rules was largely a losing battle, the COs tolerated it as long as it did not become so blatant as to make them obviously complicit. Among themselves, inmates enforced basic rules: blowing the smoke out windows, not smoking too much at once, and masking the scent with homemade air fresheners. Inmates who were serious about their smoking habit took these rules seriously, as they enabled the daily enjoyment of one of the small pleasures of city time. And it was in everyone's interest to avoid a shakedown, if for no other reason than to avoid the indignity and chaos they bring.

One day, a section of heavy smokers broke from the unspoken pact that kept everyone smoking in peace, and created a great stink. The B officer, responsible for patrolling the dormitory, visited their section and told them, almost apologetically, to keep the smoking to a minimum. They ignored her and kept at it. Shortly thereafter, perhaps by coincidence but likely not, a captain came through and ordered them to stop smoking. Dissatisfied with their response, she stormed out. Several minutes later, like clockwork, the men heard, "On your stomachs, eyes on the window, and dream of home." An armored probe team proceeded immediately to the section of smokers, and dumped all of their buckets and bedding into a big pile right in the middle of Broadway. The team insulted and berated the men, and confiscated a pair of boots that were the only shoes one man in the offending section had.

After they left, the smokers left the pile of bedding and commissary untouched for hours, in one final act of defiance. The other inmates in the back half of the dorm began to politely request that the mess be cleaned up, but the stubborn smokers refused. In response, an overwhelming and vocal consensus emerged that they should clean it up, since their section had brought the raid on itself by flaunting their de facto privileges and refusing to cooperate with the COs. The renegade smokers were forced to comply.

Cool COs and Herbs

"The assertion that the ends of police violence are always identical or even connected to those of general law is entirely untrue," critical theorist Walter Benjamin observed in the early twentieth century. "Rather, the 'law' of the police really marks the point at which the state, whether from impotence or because of the immanent connections within any legal system, can no longer guarantee through the legal system the empirical ends that it desires at any price to attain."[15] The violent actions of the police, therefore, do not simply refer back to any written general statute but constitute, in a creative and productive sense, the realization of the extralegal violence at the core of law itself. An adage among New York cops, dating to the nineteenth century, puts it more bluntly: "There is more law in the end of a policeman's nightstick than in a decision of the Supreme Court."[16] These words are doubly true of the CO, who polices a population lacking even the flimsiest claims to due process. COs' discretionary power is immense, and can furnish the final word on most questions, with no serious possibility for appeal. But it is not absolute.

In a 1985 study of five prisons, sociologist John R. Hepburn found considerable variance within individual workforces in how guards practiced power. Guards were likely to refer to their legal authority as a source of power, although it is unlikely many prisoners followed their orders for this reason alone. But guards also responded in large numbers indicating that they believed their power to also rest on the reputation they cultivated among prisoners for their competence, judgment, and treatment of them.[17] David and Jarrod found this to be true of Rikers; COs who had a reputation for cutting inmates slack, or at least not going out of their way to give anyone a hard time, were respected, and in turn, their jobs were made easier.

David developed a rapport with the CO who served as his supervisor in C-74's kitchen, who not only turned a blind eye to the extra food and spices David pilfered daily; he also allowed David to go to the yard while he was on the clock, sometimes offered him things like better food, and often paid David overtime no matter how many hours he actually worked (or didn't). When David expressed his desire to quit his job to focus on writing and translation, his supervisor not only permitted him to quietly stop showing up to work (inmates are required to work, and therefore not technically allowed to quit); he even kept David on the payroll. When wages were slashed in August 2020, he began paying David overtime wages every week to make up the difference, even though David still was not actually working. This rapport and arrangement were due at least in part to David's criminal case, to which his supervisor was sympathetic. At the same time, it served to ensure that David would not rock the boat at work by flouting any institutional rules too brazenly.

This sort of arrangement was not uncommon and usually seemed to exist as a sort of favor-giving from the CO to the inmate, sometimes with the expectation of reciprocity. David's supervisor did ask David to snitch once, but kept the same arrangement even after David refused. Other COs developed more complex relationships with inmates, and might go so far as to buy them food from "the street" or even packs of real cigarettes, alcohol, and weed. Whether these things were given freely or with the expectation of pay was often unclear. (Payment, in cases like these, would be handled through outside intermediaries, not made in commissary products.) All of these things, even a slice of pizza, could be sold inside for enormous profit. Sometimes these relationships were based on gang affiliation; there were always rumored to be members of the Bloods, Crips, and Latin Kings on staff at Rikers, including very specific allegations about individual officers. Sometimes, though, favors were simply based on friendship, or something approaching it.

Other examples of "cool COs" include those who would assuage an inmate's psychological pain by telling him he "didn't belong here" or "shouldn't be here." Others engaged in various forms of play with the inmates, such as chess, trash talking the institution, performing impressions, joining jailhouse gossip, or sitting down in the day room to watch TV. One cool CO could often be found playing Xbox with the inmates in his dorm. That same CO often brought up the fact that he had been incarcerated for six months in Atlanta's Fulton County Jail on charges that were eventually dropped, further burnishing his cool-CO credentials.

Some COs would try to relate to inmates in terms of racial or ethnic solidarity. One Black CO in C-76 sported a pin in the shape of a Black Power fist on the front of his uniform. A Black female captain once launched into a tirade against the 12-Lower Crips because they had been turning away too many new arrivals at the gate, declaring, seemingly without a sense of irony, how she hated to see "Black and brown people oppressing other Black and brown people." Another captain, this one white and male, seemed to surprise an inmate of color with his candid and relatable demeanor. The inmate asked, "Captain, are you Spanish?" The captain replied, "No, I'm white, but I'm Eminem white, not Donald Trump white."

Cool COs engage in routine rule breaking. For example, the door between the changing area and waiting area for inmates receiving visitors at C-76 was supposed to be kept closed, with the inmates penned into a narrow hallway awaiting their visit. The main CO who oversaw this area during Jarrod's time, however, liked to socialize with the inmates and kept the door open, allowing them to mill around the much larger intake area freely, cracking jokes, and reading the uncensored versions of the New York tabloids. On one occasion, as a captain passed through, the CO silently gestured for inmates to step back into their designated area and shut the door. Understanding at once what they were being asked to do, they all complied, right in time for the captain to observe that everything was being done by the book.

Just as cool COs quickly get a good reputation, inmates remember when COs needlessly give them trouble. These COs are often called "herbs" or "bozos," New York slang for an uncool person. When Jarrod was in the pens awaiting release, the overseeing CO left the cell open during this basic routine of processing inmates' paperwork. A captain walked in and commanded a waiting inmate to move his foot, which protruded by several inches, back into the cell. As he walked away the inmate remarked, "It's two inches; Go Go Gadget had to say something. He knows he's a bozo!" Another rejoined, "That nigga came into 7-Main, a guy in a knee brace asked him a question, and he ignored the questions and asked 'do you have a permit for that knee brace?'" When the answer was no, "Go Go Gadget" had taken it away.

Herb COs have a much harder time of it than the cool ones. One CO, a white man with a heavy lisp named Festa, often had his speech impediment mocked by the inmates, many of whom referred to him as "Festa the Molesta." As he made his rounds doing the start-of-shift head count, inmates would sometimes call out things like, "Yo Festa! Say 'spaghetti'!" On one occasion, an inmate did not understand that Festa was directing him to reach into the immobile metal tray set in the wall separating the Bubble from the dorm, because Festa could not think of the word for it, and referred to it as "the . . . thing." When the inmate finally figured out what he meant, he scowled and asked, "Why didn't you just say the drawer?" Festa answered glibly that it was "more of a slot than a drawer," to which the inmate responded, exaggerating Festa's speech, "Well, why didn't you say 'schthlot,' then?" Though cruel, these interactions presented a rare opportunity for the inmates to get the upper hand, even if momentarily. By extension, the practice of giving (often demeaning) nicknames to COs was a constant source of empowerment and comedic relief.

Run by Females

"This supposed to be the strongest prison in New York," one inmate bemoaned to Jarrod. "How you gonna have that when it's run by females?" In a 1986 study of female guards in male prisons, sociologist Lynn E. Zimmer observed that women faced persistent vocalized skepticism from their male superiors and prisoners alike, in tandem with sexual harassment from both their coworkers and the men they were charged with guarding. Female guards were also subjected to rumors surrounding their sexual practices, including the potentially harmful insinuation that they were lesbians, or the career-threatening accusation that they were sexually involved with prisoners.[18]

Recent accounts by women guarding Rikers indicate that these practices remain, though women are far greater in number than they were in 1986, and today hold considerable positions of authority.[19] Female COs at Rikers still deal with sexual harassment from their coworkers, and also from the men they guard, which can be quite colorful. Gary Heyward recalls one prisoner yelling, "That bitch can suck my dick in a Macy's window at Christmas!"[20] While male COs often come to the defense of women harassed by prisoners—in this case, the prisoner was beaten for his provocations—there is also a perceptible male solidarity, accomplished through shrugs, eye rolls, and the occasional backroom gossip, which binds male prisoners and COs in a sexist pact against women. West, for instance, recounts how the locker-room gossip among male COs, either spoken or literally written on the wall, gets back to the male prisoners, who take part in the ritual humiliation of female COs for their sexual proclivities, real or imagined.[21] And while some male officers insisted that the inmates in their custody remain respectful of female officers, calling out sexist remarks and too-obvious glances in the halls, most were quite tolerant of the inmates' "reckless eyeball," also known as the "Rikers eyeball."

We witnessed numerous female COs at Rikers demonstrating day in and day out that they could be just as ruthless and aggressive as the men, if not more so. Contrary to what the reader may imagine, many of the most overt displays of aggression we observed came from the female COs, some of whom spent much of the day shouting insults and threats. Perhaps male COs acting this way would be perceived as more of an affront, leading to violence. It is also likely that the male COs simply did not have to try as hard to have their authority recognized. But if the female COs' constant shouting and posturing was meant to communicate strength and self-assurance, it had the opposite effect on us; like most inmates, we largely drowned them out. Jarrod got so used to ignoring the tirades of the women who guarded his dormitory that on several occasions they had to call his name numerous times, until the CO was nearly apoplectic with anger. (He also did this a few times on purpose.)

Out-toughing the tough guys is just one approach; many female COs have more than just a hammer in their toolbox. Zimmer identified distinct "adjustment strategies" through which female guards adapted to the sexism pervading men's prisons. Among them are the "institutional role," which takes the equality of male and female guards literally, dividing work with no respect to gender, and the "inventive role," in which female guards concede differences with male guards but explore the potential advantages uniquely available to women dealing with men. These advantages include the taboo on violence against women, working-class men's tendency to act as guardians of women in danger, and the absence of the machismo that often puts male guards into unnecessary conflict with male inmates.[22] Serving our city time roughly three decades after Zimmer's study, we identified considerable evidence of the institutional role and the inventive role among female COs. Of particular note, we persistently observed an obvious aspect of the inventive role that Zimmer does not mention: the female COs' use of the attention and affection of sex-starved men as a lever of power.

During David's time in 12-Lower, one of the steady floor officers was an attractive rookie CO in her early twenties. A Staten Islander of Italian descent, she was animated, playful, and clearly enjoyed having a small crowd of men vying for her attention. Flirting with this officer was a nightly ritual in 12-Lower, and could drag on for hours, a small gaggle of imprisoned men in their gym shorts and durags circulating around her post at the plastic table at the front of the dorm, by turns cracking jokes, commenting on her appearance, and offering to perform minor services for her.

"That's the fishhook," one inmate scolded a group of men in Jarrod's dorm, of a different CO who was playing much the same game. "She is putting it out there for y'all niggas to chat with her, then she snitch on you. Y'all niggas ain't supposed to be mingling!" While we did not see much evidence of elaborate entrapment, many female COs did indeed use the strange power this dynamic afforded them to enlist the help of the men fawning over them in performing minor services like cleaning, or providing them with snacks from their commissary bucket. Recall how one of the 12-Lower steady officers, an attractive young Black woman, solicited a team of volunteers from her fan club in the dorm to help her decorate the dorm for Christmas. Soon, perhaps a dozen men were happily taping wrapping paper to the cold concrete walls and hanging decorations from all kinds of places as she looked on approvingly, offering occasional instructions.

This dynamic can become quite toxic. One female steady officer in Mod 4 seemed to enjoy a sort of cyclical attraction-rejection-aggression model for the mini-relationships that arose between her and some of the inmates. After a brief reciprocal courtship, she often flew into a rage at the first disagreement with those she had until recently been flirting and bantering with. She then escalated the petty spat to the level of name calling and mocking the men for being incarcerated while she made large amounts of money, according to her, for keeping them locked up.

Similarly, we observed an explosive, sporadic ritual of exchanging sexually explicit insults. This usually involved women, especially Black women, mostly from the same working-class neighborhoods and backgrounds as the men, giving it back tit-for-tat when the men made lewd comments about their bodies, often in equally vile terms and frequently about the men's penises. The inmates, for example, are quick to refer to a female officer who has provoked their ire as a "fatass bitch" or "nasty-ass bitch." The female COs might retort with a string of invectives like "Your mother's a bitch," "Little dick-ass havin' nigga," or "You can't get no pussy anyway."

Rikers Island offers no magical respite from the patriarchal social relations that structure the outside world. But the growing predominance of women in the CO force, particularly women of color, cannot be understated. "Listen, it's your first day," the hard-nosed female officer Captain Perry consoles new CO Tiffany Thompson in *Across the Bridge*, a 2021 novel by former Rikers CO Steven Dominquez. "I came off rough, but like you, I'm a woman in a department where we might be looked at as weak. You'll realize that we dominate here though. We're the ones in higher positions, we're the ones with the promotions, and we maintain order here."[23]

Stick-Ups

A "stick-up" is a catchall term used by Rikers inmates to refer to any direct refusal, individual or collective, to cooperate with institutional policy. Refusing to remove one's piercing or jewelry upon intake, or refusing to be transferred to another unit or building, for example, would be considered sticking it up, but stick-ups also include labor disputes like slowdowns, stoppages, strikes, sabotage, and so on.

The strike David helped organize is the most developed and largest-scale stick-up either of us experienced directly. As the full scope of the COVID-19 pandemic came into focus during the first wave, people inside Rikers, like those outside, became increasingly anxious about protecting their health at all costs. Unfortunately, the DOC showed itself to be largely indifferent to the fate of those in its custody, even as its public face claimed that the institution was doing everything in its power to provide humane and sanitary conditions. As inmates' piecemeal and intermittent demands for masks, COVID-19 tests, and the cessation of inmate transfers between units grew louder, people in David's unit and the one across the hall began to get sick. News stories of panic and even physical confrontations at grocery stores in the outside world began to trickle in, as did accounts of prisoners rioting or being released en masse from facilities around the world.

One guy in David's dorm had been told by his girlfriend of a report of a small stick-up in C-95; this was later revealed to be eight men refusing to "lock in," and demanding medical care in the wake of possible exposure.[24] Shortly thereafter, a shotcaller in the dorm across the hall began telling people that his girlfriend had told him of a hunger strike in a Hudson County, New Jersey, facility; this action was undertaken by immigrants in ICE detention.[25] With frustration—and the awareness that these were extraordinary conditions—mounting, all it took was a spark, which came in the form of the dorms' running out of cleaning supplies, and the arbitrary cutoff of the dorms' phones on March 21, 2020. Talk of some sort of action, ranging between a simple refusal to go to work or chow to a full-blown hunger strike, had been swirling for days. The inmates, with near-unanimity, decided to refuse both work and chow, agreeing to stay in the dorm and eat only food they had purchased at commissary.

At David's suggestion, they drew up a loose list of demands, and once the phones came back on, he communicated these demands to an activist friend on the outside. Their demands included social distancing, masks, COVID-19 tests, cleaning supplies, and the early release of as many inmates as possible, in line with the recommendation of the DOC's oversight panel, the Board of Correction. The inmates' demands spread through activist spaces on social media before entering mainstream media. By that afternoon, they had reached Mayor de Blasio and Congresswoman Alexandria Ocasio-Cortez.

Though there were certainly interpersonal tensions during the strike, most inmates showed a surprising amount of cohesion and determination in facing off against the institution, and fully expected some form of retribution, such as transfer, box time, or loss of good time. However, the strike actually succeeded in most of its demands; in the face of overwhelming public pressure, masks and cleaning products were provided by that evening, and approximately 75 percent of all sentenced inmates, including the same proportion of the men in the striking dorms, were released two days later.[26]

Not all stick-ups are this large or this successful; most come and go with no news or list of demands being passed to the outside world. A smaller stick-up, for example, and the first one David witnessed, took place on the day before Christmas Eve in 12-Lower. The dorm was almost passed over for its regularly scheduled commissary visit. The Crips who ran the dorm refused to believe that the dorm would be taken the following day, as many services close for public holidays in jail just as they do in the outside world, and quickly placed themselves between the escort officer trying to leave the housing unit and the gate, refusing to budge until he took everyone to commissary. Several others soon joined them, calls and radio calls were made up the chain of command, and within minutes 12-Lower was actually on its way to commissary.

"Picking a herb" is another way of sticking it up, if one much less reliant on social cohesion. Picking a herb, a highly individualistic strategy of defying the institution, means announcing to the COs that you will begin beating up someone who likely will not fight back if they do not respond to your demands. For example, "Yo, CO! If y'all don't get me outta this bullpen, I'm gonna pick a herb." This raises the specter of paperwork, liability, and other headaches for the COs, meaning that they are in fact likely to respond to the threat.

Retribution

There was widespread agreement among those who had been coming to Rikers since before the advent of ubiquitous security cameras that the use of force by staff had decreased with the cameras' arrival. Staff violence against inmates surely persists, but the COs also have a number of more subtle tools for retribution in their kit, most notably searches and transfers.

Searches are the institutional weapon of retribution par excellence. Inmates who have disrespected individual COs prior to the search are very likely to find their beds being searched by those same COs, and perhaps be strip searched by them as well, sometimes accompanied by taunting remarks. The same holds true for inmates who offer the slightest resistance during a search: their bunks are unceremoniously trashed. They may be taken to Intake in handcuffs to await transfer elsewhere, or to be returned to the dorm only after their belongings have lain all over the floor, up for the taking, for several hours, or their commissary products seized and thrown away. David, in his prior career as a funeral director, had a colleague who had worked as a Rikers CO for two years some twenty years earlier. After David's release, they were discussing searches, and the colleague chuckled. "I used to love those searches," he confessed. "If I had beef with a inmate, I'd open up a brand-new jar of his peanut butter, lick my finger, stick it in there."

Forced transfers, or institutional pack-ups, are the institution's second favorite weapon of retribution. An inmate who has had a fight, been problematic during a search, mouthed off to an officer, or otherwise run afoul of DOC staff is liable to hear his name called at random, followed by the ominous words, "Pack up!" Despite his protestations, if any (some are keen to insist "I'm good anywhere I go!"), he will be given no clue as to where he is going or in what time frame. He might well spend days in Intake before being knowingly sent to a unit where he will have a hard time. Transfers to the Boat and the Five were particularly hated. When those returning to the dorm from work or programs ask where the man has gone, the somber reply is always, "The COs packed him up."

Then there are the why-me pens, whose name sums up the feelings of self-pity that come naturally to those held in them. A why-me pen is a tiny isolated holding cell in Intake designed to be as uncomfortable as possible. The why-me pen in C-76 was about the size of a closet and had no windows or space to lie down, only a tiny metal bench. By the account of one inmate who spent time there after being accused of stealing from a CO, he had all his commissary items confiscated, over three hundred dollars' worth of goods, and thrown in the trash in front of him (another favorite method of DOC retribution) before spending all night in the why-me pen, where the air conditioning was kept blasting so cold he shivered. One inmate described being sent to a closet-sized cage with no bench and a shower in it in C-74, another type of why-me pen.

COs also try to "pedo-bait" certain inmates they have beef with, exposing them to potentially disastrous repercussions from their fellow inmates. One man who apparently had some dispute with a CO made a faux lunge at him in the hall, trying to get him to flinch. The CO, unfazed, simply told him to "get the fuck out my face," and called him a "child toucher" in front of a line of inmates waiting to enter the mess hall. Whether there was truth to the allegation or not is unknown, but the social factor in the CO's choice to make the claim out loud was clear. Another inmate, getting into an argument with a CO over when he would be given his methadone, slunk off in disgust as it became clear that she would be of no help to him. "Probably one of those guys in here for touching little boys or something," she muttered as he walked away. "I got a jacket a mile long, bitch," he shot back, spinning around, "and touching little boys ain't on it. You can see my rap sheet. I'll tell you what is on there, though—slapping the shit out of dumb motherfuckers like you."

By the Book

There is a certain reluctance on the part of many inmates to complain about their conditions. Common utterances like "This is jail!" and "You ain't supposed to complain" attest to a mindset that celebrates quietly suffering through the ordeal. COs sometimes try to frame filing a complaint with a captain, via the grievance process or with 311, as "snitching," invoking a sense of solidarity between themselves and their captives. Yet despite this, and despite most inmates' reluctance to acknowledge the legitimacy or moral superiority of the institution, many see using the institution's system against itself as a strength, and cling to the letter of the law when it serves them. They know what will or will not fly on paper, and how to use the official channels to fight back. These include filing grievances, making 311 calls, or invoking the specter of a lawsuit or simply a potential headache for a CO.

The internal grievance process was created in 1977 as part of an overhaul expanding the Board of Correction's authority and autonomy.[27] Whether it has ever yielded a concrete form of recourse for inmates we cannot say, though we profess our deep skepticism. What is certain is that filing a grievance form (form 7101R-A) was almost sure to be a fruitless pursuit for inmates during our periods of incarceration on Rikers. If they received any response, it was likely to be a negative one. Precisely because grievances are so ineffective, and because they have so much time on their hands, inmates, in return, often file frivolous grievances as a way of making life harder for DOC personnel. See in figure 12.1 David's grievance form filed for a number of colored pencils seized during a search. Note in particular the document's poor copy quality, and the response: "Non-grievable."

ATTACHMENT -B-1

CITY OF NEW YORK - DEPARTMENT OF CORRECTION
OFFICE OF CONSTITUENT AND GRIEVANCE SERVICES
INMATE STATEMENT FORM

Inmate's Name: DAVID CAMPBELL
Book & Case #: 3101900657
NYSID #:
Facility: RNDC
Housing Area: M4LS
Date of Incident: 6/2/20
Date Submitted: 6/3/20

All grievances must be submitted within ten business days after the incident occurred, unless it's a sexual abuse or harassment allegation. The inmate filing the grievance must personally prepare this statement. Upon collection by the Office of Constituent and Grievance Services (OCGS) staff, OCGS staff will time-stamp and issue it a grievance reference number. OCGS staff shall provide the inmate with a copy of this form as a record of receipt.

Grievance: During search yesterday under Capt. Clarke's supervision, 4 of my 6 colored pencils were taken. These were received through the mail and approved and fit the regulations as described on p. 32 of the Inmate Handbook – golf pencil size, no eraser. Furthermore, I have been keeping a color-coded calendar using these pencils and am now unable to complete it. This is causing me unnecessary and extreme stress and anxiety.

Action Requested by Inmate: Return my colored pencils to me. If that's not possible, compensate me for my pencils + emotional injury

Please read below and check the correct box:

Do you agree to have your statement edited for clarification by OCGS staff? Yes ☐ No ☒
Do you need the OCGS staff to write the grievance for you? Yes ☐ No ☒
Have you filed this grievance with a court or other agency? Yes ☐ No ☒
Did you require the assistance of an interpreter? Yes ☐ No ☒

Inmate's Signature: [signature]
Date of Signature:

FOR DOC OFFICE USE ONLY

OCGS MUST PROVIDE A COPY OF THIS FORM TO THE INMATE AS A RECORD OF RECEIPT.

THIS FORM IS INVALID UNLESS SIGNED BY THE INMATE AND GRIEVANCE COORDINATOR

TIME STAMP
Grievance Reference #: Non-grievable
Category: Staff
Office of Constituent and Grievances Services Coordinator/Officer Signature: [signature]

Figure 12.1: A grievance form David filed seeking the return of confiscated colored pencils. Courtesy of the authors.

Calling 311, NYC's nonemergency information and complaint hotline, is a more reliable way to provoke a response from the DOC, sometimes even a favorable one. The degree to which DOC staff complain after they get wind of an inmate's 311 call attests to how this form of recourse actually has some teeth, as the appeal is made directly to an outside agency.

However, the DOC is equally adept at claiming to have resolved the issue while actually changing precious little about the conditions that gave rise to the complaint in the first place. Some captains also threaten inmates for making 311 calls, as their name and book and case number usually appear on the complaint. In one case during David's sentence, a captain threatened to begin transferring men from his dorm at random if they did not stop making 311 calls about the COVID-related conditions, such as overcrowding and the lack of masks. Additionally, because inmate phone time is limited, 311 calls often cut off before a caller has a chance to speak to anyone, or before the caller finishes filing the complaint. This was particularly the case during the height of the first wave of COVID-19.

Though inmates may seek to resolve an issue through unofficial channels by appealing directly to a cap, dep, warden, or other ranking member of the DOC hierarchy, they may also hint at a lawsuit, or actually follow through: inmates file lawsuits against the DOC with some degree of frequency. At the risk of denying the very real dangers of the conditions on Rikers, and the fact that people do indeed have debilitating accidents there, it bears noting that some of these suits, such as "slip and falls," can be fairly frivolous. One inmate in 12-Lower who had had a rusty nail pierce his foot walked with a cane everywhere he went except the camera-free bathroom, where he placed his cane against the wall and walked upright without a limp. Once, when the CO driving the SOD bus began accelerating with David hanging out the open back door, this same inmate told David he was "stupid as fuck" for not pretending to fall and injure himself. A Rikers veteran once told David that he had been incarcerated there in the eighties, entered the bathroom to find a puddle on the floor, and simply "laid down and started screaming."

There are also a number of lawsuits over moldy and expired food sold at commissary. Some people actually get sick from these items; others are clever enough to notice their condition beforehand and use them to their advantage. David met one man who had gotten a moldy bag of chips from commissary, identifiable through the clear plastic window on the front of the packaging. He opened it in the bathroom, off camera, then claimed to have eaten a few chips before realizing they were expired, and gotten sick. He spent about a month getting intermittently shuffled back and forth to the prison ward at Bellevue Hospital in Manhattan, and spent a lot of time on the phone with his lawyer, but eventually received a settlement for a thousand dollars. "That ain't bad for a fifty-cent bag of chips," he mused. "And besides, what the fuck else we got to do?"

Forty-Eightin'

The common denominator in institutional relationships for both inmates and COs is plausible deniability. COs let lots of things slide, like smoking in the bathroom or at the yard, or stealing things from the kitchen, as long as they are not so obvious they can't tell their superiors they didn't see them. Similarly, it behooves any inmate to broadcast his ignorance of certain things, even if he has, in fact, seen them. While on the phone about a month into his sentence, David witnessed three men testing out a new shank in the bathroom. They noticed him noticing them, and paused, but after David performatively turned his head away and continued his phone conversation, they carried on as if nothing had happened.

The inmate's default response to inquiries by staff about an item's provenance becomes something plausible but unarguable: "Where'd you get this?" is met with "I found it," "I don't remember," or, rarely, "Someone gave it to me." When this latter statement is pursued with "Who?" the answer is either "I don't remember" or "He went home already." This becomes deeply ingrained after only a few months. Near the end of his sentence, David handed a plastic ice bag to the CO overseeing inmate-workers in the mess hall, asking him to fill it up with ice for his milk fridge. This was common practice in the C-74 during the summer months. Most inmates used clean trash bags, but since David worked in the kitchen, he had been able to snag a bona fide ice bag with a scarf-toting penguin logo on it. The CO, surprised to see this instead of a standard trash bag, asked David where he got it. Taking an ice bag from the kitchen was not a big deal, and David would not have gotten into trouble for it, but he immediately and unthinkingly responded, "Don't worry about it."

"Don't worry about it?" the CO replied, taken aback. "I could just as easily tell you 'don't worry about it' and not give you any ice."

"You could," David admitted with a shrug, remaining noncommittal. The CO ultimately filled his ice bag and handed it back with a frown.

This sort of refusal to engage by giving vague answers, or telling outright lies, is often referred to as "forty-eightin'" by the inmates, especially when it is directed at them by staff, as it usually is. (We never figured out the etymology of this expression.) Ironically, COs often selectively try to appeal to the inmates' sense of solidarity. "I'm in here, same as you," they might say to someone who asks when chow, yard, or methadone will be called, as a way of saying they don't know. On a number of occasions, David witnessed the very same COs who had invoked their ostensible similarity of status take the opposite tack when it suited them, offering inmates who complained about the temperature or the fire alarm going off for hours on end cynical advice like, "Don't come to jail."

The institution as a whole often takes a placating attitude to those in its custody, which can itself be considered a form of forty-eightin', as it is often a refusal to address the real issues leading to or exacerbated by incarceration. A number of copies of the superficial, magical-thinking self-help book *The Alchemist* could be found floating in any given dorm; when asked, those with the book would answer that every inmate in C-95 had been issued one at some point in the recent past. In the difficult period following the first wave of COVID-19, the mass release, and the first lockdown, the DOC showed little interest in providing masks or sanitary living conditions, but began issuing off-brand 400-game-in-one Gameboys to every inmate instead. Unsurprisingly, they were incompatible with the headphones sold at commissary.

13

Release

The day of their release is an obsessive fixation among city-time inmates, who await it with all the zeal of evangelicals anticipating the Second Coming. In the case of city time, the day of deliverance actually comes, though its anticipation is perhaps no less challenging to one's faith. David and Jarrod both observed and experienced how the approach of an inmate's last day can be the greatest test of the time-doing strategy he has developed. Some people, especially those with longer sentences, became noticeably agitated as their final hours ticked away, and the euphoria of impending release was offset by the return of familial, employment, and housing demands, on top of the necessity to rebuild one's life following a disruptive period of incarceration. Given that the typical city-time inmate is locked up for a crime associated with life on the margins of society, and that time behind bars at Rikers offers virtually nothing to make one's situation any better on the outside, inmates facing release typically approach an arrangement similar to the one that led them to city time in the first place, only worse.

New York City began investing in discharge planning services as we experienced them in 2003, after it was discovered that nearly a third of people entering city homeless shelters had previously spent time in city jails (apparently—and concerningly—this came as a surprise to the commissioners of correction and homeless services). A June 2009 report by the city's Independent Budget Office noted that "city spending on discharge planning and reentry has increased steadily from $4 million in 2005 to a budgeted $14.5 million in 2009."[1] These programs saw several years of substantial expansion; the city's three-year financial plan for 2020–2023, released in November 2019, included $34 million for "re-entry and discharge planning improvements," in addition to $10.5 million transferred from the DOC to the Mayor's Office of Criminal Justice for "new re-entry planning services."[2] But this seems to have been the high-water mark: in June 2023, the DOC slashed $17 million from its

2024 budget by terminating contracts with six nonprofits providing programming and reentry services, such as the Fortune Society and the Osborne Association.[3]

Much of the entirely warranted public criticism of these cuts has focused on the claim that these programs do in fact work. But these programs, well-intentioned though they may be, serve as little more than damage control for a problem that should not exist. Even in the best of times, they are overburdened and underfunded: $17 million, for example, is a drop in the bucket of the DOC's $1.2 billion budget for the same period, roughly 85 percent of which is spent on its highly bloated staff.[4] David, trying to fix an error on his rap sheet after his release, contacted a number of nonprofits providing reentry services. The process generally consisted of sending an email or leaving a voicemail and hoping for a brief response from an overbusy representative. Even after several months of persistent follow-up, he was unable to get the help he needed. This fairly minor process was difficult and ultimately fruitless even for a person with a stable phone number, address, and email account. We can only imagine what trying to receive postrelease support must be like for those dealing with substance abuse or mental health issues, homelessness, language barriers, or racialized poverty.

All inmates receiving mental health services are entitled to discharge planning services under the *Brad H.* settlement.[5] Whether they received it or not was unclear, in our experience, though it seems unlikely that they did.[6] So, too, was the question of whether non–Brad H. inmates were entitled to discharge planning services. About a month into his sentence, David was summoned to C-76's discharge planning office, where he was given a form to request food stamps and Medicaid after his release, a plain white T-shirt, and an HIV test. As his release date finally approached, eleven months later and in C-74, David repeatedly tried to schedule an appointment with discharge planning but was forty-eighted at every step along the way, often told that only Brad H. inmates were afforded these services. His partner in this endeavor, a friendly inmate with the same release date, fared no better despite the fact that he was labeled Brad H.

The DOC claims that reentry services were heavily reduced during this period due to COVID-19, but if the answer is that simple, why no one ever provided it to David or the other inmate remains a mystery.[7]

As for David's earlier discharge planning visit, though it occurred in the comparatively favorable and well-funded climate of late 2019, it seems not to have amounted to anything: he ended up having to apply for food stamps and Medicaid on his own after his release.

The DOC claims to hand out copies of its "Beyond the Bridge" brochure, which contains information on employment, housing, and public benefits, to every new arrival, and to distribute copies of the New York Public Library's *Connections Handbook*, an annual compilation of various resources for those recently released from incarceration in New York, to all inmates before they leave.[8] David actually received a copy of the former, but quickly lost it; in any case, the idea that this booklet is supposed to survive the countless random searches, transfers, and confiscations attendant to a city sentence is all but laughable. Despite being valuable resources, these publications, like the various reentry services themselves, are a wholly inadequate response to the needless havoc wreaked by city time.

In the days before his release, Jarrod was told that he was required to visit the Rikers Island Discharge Enhancement (RIDE) office to meet with a civilian social worker. RIDE, which is actually voluntary and not mandatory as Jarrod had been led to believe, is a seemingly good-hearted effort to plug inmates into public-assistance and substance-abuse programming available on the outside, mediated through postrelease nonprofits like the Osborne Association.[9] Jarrod sat in the packed RIDE waiting room for a long time, the inmates largely fixated on a talk show host attempting to rehabilitate Johnny Depp's image in the wake of domestic violence allegations. The room smelled like mold and body odor. A CO sprayed Lysol, to little avail. One inmate got sick of waiting and tried to get up to leave. The CO chastised him: "You don't even know what this is and you don't want it?" The inmate called his bluff and asked what RIDE was. The CO replied, "I don't know, but everyone else leaves happy." Another responded, "Unless you got freedom, we ain't interested."

What You're Supposed to Do

David once heard from multiple inmates he worked with that one of their number, a particularly popular guy, had been feted on his last night by their entire dorm, 10-Lower, with hooch, joints, and sticks, and cheered and applauded down Broadway as he walked to the gate. But this is a notable exception. There are generally no parties upon a person's release, and celebration is frowned upon. We surmised during our time inside that this was the case because the reality of a friend going home only served to bring into stark relief the continuation of the others' captivity. David certainly felt that way after experiencing the mass release during the pandemic, during which most of his friends left literally overnight. As happy as he was for them, he was equally distressed to be left behind. One friend of David's who was released early celebrated publicly in the dorm, doing a little dance and gleefully chanting, "I'm going home! I'm going home!"

"He did exactly what you're not supposed to do," a Rikers old head who had also served time upstate later muttered. "Upstate, they would've given him something to take home [slashed his face] for that." Veterans who had spent time in state or federal prison sometimes refused to provide their exact release dates, even to close friends, for fear of being attacked on their way out the door.

For some, release can be a daunting prospect. David witnessed one inmate, whose release date fell during the first wave of COVID-19, actually ask a captain if he could stay in jail. Jarrod similarly beheld a strange incident upon the release of a young Korean American man with a hard-drug addiction. This man was scheduled for release from the intake dormitory, 1-Upper, along with a group of "weekend warriors" serving their time in weekend increments. When his time came to pack up, he fumbled with his belongings for nearly an hour, packing and unpacking them, and said long, elaborate goodbyes to every person around him. The typical inmate prepares for release by packing up long in advance of their name being called, and does not need to be told twice to vacate the dormitory. Not so in this case.

Soon, everyone else scheduled to be released was waiting at the gate. The CO in charge called the man's name several times, and then lost patience, shouting, "Get the hell out of my house!" The man just ignored the CO and continued dragging his feet in the same way, saying long goodbyes and fussing with his bundle of possessions. The CO, incensed, continued shouting, and eventually even the inmates joined in. One mentally challenged man paced around yelling, "Chino doesn't wanna go home!" over and over again. All eyes in the dormitory fell on this scene, which took on the absurd dimensions of a high school humiliation nightmare. At last, the CO approached him, flanked by the big homie, who volunteered himself as backup muscle to make this disturbance go away. The CO physically pushed the young man toward the exit, as the top shotcaller stood shoulder to shoulder with their mutual captor. This case, though extreme, speaks volumes; for some city-time inmates we met, incarceration seemed less onerous than whatever was waiting for them on the outside.

Far more typical, however, was a phenomenon both David and Jarrod witnessed and experienced: the torturous expansion of time. David felt this especially in his final weeks, and Jarrod in his final days. Beginning almost imperceptibly, days, and then hours, trickled ever more slowly by. Just as the pre-Socratic philosopher Zeno posited that a person can never truly cross a room—because one can only cross each successive increment of space by half, and never eliminate the remainder altogether—the approach of release from city time had the uncanny effect of making the remaining time seem interminable.[10] Time strategies, no matter how efficient, became more difficult to maintain as their true nature, distraction from the hardship of life in a cage, became impossible to ignore against the impending experience of freedom.

Last Call

During Jarrod's time, city-time inmates were given two options for release. The first involved packing up in the early evening, spending the night in the intake pens, and eventually being ferried to one of the borough courthouses in the predawn hours. The second option involved sleeping in the dormitory, getting packed up in the morning, and being released on the other side of the bridge some time before noon. Jarrod did not encounter anyone planning the second, though it was the far more comfortable option, at least in theory. It seemed just about everyone was content to suffer the pens, as they had upon intake, and get off Rikers Island as quickly as possible.

Jarrod, too, chose a nighttime release. A celebratory mood pervaded his section that afternoon and Jarrod suddenly became quite popular, in part because his departure meant he would no longer need many of his items. His food, blankets, and, above all, mattress, had been requested by fellow inmates long in advance. Jarrod's Russian dormitory neighbor, who had done time back home, told him to take everything he had with him instead of giving it away, and to throw it away before reaching home. "What's the word . . . ," he asked. "Superstition?" It was a slightly different take on a piece of Rikers conventional wisdom Jarrod had encountered many times before: "If you found that shit in jail, leave that shit in jail."

Jarrod chose to follow the conventional city-time practice and found good homes for these items, as well as his reusable bowl, writing utensils, paper, stamps, and a stand-alone eraser, which were difficult to come by. He returned a contraband pen to his neighbor, who insisted Jarrod keep it as a gift, but Jarrod replied that they were a bit easier to get on the outside, and they both laughed. He threw most of his clothing away. By midafternoon, Jarrod's bed had been stripped, his mattress quickly vanishing beneath another inmate's bedroll, and aside from a clear trash bag containing his books, notepads, and a few stray keepsake items, it was as though he had never been there at all. By 5:30 p.m., when he was instructed to pack up, he did not need to be told twice.

The departure itself was surprisingly emotional. Jarrod had not reflected very deeply on the bond he had formed with the men he was locked up with, but parting ways from them dredged up a sentimentality that surprised him and seemed comical in the context of the miserable environment he was finally about to leave. These feelings were mutual, and his neighbors began waxing poetic. One told him that he would always remember this time, the time they had spent together. When his name was called, Jarrod was received by a line of men shaking his hand, and admonishing, "Don't come back!" This command followed him down the halls as he and a handful of other inmates being released made their way to the pens, with strangers who had overheard the news stopping to offer congratulations and a playful warning not to return.

Jarrod's escort to the pens teased the men that he could not believe how slowly they were walking, considering that they were on their way to get their street clothes back. The return of these clothes was valuable both symbolically and practically. They represented, on the one hand, the reversal of the intake process, which Goffman called "a leaving off and a taking on," the return of garments central to the inmate's sense of self outside the institution.[11] And then, they were also just a lot more comfortable.

Putting on real shoes, especially, was almost a shock. On the outside, Jarrod had long been in dire financial straits, and had worn the same pair of sneakers for almost eighteen months, wearing their soles down to almost nothing. But compared to the Patakis, they felt like walking on a cloud! The return of street clothing occasioned a festive atmosphere that dissipated, gradually, as the reality of sitting in intake pens for upwards of ten more hours set in. Soon enough, the penned inmates had been seized once more by the alternatingly listless and agitated disposition that characterizes protracted time spent in squalid pens with nowhere to even comfortably sit down, albeit in street clothes.

Cockroaches patrolled the pen's perimeter as men lounged on their dormitory sheets, spread out across the floor for a modicum of sanitation. The sink was filled with trash: an apple, toothbrush, paper cup, and wet toilet paper. Meanwhile, the familiar cool, verdant breeze blew in from an overgrown courtyard. A group of boosters who had just met each other compared notes and decided to work together on a heist targeting a suburban mall one of them had been casing before getting locked up. Jarrod had, somewhat selfishly and at the risk of bad luck, held onto his radio, and became increasingly dependent on it for energy as the night wore on. After midnight, he and the others were herded into another pen with adolescents, who were energetically celebrating their release. They rolled a cigarette and everyone passed it around. Even Jarrod, who doesn't smoke, took a few drags. The adolescents started clapping and chanting, "I'm getting out / Fuck DOC / Fuck Rikers Island" over and over again. Naturally, Jarrod joined in.

The group was moved into another pen, this one close enough to hear buses idling outside. This ratcheted up the excitement considerably, but also occasioned multiple false alarms, as a number of buses departed, leaving disappointment in their wake. Around 4:00 a.m., some ten hours after Jarrod had arrived in the pens, the inmates were at last called to line up and prepare for departure through the loading dock where intake on the island begins. The outside air was misty and moist with dew, catching in the harsh streetlights of the otherwise dark island to create an ambience of otherworldliness. "I have never seen, and will never see again, this landscape of a world between," recalls Victor Serge, of his early-morning release, "this landscape immersed in deep shadows and the pale glimmers of the night."[12]

At this sight, men who had spent months performing dispassionate masculinity laughed and bounced along the cement toward the bus waiting to transport them out of their pointless ordeal. Just before boarding, one of the adolescents spun around to face C-76. Raising cupped hands to his face like a megaphone, he shouted, "Rikers Island, suck my dick!"

ACKNOWLEDGMENTS

This project would not have been possible without the communities we call home. We wish to acknowledge the support of our families, friends, and comrades, especially Jack Norton, Tanzeem Ajmiri, Zhandarka Kurti, May Shanahan, Stephen Campbell, Zach Campbell, John Garvey, Erin Schell, Maud Pryor, Julia Buck, Eleni Vradi, Daniel McGowan, Jerry Koch, Chloé Maës, Andy Gittlitz, Craig Hughes, Nate McDonough, CUNY Struggle, Boston Hardcore, the David Campbell Defense Committee, the International Anti-Fascist Defence Fund, the Metropolitan Anarchist Coordinating Council, and NYC Anarchist Black Cross. This project also enjoyed vital support from Jarrod's Environmental Psychology cohort (plus Brendan Tuttle) and the Critical Psychology Cluster at the CUNY Graduate Center, as well as the Faculty Research Seminar at Governors State University. We both wish to thank Ilene Kalish and Priyanka Ray at NYU Press, and the book's anonymous peer reviewers, for their helpful feedback. Lastly, we are both extremely grateful to the former prisoners who helped us prepare for incarceration, and our fellow prisoners who helped us navigate it.

GLOSSARY

[Air] Patakis: Standard-issue footwear for those in DOC custody
To Bang: To be a member of a gang
Banger: A small slashing implement
Bartender: An inmate with an impressive workout on the pull-up bar
Big Homie: The head inmate in a housing unit
To Boof: To hide something in one's rectum
Book and Case [Number]: A DOC-issued inmate ID number
Box Time (the Box): Solitary confinement
Brad H (MO, Seven-Thirty): A person with mental health issues
Broadway: The main aisle running down the center of a housing unit; also used more broadly to describe any main thoroughfare
The Bubble: An enclosed control and observation booth
Bucket: A DOC-issued fourteen-gallon Rubbermaid Roughneck plastic storage bin
Buck-Fifty: A large, prominent facial scar, usually from a fight behind bars
Bugout: A person with severe mental illness (pejorative); also used as a verb
Cambro: An insulated drink dispenser, so named for its manufacturer
Cap: A DOC captain
Chinita (Subs): Suboxone
Chow: Institutional meals
City Time (City Sentence): A short criminal sentence served in a New York City jail, rather than a New York state prison
CO: A DOC guard
Corcraft: Standard-issue bar soap, so named for its manufacturer
C-74 (the Four, the Four Building, the Robert N. Davoren Center, RNDC): One of the buildings on Rikers,

used primarily for housing adolescent (eighteen- to twenty-one-year-old) detainees

C-76 (the Six, the Six Building, the Eric M. Taylor Center, EMTC): One of the buildings on Rikers, used exclusively for housing city-time inmates

Dancefloor (Dancehall): The visiting room

Dep: DOC Deputy warden

To Forty-Eight (Someone): To give vague, noncommittal, or entirely fabricated answers; similar to giving someone "the runaround"

Good Time: Time reduced from a sentence for good behavior; for city-time inmates, this is one-third of their total sentence

GP: General population

Greens: Sentenced inmates serving city time, usually invoked in opposition to Tans; also refers to the institutional clothing they wear

Hooch: Jailhouse liquor

House: Housing unit

House Bucket: A white plastic bin containing toothpaste, toothbrushes, soap, and toilet paper, left in the dorm for inmates to take as they need

House Gang: A housing unit's dedicated inmate cleaning crew

Inmate: An incarcerated person

Intake: The area of a jail facility where new arrivals are processed, but also where inmates are held in pens while awaiting transfer or release, or for punitive reasons

Juice: Recycled liquid methadone

KEEP (DOT): The name for methadone treatment in C-76; elsewhere, "DOT" is used

Kite: An unauthorized written inmate communication

The KK: The kitchen

K2 (Plane, Deuce, Spice): A synthetic cannabinoid widely used as a recreational drug

Mag: A walk-through metal detector

Meth: Methadone

Methheads: Methadone users

Neutral (Five-Fifty): Someone who is not gang affiliated

OG: An older or elderly inmate

One-Piece: A jumpsuit issued to new arrivals; used to distinguish them as such by other inmates

To Pack (Someone) Up: To force an inmate out of a housing unit, engage in a pack-up

Pen (Bullpen): A temporary holding cell or cage

To Pick a Herb: To assault another inmate one believes unlikely to fight back as a way of forcing the COs to respond to one's demands

To Play the Bathroom: To fight in the bathroom

To Rep: To signal one's gang allegiance, usually via color-coded clothing or jewelry

Section: The area around one's bed and a number of neighboring beds

Shotcaller: A gang-affiliated inmate with some authority

Slot Time: A period, usually at the end of the day, when phone use is strictly regulated

Steady Officer: An officer whose regular post is in the housing unit

Stick: A homemade cigarette

To Stick It Up: To refuse to cooperate with institutional policy, engage in a stick-up

The/That Sticky: Marijuana

Suitcase: One's rectum (as a place for hiding contraband)

Tans: Pretrial detainees, as distinct from Greens; also refers to the institutional clothing they wear

Turtles: COs in riot gear, dispatched during searches and emergencies

VI: Visit

White Bucket: A DOC-issued 12-quart Sterilite plastic dishpan

Why-Me Pen: A small, uncomfortable cell in Intake, generally used for punitive purposes

Work House (Working Dorm): A dorm in which all residents are required to work

NOTES

INTRODUCTION

1 "People in Jail in New York City: Daily Snapshot, September 21, 2023," Vera Institute of Justice, https://greaterjusticeny.vera.org.

2 Luke Scrivener, Shannon Tomascak, Erica Bond, and Preeti Chauhan, "New York City Jail Population in 2019," 3, Data Collaborative for Justice, July 2021, https://datacollaborativeforjustice.org.

3 David C. May, Brandon K. Applegate, Rick Ruddell, and Peter B. Wood, "Going to Jail Sucks (And It Really Doesn't Matter Who You Ask)," *American Journal of Criminal Justice* 39, no. 2 (June 2014): 252, doi:10.1007/s12103-013-9215-5.

4 Orisanmi Burton, *Tip of the Spear: Black Radicalism, Prison Repression, and the Long Attica Revolt* (Oakland: University of California Press, 2023), 34.

5 Goldfarb's largely anecdotal analysis has been augmented in the years since by a number of studies focused on the high density of mentally ill, substance-dependent, and homeless populations in US jails, and the overwhelming racial disparities in which the populations of US jails and prisons skew with stark disproportion toward working-class Black and brown people. See: Ronald Goldfarb, *Jails: The Ultimate Ghetto* (New York: Doubleday, 1975); David Michaels, Steven Zoloth, and Phil Alcabes, "Homelessness and Indicators of Mental Illness among Inmates in New York City's Correctional System," *Hospital and Community Psychiatry* 43 (1992): 150–55; Marilyn Chandler Ford, "Frequent Fliers: High Demand Users of Local Corrections," *American Jails*, July/August 2008, 18–26; Douglas Shenson, Nancy Dubler, and David Michaels, "Jails and Prisons: The New Asylums?," *American Journal of Public Health* 80, no. 6 (1990): 655–56; Freda Adler, "Jails as a Repository for Former Mental Patients," *International Journal of Offender Therapy and Comparative Criminology* 30 (1986): 225–36; Nicholas Freudenberg, "Jails, Prisons, and the Health of Urban Populations: A Review of the Impact of the Correctional System on Community Health," *Journal of Urban Health* 28, no. 2 (2001): 214–35.

6 John Irwin, *The Jail: Managing the Underclass in American Society* (Berkeley: University of California Press, 1985), 1–17.

7 Ruth Wilson Gilmore, *Golden Gulag: Surplus, Crisis, and Opposition in Globalizing California* (Berkeley: University of California Press, 2007).

8 Kelly Lytle Hernández, *City of Inmates: Conquest, Rebellion, and the Rise of Human Caging in Los Angeles, 1771–1965* (Durham: University of North Carolina Press, 2017); Judah Schept, *Progressive Punishment: Job Loss, Jail Growth, and the*

Neoliberal Logic of Carceral Expansion (New York: New York University Press, 2015); Jack Norton, Judah Schept, and Lydia Pelot-Hobbs, eds., *The Jail Is Everywhere: Fighting the New Geography of Mass Incarceration* (London: Verso, 2023); Lydia Pelot-Hobbs, *Prison Capital: Mass Incarceration and Struggles for Abolition Democracy in Louisiana* (Durham: University of North Carolina Press, 2023); Melanie D. Newport, *This Is My Jail: Local Politics and the Rise of Mass Incarceration* (Philadelphia: University of Pennsylvania Press, 2022); "In Our Backyards Stories," Vera Institute of Justice (blog), 2023, https://www.vera.org.

9 Jarrod Shanahan, *Captives: How Rikers Island Took New York City Hostage* (London: Verso, 2022).

10 Michael Walker, *Indefinite: Doing Time in Jail* (New York: Oxford University Press, 2022), 11–12.

11 Jennifer Wynn, *Inside Rikers: Stories from the World's Largest Penal Colony* (New York: St. Martin's Press, 2001), 4.

12 Loïc Wacquant, "The Curious Eclipse of Prison Ethnography in the Age of Mass Incarceration," *Ethnography* 3, no. 4 (2002): 371–97.

13 Manuela Cunha, "The Ethnography of Prisons and Penal Confinement," *Annual Review of Anthropology* 43 (2014): 225.

14 Keith Farrington, "The Modern Prison as Total Institution? Public Perception versus Objective Reality," *Crime & Delinquency* 38, no. 1 (1992): 18–23; Jason Warr, "Afterword," in *The Prisoner*, ed. Ben Crewe and Jamie Bennet (London: Routledge, 2013), 142–48.

15 Michelle Brown, *The Culture of Punishment: Prison, Society, and Spectacle* (New York: New York University Press, 2009), 16.

16 Ruth Wilson Gilmore and James Kilgore, "Some Reflections on Prison Labor," *Brooklyn Rail*, June 2019. Similar canards abound about the prevalence of private prisons, which represent roughly 8 percent of human cages in the United States. See: Craig Gilmore, "On the Business of Incarceration," *Commune* 5 (Winter 2020).

17 To get a better sense of what we mean, we encourage the reader to watch the acclaimed 2016 HBO series *The Night Of*. It depicts the true injustice of Rikers as coming from the contaminating immersion of a lone innocent person in a violent world of dangerous criminals who belong behind bars.

18 We do not wish to overstate the absence of prison ethnography, a charge sometimes made of Wacquant. This is especially so for the small but vibrant tradition of prison writing by former or current prisoners, often classed under the banner of "convict criminology." See, for example, Stephen C. Richards and Jeffrey Ian Ross, "Introducing the New School of Convict Criminology," *Social Justice* 28, no. 1 (2001): 117–90; Greg Newbold, Jeffrey Ian Ross, Richard S. Jones, Stephen C. Richards, and Michael Lenza, "Prison Research from the Inside: The Role of Convict Autoethnography," *Qualitative Inquiry* 20, no. 4 (2014): 439–48; and the *Journal of Prisoners on Prison* (www.jpp.org). Additionally, a small but vibrant group of prison ethnographers continue to center the experiences of the carceral facility, including from the prisoners' perspective. See: Ben Crewe and Jamie Bennett, eds., *The Prisoner* (London: Routledge, 2013).

19 Walker, *Indefinite*, 17.

20 James B. Jacobs, *Stateville: The Penitentiary in Mass Society* (Chicago: University of Chicago Press, 1977), 223.

21 Lil Wayne, *Gone 'Til November* (New York: Plume, 2016), 71.

22 Michael Rempel, Ashmini Kerodal, Joseph Spadafore, and Chris Mai, *Jail in New York City: Evidence-Based Opportunities for Reform* (New York: Center for Court Innovation, 2017), x, 5–6, 72, www.innovatingjustice.org.

23 See: New York City Department of Correction (DOC), "Population Demographic Reports," www1.nyc.gov, accessed February 10, 2022.

24 Even between us there are considerable differences: Jarrod's short stay ultimately amounted to a temporary annoyance, and while he lost housing as a result of his conviction, this was replaced without interruption. His graduate studies and employment at the City University of New York were not interrupted, and he was therefore able to step back into his life with relative ease. By contrast, David's year at Rikers upended his life almost entirely; for example, the conviction cost him his livelihood.

25 David Ranney, *Living and Dying on the Factory Floor: From the Outside In and the Inside Out* (Oakland, CA: PM Press, 2019), vii–viii.

26 Michael Walker, "Race Making in a Penal Institution," *American Journal of Sociology* 121, no. 2 (2016): 1058.

27 A. L. Spedding, "Dreams of Leaving: Life in the Feminine Penitentiary Centre, Miraflores, La Paz, Bolivia," *Anthropology Today* 15, no. 2 (1999): 16–17.

28 See: Alison Liebling, "Whose Side Are We On? Theory, Practice, and Allegiances in Prisons Research," *British Journal of Criminology* 41, no. 3 (2001): 472–84; Mary Bosworth, Debi Campbell, Bonita Demby, Seth M. Ferranti, and Michael Santos, "Doing Prison Research: Views from Inside," *Qualitative Inquiry* 11, no. 2 (2005): 249–64; Deborah H. Drake, Jennifer Sloan, and Rod Earle, eds., *The Palgrave Handbook of Prison Ethnography* (London: Palgrave MacMillan, 2013).

29 See Shanahan, *Captives*.

30 Richard S. Jones, "Uncovering the Hidden Social World: Insider Research in Prison," *Journal of Contemporary Criminal Justice* 11, no. 2 (1995): 107, 111.

31 Johann Wolfgang von Goethe, *Novels and Tales: By Goëthe. Elective Affinities; The Sorrows of Werther; German Emigrants; The Good Women; and A Novelette* (England: H. G. Bohn, 1854), 282.

32 "Words Matter: Using Humanizing Language," The Fortune Society, https://fortunesociety.org, accessed August 10, 2023.

33 In many state and federal prisons, "inmate" generally describes a subservient or penitent prisoner, as opposed to a "convict," who is honorable in the eyes of other prisoners. Former political prisoner Daniel McGowan, who served time in federal prison, explained to us that the term "inmate" is "self-marginalizing" there, and could even be an insult. A friend David made on Rikers, who had previously

served a long bid in New York state prison, elaborated: "Upstate, an inmate is considered to be a person that, if the CO tells you to jump, you'll be like 'How high?' Whereas a *convict*, he's gonna question why you want to make him jump in the first place."

This distinction, however, simply does not exist among city-time men on Rikers, where the different linguistic convention provides an excellent example of jail culture as distinct from prison culture. "A lotta people go through the city part of the system, never been upstate, and they just rotate in and out of that little system," David's friend explained, an observation confirmed by our experience of meeting vast numbers of incarcerated men who had been passing through Rikers for years or decades but who had never been to prison. For them, the term "inmate" was not a loaded one and just meant "incarcerated person."

This lack of a pejorative connotation to the word was often obvious in the way it was used. After David had been incarcerated for several months, other incarcerated men, including some who had served time upstate, began proudly telling him that he "looked like an inmate now," or deserved the "most improved inmate award," by which they meant he had learned to properly navigate daily life in the jail. Sometimes this could even be attested to by the term's use in downright radical scenarios: expressions like "It's inmates versus COs, and don't forget it!" were sometimes heard. During the George Floyd Uprising, one of David's dorm mates once exclaimed, "All inmates should be turning it up for Breonna Taylor! Greenlight on all COs!" ("greenlight" here means "encouragement to physically assault").

Similarly, we have elected to call the guards at Rikers "COs," short for "correction officer." This is despite the fact that we are loath to imply that DOC staff perform "correcting" of any kind. In our other writing, we have been happy to refer to them as guards, a term they don't seem to like very much. Nonetheless, "CO" is the term that virtually every incarcerated man we encountered used to reference the guards—at least when they were not using more colorful language.

34 Gabrielle Fonrouge, "Squalid, Crowded Conditions Return to Rikers Island Intake Center," *New York Post*, June 14, 2022; Gabrielle Fonrouge, "Rikers Island Inmate Found Dead, 12th Death This Year: Sources," *New York Post*, August 15, 2022.

35 Sonia Moghe, "Inside New York's Notorious Rikers Island Jails, 'The Epicenter of the Epicenter' of the Coronavirus Pandemic," *CNN*, May 18, 2020, www.cnn.com.

36 Brown and Guenther Architects, *Capital Project No. C-76, Workhouse of the City of New York, Rikers Island, New York City*, October 31, 1958, 1. Courtesy of New York City Municipal Archives.

37 Fisher v. Koehler, 692 F. Supp. 1519 (S.D.N.Y. 1988), 1523–24.

38 Graham Rayman and Reuven Blau, *Rikers: An Oral History* (New York: Random House, 2023), 44.

39 "The Architects: Brown & Guenther," Queens Modern, https://queensmodern.com, accessed November 1, 2023.

40 C. René West, *Caught in the Struggle: The Real Rikers Island* (New York: Premadonna Publishing, 2004), 157.

41 Pierre Raphaël, *Inside Rikers Island: A Chaplain's Search for God* (Maryknoll, NY: Orbis Books, 1990), 33.

42 New York City Department of Correction (DOC), *Progress through Crisis, 1954–1966* (New York: DOC, 1956), 384.

43 Brown and Guenther Architects, *Capital Project*, 25–26.

44 NYC DOC, *Jails for the '80s* (New York: DOC, 1980), III: 37, 39; New York City Board of Correction (BOC), *A Study of Violence and Its Cause at the New York City Adolescent Remand and Detention Center* (New York: BOC, 1985), 11–12.

45 Brown Guenther Battaglia Galvin Architects, *Preliminary Plans*, 15.

CHAPTER 1. INTAKE

1 Erving Goffman, *Asylums: Essays on the Condition of the Social Situation of Mental Patients and Other Inmates* (New York: Anchor Books, 1961), 16.

2 Goffman, *Asylums*, 19.

3 Goffman, *Asylums*, 18.

4 Goffman, *Asylums*, 16.

5 Harold Garfinkel, "Conditions of Successful Status Degradation Ceremonies," *American Journal of Sociology* 61, no. 5 (1956): 420–24.

6 Ed Sanders, *Fug You: An Informal History of the Peace Eye Book Store, the Fuck You Press, the Fugs, and Counterculture in the Lower East Side* (Boston: Da Capo Press, 2011), 14.

7 "Rikers Island C74 Adolescent at War: Kill or Be Killed," YouTube video, 17:13, posted by "LIONS and MEN," March 16, 2021, https://www.youtube.com/watch?v=QrSz3NFYcuA.

8 Marcos Perez, "Untitled," in *7-Upper: Writing from Rikers Island, EMTC, through the Fortune Society* (New York: New York Writers Coalition Press, 2013), 13.

9 DOC, "About," LinkedIn, www.linkedin.com, accessed November 30, 2023.

10 Training materials in our possession, dating to around 2010, contain a one-hour, forty-five minute presentation called "Games Inmates Play." This is surely a nod to Bud Allen and Diana Bosta's seminal corrections manual *Games Criminals Play: And How You Can Profit by Knowing Them* (Roseville, CA: Rae John Publishers, 1981).

11 Walker, *Indefinite*, 3.

12 NYC DOC, "Directive: Inmate Orientation," classification #3750, July 11, 2006, 2. Also available on DOC directives page, not obtained via FOIL. www.nyc.gov.

13 Gresham Sykes, *The Society of Captives: A Study of a Maximum Security Prison* (Princeton, NJ: Princeton University Press, 1958), 75.

14 Carlo de Fornaro, *A Modern Purgatory* (New York: Mitchell Kennerly, 1917), 60.

15 Michael G. Santos, *Inside: Life behind Bars in America* (New York: St. Martin's Griffin, 2006), xxv.

16 Sykes, *The Society of Captives*, 76.

17 United States Department of Justice, *CRIPA Investigation of the New York City Department of Correction Jails on Rikers Island* (New York: DOJ, 2014).
18 Gary Heyward, *Corruption Officer: From Jail Guard to Perpetrator inside Rikers Island* (New York: Atria, 2011), 154.
19 West, *Caught in the Struggle*, 100.
20 Lil Wayne, *Gone 'Til November*, 45.
21 Russell "Half" Allen, *Gladiator School: Adolescents at War* (independently published, 2021), 13.
22 Steven Dominquez, *Across the Bridge: A Rikers Island Story* (North Miami Beach, FL: Molding Messengers, 2020), 128.
23 The use of the term "work house" is fascinating; not only is the classical workhouse the historical antecedent to the short-stay men's jail, where impoverished prisoners were punished with hard labor, but technically speaking, C-76 itself is a workhouse, though nobody really used the term. In the city-time parlance, however, a "work house" or "working dorm" meant a dormitory for prisoners who had been largely classified as low risk, spent much of their day working jobs in the jail, and preferred to otherwise go about their time in peace, enjoying small pleasures and minor transgressions, free from heavy-handed intervention by COs, who were similarly content to sit back and enjoy an easy job. For more on this history, see: Jayne Mooney and Jarrod Shanahan, "Rikers Island: The Failure of a 'Model' Penitentiary," *Prison Journal* 100, no. 6 (2020).
24 Lil Wayne, *Gone 'Til November*, 139.

CHAPTER 2. THE PEOPLE OF CITY TIME

1 New York City Mayor's Office of Criminal Justice (NYC MOCJ), "Justice Brief Jail: City Sentences (Including Alternatives to Incarceration)" (New York: City Hall, 2020), 1, 3. As this report indicates, the year 2019 is more exemplary of recent trends in city time than 2020, as COVID-19 occasioned the release of some three hundred city-time inmates, who were suddenly deemed able to freely walk the streets, and arrests and sentencing dropped considerably. These trends dramatically skewed the population of city-time inmates toward those convicted of violent crimes and felonies and serving longer sentences.
2 Aaron Marks, "These 5 Neighborhoods Supply over a Third of NYC's Prisoners," *Gothamist*, May 1, 2013, https://gothamist.com.
3 Scrivener et al., "New York City Jail Population in 2019."
4 Tellingly, Jarrod, who spent far less time at Rikers than David and has undergone academic training as an ethnographer, was initially more enthusiastic about taxonomizing prisoners than David, who developed more substantive relationships during his city time, and initially bristled at the idea that these human beings could be represented so schematically.
5 John Irwin, *The Felon* (Englewood Cliffs, NJ: Prentice Hall, 1970), 11–12; John Irwin and Donald R. Cressey, "Thieves, Convicts, and the Inmate Culture," *Social Problems* 10, no. 2 (Autumn 1962): 142–55.

6 This is no trade secret. The man told Jarrod that he could read about it in the news when he got home, and sure enough, Jarrod found this story: Jamie Schram, Daniel Prendergast, and Sophia Rosenbaum, "City's Bodegas Are Stocked with Stolen, Re-frozen Ice Cream," *New York Post*, May 11, 2016, https://nypost.com.

7 New York City Mayor's Office of Operations, *Mayor's Management Report Fiscal 2023*, September 2023, 81, www.nyc.gov.

8 S. M. Katz, "Taking Back the Island (Riker's Island), Part 1," *Corrections Technology & Management* 2, no. 8 (September 1998): 34–37.

9 Rayman and Blau, *Rikers*, 69; New York City Police Department, *The Gang Manual* (New York: New York/New Jersey HIDTA, 2004), 2.

10 Jonathan Munby, *Public Heroes: Screening the Gangster from Little Caesar to Touch of Evil* (Chicago: University of Chicago Press, 1999).

11 Edwin G. Burrows and Mike Wallace, *Gotham: A History of New York City to 1898* (New York: Oxford University Press, 1998), 633–35.

12 Alice Speri, "The Largest Gang Raid in NYC History Swept Up Dozens of Young People Who Weren't in Gangs," *The Intercept*, April 25, 2019, https://theintercept .com.

13 Jarrod Shanahan, "Some Bullshit," *Hard Crackers: Chronicles of Everyday Life* 1 (Spring 2016), https://hardcrackers.com.

14 Irwin, *The Felon*, 32–34.

15 Wynn, *Inside Rikers*, 202.

16 New York City Council (Finance Division), *Report of the Finance Division on the Fiscal 2021 Preliminary Plan and the Fiscal 2020 Preliminary Mayor's Management Report for the Department of Correction*, March 16, 2020, 4, 7, www.nyc.gov.

17 Nunez Monitoring Team, *Eleventh Report of the Nunez Independent Monitor: Eleventh Monitoring Period July 1, 2020–December 31, 2020* (New York: NYC.gov, 2021), 10–13.

18 NYC Council (Finance Division), *Report of the Finance Division on the Fiscal 2021 Preliminary Plan* , 8.

19 NYC Council, "New York City Department of Correction Uniform Personnel Demographic Data October 23rd, 2019," https://council.nyc.gov, accessed May 24, 2022.

20 Ben M. Crouch, "Pandora's Box: Women Guards in Men's Prisons," *Journal of Criminal Justice* 13 (1985): 535–37; Lynn E. Zimmer, *Women Guarding Men* (Chicago: University of Chicago Press, 1986), 5–8.

21 Brooke Hauser, "On Rikers Island, a Changing of the Guard," *New York Times*, September 26, 2008, www.nytimes.com.

22 NYC DOC, "Join the Boldest: How to Qualify," www1.nyc.gov, accessed May 24, 2022.

23 NYC DOC, "Join the Boldest: Benefits," www1.nyc.gov, accessed May 24, 2022,

24 Our Freedom of Information Law request for current DOC Academy material of any kind was refused on the dubious grounds that it "relates to the supervision, safety, and security of individuals." However, we obtained a detailed audit

of DOC Academy circa 2009, conducted by criminal justice experts Gordon A. Crews, Ann M. Jones, William H. McDonald, and Eric C. Schultz, that provides a detailed sketch of the academy programming at the levels of rookie CO, academy instructor, captain, and assistant deputy warden.

25 Heyward, *Corruption Officer*, 32–33, 36.

26 New York City Department of Investigation (DOI), *Report on the Recruiting and Hiring Process for New York City Correction Officers* (New York: DOI, 2015), 2.

27 Brad Hamilton, "Ex-Guard Tells of Inmate Lovin' at Rikers," *New York Post*, March 20, 2011, https://nypost.com.

28 Yoshe, *Taboo* (Deer Park, NY: Urban Books, 2009); Yoshe, *Taboo II: Locked In* (Deer Park, NY: Urban Books, 2011).

29 Robin K. Miller, *Inside the Dark Underbelly of Rikers Island: A Retired Female Correction Officer Speaks Out* (New York: Robin K. Miller, 2016), 51.

30 Heyward, *Corruption Officer*, 146–47.

31 Simone Martin-Howard and Janet Garcia-Hallett, "The (Power) Struggle: Experiences of BIWOC Correctional Officers at Rikers Island Jail," *Women & Criminal Justice*, December 2022, doi: 10.1080/08974454.2022.2154631. The COs in this study were not identified beyond being "of color."

32 West, *Caught in the Struggle*, 157.

33 West, *Caught in the Struggle*, 37–38.

34 West, *Caught in the Struggle*, 39, 43.

35 Angela Davis, *An Autobiography* (New York: International Publishers, 1988), 43.

36 Heyward, *Corruption Officer*, 14.

37 West, *Caught in the Struggle*, 37–38.

38 Heyward, *Corruption Officer*, 14.

39 Donald Reid and Martin Small, "Rikers Island: Life and Experience of Two Retired Correction Officers," March 26, 2020, in *Road to Legacy Podcast*, podcast, 01:43:05, https://play.acast.com.

40 West, *Caught in the Struggle*, 10.

41 Walker, *Indefinite*, 110.

42 Davis, *An Autobiography*, 43.

43 West, *Caught in the Struggle*, 152.

44 Keith Williams, "We Know They're New York's Finest: But Why?" *New York Times*, May 4, 2017, www.nytimes.com.

45 Correction Officers' Benevolent Association, Inc., "About COBA," www.cobanyc.org, accessed June 3, 2022. Complaints of DOC's fusion of police and military culture go back a long way. One investigation, undertaken in the wake of a brutal 1986 staff riot, observed, "The consistent emphasis of similarities to police and military organizations during academy training should be eliminated immediately. . . . The current training overplays these similarities and fails to specify the distinctions. . . . Through such misguided practices new officers develop an orientation which emphasizes enforcement functions and technical skills, while neglecting human relations and communication skills that are necessary and compose most of the job." See: Michael J. Gilbert, *The New York City Department of Correction Training Academy: An Executive Management Presentation of a Report on the Use of Force in the New York City Department of Correction* (New York: DOC, 1987), 9.

46 West, *Caught in the Struggle*, 15–16.

47 West, *Caught in the Struggle*, 52.

48 James B. Jacobs and Harold G. Retsky, "Prison Guard," in *The Keepers: Prison Guards and Contemporary Correction*, ed. Ben M. Crouch (Springfield, IL: Charles C. Thomas, 1980), 188.

49 Assata Shakur/Joanne Chesimard, "Women in Prison: How We Are," *Black Scholar* 9, no. 7 (April 1978): 52–53.

50 Martin-Howard and Garcia-Hallett, "The (Power) Struggle."

51 This story is a central narrative in Jarrod Shanahan, *Captives: How Rikers Island Took New York City Hostage* (London: Verso, 2022).

52 NYC Council (Finance Division), *Report of the Finance Division on the Fiscal 2021 Preliminary Plan*, 7.

53 New York City Office of Management and Budget, *FY 2022 Budget Function Analysis* (New York: City Hall, 2022) 145–52.

54 These numbers are approximations, measured as "full-time equivalents," and have been rounded down from decimal points. See: New York City Council (Finance Division), *Report of the Finance Division on the Fiscal 2021 Preliminary Plan, Fiscal 2021 Preliminary Capital Budget, Fiscal 2021 Preliminary Capital Commitment Plan, and the Fiscal 2020 Preliminary Mayor's Management Report for Health + Hospitals* (New York: City Hall, 2020), 19.

55 Osborne Association, "Jail Based Services," www.osborneny.org, accessed June 2, 2022; Wynn, *Inside Rikers*.

56 Shanahan, *Captives*, 85–87.

57 Mary E. Buser, *Lockdown on Rikers: Shocking Stories of Abuse and Injustice at New York's Notorious Jail* (New York: St. Martin's Press, 2015), 141.

58 Homer Venters, *Life and Death in Rikers Island* (Baltimore, MD: Johns Hopkins University Press, 2019), 42–43, 143.

59 Kimberly L. Sue, "Violence at Rikers Island: Does the Doctor Make It Worse? A Clinician Ethnographer's Work amidst Carceral Structural Violence," *Culture, Medicine, and Psychiatry*, November 2022, 6, doi: 10.1007/s11013-022-09812-2.

60 Buser, *Lockdown*, 7.

CHAPTER 3. A DAY IN THE LIFE

1 NYC DOC, *Inmate Handbook* (HB no. 44915, revised December 2007), 32.

CHAPTER 4. DOING TIME

1 Hans Reimer, "Socialization in the Prison Community," in *1937 Proceedings of the Annual Congress of the American Prison Association* (1937), 151.

2 Walker, *Indefinite*, 147.

3 James J. Gibson, "The Theory of Affordances," in *The Ecological Approach to Visual Perception* (Boston: Houghton Mifflin, 1979).
4 MacGyver is a television character who can fashion a solution to any crisis out of ready-to-hand objects.
5 NYC DOC, *Inmate Handbook*, 32.
6 Daniel Genis reported this same technique in New York's state prison system, where the participants "strenuously denied" its homoeroticism. On Rikers, in contrast, the homoerotic element of full-body contact between men was never broached at all. See: Daniel Genis, "An Ex-Con's Guide to Prison Weightlifting," *Deadspin*, May 6, 2014, https://deadspin.com.
7 Visitors were previously allowed to bring packages for inmates, which they then surrendered to the COs for screening. As of December 2023, the DOC has banned packages on in-person visits. See: NYC DOC, "Mailing Packages to Persons in Custody," www.nyc.gov, accessed February 2, 2024.
8 Pakij Kent Ochjaroem, "Sibling Letter," in *7-Upper: Writing from Rikers Island, EMTC, through the Fortune Society* (New York: New York Writers Coalition Press, 2013), 33.
9 Reimer, "Socialization," 153.
10 Donald Clemmer, *The Prison Community* (New York: Holt, Rinehart, and Winston, 1958), 92.
11 Heyward, *Corruption Officer*, 39. In one evocative passage, Heyward recalls, "I was running through the jails swinging my dick from left to right" (88).
12 West, *Caught in the Struggle*, 37.
13 Heyward, *Corruption Officer*, 22.
14 West, *Caught in the Struggle*, 74.
15 Heyward, *Corruption Officer*, 22.
16 West, *Caught in the Struggle*, 74.
17 Goffman, *Asylums*, 67, 69.
18 Perez, "Untitled," 48.
19 Victor Serge, *Men in Prison* (Oakland: PM Press, 2014), 29.
20 Irwin, *The Felon*, 68–74.
21 Serge, *Men in Prison*, 200.
22 Goffman, *Asylums*, 50.
23 William S. Burroughs, *Junky* (New York: Penguin, 2003), 53.
24 Venters, *Life and Death*, 22.
25 Theodore Hamm, "The Man Who's Been Sent to Rikers 100 Times," *Village Voice*, January 9, 2018, www.villagevoice.com.

CHAPTER 5. WORK

1 Caroline Lewis, "Rikers Inmates Will No Longer Bury the Dead amid Hart Island Transformation," *Gothamist*, May 6, 2021, https://gothamist.com; Corey Kilgannon, "A Million Bodies Are Buried Here: Now It's Becoming a Park," *New York Times*, March 24, 2023, www.nytimes.com.

2 Lil Wayne, *Gone 'Til November*, 35. Incidentally, Lil Wayne claims to have landed this coveted position by offering to introduce an influential inmate to one of the models from a magazine he had (21).
3 NYC DOC, "Directive: Inmate Incentive Pay Plan," classification #4014R-A, April 11, 2007. Document obtained via FOIL request.
4 NYC DOC, "Directive: Assignment of Inmates to Work Details," classification #3255R, June 29, 1987. Document obtained via FOIL request.
5 NYC DOC, "Inmate Wage Incentive Plan," in *Progress through Crisis: 1954–1966* (DOC, 1966), 128–29. This did not immediately apply to all inmate-workers.
6 US Department of Labor, Wage and Hour Division, "Overtime Pay," www.dol.gov, accessed October 12, 2022.
7 David Campbell, "Decarceration Means Funding the Incarcerated," *CUNY Law Review Footnotes Forum* 25, no. 1 (Winter 2022), https://academicworks.cuny .edu; NYC Board of Correction member Dana Wax, "Wages," email message to NYC Board of Correction member Bennett Stein, September 23, 2020. Document obtained from the NYC Board of Correction via FOIL request.
8 NYC DOC, "Directive: Incentive Pay Plan for Incarcerated Individuals," classification #4014R-B, October 12, 2021, 3. Available on the DOC directives page. www.nyc.gov.
9 Portions of this chapter first appeared in: Jarrod Shanahan, "Checking Out," *Insurgent Notes*, September 7, 2016, www.insurgentnotes.com.
10 NYC DOC, "Directive: Assignment of Inmates to Work Details," 2.
11 Zoe Greenberg, "Phone Calls from New York City Jails Will Soon Be Free," *New York Times*, August 6, 2018, www.nytimes.com.
12 Rayman and Blau, *Rikers*, 163–64.
13 U.S. Attorney's Office, Southern District of New York, "9 Department of Correction Officers and Employees Charged with Taking Bribes to Smuggle Contraband to Inmates at New York City Jails," May 26, 2021, www.justice.gov.
14 U.S. Attorney's Office, Southern District of New York, "Former Rikers Correction Officer Sentenced to More Than Two Years in Prison for Taking Bribes to Smuggle Contraband to Inmates," November 2, 2022, www.justice.gov.
15 Rob Ralphs, Lisa Williams, Rebecca Askew, and Anna Norton, "Adding Spice to the Porridge: The Development of a Synthetic Cannabinoid Market in an English Prison," *International Journal of Drug Policy* 40 (February 2017): 57–69, doi: 10.1016/j.drugpo.2016.10.003.
16 K2 can be purchased on websites like legalhemponline.com, but we do not recommend it.
17 Frankie Edozien, "Jail Guards: Smoke Ban Is Un-Kool," *New York Post*, January 29, 2003, https://nypost.com.
18 In the abovementioned May 2021 federal case, one CO allegedly sold packs of cigarettes to inmates for five hundred dollars apiece, implying a resale price above five hundred dollars for any inmate looking to make a profit. See: Benjamin Weiser, "Guards Smuggled Drugs and Razors into N.Y.C. Jails, Prosecutors Say," *New York Times*, May 26, 2021, www.nytimes.com.

19 Didier Fassin, *Prison Worlds: An Ethnography of the Carceral Condition* (Cambridge, UK: Polity, 2016), 203.
20 Goffman, *Asylums*, 69.
21 The populations of men Guilbaud studied in *maisons d'arrêt* (MA) were 50 percent sentenced and 50 percent in pretrial detention, and quite similar to Rikers' in a number of ways: "The population in MAs is young (around 30) and turns over quickly (average stay is five months). Most MA inmates have been convicted of petty to moderately serious crimes (26% for theft, 18% for drugs, 16% for violence). At the time of my study, 46% of inmates had been working manual jobs, 15% clerical and 33% were unemployed when they entered prison." Fabrice Guilbaud, "Working in Prison: Time as Experienced by Inmate-Workers," *Revue française de sociologie* 51, no. 5 (2010): 41–68, appendix, doi: 10.3917/rfs.515.0041.
22 Guilbaud, "Working in Prison," 53.
23 Theodor Adorno, "Free Time," in *The Culture Industry: Selected Essays on Mass Culture* (New York: Routledge, 2001).
24 Goffman, *Asylums*, 68.

CHAPTER 6. SPECIAL OCCASIONS

1 NYC DOC, *Handbook for Detained and Sentenced Individuals* (HB no. 0339, revised December 2019), 24.
2 Bianca Pallaro and Reuven Blau, "Stiff Prices, Unfulfilled Orders: How the Private Contractor Running Rikers Commissary Serves Detainees," *The City*, June 9, 2023, www.thecity.nyc; Bianca Pallaro and Reuven Blau, "Rikers Set to Renew No-Bid Contract with Much Criticized Commissary Vendor Keefe Group," *The City*, June 22, 2023, www.thecity.nyc.
3 Shayla Mulzac, "Inquiry—status of contract with Keefe group," email message to author, September 22, 2023.
4 Wynn, *Inside Rikers*, 4.
5 Cindy Rodriguez, "After Years of Complaints, NYC Will Compensate Jail Visitors Who Were Subjected to Invasive Searches," *Gothamist*, December 17, 2019, https://gothamist.com.
6 Jarrod worked on a collaborative project with Pryor and comic artist Nate McDonough documenting the visitation process from his experience as an inmate and their experience visiting him. The result is the zine "Visiting Day" (2017), which can be accessed here: https://hardcrackers.com/wp-content/uploads/2017/06/Visiting-Day-1.pdf.
7 Joseph Ax and Nate Raymond, "Prosecutors Turn Fire on New York Prison's Culture of Violence," *Reuters*, April 19, 2016, www.reuters.com.
8 New York City Department of Investigation (DOI), "New York City Department of Investigation Report on Security Failures at City Department of Correction Facilities" (NYC: DOI, 2014); NYC DOI, "Investigation Reveals Front-Gate Security Failures at City Detention Complexes in Manhattan and Brooklyn" (New York: DOI, 2018). The latter report was distributed attached to a letter bearing the

boldfaced subtitle "DOI Found Same Failures in 2014 and Recommended DOC Make Changes, Which the Agency Never Adopted."

9 George Joseph and Reuven Blau, "When Visitors Were Banned from Rikers Island, Even More Drugs Showed Up," *The City*, February 9, 2022, www.thecity.nyc.

10 Jarrod Shanahan, "'Visiting Day' at Rikers Island," *Qualitative Research in Psychology* 15, no. 2/3 (2018): 352–354.

11 de Fornaro, *A Modern Purgatory*, 113.

12 West, *Caught in the Struggle*, 134–35.

13 Brooklyn Public Library, "Plan Your Televisit," www.bklynlibrary.org, accessed September 12, 2023.

14 As of December 2023, DOC video visits are still ongoing, and a representative for the Brooklyn Public Library confirmed via email that TeleStory is now used exclusively for inmates in the state prison system, meaning that the DOC has effectively asserted direct control over video visits for those in its custody. See: NYC DOC, "Televisit Request Form," www.nyc.gov, accessed February 3, 2024.

15 Daniel E. Slotnik, "For the First Time in More Than a Year, Visitors Can Return to New York City Jails," *New York Times*, June 25, 2021, www.nytimes.com.

16 Pierre Raphaël and Henri Tincq, *Dans l'Enfer de Rikers Island: Aumônier de prison à New-York* (Paris: Centurion, 1988), 104 (translation by David Campbell).

17 Walker, *Indefinite*, 90.

18 The Vera Institute of Justice, "A Look inside the New York City Correction Budget," May 2021, 8, www.vera.org.

19 Vera Institute, "A Look Inside," 1.

20 Office of the New York City Comptroller, "Comptroller Stringer: Cost of Incarceration per Person in New York City Skyrockets to All-Time High," December 6, 2021, https://comptroller.nyc.gov.

21 The Fortune Society, "Prepare for Release with the I-CAN Program," https://fortunesociety.org, accessed October 12, 2022.

22 NYC DOC, "I-CAN: Individualized Corrections Achievement Network," www1.nyc.gov, accessed October 12, 2022.

23 The Fortune Society I-CAN Program, "Certificate of Successful Participation," presented January 7, 2020.

CHAPTER 7. FOOD

1 This is more than simple intuition. According to the online corpus linguistics platform Sketch Engine's English Web 2021 corpus, for example, the top five modifiers of the noun "chow," excluding those that refer to the Chow Chow dog breed, all refer to animal food.

2 New York City Mayor's Office, "Mayor de Blasio, Chancellor Carranza, and Brooklyn Borough President Adams Announce Citywide Meatless Mondays," March 11, 2019, www.nyc.gov.

3 Walker, "Race Making," 1071.

4 West, *Caught in the Struggle*, 159.

5 Cambro, "Ultra Camtainers," www.cambro.com, accessed November 17, 2023.
6 New York City Department of Environmental Protection, *New York City Drinking Water Supply and Quality Report 2022* (New York: DEP, 2022), 1, www.nyc.gov.
7 Lil Wayne, *Gone 'Til November*, 54.

CHAPTER 8. HYGIENE

1 Lil Wayne, *Gone 'Til November*, 13.
2 Spedding, "Dreams of Leaving," 15.
3 Lil Wayne, *Gone 'Til November*, 60.
4 New York State Department of Corrections and Community Supervision (Division of Industries), *Corcraft Products Price & Specification Guide* (Albany, NY: NYS-DOCCS, 2020), 176, https://corcraft.ny.gov.
5 Jon Alpert and Nina Rosenblum, *Lock-Up: The Prisoners of Rikers Island*, HBO, 1994.
6 New York State Department of Corrections and Community Supervision, "About Us," https://corcraft.ny.gov, accessed February 3, 2024.
7 NYC DOC, *Inmate Handbook*, 32.
8 NYC DOC, "Institutional Uniforms," www.nyc.gov, accessed February 3, 2024.
9 NYC DOC, *Handbook for Detained and Sentenced Individuals*, 32.

CHAPTER 9. CLOTHING

1 BOC, *Study of Violence*, 12.
2 Kathleen Horan, "'Air Patakis': The City's Jail Sneaker," *WNYC News*, August 8, 2011, www.wnyc.org.
3 Irwin and Cressey, "Thieves, Convicts," 149.
4 Donald W. Winnicott, "Transitional Objects and Transitional Phenomena: A Study of the First Not-Me Possession," *International Journal of Psycho-Analysis* 34, no. 2 (1953): 89–97.
5 NYC DOC, *Visit Guide*, 20, www.nyc.gov, accessed February 3, 2024.
6 NYC DOC, *Visit Guide*, 18; NYC DOC, *Handbook for Detained and Sentenced Individuals*, 31.

CHAPTER 10. SUBSTANCE ABUSE AND MENTAL HEALTH

1 New York State Office of Addiction Services and Supports, "What Are Synthetic Cannabinoids?," https://oasas.ny.gov, accessed February 3, 2024; European Monitoring Centre for Drugs and Drug Addiction, "Synthetic Cannabinoids and 'Spice' Drug Profile," www.emcdda.europa.eu, accessed February 3, 2024.
2 Travis Linnemann, *Meth Wars: Police, Media, Power* (New York: New York University Press, 2016), 28–29.
3 Caitlyn Norman, "A Global Review of Prison Drug Smuggling Routes and Trends in the Usage of Drugs in Prisons," *WIREs Forensic Science* 5, no. 2 (March/April 2023): 7, doi: 10.1002/wfs2.1473.
4 Wynn, *Inside Rikers*, 169–81.

5 Maurice Carroll, "City Council Overrides Lindsay, Orders Jail Methadone Program," *New York Times*, September 10, 1969, www.nytimes.com; Maurice Carroll, "Councilmen Push for Methadone Plan," *New York Times*, February 15, 1970, www.nytimes.com; Edward Ranzal, "City Plans to Double Methadone Project," *New York Times*, September 30, 1970, www.nytimes.com; NYC BOC, *Crisis in the Prisons: A Commitment to Change* (New York: BOC, 1971), 9.

6 V. Tomasino, A. J. Swanson, J. Nolan, and H. I. Shuman, "The Key Extended Entry Program (KEEP): A Methadone Treatment Program for Opiate-Dependent Inmates," *Mount Sinai Journal of Medicine* 68, no. 1 (January 2001): 14–20.

7 Substance Abuse and Mental Health Services Administration, "Buprenorphine," www.samhsa.gov, accessed April 14, 2024.

8 Substance Abuse and Mental Health Services Administration, "Buprenorphine Quick Start Guide," 2–3, www.samhsa.gov, accessed February 3, 2024; Indivior UK Limited, "Suboxone Sublingual Film: Highlights of Prescribing Information," section 5.10, www.suboxone.com, accessed February 3, 2024.

9 Venters, *Life and Death*, 67.

10 Venters, *Life and Death*, 67. For a sustained historical sketch linking deinstitutionalization to the rise of mass incarceration, see: Bernard Harcourt, "From the Asylum to the Prison: Rethinking the Incarceration Revolution," *Texas Law Review* 84 (2006): 1751–86.

11 New York City Mayor's Office of Operations, "Department of Correction," in *Mayor's Management Report Fiscal 2022*, September 2022, 85, www1.nyc.gov.

12 Reuven Blau, "New Psych Units at Rikers Delayed Despite Renewed Focus on Mental Health and Justice," *The City*, February 28, 2022, www.thecity.nyc; New York City Mayor's Office of Operations, "Department of Correction," 85.

13 Michael Winerip and Michael Schwirtz, "Rikers: Where Mental Illness Meets Brutality in Jail," *New York Times*, June 14, 2014, www.nytimes.com.

14 Buser, *Lockdown*, 125–26, 192.

15 Article 730: Mental Disease or Defect Excluding Fitness to Proceed, New York State Senate (2014), www.nysenate.gov.

16 Urban Justice Center, "Impact Litigation: Brad H. v. The City of New York," https://mhp.urbanjustice.org, accessed December 3, 2022.

17 New York City Mayor's Management Report, "Department of Correction," 85.

18 Rayman and Blau, *Rikers*, 117.

19 Liat Ben-Moshe, *Decarcerating Disability: Deinstitutionalization and Prison Abolition* (Minneapolis: University of Minnesota Press, 2020), 152, 156–58.

20 Treatment Advocacy Center, "Serious Mental Illness Prevalence in Jails and Prisons," September 2016, www.treatmentadvocacycenter.org.

CHAPTER 11. INTERPERSONAL RELATIONSHIPS

1 Lil Wayne, *Gone 'Til November*, 29.

2 Orisanmi Burton, "Organized Disorder: The New York City Jail Rebellion of 1970," *Black Scholar* 48, no. 4 (October 2018): 28–42, doi: 10.1080/00064246.2018.1514925.

3 Richard Cloward, "Social Control in the Prison," in *Theoretical Studies in Social Organization of the Prison*, ed. Social Science Research Council (New York: Social Science Research Council, 1960), 33.
4 Wacquant, "The Curious Eclipse," 378.
5 Spedding, "Dreams of Leaving," 14.
6 J. B. Nicholas, "Man Who Tried to Escape Rikers Twice in Four Days 'Has No Other Choice,' Fellow Inmate Says," *Gothamist*, June 22, 2020, https://gothamist.com.
7 Walker, *Indefinite*, 135.
8 Lil Wayne, *Gone 'Til November*, 91.
9 Dana Wax, "Rikers Is Already Awful, and It's Worse If You're Trans," *New York Times*, March 7, 2023, www.nytimes.com.
10 George Joseph, "Under Eric Adams, a Rikers Unit That Protected Trans Women Has Collapsed," *The City*, January 24, 2023, www.thecity.nyc.
11 Mumia Abu-Jamal, "Caged and Celibate," in *Prison Masculinities*, ed. Don Sabo, Terry A. Kupers, and Willie London (Philadelphia: Temple University Press, 2001), 139.
12 Sykes, *The Society of Captives*, 72.
13 Sykes, *The Society of Captives*, 99.
14 Allen, *Gladiator School*, 117.
15 A 1994 report, for example, notes that when inmates tore out phones in protest of a new, more restrictive DOC phone policy, "the absence of working phones made those who destroyed them the enemies of their fellow inmates; two inmates who damaged phones had to be re-housed rather than return to face the wrath—and certain violence—of angry inmates." See: Nancy G. La Vigne, "Rational Choice and Inmate Disputes over Phone Use on Rikers Island," *Crime Prevention Studies* 3 (1994): 116.
16 In our experience, the only insult approaching "snitch" in severity, for example, was "sneak thief." Snitching can itself be thought of as perhaps the most basic form of refusing to participate in inmate solidarity. See: Thomas Ugelvik, "'Be a Man. Not a Bitch': Snitching, the Inmate Code, and the Narrative Reconstruction of Masculinity in a Norwegian Prison," in *Masculinities in the Criminological Field: Control, Vulnerability, and Risk-Taking*, ed. Ingrid Lander Signe Ravn and Nina Jon (New York: Routledge, 2016), 58.
17 Jan Ransom and Bianca Pallaro, "Behind the Violence at Rikers, Decades of Mismanagement and Dysfunction," *New York Times*, December 31, 2021, www.nytimes.com.
18 Cincere Wilson, "Rikers Island Today: Part Two; Will '3-3-3' Be a Formula for Peace?," *Urban Matters*, April 20, 2022, www.centernyc.org.
19 See: NYC MOCJ, "Justice Brief Jail," 5.
20 J. Sakai, *Settlers: Mythology of the White Proletariat*, 2nd ed. (Oakland, CA: Kersplebedeb/PM Press, 2014).
21 Noel Ignatiev and Theodore Allen, "The White Blindspot," in *Treason to Whiteness Is Loyalty to Humanity*, ed. Geert Dhondt, Zhandarka Kurti, and Jarrod Shanahan (London: Verso, 2022), 44–60.

22 Walker, "Race Making," 151–78; Walker, *Indefinite*, 48–108.

23 Jacques Derrida, *The Work of Mourning*, trans. Pascale-Anne Brault (Chicago: University of Chicago Press, 2001).

CHAPTER 12. INSTITUTIONAL RELATIONSHIPS

1 Jack Henry Abbott, *In the Belly of the Beast: Letters from Prison* (New York: Vintage, 1981), 60.

2 Neville "Storm" Redd, "Confused Anger," in *7-Upper: Writing from Rikers Island, EMTC, through the Fortune Society* (New York: New York Writers Coalition Press, 2013), 35.

3 Richard Cloward, "Social Control in the Prison," in *Theoretical Studies in Social Organization of the Prison*, ed. Social Science Research Council (New York: Social Science Research Council, 1960), 22.

4 Miller, *Inside the Dark Underbelly*, 22. The term "brainwashing" appears fairly frequently in firsthand accounts from former COs, such as the *Road to Legacy Podcast* episode cited in chapter 2, "Rikers Island: Life and Experience of Two Retired Correction Officers," and in the comments section of the DOC's LinkedIn page.

5 Miller, *Inside the Dark Underbelly*, 26.

6 John Irwin, *Prisons in Turmoil* (Boston: Little, Brown, 1980), 127–28.

7 West, *Caught in the Struggle*, 105.

8 Sykes, *The Society of Captives*, 42, 55–57.

9 Cloward, "Social Control," 32–45.

10 Brad Hamilton, "Brutal System of Teen Beatings Continues at Rikers Island's RNDC Prison," *New York Post*, May 6, 2012, https://nypost.com.

11 Stephen Rex Brown, "Rikers Island Correction Officers Run 'World Tour' Program Using Inmate Enforcers: Suit," *New York Daily News*, November 16, 2020, www.nydailynews.com.

12 Denise L. Jenne and Robert C. Kersting, "Gender, Power, and Reciprocity in the Correctional Setting," *Prison Journal* 78, no. 2 (1998): 166–85.

13 Alison Liebling, "Prison Officers, Policing, and the Use of Discretion," *Theoretical Criminology* 4, no. 3 (2000): 333–59.

14 David Correia and Tyler Wall, *Police: A Field Guide* (London: Verso, 2018), 184.

15 Walter Benjamin, "Critique of Violence," in *Selected Writings*. Vol. 1, *1913–1926*, ed. Marcus Bullock and Michael W. Jennings (Cambridge, MA: Belknap/Harvard University Press, 1996), 243.

16 Luc Sante, *Low Life: Lures and Snares of Old New York* (New York: Vintage, 1992), 247.

17 John R. Hepburn, "The Exercise of Power in Coercive Organizations: A Study of Prison Guards," *Criminology* 23, no. 1 (1985): 146–54. These results, as Hepburn indicates, largely square with Lucien Lombardo's earlier study of COs at New York's Auburn State Prison, *Guards Imprisoned: Correctional Officers at Work* (New York: Elsevier, 1978).

18 Zimmer, *Women Guarding Men*, 78–107.
19 Miller, *Inside the Dark Underbelly*; West, *Caught in the Struggle*; Yoshe, *Taboo*; Yoshe, *Taboo II*.
20 Heyward, *Corruption Officer*, 121.
21 West, *Caught in the Struggle*, 92.
22 Zimmer, *Women Guarding Men*, 108–47.
23 Dominquez, *Across the Bridge*, 89.
24 "Protest on Rikers amidst COVID-19 Outbreak," *Perilous Chronicle*, March 21, 2020, https://perilouschronicle.com.
25 "ICE Detainees Hunger Strike in Hudson County, NJ, in Response to COVID-19," *Perilous Chronicle*, March 18, 2020, https://perilouschronicle.com.
26 For a full account of the strike, see: David Campbell, "Stick-Up on Rikers Island," *Hard Crackers: Chronicles of Everyday Life*, May 1, 2020, https://hardcrackers.com.
27 NYC BOC, *A Study of the Department of Correction Inmate Grievance and Request Program* (New York: BOC, 2016), 2, www.nyc.gov; NYC BOC, "About," www.nyc.gov, accessed February 3, 2024.

CHAPTER 13. RELEASE

1 New York City Independent Budget Office, "Fiscal Brief June 2009: City Spending Rises on Programs to Help Inmates Leaving Jail," June 2009, 1–2, https://ibo.nyc.ny.us.
2 NYC Council (Finance Division), *Report of the Finance Division on the Fiscal 2021 Preliminary Plan*, 7–8, 13.
3 Dana Rubinstein and Emma G. Fitzsimmons, "Libraries Spared but Rikers Suffers in $107 Billion N.Y.C. Budget Deal," *New York Times*, June 29, 2023, www.nytimes.com; Matt Katz, "Mayor Adams Cuts Classes and Re-entry Services at Rikers to Save $17 Million in NYC Budget," *Gothamist*, May 16, 2023, https://gothamist.com.
4 NYC Council (Finance Division), *Report on the Fiscal 2024 Preliminary Plan and the Fiscal 2023 Mayor's Management Report for the Department of Correction*, March 23, 2023, 1, https://council.nyc.gov; Carlina Rivera, "Rikers Is Richly Staffed: Without a Plan to Rightsize, It Will Cost Us Dearly," *City & State New York*, August 23, 2023, www.cityandstateny.com.
5 NYC DOC, *Handbook for Detained and Sentenced Individuals*, 29.
6 Urban Justice Center, "Impact Litigation."
7 NYC DOC, "Discharge Planning Report," March 2023, www.nyc.gov.
8 NYC DOC, *Handbook for Detained and Sentenced Individuals*, 35.
9 Michael D. White, Jessica Saunders, Christopher Fisher, and Jeff Mellow, "Exploring Inmate Reentry in a Local Jail Setting: Implications for Outreach, Service Use, and Recidivism," *Crime & Delinquency* 58, no. 1 (2012): 129–30.
10 Robin Waterfield, trans., *The First Philosophers: The Presocratics and the Sophists* (Oxford: Oxford University Press, 2000), 69.
11 Goffman, *Asylums*, 19.
12 Serge, *Men in Prison*, 202.

INDEX

1-Upper, 32, 33, 40, 41–42, 47–48, 178, 179, 210, 211–212, 283

Abu-Jamal, Mumia, 232
Ack, 43, 227–228, 233, 247
Adams, Eric, 231
Adorno, Theodor, 123
Air Patakis, 32, 78, 196–197, 198, 286
alarms, 19, 20, 37–38, 133, 279
The Alchemist, 279
Allen, Russell "Half," 38, 234
argot, 44–45, 75, 101; regarding mental health status, 219–220, 221
artworks: produced by inmates, 66, 119; institutional murals, 20, 75, 93, 100, 143

beds: bedding, 18, 33, 42, 83, 138, 173, 189; bed frames, 17, 188, 205; importance of location, 17, 22, 40, 25; bed corsets, 89–90
Bellevue Hospital, 197, 277–278
Ben-Moshe, Liat, 225–226
big homies, 236, 284; gang-affiliated, 246–248; neutral, 248–249, 256, 261
Blackwell's Island, 36, 130
Board of Correction, 18, 113n7, 272, 275
The Boat, 137, 274
books, 98–100; on visits, 98, 128, 135; as social capital, 98–99; as weights 92, 94, 160, 162, 189
boosting, 48, 49–51, 108, 286
box time. *See* solitary confinement
Brad H.: as term for mentally ill inmates, 221, 222; court settlement, 222, 281; folk etymology of, 102, 221–222
Brown, Michelle, 4
Bullpens. *See* pens
Burroughs, William S., 109
Buser, Mary E., 65, 66, 220
buses, 30–31, 141, 200, 286, 287; for visitors, 128, 129, 130; SOD 72, 277

captains: making rounds, 82, 87, 209, 211, 241, 242; overseeing searches 137, 138, 262
Captives: How Rikers Island Took New York City Hostage, 6
Child Protective Services, 133
Chinita. *See* Suboxone
chow. *See* food
civilian workers, 32–33, 64–66, 167; intimidation of by COs, 65; in kitchen, 65, 154, 157, 164, 167, 169; in medical and mental health services, 33, 65–66, 220, 282; in programs and discharge planning, 65, 282
Civiliter mortuus, 27
Clemmer, Donald, 101
clinic visits, 19, 32–33, 35, 37, 184, 197, 211, 212, 213, 219; unintended consequences of, 207
clothing: CO uniforms, 193–194, 260; inmate fashion, 194–196, 198–203; inmate uniforms, 12, 27, 32, 68, 70, 72, 117, 152, 175, 187, 191–193, 201, 260; jewelry, 200–201; outside work and, 72, 121; visits and, 130, 136, 195
Cloward, Richard, 229, 260

commissary: drinks, 155, 166–167; food, 42, 76, 78, 80, 125–127, 155, 161–163, 168, 277; hygiene products, 88, 126, 176, 194; visits, 20, 40, 42, 124–127, 155, 166, 168, 279
conflict: avoidance, 150, 158, 172, 228, 230, 235, 237–238, 248–250; between COs and inmates, 180, 218, 219, 261, 273–275, 278–279; between COs and superiors: 62–63, 64; between inmates, 41, 78–79, 91–92, 107, 163, 169–170, 181, 195, 218, 227–228, 233–238, 240n15, 246, 255; between visitors, 132
contraband, 5, 20, 27, 31–32, 34, 41, 55, 61, 87, 88, 91, 93, 117, 119–120, 127, 129, 133, 157, 158, 163, 166, 168, 169, 181, 202, 229, 241–243, 260
Convict criminology, 5n18, 10, 50, 107
Corcraft: corporation, 175; soap, 79–80, 175, 180, 181, 188
Correctional Institution for Women, 63
Correctional Officers' Benevolent Association (COBA), 57, 62, 62n45, 64, 65, 129–130
Correia, David, 264
cost of city time per inmate per year, 143
COs: employment benefits, 58, 60; punished for speaking out, 62–63; race and gender demographics of, 57–58; women, 57–58, 61–62, 81, 260, 268–271
COVID-19 pandemic: effects on hygiene, 174, 183–184, 240, 277; effects on inmate pay, 113; effects on searches, 137; effects on smuggling, 129, 129n9; effects on visits and services, 118, 127–129, 135, 281; general, 6, 12–13, 67, 70, 152, 229, 272–273, 277; mass release during, 48, 57, 249–250, 257, 271–273, 279, 283
Cressey, Donald R., 198
cultural gulfs between inmates, 9–10
Cunha, Manuela, 4

Davis, Angela, 60–61
day room corner section, 21, 22
de Blasio, Bill, 56, 65, 272
Dickinson, Yolanda "Yoshe", 59
disciplinary infractions, 37, 68, 93, 180, 205, 242
Dominquez, Steven, 39, 271
dormitory power structure, 228, 246–251
DOT. *See* Methadone
drug use: general, 109, 204–217, 223, 254; k2, 80–81, 94, 109, 119–120, 120n16, 142, 179, 204–209, 223, 253, 256; marijuana, 81, 109, 179, 210, 205; prescription medications, 211–213; social elements of, 207, 216. *See also* hooch, smoking, Suboxone, Methadone

East Elmhurst, 1, 13, 31
Eminem, 224, 267
exercise, 72, 94–95, 94n6, 139, 143, 189, 191, 196, 254, 256

Fassin, Didier, 121
Fat Joe, 14
federal prison, 1, 12n33, 36, 61, 120, 252, 283
the Five, 19, 274
folklore, 100–104, 221–222
food: dietary restrictions, 33, 155–156; holiday fare, 159–161; inmate-prepared, 79–80, 161–164; institutional meals, 77, 105, 149–159; waste of, 169–170. *See also* commissary, holidays
Fortune Society, 66, 143–145, 281
forty-eightin', 278–279
Freedom of Information Law (FOIL) requests, 5, 111n3, 112n4, 58n24, 113n7
friendship, 117, 256–257

gambling, 76, 78, 95, 227–228
Gameboy, 279
Games Criminals Play, 35n10, 260
gangs: assault, 229; Bloods, 52, 202, 224, 243, 266; Crips, 52, 97, 224, 243–244, 247, 266–267; declaring status, 245; Folk Nation, 51; general, 52, 97,

244–245, 266; Latin Kings, 52, 244–245, 266; MS-13: 51; prevalence of, 51–52; solidarity and, 224, 229, 235–236, 243; Trinitarios, 51, 244
Garfinkle, Harold, 32
gender-affirming housing, 230–233
Gibson, James, 85
Gilmore, Ruth Wilson, 2
Giuliani, Rudy, 196
Goffman, Erving, 27–28, 104, 108, 122, 285–286
Goldfarb, Ronald, 1–2, 2n5
good time, 113, 115, 193, 201, 210, 216, 237–238, 255, 272
greens. *See* clothing
grievances, 192, 262, 263, 275–277
Guilbaud, Fabrice, 122–123, 123n21

hairstyles, 45, 183, 202–203
Hart Island, 34, 111
Heiss, Jasmine, 2
Hernández, Kelly Lytle, 2
Heyward, Gary, 37, 58–59, 59, 60, 102, 102n11, 103, 104, 129, 268
Hibbert, Toots, 23
Hinds, Oliver, 2
holidays: early release for, 92; general, 141–142, 238, 270–271, 273. *See also* food
homelessness, 2n5, 49–51, 162, 255, 262, 280, 281
homophobia, 102, 183, 186, 203, 230, 233, 234
hooch, 119, 141–142, 210, 211, 283
house detail. *See* house gang
house gang, 111–112, 173, 177, 224, 256
hustling, 48, 49–51

Illinois State Penitentiary, 101
Immigration and Customs Enforcement (ICE) detention facilities, 90, 272
incomprehensible order, 34–38, 92, 131
Independent Budget Office, 280
inmate deaths, 41, 103, 104, 221, 262
inmate demographics, 47–48
Inmate Handbook, 34, 83, 89–90, 137, 181, 189
institutional review boards, 3
intake (process): general, 27–46; institutional, 118; social, 102–103; visitors and, 128–129
In Our Backyards Initiative, 2
Irwin, John, 2, 10, 50, 51, 55, 107, 198, 261

Jacobs, James B., 6, 63
Johnson, Dwayne "the Rock," 98
Jones, Richard S., 10, 5n18

Kang-Brown, Jacob, 2
KEEP. *See* Methadone
Kessler, Eve, 225
kites, 101, 240–241

labor disputes, 113, 173, 271
laundry, 38, 187–189, 191, 201, 239
letters. *See* mail
lights out, 73, 80, 98, 162, 211, 239, 263; reading after, 32, 81–82, searches after, 137
Lil Wayne, 6, 7–8, 13, 38, 46, 102, 111, 111n2, 168, 172, 174, 228, 230
Linnemann, Travis, 208
Lock-Up: The Prisoners of Rikers Island, 175, 231, 232

mail, 8, 14, 20, 37, 70, 74, 88, 98, 99, 100, 119, 137, 194, 206–207, 244
Mayor, 250
Mayor's Office of Criminal Justice, 47n1, 57, 280
McGowan, Daniel, 10, 12n33
McMickens, Jacqueline, 58
mental illness: effects of city time on, 225–226; prevalence among inmates, 217–218, 217n10. *See also* Brad H., civilian workers
mess hall, 20, 112, 148, 148–153, 156–158, 164, 193, 199, 215, 240, 254, 257, 278; layout in C-76, 149–150

Methadone, 50, 51, 78, 79, 124, 212–215, 240, 275, 279. *See also* drug use
Miller, Robin K., 59, 260
misconceptions about mass incarceration, 3–5, 4n16

neutral dorms, 245, 246–247, 248–251
Newport, Melanie D., 2
New York City Department of Investigation, 59, 129, 129n8
New York City Municipal Archives, 5, 13n36, 15, 17
New York state prison, 12n33, 46, 54, 57, 66, 101, 102, 106–107, 145, 186, 243, 245, 262, 283
nicknames, 43–44, 133, 244, 268
The Night Of, 5n17
non-profit organizations. *See* programs
Norton, Jack, 2
Nunez monitor, 57, 222

Ocasio-Cortez, Alexandria, 272
OG, 43, 107, 251
Omar "OG Mack" Portee, 52
Osborne Association, 65, 143, 281, 282

pack-ups, 223, 223–224, 228, 235, 236–237, 247, 249–250, 274
Pataki, George, 196
Peace Center, 20, 143
Pelot-Hobbs, Lydia 2
pens, 29, 31, 33, 134, 140–141, 206, 285–286; why-me pens, 219, 274
Perez, Marcos, 34, 105
Ponte, Joseph, 225
Prime Minister, 224
prison ethnography, 3–4, 6, 56, 49n4
programs, 65, 66, 105, 142–147, 280–281, 282. *See also* Osborne Association, Fortune Society
Pryor, Maud, 129, 131

rabble management hypothesis, 2
race and ethnicity: social elements of among inmates, 251–256; racism, 60, 63–64, 114, 146, 247, 252
Ranney, David, 9, 10
Raphaël, Pierre, 17, 137
recidivism, 7, 109, 144
reciprocity between inmates and COs, 41, 242, 261–267, 278
reentry services, 144, 280–282
Reimer, Hans, 84, 100
Release, 92, 105–109, 204, 216, 280–287; Brad H. inmates and, 222–223, 281–282; drug use upon, 216–217; resistance to, 283–284
religion, 8, 67, 75, 142, 193, 245, 259; clothing and, 199–200, 259
Retsky, Harold G., 63
Rikers: An Oral History, 14, 225
Rikers Island Discharge Enhancement (RIDE), 282
Road to Legacy Podcast, 260n4
Rose M. Singer Center, 30, 175
routine, 94, 124, 140; as time strategy, 104–106

Sanders, Ed, 34
Santos, Michael G., 36
Schept, Judah, 2
Schiraldi, Vincent, 113
searches: as punishment, 76, 129, 139, 207, 229, 235, 262, 273–274; general, 76, 87, 89, 94, 98–99, 124, 137–139, 167, 168, 174–175, 185, 192, 195, 202, 210, 211, 275
sentence length: average, 47–48; discussing, 46, 243
Serge, Victor, 106, 108, 286–287
sexism, 63–64, 268–271
sexual assault, 48, 55, 56, 102–104, 187, 222
sexual relations: between inmates, 8–9, 102–103, 232, 233; between inmates and staff: 59, 102–104, 269–270
Shakur, Assata, 63, 99

shotcallers, 41, 78, 97, 142, 166–167, 186–187, 227–228, 229, 236, 238, 246, 247, 248, 249, 256, 261, 272, 284
showers, 15, 25, 87–89, 103, 142, 173, 175, 184–187, 250
slot time. *See* telephones
smoking, 40, 41, 80–81, 101, 120, 120n18, 141–142, 171, 179, 205–206, 229, 242–243, 264, 278, 282, 286. *See also* drug use
smuggling: by COs, 61, 119–120, 120n18, 129–130, 207; by inmates, 133–134; 205–207, 209–210, 241
snitching, 10, 52, 134, 234–235, 240, 240n16, 263, 275
social and family ties between COs and inmates, 59–63
SOD, 71–73, 80, 114, 116, 180, 195–196, 207
solitary confinement, 9, 115, 210, 216, 272
Special Search Team, 138, 194
Spedding, Alison, 9, 172, 229
stick-ups, 197, 201, 247, 271–273
strip searches, 31–32, 72–73, 129, 132–133, 138, 139, 219
STRIVE program, 145
Suboxone, 212 -213, 215. *See also* drug use
Sue, Kimberly L., 65
suicide prevention aid, 111
Sykes, Gresham, 36–37, 232, 261

Taboo, 59, 99
telephones: general, 40, 42, 76–77, 78, 105, 116, 118, 142, 146, 177, 185, 239–240, 240n15, 246, 248, 251, 272; hygiene and, 171–172, 173, 174; slot time, 78, 78–79, 105, 239–240, 246, 249
TeleStory. *See* visits
tenses: use of, 11
terminology: choice of, 11–12
Third Base. *See* Prime Minister
Tickets. *See* disciplinary infractions
Time Men, 1
time strategies, 84, 104–109, 121, 122, 204, 284
toothpaste, 33, 175, 176; as adhesive, 87, 107
transfers, 1, 12, 78, 103, 139–141, 151, 216; as punishment, 62, 115, 139, 273–274, 277
transitional objects, 200–202
Treatment Advocacy Center, 225, 226
Turtles, 79, 103, 138, 229, 247, 263. *See also* searches
TV, 40, 79, 96–98, 105, 117, 122, 205, 211, 214, 247–248, 251, 254, 266

urinalysis tests, 33, 37, 139, 206, 216

Venters, Homer, 65, 109, 217, 217n10
video games, 95–96, 107, 143, 247, 266
visits: in-person, 73, 124, 127–129, 135–137; video, 135–137

Wacquant, Loïc, 3, 5n18, 229
Walker, Michael, 3, 6, 9, 36, 61, 84, 139, 141, 164, 206, 230, 255–256
Wall, Tyler, 264
Warr, Jason, 4
weekend warriors, 47–48, 283
Weinstein, Harvey, 117
West, René C., 14, 37, 60, 61, 62, 102, 104, 132, 164, 261, 269
Winnicott, Donald, 200
Women's House of Detention, 60
work: assignment, 112–115; as time strategy, 110, 121–213; Inmate Wage Incentive Plan, 112; pay, 112–113, 112n5; perks of, 116–117, 120, 150, 157–158, 169–170, 180, 195–196, 197–198, 265; quitting, 114
workhouse, 41, 41n23, 111
working dorm, 41, 41n23, 73, 112, 114–115
Wynn, Jennifer, 3, 56, 65, 128, 213

Zeno, 284
Zimmer, Lynn E., 268, 269–270
zombies, 51, 208

ABOUT THE AUTHORS

DAVID CAMPBELL is a writer, translator, and former antifascist political prisoner. He was a PEN America Writing for Justice 2021 fellowship finalist, and his writing has appeared in numerous publications, including *Slate*, *Huffington Post*, *Truthout*, and *The Appeal*. While incarcerated, he translated *Revolutionary Affinities* by Michael Löwy and Olivier Besancenot. He is currently writing a memoir of his time on Rikers Island.

JARROD SHANAHAN is Assistant Professor of Criminal Justice at Governors State University in University Park, Illinois. He is the author of *Captives*; coauthor, with Dr. Zhandarka Kurti, of *States of Incarceration* and *Skyscraper Jails*; an editor of *Treason to Whiteness Is Loyalty to Humanity*; and a founding editor of the journal *Hard Crackers: Chronicles of Everyday Life*.